DATE DUE

JUN 0 5 2013			

Demco

DIARY OF A
PHILOSOPHY STUDENT

Simone de Beauvoir

DIARY OF A PHILOSOPHY STUDENT:
VOLUME 1, 1926–27

Edited by Barbara Klaw,
Sylvie Le Bon de Beauvoir,
and Margaret A. Simons,

with Marybeth Timmermann

Foreword by Sylvie Le Bon de Beauvoir
Translations, Notes, and Annotations by Barbara Klaw
Transcribed by Barbara Klaw and Sylvie Le Bon de Beauvoir

University of Illinois Press
Urbana and Chicago

English-language translation of *Les cahiers de jeunesse, 1926–1927,*
by Simone de Beauvoir

Library of Congress Cataloging-in-Publication Data

Beauvoir, Simone de, 1908–1986.
[Carnets de jeunesse. English]
Diary of a philosophy student / Simone de Beauvoir ; edited by
Barbara Klaw, Sylvie Le Bon de Beauvoir, and Margaret A. Simons,
with Marybeth Timmermann; foreword by Sylvie Le Bon de Beauvoir;
translations, notes, and annotations by Barbara Klaw; transcribed by
Barbara Klaw and Sylvie Le Bon de Beauvoir.
p.   cm. — (The Beauvoir series)
Includes bibliographical references and index.
ISBN-13: 978-0-252-03142-7 (cloth : alk. paper)
ISBN-10: 0-252-03142-3 (cloth : alk. paper)
1. Beauvoir, Simone de, 1908–1986.
I. Klaw, Barbara.
II. Le Bon de Beauvoir, Sylvie.
III. Simons, Margaret A.
IV. Title.
B2430.B344A313   2006
194—dc22[B]   2006021222

The editors gratefully acknowledge the support of a grant from the
National Endowment for the Humanities, an independent federal
agency; a translation grant from the French Ministry of Culture; and a
Matching Funds grant from the Illinois Board of Higher Education.

Contents

Foreword to the Beauvoir Series

Sylvie Le Bon de Beauvoir

TRANSLATED BY MARYBETH TIMMERMANN

It is my pleasure to honor the monumental work of research and publication that the Beauvoir Series represents, which was undertaken and brought to fruition by Margaret A. Simons and her team. These volumes of Simone de Beauvoir's writings, concerning literature as well as philosophy and feminism, stretch from 1926 to 1979, that is to say, throughout almost her entire life. Some of them have been published before and are known, but they remain dispersed throughout time and space, in diverse editions, newspapers, or reviews. Other pieces were read by Beauvoir during conferences or radio programs and then lost from view. Some had been left completely unpublished. What gives all of them force and meaning is precisely having them gathered together, closely, as a whole. Nothing of the sort has yet been realized, except, on a much smaller scale, *Les écrits de Simone de Beauvoir* (The Writings of Simone de Beauvoir), published in France in 1979. Here, the aim is an exhaustive corpus, as much as that is possible.

Because they cover more than fifty years, these volumes faithfully reflect the thoughts of their author, the early manifestation and permanence of certain of her preoccupations as a writer and philosopher, as a woman and feminist. What will be immediately striking, I think, is their extraordinary *coherence*. Obviously, from this point of view, *Les cahiers de jeunesse* (The Student Diaries), previously unpublished, constitute the star document. The very young eighteen-, nineteen-, or twenty-year-old Simone de Beauvoir who writes them is clearly already the future great Simone de Beauvoir, author of *L'invitée* (She Came to Stay), *Pour une morale de l'ambiguïté* (The Ethics of Ambiguity), *Le deuxième sexe* (The Second Sex), *Les Mandarins* (The Mandarins), and *Mémoires* (Memoirs). Her vocation as a writer is energetically affirmed in these diaries, but one also discovers in them the roots of her later reflections. It is particularly touching to see the birth, often with hesitations, doubt, and anguish, of the fundamental choices of thought and existence that would have such an impact on so many future readers, women and men. Beauvoir expresses torments, doubt, and anguish, but also exultation and confidence in her strength and in the future. The foresight of certain passages is impressive. Take the one from June 25, 1929, for example: "Strange certitude that these riches will be welcomed, that some words will be said and heard, that this life will be a fountainhead from which many others will draw. Certitude of a vocation."

These precious *Cahiers* will cut short the unproductive and recurrent debate about the "influence" that Sartre supposedly had on Simone de Beauvoir, since they incontestably reveal to us Simone de Beauvoir *before* Sartre. Thus, the relationship of Beauvoir and Sartre will take on its true sense, and one will understand to what point Beauvoir was even more herself when she agreed with some of Sartre's themes, because all those lonely years of apprenticeship and training were leading her to a definite path and not just any path. Therefore, it is not a matter of influence but an encounter in the strong sense of the term. Beauvoir and Sartre *recognized themselves* in one another because each already existed intensely independently and intensely. One can all the better discern the originality of Simone de Beauvoir in her ethical preoccupations, her own conception of concrete freedom, and her dramatic consciousness of the essential role of the Other, for example, because they are prefigured in the feverish meditations that occupied her youth. *Les cahiers* constitute a priceless testimony.

I will conclude by thanking Margaret A. Simons and her associates again for their magnificent series, which will constitute an irreplaceable contribution to the study and the true understanding of the thoughts and works of Simone de Beauvoir.

Acknowledgments

Barbara Klaw writes: I applaud the numerous individuals who helped in the production of this annotated translation. First, I thank Sylvie Le Bon de Beauvoir for her kind encouragement in my continued work on Beauvoir's 1926–30 diary. I am grateful to the staff in the Manuscript Room of the Bibliothèque Nationale in Paris and especially to Mauricette Berne for facilitating my study of the manuscripts.

I am grateful to colleagues and students who have commented on my translations and scholarly presentations related to my introduction that precedes the 1926 diary, including those at the Simone de Beauvoir Society, the American Translation Association, the Kentucky Philological Association, and Northern Kentucky University. To Alan Hutchison, Tony Russell, Margaret Simons, Marybeth Timmermann, and the anonymous reviewers for the University of Illinois Press, I am indebted for comments on earlier versions of my translation, annotation, and introduction. I sincerely appreciate the invaluable suggestions and questions of Carol Betts at the University of Illinois Press. For their help in finding references for the works or places that Beauvoir cited, I acknowledge Nathalie Bague, Wilson Baldridge, Nina Hellerstein, Nancy Jentsch, Madeleine Leveau-Fernandez, Tamara F.

O'Callaghan, Michele Peers, Richard Shryock, Louise Witherell, and Tom Zaniello. The Interlibrary Loan Department of Northern Kentucky University deserves praise for its success in making requested translations available for use. I am beholden to Gisèle Loriot-Raymer for her aid with translations, to Katherine C. Kurk for her editorial expertise, to Roxanne Kent-Drury for her computer skill, to Danny Miller for his moral support, to Vanessa Johnson for her administrative assistance, and to Alan Hutchison for his help with translations and his moral support.

I wish to thank all of my former professors at the University of Pennsylvania, where I obtained my doctorate in French literature in 1990, for teaching me so well and for making it possible for me to live and work in France repeatedly. I am most grateful to Gerald Prince, who first introduced me to Beauvoir's works in 1986 and later offered advice and recommendations that helped me to obtain grants and to publish; to Lucienne Frappier-Mazur, for suggesting in 1990 that I consult the manuscripts for Beauvoir's 1926–30 diary; and to Kate McMahon, who has been a friend and role model for years.

For encouraging me in countless ways I also thank Myriam Crave, Christine Delphy, Kathi Godber, Geneviève Guido, Henri Guido, Nadia Ibrahim, John Ireland, Claire Jouffroy, Rick Hutchison, Joyce Kornel, Linnett Leisner, Angela Lucarelli, Claire Marrone, Joseph Martin, Kathy Maystadt, Amy McIntosh, Mary Carol Meinken, Desirae Mercer, Katy Moeggenberg, Yolanda Patterson, Valérie Santoni, Andrew Taylor, and Yvette Van Ness.

For the funding of my continued work on this book for the past years, I express gratitude to the American Philosophical Society, the National Endowment for the Humanities, Northern Kentucky University, and the Southern Regional Education Board.

Margaret A. Simons writes: I gratefully acknowledge the generous support of a Collaborative Research Grant from the National Endowment for the Humanities (NEH), an independent federal agency; a translation grant from the French Ministry of Culture; and a Matching Funds grant from the Illinois Board of Higher Education, allocated by the Graduate School of Southern Illinois University Edwardsville. I sincerely appreciate the kind assistance of Mauricette Berne with my efforts to decipher Beauvoir's diary at the Bibliothèque Nationale, the expert advice from Marybeth Timmermann on translations, and the invaluable suggestions by the anonymous readers for the University of Illinois Press. I have benefited from helpful, critical discussions of my work on Beauvoir's early philosophy at Philosophy Department Colloquia at Southern Illinois University Carbondale, Southern Illinois University Edwardsville, and Webster University, as well as conferences of the Society for Phenomenology and Existential Philosophy, and the International Simone de Beauvoir Society.

I am particularly grateful to the SIUE Graduate School for the support of the Vaughnie J. Lindsay Research Professor Award and to the following persons for their encouragement and assistance: Margot Backas and Michael Hall of NEH; Anne-Solange Noble, Florence Giry, and Liliane Phan of Éditions Gallimard; Joan Catapano and Carol Betts at the University of Illinois Press; and at Southern Illinois University Edwardsville, Steve Hansen, Jo Barnes, Sharon Hahs, Kent Neely, Bob Wolf, and especially Janette Johnson for her assistance with administering the grants. I thank the members of the Beauvoir Series Editorial Board for their guidance: Kristana Arp, Debra Bergoffen, Anne Deing Cordero, Elizabeth Fallaize, and Eleanore Holveck. Marybeth Timmermann deserves a special note of thanks for her fine editing work on the translation. Finally, I would like to express my profound gratitude to Barbara Klaw for her tremendous achievement in this volume and to Sylvie Le Bon de Beauvoir, who has made both this volume and the Beauvoir Series possible.

DIARY OF A
PHILOSOPHY STUDENT

Introduction

Margaret A. Simons

Some readers may be surprised to find a teenage diary included in a series on the philosophy of Simone de Beauvoir, but a fully annotated, scholarly translation of Beauvoir's student diary, dating from her years as a philosophy student at the Sorbonne, has been a key part of the Beauvoir Series from the beginning. In addition to revealing previously unknown details about the life of one of the twentieth century's most important and fascinating writers, Beauvoir's student diary provides access to her early philosophy, written years before her first meeting with Jean-Paul Sartre, whom most critics have credited with originating the existential philosophy in her work.

In a sense, the Beauvoir Series project began in 1986 with Sylvie Le Bon de Beauvoir's discovery of her adoptive mother's handwritten diaries and letters following Beauvoir's death. Beauvoir herself had made portions of her once private diary and correspondence public years earlier by quoting from them extensively in *Memoirs of a Dutiful Daughter* and her other auto-biographical writings.[1] In 1990 Sylvie Le Bon de Beauvoir donated the student diary along with other manuscripts to the Bibliothèque Nationale in Paris, where they were made available for scholarly research. Further fueling a renaissance of scholarly interest in Beauvoir's philosophy was the publication, also in 1990, of Le Bon de Beauvoir's editions of Beauvoir's *Journal de guerre* (Wartime Diary) and *Lettres à Sartre* (Letters to Sartre). These publications play a central role, for example, in Edward Fullbrook and Kate Fullbrook's 1993 study tracing the chronology of Beauvoir's novel *She Came to Stay* and Sartre's essay *Being and Nothingness,* both published in 1943. The Fullbrooks discovered that Beauvoir's metaphysical novel, long assumed to be a literary application of the philosophy in Sartre's essay, was actually written first, thus undermining the traditional interpretation of Beauvoir as Sartre's philosophical follower.[2]

Reading of the Fullbrooks' discovery, I thought of a way to test their conclusion. If the philosophy in Beauvoir's novel, written during 1939–41, was indeed her own creation and not Sartre's, then her 1927 student diary, written twelve years earlier and two years before her first meeting with Sartre, might contain an early form of the same philosophy. So in the summer of 1994 I went to the Bibliothèque Nationale to find out. It wasn't until my last day in Paris, after days of struggling to decipher Beauvoir's notoriously difficult handwriting, that I made my most important discovery.

In the diary entry for July 10, 1927, Beauvoir recorded her determination to put her philosophical ideas in order and probe more deeply into the problems that attracted her: "The theme is almost always this opposition of self and other that I felt upon starting to live." This passage, which is not mentioned in Beauvoir's *Memoirs,* is tantalizing evidence of Beauvoir's early concern with the problem of the Other, the theme of *She Came to Stay* and a central problem of her philosophy. But my stay in Paris was ending with my work on the diary barely begun.

Fortunately I was not the only Beauvoir scholar working on Beauvoir's unpublished diaries that summer. Barbara Klaw, then assistant professor of French at Northern Kentucky University, was just arriving in Paris to begin a research project on the diaries. I told her of my exciting discovery and shared with her my fragmentary transcription of a few pages of the 1927 diary. To my delight, Barbara Klaw sent me her rough transcription of the entire 1927 diary in the fall of 1994. Our collaborative work had begun.

At a panel on Beauvoir's philosophy at the Pacific Division of the American Philosophical Association the following spring, I presented a preliminary analysis of Beauvoir's philosophy in the 1927 diary based on Barbara Klaw's draft transcription. Inspired by our discoveries, those attending the session formed a scholarly society, the Simone de Beauvoir Circle, to encourage research on Beauvoir's philosophy. We knew that one of our first objectives would be to find a way to bring out accurate, scholarly translations of Beauvoir's works, since the lack of such translations posed a serious barrier to Beauvoir research in the United States.

In the 1960s when the popularity of French existential phenomenology was at its height and scholars were writing its history, Americans read English translations of essays by Sartre (1955) and Maurice Merleau-Ponty (1964), Beauvoir's colleagues first as philosophy students then as co-editors of the journal *Les temps modernes*.[3] But most of Beauvoir's essays from the same period were still untranslated and her contributions to *Les temps modernes* and, more generally, to the development of French existential phenomenology, largely overlooked. Furthermore, in the popular translations of Beauvoir's work by commercial publishers, the accurate and consistent translation of philosophical terms has not been a priority.

As I detailed in a 1983 article, more than 10 percent of the French text is missing from the sole English edition of *The Second Sex* (first published in 1952 by Knopf) and key philosophical terminology is mistranslated.[4] The translator, H. M. Parshley, an eminent zoologist, justified his disregard for philosophy in the preface: "Mlle de Beauvoir's book is, after all, on woman, not philosophy." Unfortunately this trend of providing popular editions at the expense of the integrity and accurate translation of Beauvoir's texts has continued.

The 1992 English translation of Beauvoir's *Letters to Sartre* (1990) deleted one-third of the French text. Despite the translator's aim of preserving "all discussion of De Beauvoir's own or Sartre's work," thirty-eight references to Beauvoir's work on her metaphysical novel *She Came to Stay* (1943) have been deleted from letters in November and December 1939 alone. There are also mistranslations. Beauvoir's description of "the central subject" of her novel, "Françoise's problem with consciousnesses," is mistranslated as the "problem with consciousness," thus misconstruing a social problem as an individual one.[5] Beauvoir's discussion of love based on a "metaphysical and moral" need for the other is obliterated in the English edition, which translates the adjectives, nonsensically, as nouns: "metaphysics and ethics."[6]

Such mistakes are all too typical of translations of Beauvoir's texts by translators lacking the requisite philosophical background and required by commercial publishers to make substantial cuts. So we understood that making full, scholarly translations of Beauvoir's works available to the English-reading public would be essential to encouraging scholarly work on her philosophy.

Another barrier to scholarly research in Beauvoir's philosophy, we recognized, might be her philosophical methodology. Beauvoir rejects traditional philosophical system building, which she characterizes as "a concerted delirium" requiring that philosophers stubbornly give their "insights the value of universal keys."[7] Beauvoir turns instead to a conception of philosophy as a way of life. "In truth, there is no divorce between philosophy and life," Beauvoir writes in the preface to a 1948 collection of her essays: "Every living step is a philosophical choice and the ambition of a philosophy worthy of the name is to be a way of life that brings its justification with itself."[8] In order to present the opacity, ambiguity, and temporality of lived experience, Beauvoir often wrote her philosophy in literary form, as in *She Came to Stay* (1943).[9] Even later, when she began writing philosophical essays as well, she focused on concrete problems, pioneering the phenomenological description of oppression in *The Second Sex* and writing her ethics as lessons in the art of living through her autobiographical texts. We thus understood that we could not be limited by disciplinary boundaries either on our team or in the texts to be translated, but must broaden the scope of our effort to include literary genres other than the conventional philosophical essay.

So the work began of assembling a team and selecting texts. Sylvie Le Bon de Beauvoir accepted the invitation to join me as co-editor of the Beauvoir Series, and she agreed to play a special role as co-editor of the two volumes of Beauvoir's student diaries. Joan Catapano, of the University of Illinois Press, and Anne-Solange Noble, of Éditions Gallimard, secured the necessary rights and arranged for publication of the series, which eventually numbered seven volumes. Then in 2000 the Beauvoir Series won a Collaborative Research Grant from the National Endowment for the Humanities, a Matching Funds grant from the Illinois Board of Higher Education, and a translation grant from the French Ministry of Culture, which made the series a reality.

The first volume in the series, Beauvoir's *Philosophical Writings,* was published by the University of Illinois Press in 2004. In addition to the present volume, the first of two volumes of Beauvoir's student diary (the second volume covers diary entries dating from 1928–30), we are translating Beauvoir's wartime diary, which records the writing of *She Came to Stay* and her developing sense of social responsibility during the Nazi Occupation, and three volumes of Beauvoir's writings on literature, politics, and feminism. We hope that our introductions to Beauvoir's texts will encourage a reexamination of Beauvoir's place in the history of twentieth-century philosophy and that our fully annotated translations will encourage commercial publishers who own exclusive English-language rights to other texts, including *The Second Sex,* to authorize new scholarly English editions.

NOTES

1. Beauvoir first mentions her diary in *Mémoires d'une jeune fille rangée; Memoirs of a Dutiful Daughter,* trans. Kirkup, 188: "I began to keep a private diary; I wrote this inscription on the fly-leaf; 'If anyone reads these pages, no matter who it may be, I shall never forgive that person.'"

2. See Fullbrook and Fullbrook, *Simone de Beauvoir and Jean-Paul Sartre,* and E. Fullbrook, "*She Came to Stay* and *Being and Nothingness,*" 50–69.

3. See Sartre, *Literary and Philosophical Essays,* trans. Michelson, and Merleau-Ponty, *Sense and Non-Sense,* trans. Dreyfus and Dreyfus.

4. My 1983 article later appeared as Simons, "The Silencing of Simone de Beauvoir: Guess What's Missing from *The Second Sex.*" See also Fallaize, "The Housewife's Destiny: Translating Simone de Beauvoir's 'The Married Woman'"; Moi, "While We Wait: The English Translation of *The Second Sex*"; and Patterson, "The Man behind *The Second Sex*" and "H. M. Parshley et son combat contre l'amputation de la version américaine."

5. Beauvoir, *Lettres,* 1:178, trans. Hoare, *Letters to Sartre,* 111.

6. Beauvoir, *Lettres,* 1:254, trans. Hoare, *Letters to Sartre,* 160.

7. Beauvoir, *Force de l'âge,* 254.

8. Beauvoir, "Préface," 11, trans. Timmermann, "Preface," 216–18. The preface is to four of Beauvoir's articles reprinted from *Les temps modernes:* "L'existentialisme et la sagesse des nations" [Existentialism and Popular Wisdom], "Idéalisme moral et réalisme politique" [Moral Idealism and Political Realism], "Littérature et métaphysique" [Literature and Metaphysics], and "Oeil pour oeil" [An Eye for an Eye], all of which are translated in Beauvoir's *Philosophical Writings.*

9. Beauvoir, *L'invitée,* trans. Moyse and Senhouse, *She Came to Stay.*

The Literary and Historical Context of Beauvoir's Early Writings: 1926–27

Barbara Klaw

Simone de Beauvoir is the Paris-born author of five novels, one play, two collections of short stories, numerous volumes of autobiography, lengthy volumes of correspondence with several men, a war diary, and a wide variety of philosophical and political essays. Her most revolutionary sociopolitical essay, *Le deuxième sexe* (The Second Sex), concerns the mythical and real relationships between men and women in society. It laid the foundation for twentieth-century discourses concerning sexuality and gender relations, and for feminism after 1949. There are those who hold that Beauvoir has yet to be fully understood and that in *Le deuxième sexe* she not only created a new type of philosophy but suggested something quite other than a sex–gender dichotomy. They believe that she argued that the kinds of projects one may realize do depend upon one's body, but that, more important, it is the interaction between each body and the world around it that continuously constructs and remodels individual choices or social and ethical norms at any given moment.[1]

Since Beauvoir's death in 1986, her scholarship, political activities, fictional and autobiographical works, letters, diaries, and personal life have all undergone intense scrutiny, and they continue to be analyzed. The posthumous publication of her letters to Sartre and her war diary, in 1990, caused her French and American public to reevaluate her on many levels. Her admirers could no longer keep her on the pedestal of feminism, political activism, and altruism. Whereas it was once thought that she was in an unequaled, loving relationship with Sartre, it now became evident that Beauvoir had had a variety of male and female lovers during her fifty years with Sartre. Many scholars had formerly assumed that Beauvoir was simply copying or illustrating Sartre's ideas in her works, but some started to argue that, on the contrary, Sartre had been appropriating ideas from Beauvoir.[2] The publication of her letters written in English to Nelson Algren, the Chicago-born author who was Beauvoir's lover for many years, and their subsequent translation and publication in French endeared her to a public who saw a new, softer side of Beauvoir. New controversies developed and old ones were reworked. Was Beauvoir misogynist or feminist, victim or torturer, male- or female-identified, homosexual, bisexual, or heterosexual? Do her writings and activities prove her to be frigid, frustrated, or sexually fulfilled, an innovator or imitator of ideas, a philosopher or a novelist, a great or a poor writer? Finally, was she significantly influential or of lesser consequence as a twentieth-century writer, philosopher, and historical persona?[3] As scholarship flourishes and attempts to answer these questions, Beauvoir's student diary, now available to the public at large, will be an invaluable tool in determining her intellectual and moral influence on the world. It is particularly important for tracing her intellectual development prior to meeting Sartre, whom she did not encounter until 1929.

In the present essay, I will summarize Beauvoir's educational background before and during the writing of this diary to highlight the originality and development of her thoughts and the change in her emotions as she acquired more expertise in understanding philosophy, literature, and mathematics through her studies, her reading, and her peers. I will discuss the importance of Beauvoir's diary to literary studies and to tracing the genesis of her subsequent writings, and I will provide a variety of ideas for future research and ways of reading this portion of the diary. Finally, I will situate her diary in its literary and historical moment in her life.[4] In the second essay, Margaret Simons will further discuss Beauvoir's education, analyze Beauvoir's thoughts in the 1926–27 diary in light of the history of philosophy, and show the philosophical impact of her ideas.

Between 1926 and 1930, or between the ages of eighteen and twenty-two, when Beauvoir only dreamed of becoming a published writer, she kept a diary in four small (roughly 17 × 22 cm) notebooks of various colors and lengths. It is the diary entries of the first two years that are the focus of the present volume. (Beauvoir refers to a 1925 notebook of her diary, but that notebook has yet to be found.) The 1926 diary runs from Friday, August 6, through Thursday, December 2; the 1927 diary, from April 17 through October 21. When Beauvoir began to write her 1926 diary, she already had completed specialties in French literature and Latin studies and had finished the equivalent of roughly half of a four-year degree in an American university today.[5] Beauvoir had studied philosophy in high school classes at Cours Désir, but, if her memoirs are to be believed, she had such abysmal instruction that she learned little more than a rapid summary of human errors and the truth according to Saint Thomas Aquinas.[6] In 1925, due to her mother's belief that philosophy corrupted the soul, Beauvoir studied mathematics instead at the Institut Catholique and classics at the Institut Sainte-Marie in Neuilly. At the latter institute in 1926, she met Jeanne Mercier, an instructor who encouraged her to return to her love of philosophy.[7]

In her August 13, 1926, diary entry Beauvoir implies that she now dislikes philosophy because of discussions that remain in a vacuum, and she expresses her hope that she will find new reasons to like it. Her diary entry of July 18, 1927, mentions that she has been doing philosophy for barely ten months, which suggests that her study of what she is calling philosophy began in September or October of 1926. Already in the spring of 1927 Mlle Mercier asked her to teach part of her 1927–28 baccalaureate class in psychology. During the writing of the 1927 diary, Beauvoir was studying for an extraordinary number of college and graduate specialties, including the general history of philosophy, Greek studies, and the general philosophy of logic. Furthermore, as the diary for that year opens, she was able to speak and read English, although the quotes she provided indicate that she often read English-language texts in French translation. She could already read and translate Latin and was teaching herself Greek.

Beauvoir either quoted or mentioned a wide variety of authors, texts, artists, and musicians in her diary, making it an unequalled resource for tracing the development of her thought and the genesis of her published writings. Although critics have argued that Beauvoir's fiction is more or less a retelling of her own experiences, her diary shows that she had many of the ideas for this fiction long before she had the experiences. Seeds for plots, characters, and themes of all of her short stories and novels can be found in her 1926–27 diary, which also contains nascent ideas for her future philosophical essays and the raw data and feelings for what will become part of Beauvoir's autobiography. The numerous authors, texts, and quotations alone provide subjects for vast research tracing the intertextuality involved in Beauvoir's works.

Paintings, cinema, theatrical productions, music, and the people around her all fascinated Beauvoir. At the time of writing this diary she was very fond of symbolism, surrealism, and fauvism. Symbolism can be seen as art or discourse that renders something other than what is immediate and visible.[8] It stands in for something absent or transposes a caricature, becoming the passionate equivalent of an emotion.[9] Beauvoir likewise seems to create a work with disparate parts and shades, meant to render the passionate equivalent of a received sensation. Narrative is not important. The recording of thoughts, feelings, and aspirations becomes paramount. Although her published memoirs mention many of the same authors and texts and a few of the quotes, the 1926–27 diary offers more precise references and many more of them. All of the works and ideas found in it inform the development of her thought. These aspects of her passion affect how she composes her thoughts in her diaries. Reading her 1926 diary might be compared to entering into a symbolist painting of the same time period. Little seems to fit logically together. The pages are filled with a multitude of quotations by others, disparate thoughts, short narratives recounting her activities, and an overflow of emotions. In short, one meets a delightful, highly intelligent, and independent eighteen-year-old who wavers between aspirations of becoming someone great and the desire to let herself be lazy and comfortable. Throughout, she obviously believed in herself with a passion that carried her to originality and success.

The passion, self-love, and self-confidence that shine out of the diary and that ultimately overcome all feelings of self-doubt render it an autobiographical self-help book before the genre became popular. Such an interpretation explains why so many women would later turn to Beauvoir's public life and writings to learn how to live as liberated and independent people.[10] Lessons could be learned even from the teenaged Beauvoir, in the advice she is constantly giving herself: "Don't let myself be absorbed by others; take from them only what is useful for me. . . . Never take an attitude; never act without knowing exactly why" (July 29, 1927); "Move forward. Don't endlessly turn back to see if it wouldn't be better to commit myself to another path that I've left behind" ([May] 11, 1927); "It seems to me that love should not make all else disappear but should simply tint it with new nuances; I would like a love that accompanies me through life, not that absorbs all my life" (August 17, 1926). There is a healthy and human contradiction evident in Beauvoir's diary that gives it great universal appeal: on some days, like

September 14, 1926, she details moments of anguish and of feeling useless, and on others, such as November 17, 1926, she exudes self-confidence and the certainty of being very special and talented.

This diary could also be read as field notes to an archeological excavation that reveals the development of Beauvoir's interest in sex roles. In essence, her diary chronicles the inception of her most famous essay, *Le deuxième sexe*, which she nourished for years until it reached maturity. Sartre, rather than giving Beauvoir the idea for her most celebrated essay, provided the emotional support she needed to develop it. Gender roles are consistently a theme of her 1926–27 notebooks. As the diary shows, her earliest ideas for stories involve a young girl who is passionately in love without being able to actualize it, or who dreams of a love made of mutual admiration and moral independence and who loses herself and her self-esteem in the actual love affair. These are among the very situations experienced by women in *Le deuxième sexe*.

Beauvoir imagines depicting "a soul who would like *to be* and who must resign itself to appearing" (September 6, 1926). This interplay between being and appearing constitutes a major theme illustrated by the characters Françoise and Xavière in *L'invitée* (She Came to Stay), by the actress Regina in *Tous les hommes sont mortels* (All Men Are Mortal), and again later by Laurence in *Les belles images* (Pretty Pictures).[11] In general in 1926, Beauvoir wants to portray a young girl who believes that she is in love solely because people tell her so, a girl who has moments of doubt and tries to escape marriage, but who marries anyway. Similarly, Françoise of *L'invitée* constantly struggles with the difference between what she feels and what others tell her, and in effect tries to kill Xavière to avoid being influenced by her. Beauvoir's struggle to reconcile her own Catholic upbringing and her reason resulted in her desire for God and her simultaneous fear that God's existence would render life meaningless, both of which inform *Tous les hommes sont mortels*. These instances alone suggest the wealth of ideas budding in the 1926–27 diary and how Beauvoir later transformed them into literary works.

The authors Beauvoir reads and cites and her notions of self expressed in her 1926 diary reappear in the unique discursive voice she created in *Le deuxième sexe*. Overall in her 1926 diary, Beauvoir imagines a sexless self. She identifies with male authors (both homosexual and heterosexual) who focus on developing the self, the search for God (either a God in the universe or a God within), and a type of platonic love in which two souls unite. There is no stated attention to physical love, although this may be due to her initial inability to write about her private difficulties or things she was feeling too strongly. She envisions love between a male and a female as achieving its ultimate in marriage. She also interrogates her love for her female friends. Her focus is on love and the desire for self-realization. The 1926 diary shows a young Beauvoir who reads extensively and admires certain writers and heroines for particular traits. The plots of the novels she mentions and the personalities of their characters point to Beauvoir's fascination with works that focus on masculine and feminine reactions to societal constraints or with authors who discuss gendered concepts such as the Eternal Feminine. Jules Laforgue, a nineteenth-century French poet noted for combining audacity and fantasy, for example, is not only one of Beauvoir's favorite authors in the 1926 diary, but he also appears in several notes in *Le deuxième sexe* referring to the Eternal Feminine.[12]

Her 1926–30 diary provides ample evidence that she possessed much more intelligence, creativity, fascination with gender roles, and passion for philosophy than suggested by the portrait she provides in her *Mémoires*. It also shows the difficulty of determining if philosophy, fiction, poetry, autobiography, letters, private journals, or art most influenced Beauvoir's journal writing, especially in 1926. There is little evidence in the 1926–27 diary entries that indicates Beauvoir's expertise in philosophical concepts at that time. However, her diary proves that she had exposure to a variety of philosophical ideas that continually reappear in the poetry and fiction that she cites, and that her exploration of philosophical ideas grows more mature and profound as the 1926–27 diary progresses. Many of her favorite authors were novelists and poets who had studied philosophy or were later appropriated by philosophers. Hegel's name and some of his ideas, for example, are mentioned in the poetry of Jules Laforgue (entry of October 17, 1926) and in the fiction of Louis Aragon (April 17, 1927), and there are frequent references to Hegel in the *Propos* by Alain, which Beauvoir is obviously reading or hearing about as she writes the 1927 diary. She also cites one of Hegel's ideas (without mentioning Hegel's name) on November 21, 1926. Although she does not reference quotes concerning Hegel from either Aragon or Alain, one might surmise that she had exposure to them since they are found in the same works from which she noted other ideas.

Beauvoir's strong interest in psychology strengthened her background in philosophy. In 1926 and 1927, in fact, she viewed psychology as her major interest. In its earliest stages, the study of psychology consisted primarily of philosophical and theological discussions of the soul, a topic that reappears frequently in the 1926–27 notebooks. Before the late nineteenth century (1890), psychologists did not look at consciousness as an evolutionary process, and people did not view psychology as a field separate from philosophy. Beauvoir would have been well versed in the theories concerning body and mind held by René Descartes, Baruch Spinoza, and G. W. Leibniz, which all played dominant roles in the development of modern psychology, where the relation of the human mind to the body and its actions have been prominent subjects of debate. Perhaps due to the influence of Mlle Mercier, who was doing her dissertation on Leibniz in November 1928, Beauvoir eventually wrote a thesis on him in April 1929.

Similarly, although Beauvoir would have denied being a feminist at the time she kept her 1926–30 diary, it is apparent that the turn-of-the-century malaise concerning women's role in society and in the male imagination informed her ideas on sex roles and planted seeds for her future fiction, characters, philosophical essays, and other work.[13] The end of the nineteenth century and the beginning of the twentieth were periods of rapid change in women's possible roles in society. Women had proven that they could successfully assume what had been considered men's responsibilities before the Industrial Revolution and World War I. But it was also an era of blatant misogyny, as men sought new ways to control these modern, independent women, not knowing how to maintain their own social status. Higher education remained very sexist. In 1914, for the first time in France, a woman, Léontine Zanta, received a doctorate in philosophy, leading the way for others. Yet no woman, despite her best efforts or credentials, was appointed chair of a college in France until 1926.[14] Similarly, after World War I, there were both laws and honors created to force women back into the home and away from traditionally male tasks. Under a French law of July 31, 1920, anyone who advocated abortion in any form could be imprisoned for from six months to three years and fined from one hundred to three thousand francs. The same law promised severe punishment to all who advocated or provided contraception to anyone. Also in 1920, the government created a national medal to honor mothers and offered the greatest rewards to women who produced five to ten offspring.[15]

This uneasiness with women's independence is apparent in symbolist paintings and revolutionary novels of the time. Beauvoir's notebooks indicate that during 1926–27, she frequented museums and salons to develop her knowledge of modern art. Most of the painters mentioned span the mid-nineteenth through the early twentieth century, the time period when symbolism, fauvism, and surrealism are in vogue. Such paintings portray a woman as a defective man, a superhuman goddess, or, worst of all, an absurd and immaterial being such as a dangerous and castrating woman who often has teeth, claws, and monsters protruding from her sexual parts.[16] In 1922 Margueritte's novel *La garçonne* introduces a new independent woman who achieves fame, fortune, and the lifestyle of a man, and yet, even she, upon finding true love, willingly returns to the stereotypical vision of woman. Popular music similarly mocks liberated woman. On October 14, 1926, Beauvoir refers to the fox-trot song "Dolorosa," copyrighted the previous year, which describes a femme fatale who is mysterious, mocking, and more seductive than all others, and who will only cause pain to those who love her. On May 24, 1927, Beauvoir notes that she saw a Jean Epstein film, $6\frac{1}{2} \times 11$. This black-and-white silent film depicts the evilness of women as it enacts the story of a woman's infidelity that causes a man to commit suicide. The 1926–27 diary thus offers strands for several different studies concerning the influence of representations of the sexes in painting, fiction, poetry, prose, plays, popular music, and even cinema on Beauvoir's future writings and actions.

In 1926 she often identified with male writers who questioned certain aspects of the status quo: Claudel, Gide, Rivière, Mauriac, Jammes, Arland, Cocteau, and Bergson. Most of these writers were novelists and poets. Both Gide and Cocteau were openly homosexual. Claudel, Gide, Mauriac, and Jammes had all struggled intensely with their faith in God. Only Bergson was a philosopher. Already in 1926, Beauvoir was seeking to explain the relationship between philosophy and fiction and envisioning how they complement each other in a reader's mind. One could perceive this thought as the first step towards what would eventually become her own personal blend of philosophy, autobiography, and fiction. Having just read Bergson, she commented:

> First, I want to point out the pleasure of being able to establish the connection between an artist, a poet, and a philosopher. I thought about Barrès in terms of language, about Tagore in terms of the two forms of the self, about Alain-Fournier, etc. What one encountered by chance, the other explains scientifically. There is a joyous astonishment in noting that these mysteries of the soul suggested by the artist have more than a subjective existence, and reciprocally that the abstract formulas of philosophy begin to live when they are clarified by quotes which resituate them in the current of individual consciousness. (August 13, 1926)

The fiction writers that Beauvoir most praised in 1926 were filled with sexist notions that still heavily influenced her and that she would struggle through the years to reject.[17] For instance, she exalted Claudel and quoted much of his very Catholic poetry. His work talks about love and suffering, as in the poems from *Les feuilles de saints*, but it is a love that is a union of souls, a simultaneous suffering for union. Beauvoir writes, "Ah! Claudel and what he said about love: 'everything, always' (p. 47–48, first notebook) 'Ah! let it stay a bit in the distance.' ... I reread these quotes and it is all of my soul that repeats them. Peace descends. Claudel always brings me answers. 'There is this need in man above all which is to escape happiness!'" (October 15, 1926).

Yet if one starts to read the Claudelian works that she read in their entirety, it quickly becomes apparent that it is women, not men, who are expected to suffer, escape happiness, and give the most. Claudel's play *L'échange* (The Trade [1995]), for example, is a masterpiece of misogyny in which the main female character, Marthe, does nothing but serve her man, Louis Laine, and finds this entirely normal. Beauvoir quotes as an epigraph before her August 6, 1926, diary entry the words Marthe speaks when she learns that Louis Laine is leaving her: "You say that you do not want to give me pain and suffering / But it is that which I expect from you and that is my role." Similarly, the line Beauvoir chooses to quote from "Canticle for Three Voices" focuses on female suffering. Fausta says, "and if you had had to bring me joy, was it worthwhile for me to learn to suffer?" Beauvoir then directs a comment to her cousin Jacques, with whom she is in love throughout the 1926–27 diary: "Thank you for not bringing me joy" (October 9, 1926).

Twenty years later, in the first volume of *Le deuxième sexe*, Beauvoir devoted a whole chapter to Claudelian myths. Her diary suggests that this is because Claudel had dominated and distorted the worldview of relationships between men and women that she shared with her female peers in her youth. In the chapter on Claudel, Beauvoir proceeded much as in her journal, but what is only sketched in her journal is more widely developed in *Le deuxième sexe*. In addition, she quotes many of the same works in the late 1940s as she did in the 1926 and 1927 notebooks—*L'échange*, *Les feuilles de saints*, and *La cantate à trios voix*—and even uses some of the same quotes.

Beauvoir's other comments on what she was reading explore gender roles and definitions and show the power that novels exercised over her understanding of the sexes. Remarking on *Le coeur gros* (The Heavy Heart) and *Le maître de son coeur* (The Master of His Heart), she said, "I am so moved when I dream that I too will become a woman. ... Oh! I would not have wanted a youth full of illusions that would have been only a continuation of my childhood, the youth of young girls from yesteryear for whom the age for all novelties brought love, and even then a love synonymous, for them, with

15

happiness. I passionately wished to be a young man because of the suffering that I knew young men experienced" (August 17, 1926). When Jacques tells her he doesn't like girls, they talk about Marcel Arland's *Monique* repeatedly. *Monique* is a novel named for its heroine, who struggles against love and marriage to her beloved because it will reduce her to being, like all other women, the possession of a man (October 3, 1926).

Beauvoir consistently read works by Barrès and Cocteau that combatted Catholic doctrines but encouraged spirituality with their talk of having a god within. She appropriated this inner god for herself, although her stress on looking like a girl despite this inner strength implies a definite awareness (perhaps encouraged by Catholicism and sexist literature) that being both a girl and a god is not normally possible: "And I would have wanted to cry out, 'I look like a young girl who does one thing or another; but within me I carry a god'" (October 5, 1926).

Similarly, she reacted against certain ideas that she found sexist or faulty in Cocteau, a poet, playwright, artist, cinematographer, and essayist. For example, Beauvoir was intellectually certain that she did not need anybody else to complete her existence, and therefore she spoke passionately against such notions that Cocteau expressed: "Truly, I completely contradict this stupid verse, 'To love, for a woman, means that one loves her'" (October 16, 1926). Beauvoir responded to Cocteau's sentiment:

> I am pleased to love without being loved; I desire only to give. But precisely, I have very little need to receive, to hang on to someone else. . . . In reality, there are in me two very different moments: the one in which I simply suffer and love—the one in which I no longer suffer, in which I still love but in knowing and controlling it. . . . It must be beautiful to be able to love while forgetting the self (by renunciation and forgetfulness, because one can relinquish oneself without forgetting oneself), with more resignation than harshness. (October 16, 1926)

Yet, she was also tortured by the belief that a man would save her and mold her, just like the young girls described in the 1949 publication *Le deuxième sexe,* in which a young girl idealizes love and wants a man because he is her superior, because he is elite.[18] Certain young girls feel a concrete need for a guide or master. With Beauvoir, her guide was first Jacques (1926) and later, as the second volume of her diary will reveal, Sartre (1929). She addresses Jacques in her journal entry of November 10, 1926: "Very exactly, none of it *exists* for me . . . You alone and me. The girls who have not found you glance around themselves to find someone of whom they will be able to dream; my dream was born with you—not because of you, with you, which is much better. And I can—I will be able to suffer. But thanks to you, this will not be mundane suffering. You saved me from the common herd (banal friendships—acts—studies)."

Her 1927 diary shows her continued efforts to rethink herself and the relationship between the sexes. She still identifies with male authors, however, often those who have gone through religious crises and who project very misogynistic views of the world into their works. She seems drawn to negative stereotypes and expectations depicting women as lesser than men. She writes, for example, "But I too would so much like to have the right to be very simple and very weak, to be a woman" ([May] 19, 1927). Her writing reveals a deep interest in defining self, a continued vacillation between needing nobody and being wildly in love, and occasional self-analysis reflecting an awareness of sexual stereotypes and tautologies. But she is still most fascinated by the mental or spiritual side of beings.

What one might physically do in a love relationship between a man and a woman did not concern her enough to discuss it in 1927, or perhaps it obsessed her too much to record. She did write, however, about feeling physically independent and experiencing sensual pleasure: "In the brilliant sunshine I felt the desire to take walks in muslin dresses completely soaked with my sweat, to stretch myself out in the grass without a thought, to take refuge in this sensual pleasure, in my body which doesn't need to depend on anybody" (April 28, 1927). Mentally, too, she noted her self-sufficiency: "I would like to know Arland, Mauriac . . . I say that, but I really feel that I know myself too well to be able to expect anything from anyone else. Oh, except intellectual pleasure, etc. but nothing profound. Rivière however, and Fournier? Yes, these men remain my friends in spite of everything" (April 28, 1927).

Many of her other comments show a keen awareness of identifying gendered behaviors, and unexpectedly, of praising women for traits often viewed as negative. She reveals her belief that women are idealists and too obsessed with their feelings: "I am still too much of a woman. I say, 'I am seeking what I need and not what is, but I know that what I need cannot be.' I too am setting forth a postulate: it is first necessary to seek what is, then I will see if I must still despair" (July 18, 1927). Yet, the next day, she implicitly applauds women for having to satisfy simultaneously their reason and their sensitivity. For her, a highly developed sensitivity is to be praised: "And then, my dear friends, you don't like young girls, but remember that they not only have a reason to satisfy but also a heavy heart to subdue—and in this way I want to remain a woman, still more masculine by her brain, more feminine by her sensibility. (Moreover, everyone recognizes in approaching me that I am not like other young girls)."

She viewed women not only as more sensitive, but also paradoxically as more practical than even the most sensitive of her male friends, Merleau-Ponty: "Drama of my affections, pathos of life and this unreal Alain-Fournier whom I often am. Indeed, I have a more complicated, more nuanced sensibility than his and a more exhausting power of love. Those problems that he lives in his mind, I live them with my arms and my legs. Has he ever known months when all the days were only tears? I do not want to lose all that" (July 28, 1927).

Similarly, for her, women are more profound than men: "In my intelligence, I am similar to men; in my heart, how different! It seems to me that they have a wider and less profound heart. More cordiality, an easier access, more indulgence, more pity, but also this does not descend into them as in me. For me, to love is the painful thing that Benda describes and blames, this identification with the other, this total 'compassion.' This hardly touches them, does not penetrate into their internal universe: a refuge, a pleasure, not an avidity of the soul" (July 29, 1927).

Her 1927 diary shows her contradictory desires to profit from social categories and to remain outside of them. On the one hand, she told herself, "Don't be 'Mlle Bertrand de Beauvoir.' Be me. Don't have a goal imposed from outside, a social framework to fill. What works for me will work, and that is all. Remain haughty and pitiful" (June 29, 1927). On the other hand, she was aware of the role that situation and education play in one's development, for she praises herself for coming so far: "You see, you must give me credit after all, because I have only been doing philosophy for barely ten months, because I have almost never chatted with intelligent people. I made myself in spite of barely favorable circumstances, and in spite of others, in a great intellectual solitude" (July 19, 1927).

In analyzing the legacy of Beauvoir's diary and the genesis of her autobiography, one must explore Beauvoir's psychological, historical, and sociological setting at the time she kept the journal. Why, how, and in what personal situation did Beauvoir construct the text of her 1926–27 diary? The first page of her 1926 notebook indicates that she is not writing for any reader but herself and that she does not want anyone else to read it. She warns, "If someone, anyone, reads these pages, I will never forgive him."[19] Unlike later, when Beauvoir shared her diary with Sartre, in 1926–27 she was writing her diary for herself alone. Her diary thus offers an uncharted journey into her mind as she explored her theories on the world around her and the relationship of those theories to writing. She constructed her diary under psychological and familial constraints that produced a particular diary form. One encounters challenges in reproducing the form and translating the meaning for publication.

Two major factors influenced the construction of Beauvoir's 1926–27 diary, and together they serve as another reason why her diary deserves to be read and studied for its differences from her published autobiography. The first factor is psychological; in her 1926–27 explanations of why she writes, one can find her earliest theories on writing. For Beauvoir, writing is therapeutic. It helps her to understand her thoughts, herself, and the self and life in general. It guards against loss and death. In the first two notebooks alone, Beauvoir reflects constantly about why she writes, what constitutes good writing, and how keeping her journal differs from writing essays, letters, novels, or anything else.

Her 1926 diary entries reveal her effort to understand herself and how the keeping of a diary relates to it. In August 1926, a reader learns, Beauvoir refrains from recording her private difficulties because of excessive modesty. She tries to reveal certain emotions to herself by comparing her attempts to do things with her hopes of realizing them. She finds that her written image of herself corresponds poorly to her real self and that writing cannot possibly reflect the intensity of feeling; but she discovers that such writing will help her to remember things differently when she is old and bitter. Writing in her journal gives meaning to her life. In October 1926 Beauvoir starts to write with more abandon; she shows her awareness of a tradition in which young girls keep diaries, and she expresses her guilt for resembling those girls. Is she wrong to write down impressions of the moment, she inquires. She notes that it is when she feels no need for people that she writes. November 1926 reveals that although she writes to see herself clearly, she also writes when she is sleepy, achy, and incapable of thinking well. This means that her diary passages are often ambiguous and awkwardly written, and I have tried to reflect this in my translations of them. She criticizes herself, her mother, and several of her friends and acquaintances in writing. She implies that she writes for her mental health, and that the less she writes, the more she knows that things in her life are going better.

Her 1927 notebook indicates a shift in mentality. She writes less about the keeping of her journal and more readily accepts her own inconsistencies. She writes thoughts she no longer simply thinks; she finds herself to be unjustly critical of herself and others; she discloses herself to her journal as she desires. She constantly judges her role as diarist and tries to use her time better, vowing to "keep a journal every day with precise descriptions of what I have done, seen, thought (and not lose myself in vague raptures and imprecise ramblings)" (July 7, 1927). But overall, she contemplates the thoughts and writings of others and discusses philosophy in an overt fashion.

The second factor influencing Beauvoir's diary creation is her familial situation. Both her psychological and her material situations evoke certain questions about the formation of her text and suggest some responses as to why the versions of the self presented there are much more vibrant, messy, endearing, and believable than the versions offered elsewhere. Just as our thoughts, words, and actions are often inconsistent and illogical in real life, so too are those of the self revealed by the diary. In contrast, the self depicted in her autobiography is constructed after the fact, and since meaning is imposed from the ending back to the beginning, it is a much more unified and unquestionable self.

As she wrote the 1926–27 portion of her diary, Beauvoir lived with her family in a tiny sixth-floor flat. Her mother still opened, explored, and censored or discarded her mail.[20] In essence, Beauvoir's only privacy was psychological. Beauvoir's expressed fear that someone (probably her mother) would read her diary may be why she writes so little about her mother and father in it. Her readers will never know for sure. What is apparent, however, is that Beauvoir did not write in her diary on a daily basis or at the same time of day or always in the same setting. Her diary suggests that she carried it with her in Paris, but that she often did not take it along on vacation. Whole sections were written retrospectively; she would head an entire entry with a date from two weeks later and then create subdates to fill in the time she hadn't recorded. For clarity and ease in reading, I have put these entries in chronological order with explanations in footnotes. Although Beauvoir may have played with self-expression in her diary, it was on a moment-to-moment basis during a typical day in her life. It is not likely that she had a master plan for the presentation of self, as one might for an autobiography or for a character in a novel.

The haphazard presentation of the scattered and contradictory self seen in this diary can be used as a point of departure for future research concerning the political, psychological, and gendered implications of the construction of self in different genres as well as for specific research on Beauvoir's writing. Unlike biographies concerning Beauvoir or her own autobiographical works, which impose order and explication on events years after they happen, her diary shows feelings and thoughts about events as they occur, or at least very soon thereafter. Her diary evokes an image of Beauvoir in the making, her desires, her aspirations, and her personal struggles with her contradictory emotions, thoughts, and lifelong goals. As such, the reader sees a much more universal Beauvoir, one who is more like other young girls with similar backgrounds, rather than the feminist icon created for her *Mémoires* and other autobiographical tomes. Many of the works, authors, and people in her diary reappear in her autobiography years later. However, the advantage of the diary is that a reader has access to all the original quotes that were meaningful to Beauvoir, and her thoughts about them, her family, acquaintances, and friends, before their transformation for the presentation of her public persona in her memoirs. This means that Beauvoir's friends and acquaintances appear much more endearing and vivid in the diary than thirty years later in her memoirs.

Her love for her cousin Jacques, for instance, is organized, sanitized, and marked by irony in her *Mémoires*. Although thirty years later the older and wiser narrator Beauvoir still quoted certain passages from her diary, she immediately discounted their value as though to assure her reader that it was impossible for her to have felt what she recorded at eighteen. She recalled, "Instead of telling myself: 'Every day I feel less certain of being able to find happiness with Jacques,' I wrote: 'I dread happiness more and more,' and 'The prospect of saying yes or no to happiness causes me equal distress.' . . . I was afraid that my affection for him would trap me into becoming his wife, and I savagely rejected the sort of life that awaited the future Madame Laiguillon."[21] In short, Beauvoir's autobiography removes the ambiguity from her feelings and her past. It tells a single version of her past whereas her diary presents similar events and sentiments in the glory of their confusion. For example on July 7, 1927, Beauvoir wrote, "But every time that his presence succeeds his slightly dormant image in the depths of myself, a great wave of love washes over me. . . . I will sacrifice my exams for him, but not my written work if I can do one, nor myself." Later (presumably in 1929, for that is when most of the marginal comments are dated) Beauvoir wrote a note in the margin showing how appalled she was only two years later that she had been going to sacrifice her exams for him. Beauvoir's diary, unlike her *Mémoires*, thus shows that she did and did not want to be married; that she constantly contemplated her love for Jacques, their differences, and their similarities; and that she had conflicting desires to give and yet to keep all of herself in a love relationship.[22]

Her presentation of her relationship to God serves as another striking example of the differences between her experiences as recounted in her diary and as reorganized for her autobiography. With a strict Catholic for a mother, and a very outspoken atheist for a father, Beauvoir manifested a schizophrenic attitude towards God for much longer than her autobiography implies. Her disbelief did not materialize between one day and the next. Brought up as a strict Catholic but exposed to her father's blatant atheism, she wavered at length between an ardent belief in God and total disbelief. With great admiration, she quoted Claudel's verses colored by basic premises of Catholicism such as self-denial and suffering for the love of another. On August 21–23, 1926, she copied several verses of Claudel's "Saint Louis" about God's depositing obedience and a personal calling in every man. She quoted with equal passion Barrès's notion that each person contains a god within, but then averred, "*I have no other god but myself*" (May 21, 1927). She struggled ardently between her desire for God and her inability to accept that God is logically possible. On July 22, 1927, she confessed, "I would want God, and yet God frightens me because then this pain, this love, this past minute would be little ephemeral things and would no longer contain infinity."[23]

A quick overview of the history of writing diaries in France can be helpful for identifying how Beauvoir continued or modified the function of keeping a journal in the early twentieth century. She created her diary as a completely private space for the contemplation of self, others, and the world around her. As such, her diary became a means for her to develop and to love herself more fully as well as to explore all the possible selves that simultaneously resided within her. The journal form evolved from a sixteenth-century Catholic and Christian tool for examining and correcting one's behavior, to a late eighteenth-century secular means of self-expression and self-study, to a nineteenth-century medium for remembering and recording all daily sensations: actions, words, passions, pleasures, and pains, a method resulting in a self scattered into bits and pieces.[24] A tradition existed between 1850 and 1914 in which adolescent girls often kept one of two types of diary as a normal part of their education to learn ethical behavior and to improve their skills of observation and writing: a spiritual diary, founded on the negation and hatred of the self and designated to examine one's conscience for self-purification, and a secular diary, based on respect for the self and designed to reflect and question life in ways impossible for the spiritual diary. A secular diary may interrogate time, individuality, memory, and psychological curiosity besides chronicling social and worldly life and providing portraits of others.[25] The only envisioned readers of these diarists were the girls themselves and their mothers. According to Beauvoir's *Mémoires*, her Catholic upbringing had introduced her to the diary as a mode for the outpourings of her soul and her resolutions for sainthood, and her reader during that time may have been her mother.[26] However, by the beginning of the 1926 diary, Beauvoir was not writing to share anything with her mother; and the few critical comments about her mother suggest that her diary may be one of the few private spaces possessed by Beauvoir. Rather, Beauvoir used her diary to record momentary impressions of all kinds, to comment on the incoherency of the self in general, and for self-analysis. It is never evident that she plans to change her behavior for religious reasons. On the contrary, any desire to change emanates from her own personal ethics in the making. On July 19, 1927, for example, she judges herself severely: "I have examined my conscience, and here is what I have found: prideful, selfish, and not very good. . . . Yes. I often have disgust for myself. I think that I could be very humble before God, but I am not humble before men." Unlike the nineteenth-century diarist who often used the diary primarily to account for use of time, Beauvoir tries to account for the impossibility of defining or classifying the self by the standards of anyone but herself. She writes, "My unity comes neither from any principle nor even any feeling to which I subordinate everything. This unity forms itself only in myself" (April 30, 1927); "I must make *my* unity. I must not care about what others think and do. . . . I mean that I must adopt my own system of values without ever judging in function of a neighbor's system" (May 11, 1927).

It is difficult to ascertain if Beauvoir is imitating the diary of any man or woman in particular. She reveals herself to be an avid reader of male authors who wrote journals, such as Maine de Biran, Léon Bloy, Stendhal, Amiel, Gide, Rivière, and Barrès. Yet, it often remains uncertain whether she read their diaries and if so, if it was before or after beginning her own of 1926.[27] It was common in her day for male authors to cite other authors and discuss their texts in their letters and journals. Beauvoir's diary shows that she was an avid reader of the letters between Rivière and Alain-Fournier, and she even copied quotes from these letters concerning the contradictory desires and behaviors inherent in the self (November 3–4, 1926). Less is known about the practices of female authors or diarists, nor is it clear if Beauvoir read any of their journals since so few of them were mentioned in her diary. Of the few published diaries by women written before 1789, only three of them remain in existence today: those of Albertine de Saussure, the future Germaine de Staël, and the future Lucile Desmoulins.[28] At the time that Beauvoir wrote her 1926 diary, she could have read them and the diary of Marie Bashkirtseff that she cited in *Le deuxième sexe* as well as the journal of Eugénie de Guérin that she cited in the *Mémoires*, but there is nothing in her diary to indicate that she knew of Bashkirtseff or Guérin at that time.[29]

Some knowledge of Beauvoir's family situation gives readers insight into attitudes manifested in her early diaries. For example, her changing social status and her family's history encourage a reader to view her comments about marriage and Jacques as prolongations of a family myth in which she would fulfill her mother's desire by loving and marrying him. Beauvoir was born on January 9, 1908, at 4 A.M. in her mother's bedroom and baptized six weeks later as Simone Ernestine Lucie Marie Bertrand de Beauvoir.[30] She eventually had one sister, younger by two years, referred to in her journal as Hélène, Henriette, or Poupette. As the first child, Simone de Beauvoir was born into a position of superiority. Her father, Georges Bertrand de Beauvoir, belonged to the lower ranks of the aristocracy. Françoise Brasseur, her mother, had grown up in a wealthy bourgeois family. Her parents thus raised Simone to believe that she was part of the elite.

For the first eleven years of her life, Beauvoir lived in a spacious apartment surrounded by her parents, her younger sister, several servants, and a nanny. In the summer of 1919, however, her family suffered a major financial blow that caused them to abandon their comfortable lifestyle. They moved into a tiny sixth-floor flat without heat, running water, or servants. Beauvoir then shared a minuscule room with her sister and learned to do her homework in the study amidst a constant stream of conversation and visitors. As part of the elite, she had been raised to be a social dilettante and upstanding wife and to marry someone elite, well educated, and financially secure. Once her family lost its fortune and status, the prospect of a good marriage became unlikely for her; it was probable that she would have to work. Thus, she grew up surrounded by conflicting social values and desires, which were further complicated by her mother's past. Jacques Champigneulles, the Jacques so frequently invoked by Beauvoir, was her cousin.[31] Her mother, Françoise, had been in love for a short while during her teen years with her own cousin Charles (Jacques's future father) and had hoped to marry him. Françoise's hopes had died when Charles chose to marry her cousin Germaine. As Beauvoir blossomed into adolescence, her mother, perhaps to compensate for her own inability to marry her cousin, began to hope that Simone could marry Jacques and pressured her accordingly.[32]

Methodology

Beauvoir's diary is written in a series of notebooks that could be easily carried everywhere. The ink is faded and the pages are often crumbling and stained with what appears to be food and liquid. It would be difficult to believe that the manuscript is counterfeit since Beauvoir obviously transformed parts of it to produce *Mémoires*. In addition, her style suggests an authentic diary: Beauvoir writes at eighteen and nineteen as a young person might speak, with frequent repetitions, incoherencies, fragments, and incomplete thoughts. Her style tends to improve as the diary progresses, but she persists in her tendency to avoid ending sentences and to overuse dashes and ellipses. I have preserved her ellipses as they appear in the diary, where she commonly uses ellipsis points, or dots, following a space after a word, which suggests a trailing off, not an omission. She comments on this in her entry for November 13, 1926, when she vows to "not pour out my feelings with a great number of ellipses." Where Beauvoir used ellipses in any other way, I have noted this in the text. It is evident from Beauvoir's remarks in the text and the margins that she frequently reread her entries and commented on them. Vertical lines frequently appear in the margins in an ink unlike that used for writing the text, suggesting that Beauvoir marked her diary as she prepared future works. Words that she underlined in her diary have been italicized in this published version.

For the sake of readability for an Anglophone reader, I have altered her style and punctuation when translating the text more literally would create difficulty or confusion that was not in the original manuscript. In most cases, I have tried to reproduce her style, including alliterations and levels of language, and I have preserved the ambiguity of her vocabulary and syntax as closely as possible. I leave it to future scholars to argue for the limiting of her meaning in certain contexts. Although Beauvoir used this diary as a basis for her future writings in all genres, I do not assume that her later writings provide a key for knowing her earliest thoughts.

It is uncertain if Beauvoir wrote chronologically as the text appears in her journal, and thus exact reproduction of the manuscript is difficult. As the diary opens, for example, there are a number of quotes from a variety of authors, which she often does not discuss for several pages if at all. It is impossible to know if she added the quotes as she found them to blank spaces at the beginning, or if she started her journal by copying quotes that appealed to her. Although the physical construction of the manuscript is a treasure itself because there are so many additions in the margins and quotes on facing pages, cost prohibits the placement of these quotes and comments across from the diary entries in the published translation of her text. I have chosen to place the quotes near the date of the entry they accompanied, with a note of explanation, although this unfortunately alters the look of the text. I have relegated to footnotes Beauvoir's comments referring to certain passages and written years later in the margins, and I have also recorded there the evidence of the highlighting of certain passages, which Beauvoir marked for emphasis with vertical single, double, or triple lines in the adjacent margin on the same page or on the facing verso. I have composed numbered endnotes to explicate for the modern reader many of the people, events, and works that Beauvoir mentions in her diary.

Beauvoir was a voracious reader and loved interacting with her peers. The information in this diary implies that she often cites passages from memory, for there are sometimes blanks left or slight changes in wording in her quotations. It is impossible to know in certain cases if Beauvoir read the quoted material in the original work of which it was a part, or if she read it in secondary literature or simply heard it quoted by friends, acquaintances, or professors. On occasion, I found the same quotation in a variety of the works that she discusses. I have provided published English translations of texts cited by Beauvoir when the translations pertained to the French that she recorded. In certain instances, she provided both author and title, in others only the author, and in still others only a quotation. Additional information is sometimes available in her published memoirs, but finding the sources was often difficult. When Beauvoir cited French translations of German authors, the English translation of the same author and text is, of course, often slightly different. I have indicated significant differences in translations from Beauvoir's citations and from the English edition texts that I have used. In instances where the French terms carry both a philosophical significance and a common meaning, and where one of these meanings would be lost in English, I have added the French words in parentheses or in an endnote.

The 1926–27 portion of Beauvoir's diary contains a wealth of feelings, ideas, activities, and artistic works that lend themselves to a variety of interpretations. It not only proves Beauvoir's originality as a writer and budding philosopher; it is also testimony to how a reader might easily make self-reflection, literature, music, painting, and philosophy an integral part of one's life to live more fully, more ethically, more intensely, and in a more self-loving and thinking manner.

NOTES

1. See, for example, Moi, "What Is a Woman" and "I Am a Woman," in *What Is a Woman?* (40, 56); see also both entire essays in *What Is a Woman?* (3–120, 121–250, respectively). Part of that new philosophy involved Beauvoir's attempt to undermine the patriarchal order with her fiction, and more particulary in writing her novel, *L'invitée* [She Came to Stay], as I argued in a presentation to the Simone de Beauvoir Society in 1993, which was later published. See Klaw, "The Rewriting of Sexual Identity from Colette's *Chéri* to Beauvoir's *L'Invitée.*"

2. See, for example, Fullbrook and Fullbrook, *Simone de Beauvoir and Jean-Paul Sartre.*

3. See Klaw, "Update on Simone de Beauvoir," for an overview of recent publications devoted to these issues.

4. See Klaw, *Le Paris de Beauvoir/Beauvoir's Paris,* which combines excerpts from the manuscripts of Beauvoir's student diary, my translation of them, and a wealth of other data drawn from Beauvoir's contemporaries, life, and published writings to situate Beauvoir in the historical moment of places in Paris.

5. Moi, *Simone de Beauvoir,* 50. See Bonal and Ribowska, *Simone de Beauvoir,* 39, for reproductions of Beauvoir's diplomas.

6. Ibid., 47; *Mémoires d'une jeune fille rangée,* 223; *Memoirs of a Dutiful Daughter,* 157.

7. Moi, *Simone de Beauvoir,* 48–50.

8. Gibson, *Le symbolisme,* 24.

9. Ibid., 31, 49.

10. The tendency of many women to base their own standards and lives on the ideas and public image of Beauvoir became especially clear during the outcry against Beauvoir when her private life was first revealed in her war diary and her letters to Sartre. See Galster, "'Une femme machiste et mesquine,'" and Barnes, "Simone de Beauvoir's Journal and Letters."

11. See Klaw, "Intertextuality and Destroying the Myth of Woman," 549–66, which demonstrates that Beauvoir's construction of *Tous les hommes sont mortels* shows how profoundly literary myths influence women to appear (as if on stage like the main female character of the novel) rather than to be (something authentic in life).

12. Beauvoir, *Le deuxième sexe,* 406.

13. This malaise seemingly influenced Beauvoir's public portrayal of herself for most of her life, and it encouraged her to depict the originality of her life and eroticism in her published fiction rather than in her published autobiographical volumes during her lifetime. Moreover, such unease concerning women's roles caused some of the cuts and errors in the English translation of *Les Mandarins.* See Klaw, "Sexuality in Beauvoir's *Les Mandarins,*" 193–221.

14. Maleprade, *Léontine Zanta,* 106, 108.

15. Bell, *Women, the Family, and Freedom,* 308–10.

16. Gibson, *Le symbolisme,* 40–41.

17. See Klaw, "Simone de Beauvoir and Nelson Algren," for a detailed interpretation (incorporating portions of Beauvoir's 1926–30 diary) of the influence of these myths on Beauvoir's later life.

18. Beauvoir, *Le deuxième sexe,* 2:117.

19. The context of this diary suggests that this general warning is perhaps most directed at Beauvoir's mother. Nevertheless, Beauvoir stated it using the French equivalents of "some-

one" (quelqu'un) and "he" (lui), and I have chosen to respect Beauvoir's ambiguity in my translation.

20. Patterson, "Entretien avec Hélène de Beauvoir," 5, 18.

21. *Mémoires*, 322–23; *Memoirs*, 233.

22. For other examples of the conflicting attitudes about love that Beauvoir portrays in her diary, see Klaw, "Simone de Beauvoir and Nelson Algren."

23. For other examples of inconsistencies in the presentations of events in Beauvoir's journal and autobiography, see Klaw, "Simone de Beauvoir, du journal intime aux *Mémoires*."

24. Simonet-Tenant, *Le journal intime*, 12, 33–42.

25. Lejeune, *Le moi des demoiselles*, 20–22.

26. *Mémoires*, 102; *Memoirs*, 74.

27. As noted earlier, in the 1926 notebook Beauvoir makes references to a 1925 notebook that has not yet been located. In light of this, the official beginning date of her diary would be 1925.

28. Simonet-Tenant, *Le journal intime*, 38.

29. *Le deuxième sexe*, 1:226; *The Second Sex*, 132; *Mémoires*, 197; *Memoirs*, 142.

30. Bair, *Simone de Beauvoir*, 33.

31. Jacques is referred to as Jacques Laiguillon in Beauvoir's autobiography.

32. Bair, *Simone de Beauvoir*, 98–99. For a more detailed look at Beauvoir's relationship to her mother, see Klaw, "Desire, Ambiguity, and Contingent Love," 110–23.

Beauvoir's Early Philosophy: 1926–27

Margaret A. Simons

For philosophers familiar with the traditional interpretation of Simone de Beauvoir as a literary writer and philosophical follower of Jean-Paul Sartre, Beauvoir's 1926–27 student diary is a revelation. Inviting an exploration of Beauvoir's early philosophy foreclosed by the traditional interpretation, the student diary shows Beauvoir's dedication to becoming a philosopher and her own formulation of philosophical problems and positions usually attributed to Sartre's influence, such as the central problem of "the opposition of self and other," years before she first met Sartre in 1929.

Also challenging the traditional interpretation of Beauvoir's work is the wide range of authors quoted in her diary. On the first pages of the 1927 diary alone are quotations from French (Alain, Lagneau, and Bergson) and German philosophers (Schopenhauer, Eucken, and Nietzsche), as well as poets and literary writers (Valéry, Mallarmé, Aragon, Maeterlinck, Claudel, Rilke, Arland, Mauriac, and Alain-Fournier). These quotations argue for a broadening of the context of interpretation of Beauvoir's philosophical work not only beyond Sartre, but also beyond a narrow, hermetic conception of philosophy as a discipline.

Reading the student diary within a larger historical context, we discover that it reflects Beauvoir's experience as a member of the first generation of French women to gain full access to the academic world of philosophy, an experience that problematizes her identity as a woman. The diary shows Beauvoir struggling to accommodate herself to the male world of philosophy while striving to make philosophy her own. For Beauvoir this means following Henri Bergson in rejecting a philosophy that engages only the abstract intelligence. Defining her own unique literary philosophical methodology, Beauvoir vows to create a philosophy that is able, like literature, to encompass emotion as well as reason.

This creative process begins in her diary where Beauvoir describes the concrete realities of her own lived experience. Searching for a sense of self in the "nothingness of everything human," Beauvoir grapples with the existential problem of despair and the temptations of bad faith, or self-deception. Celebrating her newly found freedom and academic achievements, Beauvoir still struggles with the masochistic asceticism of her Catholic upbringing and longs for love, fearing a solitary future bereft of the comforts of woman's traditional role. Beauvoir's student diary thus allows us to trace the development of her early philosophy within the context of her life, while providing an intimate view of an academic world in transformation.[1]

In *Memoirs of a Dutiful Daughter* Beauvoir writes that she first became interested in philosophy during her 1924–25 senior year at the Institut Adeline-Désir, or Cours Désir, a private Catholic girls' school that she had attended since the age of five. The yearlong philosophy class prepared the students for the difficult philosophy *baccalauréat* exam, required for access to the university and entrance to the professions.[2] The class was taught by an elderly priest who, Beauvoir writes, "disposed of" the four subject areas of the philosophy syllabus (psychology, logic, ethics, and metaphysics) "at the rate of four hours of classes per week,"[3] half of the standard eight-hours-a-week class offered in the boys *lycées*.[4] Their philosophy textbook was, according to Beauvoir, no more "encumbered with subtleties" than their instructor: "regarding each problem [the textbook] made a rapid inventory of human errors and taught us the truth according to Saint Thomas" (*Mémoires*, 219).[5]

Despite its shortcomings, the course inspired Beauvoir to dream of studying philosophy at the Sorbonne and teaching philosophy in a *lycée*. "I read a magazine article about a woman philosopher, Mlle Zanta, who had earned her doctorate," Beauvoir writes in *Mémoires*. "In those days you could count on one hand the number of women who had passed the *agrégation* [graduate teaching] exam or earned a doctorate in philosophy:

I wanted to be one of those pioneers" (222).[6] Pursuing a degree in philosophy in 1925 would indeed make a French woman a pioneer, since university education had been fully opened to French women only in 1924 following years of feminist struggle. Until then French schools had been governed by the eighteenth-century educational ideal of a separate, domestic sphere for women. Girls and boys attended different schools with different curricula and even took different state-administered exams. Secondary schools for girls traditionally prepared girls not for the *baccalauréat* degree, but only for a finishing-school diploma with no practical value.[7] It was not until 1905 that a woman first competed in the men's *agrégation* exam in philosophy.[8]

The situation began to change during World War I when women with the *licence* degree in philosophy were allowed to teach in the boys *lycées*. After the war, the government tried unsuccessfully to force the women back into the domestic sphere, closing the men's *agrégation* exams to women in every field except modern language. But after protests by the university faculty, the women were allowed, as an exception and under a separate classification, to compete in the men's *agrégation* exam in philosophy.[9]

World War I actually spurred reform of women's education in France as the *baccalauréat* came to be seen as offering a respectable alternative—a "dowry substitute"—for unmarried women whose families had been impoverished by the war. According to the historian Karen Offen, the war laid bare "the unpalatable fact" that a sizable number of upper-class women "might never marry and might, therefore, have to support themselves."[10] In her *Mémoires,* Simone de Beauvoir writes that she and her younger sister faced this very situation. "My father was not a feminist," she writes. "He admired the wisdom of novels . . . where the woman lawyer or doctor ended up sacrificing her career to domestic harmony. But necessity made the rule: 'You, my girls, will not marry' he often repeated. 'You have no dowry and will have to work'" (145).

In 1924 the historic Bérard decree provided a new curricular option in the public girls' *lycées,* offering for the first time the courses in Latin and philosophy required for the *bac.*[11] Reforms at the post-secondary level followed soon after. Henceforth, women, no longer classified separately from men, would be permitted "to take all of the *agrégation* exams and all of the *certificats* previously reserved for men."[12] Offen describes the 1924 reforms as "a triumph for Third Republique feminism." Thus when Beauvoir took the *baccalauréat* exams in philosophy and mathematics in the spring of 1925 and prepared to enter the university the following fall, she was the heir to a feminist struggle against an educational system based on sexual difference, an experience that interestingly prefigures her own later rejection of a feminism based on difference in *The Second Sex*.[13]

The effects of the 1924 reforms were so dramatic that in 1930 a professor at the Sorbonne described the "invasion of the university by women" as the "greatest revolution" of the postwar era. Rarely seen at the Sorbonne in 1900, by 1930 women comprised almost half of the student body.[14] But while many young women took advantage of the new opportunities for higher education and access to the professions, the reforms were realized, according to Offen, in "an adverse political and cultural climate." Offen writes, "France in the interwar period remained an intransigently conservative society." Many French people saw the reforms as "a political concession to bittersweet socio-economic realities that had rendered unattainable, though no less desirable, the republican ideal of a complete sexual division of labor in the family and society."[15] The result was what Françoise Mayeur describes as the "disarray" of families caught up in the social change, a description that applies to Beauvoir's family.[16]

Beauvoir's ambition in 1925 to study philosophy at the Sorbonne was opposed by her religious mother, who had heard that "philosophy mortally corroded the soul" (*Mémoires*, 223). Beauvoir reluctantly agreed to "sacrifice philosophy for literature" and enrolled in October 1925 at the Institut Sainte-Marie, a Catholic girls' school in the Paris suburb of Neuilly, to prepare for a degree in classics, while also studying mathematics at the Institut Catholique in Paris, and learning Greek (223).[17] Beauvoir's father, instead of encouraging her academic efforts, insisted that she fulfill all of the social obligations of a proper young lady and angrily accused her of "denying her sex" when she refused to do so (247).[18] Deeply hurt by the loss of her father's support, Beauvoir writes in her *Mémoires* that she felt "ill at ease in my own skin and full of resentment" (248–49). The familial "disarray" evident in her father's charge that she was "denying her sex" in seriously pursuing a career is also reflected in Beauvoir's student diary, where she grapples with the problematizing of her gender identity. Her efforts to reconcile her identity as a woman with her career in philosophy may have laid the experiential ground for her later question in *The Second Sex*: "What is a woman?"[19]

While at Neuilly in 1925, Beauvoir found her first intellectual mentor. Robert Garric was a charismatic literature professor, veteran of the World War I trenches, and founder of an idealistic movement, the Équipes Sociales (Social Teams), which sought to overcome class divisions by bringing together young people from different classes. Inspired by Garric's example, Beauvoir vowed in her diary to dedicate her own life to serving humanity. She emulated Garric's asceticism, neglecting her health and appearance, and joined the Équipes Sociales, teaching literature to a group of girls in the working-class suburb of Belleville in 1926–27. Beauvoir's father condemned her actions and Garric's politics as undermining the bourgeois values of family and class loyalty. "Stunned and painfully disoriented" by her father's condemnation, Beauvoir writes in her *Mémoires* that her rancor gradually "turned into rebellion" (264). Thus Beauvoir's life in 1925–26 is characterized by academic achievement and ascetic self-denial, by familial "disarray" and conflict reflective of an era of radical change in women's roles.

By the spring of 1926, after passing the exams for *certificats d'études supérieurs* in French literature, mathematics, and Latin, Beauvoir, with the consent of her parents and the encouragement of the philosophy professor at Neuilly, Jeanne Mercier, was able to return to her original project of preparing for the *license* in philosophy.[20] She began studying philosophy at the Sorbonne in the fall of 1926 while taking courses in logic and history of philosophy from Mercier at Neuilly (*Mémoires*, 256, 282).[21]

When the diary opens, with an entry dated August 6, 1926, Beauvoir is grappling with a central problem of her early life and philosophy, the conflicting moral obligations to self and others. Recounting a pilgrimage to Lourdes with an aunt, Beauvoir recalls feeling "ashamed" when faced with the physical suffering of the invalids: "[O]nly a life that was a complete gift of oneself, a total self-abnegation, seemed possible to me." But then, anticipating her critique of self-abnegation in *The Second Sex,* Beauvoir rejects it, describing the "absolute gift" as "moral suicide." She vows, instead, to achieve an "equilibrium" between the duty to self and the duty to others.[22] In the August 12, 1926, diary entry, Beauvoir frames the problem in metaphysical terms, referring to one part of herself "made to be given away," and another "made to be kept and cultivated." Later, in the November 5, 1926, entry, Beauvoir returns to the problem, describing her existence as divided "into two parts": one part, she describes as "for [her]self," and the other part as "for others," that is "the bonds that unite [her] with all beings."

Beauvoir's 1926 description of existing "for herself" and "for others" lays the ground for her later philosophical work on the problem of the Other, as in her 1943 metaphysical novel *She Came to Stay,* where the female protagonist struggles to reclaim an existence for herself instead of existing solely for others, and in *The Second Sex* (1949), where Beauvoir argues that women are forced to assume themselves not as they exist for themselves but solely as they exist for men, thus as the absolute Other.

During the course of the 1926 diary, Beauvoir's efforts to reconcile these two "parts" of her existence are complicated by various influences, including her reading of Henri Bergson, the leading French philosopher of the early twentieth century. Beauvoir quotes at length in her 1926 diary from Bergson's *Essay on the Immediate Data of Consciousness,* which she describes, on August 16, as a "great intellectual rapture."[23] This diary entry may surprise those who remember the reference to Bergson in Beauvoir's *Mémoires:* "I would not have been at all pleased if someone had prophesied that I would become a kind of Bergson; I didn't want to speak with that abstract voice which, whenever I heard it, failed to move me" (288). In this case as in so many others, Beauvoir's diaries present a very different picture.

In the August 16 diary entry, Beauvoir is critical of Bergson's impersonal philosophical voice. But she lauds his methodological "appeal to intuition," which brings philosophy in contact with the "palpable reality" of life, as more characteristic of literature than philosophy. On August 9, Beauvoir quotes Bergson's celebration of the "bold novelist" able to tear aside "the cleverly woven web of our conventional self" and reveal the "fundamental absurdity" of impressions underneath. "Nobody has better than he . . . defined the art of the modern novelist," Beauvoir writes, suggesting Bergson's influence on Beauvoir's developing literary philosophical method.[24]

Beauvoir writes, in the August 16 entry, that she is "thrilled" by Bergson's "analysis of the two aspects of the self," the authentic inner self and the external social self. For Bergson, unlike Beauvoir who is concerned with serving others as well as the self, our responsibility is wholly to the self and its freedom, which we discover only by breaking through what Bergson calls the superficial "crust" of the social self. If his ethic of individual freedom complicated Beauvoir's search for an "equilibrium," in the relation of self and other, Bergson's methodological turn to intuition and rejection of philosophy's sole reliance on reason might have appealed to a young woman trying to enter the male world of philosophy and make it her own.

As classes begin in the fall of 1926 her earlier passion for philosophy gradually returns. "I got caught up again in philosophy last night," she writes on October 6. An important influence in this interest is her philosophy professor at Neuilly, Jeanne Mercier. While Beauvoir's *Mémoires* describes Mercier's influence as limited by her religiosity (309), the student diary reveals a much closer, and more problematic, relationship with her teacher, whose mystification of romantic love complicates Beauvoir's efforts to balance her existence "for [her]self" and "for others." "This long chat with a mademoiselle Mercier previously unknown to me transported me to this region I will call 'Claudelian,'" Beauvoir writes on November 16, "because as in

Claudel's universe, life appears to be a necessary drama that infinitely surpasses the poor humans who live it." It is also a universe where, as Beauvoir will explain in the chapter on Claudel in *The Second Sex*, woman is a model of "perfect devotion" "made for giving of herself and not for taking."[25] "She told me of the grandeur of love," Beauvoir writes on November 17, ". . . and that this need two people have for one another is really majestic, and their union is a really complete and beautiful thing, the most beautiful. And if one is truly designated, called by a being, that is where one must go."

Beauvoir applies Mercier's Claudelian model to her relationship with her cousin, Jacques, whom she dreams of marrying: "In my soul's mystical attraction to his, nothing about him can stop me anymore. At moments, he appears to me as only the pretense for a higher necessity to which I bow my head" (November 16, 1927). It is thanks to Mercier, Beauvoir writes, that she dares "*to demand* . . . one of 'these beautiful unions' described by Mademoiselle Mercier." Under Mercier's influence Beauvoir's need for Jacques is exaggerated: "I need him in order to live," she writes. The result is a problematic complication of Beauvoir's effort to achieve an equilibrium between her existence for herself and for others.

The diary suggests that Mercier was also affected by the social "disarray" of women's changing roles. "Do you believe that a woman can have a normal life outside of marriage?" Mercier asks in a question recounted in both the November 17 diary entry and in Beauvoir's *Mémoires* (309). Rather than discouraging her student, Mercier's personal remark seems to have helped Beauvoir, who marvels at hearing such passionate words from a woman she had "believed to be purely intellectual!" Mercier encourages Beauvoir to value her own emotions, a traditional element of womanly identity disparaged by philosophers: "She told me that my weaknesses—these crying fits, these feelings of disgust—were valuable, that I am complete because I think my life, and at the same time, I live intensely." But Mercier's message of self-respect is undermined by her mystification of love: "Only, while showing me my riches," Beauvoir writes on November 17, "she increased my ardent desire for *him* to come take them."

In the spring of 1927, Mercier will invite Beauvoir to teach the psychology part of the *baccalauréat* philosophy class at Neuilly the following year (*Mémoires*, 359). Beauvoir accepts, but her relationship with Mercier will become strained during that year. On July 10, 1927, Beauvoir writes of Mercier's efforts to "convert" her. In the September 30, 1927, entry, Beauvoir writes about Mercier, "her God is far from me," and adds that she has been "[f]reed from those who want to lead me astray, far from myself." The portrait of

35

Mercier that emerges from the 1926 diary resembles Chantal Plattard, a character from Beauvoir's 1935–37 novel *When Things of the Spirit Come First.* Plattard is a teacher whose bad-faith mystification of sexuality has tragic consequences for her young woman students, who take literally what she meant spiritually. Beauvoir's novel remained unpublished until 1979. But Beauvoir's relationship with her former mentor had clearly soured by 1945 when Mercier wrote an article condemning the existentialism of Beauvoir and Sartre as "satanic," a "blaspheme," and a "betrayal of the spirit."[26]

When Beauvoir's 1927 diary begins, in April that year, following her success on the history of philosophy exam, the themes of her later existential philosophy continue to be apparent: the sense of nothingness and the struggle against despair, the search for self and the temptations of bad faith, and the conflicting demands of an existence for herself and for others. "What did this year bring to me intellectually?" she asks on April 20. "A serious philosophical formation which ... sharpened my (alas!) too penetrating critical mind and my desire for rigor and logic. ... Everywhere I observed only our inability to found anything in the order of knowledge as in the order of ethics."

The erosion of philosophical absolutes, following the earlier erosion of her religious faith, leaves her with a frustrated awareness of the uselessness of her existence, as in the April 30 entry: "I am really in a paradoxical situation; I feel my intelligence and the positive power that it could have. ... Only these very qualities which require to be of use also show me what an illusion it is to claim to be of use for anything." "I am intellectually very alone and very lost at the entrance to my life" she writes on May 6, recounting an appeal to a friend. "I feel that I have worth, that I have something to do and say, but my thoughts spin aimlessly." A frustrated yearning for an absolute justification for her life can lead to despair: "These miserable efforts for being!" she writes on May 19, "... in my depths, masked by this day's diversions, the same emptiness!"

Beauvoir reports in an April 28, 1927, entry that she finds the "most resources" in the "self-worship" (*culte du moi*), a Bergsonian position popularized by Maurice Barrès. But for Beauvoir, the self, as a construct of consciousness and not a given, is a problematic resource. "[W]hat am I?" she writes on April 30. "My unity comes from neither any principle nor even any feeling to which I subordinate everything. This unity forms itself only in myself." A sense of detachment from her own memories means that the appeal to memory offered by Bergson as a solution to the problem of constructing an enduring self is unavailable to her. Entering the male world of academic philosophy has cut her off from her past: "My past is behind me like a thing that has left me," she writes on April 28, "something I can't do anything about anymore and that I watch with foreign eyes."

Against the disintegration of the self, Beauvoir turns for support, perhaps surprisingly, to friendship, acknowledging the affective bond uniting self and other that will be an important feature of her later ethics, as in her 1944 essay *Pyrrhus and Cineas,* where responding to the appeal of the other opens a path out of solipsism. In the April 18, 1927, diary entry, Beauvoir describes herself as finding comfort and encouragement in the other's gaze: "I am lonely to the point of anxiety today. . . . To console myself, I must glance at this self with the multiple faces which my friends' eyes reflect." On May 20 Beauvoir writes that "even simple companionship is a very precious good! In it alone I can tear myself away from my own manner of thinking." Thus the look of the other can be a solace, and not always the threat to the self as recounted in Beauvoir's metaphysical novel *She Came to Stay.*

As in the case of friendship, love can provide a support against nothingness and despair, while also posing even more of a threat to the self. On June 3 Beauvoir writes of her love for Jacques: "we will support one another so strongly that we will know how to withstand the great vertiginous void. We will not fall into the abyss." But love is not an unproblematic resource. Feelings can change and passions dissipate. "There is nothing in which I believe," she writes on April 30. "Not even in myself. I can love . . . and act according to my love: this is what allows me to be lively and passionate. But I do not master love, and once it stops, I have nothing to hang on to."

The problem of love is heightened by the Claudelian masochistic ideal embraced by Beauvoir that demands woman's self-abdication and fusion with the other. In the April 18, 1927, diary entry Beauvoir describes Jacques as "everything—my only reason to live" and adds, "I wait so impatiently for the day when you will no longer be 'the other' or 'self,' but it will only and definitively be 'us.'" The May 6 diary entry shows Beauvoir struggling with the threat posed by this masochistic ideal: "[M]y *self* does not want to let itself be devoured by his." Beauvoir recounts having witnessed the erosion of her ambitions the previous winter under the influence of this ideal. Now she fears that marriage to Jacques would be "the supreme defeat!" But the problem seems unsolvable when Beauvoir defines loving, as she does in the August 1, 1927, entry, as "feeling dominated," a position that she will later critique in *The Second Sex.*

Beauvoir's struggles against despair in 1927 present her with the temptation to self-deception, or bad faith, the subject of *When Things of the Spirit*

Come First and a central theme of her later ethics, including *The Second Sex,* where bad faith drives both men's oppression of women and women's complicity. The April 30 diary entry reveals Beauvoir's envy of friends who are able to build their lives on "some convictions that they hang on to." Comparing herself to them, Beauvoir writes that she "felt ashamed for lacking certainty." This yearning for absolutes is the origin of bad faith. As the passage continues, Beauvoir moves beyond the shameful recognition of her inadequacies in the eyes of her friends: "I cannot keep myself from envying them," she writes, "because it seems that in faith and happiness, there is something more complete than in doubt and restlessness [*inquiétude*]. However I do indeed *know* that their God is not. . . . . No, really; what I like more than anything is not ardent faith. . . . It is intelligence and criticism.. . . . It is the beings who cannot let themselves be duped and who struggle to live in spite of their lucidity." In condemning bad faith in the name of lucidity, Beauvoir establishes a central theme of her philosophy. From Marguerite's turn away from mystification in *When Things of the Spirit Come First,* to Beauvoir's call in *The Second Sex* for men and women to assume the ambiguity of their embodied existence with a "lucid modesty" (*DS,* 2:573), Beauvoir calls to her readers to face life without illusions.[27]

In 1927 Beauvoir finds the most effective recourse against despair in her work in philosophy. Reflecting a Bergsonian turn to the description of immediate experience, Beauvoir uses her diary to discover herself: "Oh! I love myself and I love my life," she writes in the April 30 entry. "I just reread the pages written in this notebook, and combined with the recent reflections on myself, it all results in a marvelous drunkenness." Beauvoir's descriptive methodology is particularly evident in the May 6 entry describing "a strange minute" involving a fellow philosophy student, Barbier. "I had just seen Barbier again. . . . He talked to me about myself, philosophy, and literature. . . . And then, . . . for an instant, I held a completely new life in my hands. . . . I thought about the love that could have been between us; I *saw* myself between his and Jacques's love. Well really! I was not chained to the past. A new passion was blossoming in me. Splendid. I loved him."

In recounting this experience of existential freedom, of being no longer "chained to the past," Beauvoir practices her descriptive methodology: "How can I put it?" she writes. "It was not speculation or reasoning, or dream or imagination. For an instant, it was. Still a bit even now." Anticipating her claim in *The Second Sex* that the only "justification for present existence is its expansion towards an indefinitely open future" (*DS,* 1:31), Beauvoir writes: "my life is no longer a traced path. . . . It is an unmarked trail that my walking alone will create." Beauvoir acknowledges it is "Bergson's *élan vital* that I am rediscovering here." Linking "free decision" and the "interplay of circumstances" in a way that anticipates the compatibilism of freedom and determinism in *The Second Sex*, Beauvoir's famous critique of marriage is also anticipated in this passage: "The horror of the definitive choice is that we engage not only the self of today but also that of tomorrow. And that is why marriage is fundamentally immoral."

Beauvoir analyzes her attraction to Barbier as representing the possibility, ridiculed by Jacques, of developing her own philosophy. She writes on May 6: "There is the serious possibility [*possible*], austerity—philosophy—Barbier; oh, its very strong attraction, my need to realize what I feel within me, to do something, to believe in something! My intellectual passions, my philosophical seriousness!" Challenging Jacques's ridicule of philosophy as a vain search, she counters that it imposes itself on her "as a living presence."

Beauvoir's turn to philosophy in response to despair grows ever clearer as the diary continues. "Mademoiselle Mercier spoke yesterday of . . . the horror of collapsed syntheses for anyone who does not have the strength to reconstruct any of them. I must reconstruct," she writes on May 11. Using her diary as a tool for self-discovery, Beauvoir is inspired to believe in her ability to undertake a serious philosophical work. "Rereading the first pages of this notebook," she writes on May 13, "I marvel . . . at my gift for describing the states that I was going through. I am moved by this as though these pages were written by another. Thus, could I too do something? I must work on a work in which I believe." As the May 13 entry continues, we discover Beauvoir's early formulation of her literary-philosophical method: "Write 'essays on life' that would not be novelistic, but rather philosophical, by linking them vaguely with fiction. But let thought be the essential and let me seek to find the truth." The philosophical work that Beauvoir is planning here in 1927 anticipates her literary-philosophical methodology employed in *She Came to Stay* and defended in her 1946 essay "Literature and Metaphysics."[28]

The student diary reveals a previously unknown influence on Beauvoir's early philosophy, her Sorbonne philosophy professor Jean Baruzi. The April 18, 1927, entry states, "Baruzi attracts me this year with his scrupulous and profound faith . . . and his manner of living his thoughts to his fingertips." On April 30, Beauvoir comments, "Baruzi's class, where beautiful and austere ideas give me a serious and passionate fever." On June 29, in laying out her projects for the next academic year, Beauvoir refers to doing work for

Baruzi and on July 7 identifies him as someone who "will criticize" her and "take [her] seriously." In the July 29 entry Beauvoir declares her intention to "link up with Baruzi" and writes of mysticism as a "tempting" alternative to skepticism and indifference. But who was Jean Baruzi?

A student of Bergson and a scholar of Leibniz's philosophy of religion and William James's psychology of religion, Jean Baruzi was the author of a controversial 1924 dissertation, published in 1931 as *St. John of the Cross and the Problem of Mystical Experience,* giving an existential-phenomenological description of religious anguish and the "lived experience" of the mystic. Baruzi was also a student of Edmund Husserl's phenomenology and might have introduced it to Beauvoir,[29] who makes prominent use of phenomenology in her later philosophy, including *The Second Sex,* the second volume of which is entitled "Lived Experience."[30]

Evidence of the social "disarray" accompanying women's changing roles continues in 1927. In the May 19, 1927, diary entry, Beauvoir imagines her future of solitary isolation, cut off from the intimate relationships in a woman's traditional role: "But yesterday how I envied M. de Wendel for being so pretty and so simple! Without pride or envy, I cried at the thought of the destiny reserved for me, the strength and the tension required for me to be able to find it preferable to all others." There's a sense in this passage of Beauvoir reconciling herself to a destiny that has been imposed on her, a destiny that requires an exhausting effort to assume as her own.

But later in the same entry, Beauvoir describes her joy in actively shaping her own future: "Friday in a moment of strength I established a program for living. In such instances my solitude is an intoxication: I am, I'm in control, I love myself, and I scorn everything else." This exhilarating experience of empowerment anticipates Beauvoir's description of human reality in *The Second Sex:* "Every subject posits himself concretely as a transcendence through projects" (*DS,* 1:31). As the May 19 diary passage continues, it reveals the ambiguity of freedom, with Beauvoir once again yearning for the warmth and security of a woman's traditional role: "But I too would so much like to have the right to be very simple and very weak, to be a woman. In what a 'desert world' I walk, so arid, with my bouts of intermittent esteem for myself as my sole oases." Beauvoir is thus rejecting a naturalized sense of gender identity. Being a woman is not a given for a female human being, but an option, a "right" that can be denied.

This passage also reveals Beauvoir's own experience of a woman's temptation to complicity with her oppression that she will later analyze in *The Second Sex.* The depth of her anguish is evident in the concluding lines of this passage: "I count on myself; I know that I can count on myself. But I would really like not needing to count on myself." A marginal notation, dated May 18, 1929, highlights her despair: "Could I stand to suffer again like I suffered in writing these lines?" Denied a woman's traditional dependency, Beauvoir experiences a sense of isolation. Intoxicated by her power and freedom, she still yearns to escape the need for it. The feminist philosopher Karen Vintges argues, in *Philosophy as Passion*, that Beauvoir's most important contribution to ethics lies in her practical guidelines for young women in reconciling love and freedom. If Vintges is correct then it may be in 1927 that Beauvoir herself learned the lessons of the "art of living" that form the experiential foundation of her ethics.

As the diary continues, Beauvoir recounts her efforts to make herself a philosopher, focusing on her own experience. In a May 20 entry, Beauvoir reflects on friendship ("In it alone I can tear myself away from my own manner of thinking"), proposing to make it a subject of study: "It would be curious to study how this education of one another takes place." As noted above, Beauvoir's interest in the ways in which relationships with others can sustain the freedom of the self is an important part of her later philosophy. In *The Second Sex*, for example, Beauvoir defines the human being as "an autonomous freedom," but she argues that we can "only accomplish" our freedom by a "perpetual surpassing towards other freedoms" (*DS*,1:31). It is in *The Second Sex*, of course, that Beauvoir has developed a political philosophy, arguing that women's collective action is necessary to overcome the "limits" of their individual freedom. But in 1927 her philosophy is resolutely apolitical: "I will not make one move for this earthly kingdom," she writes on May 24, 1927; "only the inner world counts."

By May 21, Beauvoir's determination to find an alternative to despair as she turns to philosophy has become apparent. She vows to "overcome the inexplicable" and use her despair as the basis for building her joy. "I myself know that there is only one problem and one that has no solution," she writes in the same passage. "I would want to believe in something—to meet with total exigency—to justify my life. In short, I would want God. ... But knowing that this noumenal world exists, that I cannot attain, in which alone it can be explained to me why I live, I will build my life in the phenomenal world which is nevertheless not negligible. I will take myself as an end." As she defines philosophy as her life's work and the problems arising from her own life as her focus, a central theme emerges that will characterize her work for the next two decades, that is, the conflict of self and others, especially as exacerbated by a masochistic ideal of love. In the

41

May 28 entry, Beauvoir declares her intention to write her thesis, or *diplôme*, on the problem of setting limits to love: "even for the most beloved there is a measurement [of love] since he is not God. In fact, maybe not . . . I will go more deeply into this for my thesis."

In June 1927, Beauvoir passed the exams for her certificates in Greek and general philosophy and logic, placing second in the philosophy exams after Simone Weil and ahead of Maurice Merleau-Ponty, both of whom, unlike Beauvoir, were preparing for the entrance exams to the prestigious École Normale Supérieure. She writes in her *Mémoires* that "Mlle [Mercier] exalted, my parents smiled; at the Sorbonne, at home, everyone congratulated me" (339). Beauvoir's competitive success increased her confidence of success in this male world of philosophy, as she writes on June 29: "Exams. . . . Slightly feverish excitation . . . ; it seemed for a moment desirable for me to study for the *agrégation* and I felt like I had the soul of a Normalian!" But the reaction of her fellow students is disconcerting: "I feel . . . a bit diminished by my successes that were too deeply felt by my companions, and diminished by the sympathetic curiosity that they feel towards a 'young girl of worth.'" One such companion was apparently Merleau-Ponty, whom Beauvoir describes as "offended at being beaten" by her.

After her success on the exams, Beauvoir reaffirms her interest in philosophy, describing on July 7 "the liking for and the habit of philosophy" as one of her accomplishments. In laying out her plan of study, she once again focuses on the question of love and friendship, "in brief, how souls can interact with one another." That she still struggles with masochistic love is also evident in the passage, as Beauvoir writes of Jacques: "I will sacrifice my exams for him, but not my written work if I can do one, nor myself. . . . [R]efusal to submit to any slavery. And deep down I don't know—maybe I will sacrifice everything, everything for him, and it will not be a sacrifice."

In an important diary entry dated July 10, Beauvoir returns to the problem of bad faith, this time in the context of her childhood religious faith: "Mademoiselle Mercier is trying to convert me . . . and I think of the words of G[eorgette] Lévy, 'You will be tempted in that domain.' It's true. This morning . . . I passionately desired to be the young girl who receives communion at morning mass and walks with a serene certainty. Mauriac's and Claudel's Catholicism . . . how it has marked me and what place remains in me for it! And yet, I know that I will no longer know this; I do not desire to believe. An act of faith is the greatest act of despair that could be and I want my despair to preserve at least its lucidity. I do not want to lie to myself." Beauvoir's linking of faith with the temptation "to lie to [her]self" provides key elements in the concept of bad faith that is central to her later philosophy.

Rereading her diary, Beauvoir vows to "clearly spell out [her] philosophical ideas . . . and go more deeply into problems that enticed me, to which I gave overly hasty solutions." The problem that she discovers is one that will occupy her work for the next two decades: "The theme is almost always this opposition of self and other that I felt upon starting to live. Now has come the time to make a synthesis of it." Paradoxically omitted from her *Mémoires*, this important early formulation of the "problem of the Other" builds on Beauvoir's August 1926 goal of achieving an "equilibrium" between duties to self and others, and her November 1926 description of her existence as divided between parts "for myself" and "for others." Usually credited to Sartre, who takes up the theme in *Being and Nothingness* (1943), the theme of the opposition of self and other is central to many of Beauvoir's philosophical works, including *She Came to Stay* (1943), where it defines the struggle between Françoise and Xavière, and *The Second Sex* (1949), where it defines woman's oppression as the Other.[31]

Although Beauvoir does not mention Hegel in her diary, the theme in this passage of achieving a synthesis of opposing terms suggests Hegel's philosophy, which is discussed, however briefly, in the philosophy texts of the era, including her philosophy textbook from the Cours Désir.[32] Furthermore, as Barbara Klaw points out above, references to Hegel's philosophy are also found in many of the literary works quoted in Beauvoir's diary. The 1927 diary also suggests, as we have seen, that for Beauvoir, unlike Sartre, the opposition of self and other arises as a problem within the context of intimate relationships. Tempted to return to her childhood faith under pressure from her mentor who is "trying to convert" her, Beauvoir instead rejects bad faith and vows to retain her lucidity. The differentiation of self within an intimate relationship thus provides the immediate context of Beauvoir's definition of the theme of the opposition of self and other, a context that may shed light on Beauvoir's approach to the problem in her later work.

The July 10 passage is also significant as evidence of Beauvoir's early interest in how childhood experience shapes consciousness, an important and unique aspect of her philosophy opening existential phenomenology to an understanding of situated consciousness. The passage also confirms an observation by Debra Bergoffen that Beauvoir conceives of bad faith as historically grounded in a nostalgic yearning for childhood absolutes and thus avoidable, unlike Sartre, who describes bad faith as ontologically grounded.[33] Describing the concrete realities of her own existence, Beauvoir locates an alternative to bad faith in the joy of disclosing being.

Many of the themes in the 1927 diary are crystallized in Beauvoir's account of her developing friendship with Maurice Merleau-Ponty, a friendship that challenges Beauvoir to defend her philosophy and her identity as a woman. Scholars have noted the similarities in the philosophies of Merleau-Ponty and Beauvoir, in particular their notions of embodied subjectivity and situated freedom. But Merleau-Ponty's philosophy, as recounted in Beauvoir's 1927 diary, has little resemblance to his later position. On July 18, for example, Beauvoir defends herself against Merleau-Ponty's criticism of her womanly reliance on emotion and her rejection of Catholicism: "Ponti [*sic*] is right. *I do not have the right to despair.* I accepted that despair was justified, but it demands to be demonstrated. . . . I am still too much of a woman." Beauvoir responds to him, arguing ironically in the style of the medieval theologian, Thomas Aquinas: "*But:* if in trying to think without passion I say, 'I have no reason to choose despair,' I also say, 'I have no reason to move towards Catholicism rather than any other way.' . . . And on the contrary, it is because Catholicism speaks too much to my heart that my reason distrusts it." Beauvoir concludes her argument by challenging Merleau-Ponty's abstract rationality, exposing both the emotional basis of his beliefs and their origins in his childhood socialization: "Raised differently, Merleau-Ponti [*sic*], would your reason stripped of all passion attract you to Catholicism?" This passage reveals Beauvoir's early critique of philosophy as pure reason, and her early philosophical understanding of the importance of the situation in human existence.[34]

The 1927 diary shows Beauvoir welcoming Merleau-Ponty's enthusiasm for philosophy without sharing his fondness for metaphysical absolutes: "Ponti says, 'It is better to sacrifice becoming than being.'" Beauvoir writes on July 19, "Me, once I see a defect in a system, I want to sacrifice the entire system." Beauvoir rejects Merleau-Ponty's appeal to faith in both Catholicism and reason. "Ponti supports his [philosophy] with faith in reason," Beauvoir writes on July 19, "I on the powerlessness of reason. Who proves that Descartes prevails over Kant? I am maintaining what I wrote for the Sorbonne—use your reason, you will end up with remainders and irrational elements." In rejecting Merleau-Ponty's appeal to faith, Beauvoir claims a modernist position, affirming the process of becoming and the critique of reason.

Beauvoir also affirms, against Merleau-Ponty, the value of her woman's emotions as she tries to accommodate herself to the cold rationality of philosophy: "And then, my dear friends, you don't like young girls, but remember that they not only have a reason to satisfy, but also a heavy heart to subdue—and in this way I want to remain a woman, still more masculine by her brain, more feminine by her sensibility." We see in this July 19 passage, once again, evidence of the problematizing of gender identity following the change in women's roles. The way in which Beauvoir will "remain a woman" is a matter of choice, not a natural fact, not simply a given. "Oh! Tired, irritated, sure of getting nothing out of this desperate recourse to philosophy," she writes on July 20, "and yet I *want*, I owe it to myself to do it. . . . Reason coldly. Ah! There is a lot to do to make a philosopher of me!" Beauvoir's dedication to becoming a philosopher is clear, whatever the cost.

Beauvoir's situation outside of a woman's traditional role in society sets her apart from Merleau-Ponty, who "lives a tranquil life next to a tenderly cherished mother," as she writes on July 28: "'Aristocrat' did he say to me? It is true. I cannot get rid of the idea that I am alone, in a world apart, witnessing this world as if at a show." Claiming the value of her emotions, once again as a woman, Beauvoir defends a notion of embodied consciousness that anticipates both her own mature philosophy and that of Merleau-Ponty, as the July 28 entry continues: "He forbids himself dreams. Ah! I myself find riches in them that I do not want to do without. Drama of my affections, pathos of life. . . . Indeed, I have a more complicated, more nuanced sensibility than his and a more exhausting power of love. Those problems that he lives in his mind, I live them with my arms and my legs. . . . I do not want to lose all that." Beauvoir's defense of "living" a philosophical problem not only with one's brain, but with one's arms and legs, provides not only a key element in her own concept of embodied, situated consciousness but also anticipates Merleau-Ponty's later concept of the lived body.

The July 29 diary entry also contains Beauvoir impassioned dedication to philosophy, encouraged by Merleau-Ponty: "Oh! I see my life well now: not action, the professoriate or whatever. But a passionate, boundless research. . . . I was unaware that one could dream of death out of metaphysical despair, sacrifice everything for the desire to know, and live only to save oneself. I didn't know that every system is something ardent and tormented, effort of life, of being, drama in the full sense of the word, and does not engage only abstract intelligence. But I know it at present, and that I can no longer do anything else."

At the diary's end, Beauvoir's struggle with despair, and the temptation to self-abdication in love continue, along with her new confidence in philosophy, as she writes to a friend on August 2: "I wrote . . . telling him my story, my initial intoxication with living, then my despair before a meaning-less life, my desire to die, . . . and finally . . . my act of faith in philosophy." Beauvoir credits Merleau-Ponty with encouraging this change, writing on September 7 that discouraged by "love, the only great human thing in which I felt the nothingness of the entirety of what's human," Merleau-Ponty gave her "the strength" to affirm "the desire to seek, the confused hope that there was something to do." In one of the last diary entries, dated September 5, Beauvoir affirms the value of friendship, finding an enduring sense of self in her long friendship with her childhood friend Zaza: "the past that still lives and to which one offers this future that he imagines, and that has become part of the present."

In the October 3 diary entry, Beauvoir, having returned to Paris after sum-mer vacation, meets with Merleau-Ponty, who encourages her once again in her philosophical work. But she also sees Jacques, who dismisses her plans: "It would be impossible to live like that," he tells her. "He is the one I love," she writes, "and . . . I am a bit afraid."[35] Contemplating her future, on Octo-ber 3, Beauvoir despairs of finding happiness outside of woman's traditional role: "I have before me three burdensome years of study. . . . Then . . . prob-ably an indefinite solitude instead of that tenderness that was offered one day. A husband, children, a warm hearth . . . Does one marry a woman like me?" The dream of masochistic devotion encouraged by her Catholic heri-tage is still alive: "I dream of immense sacrifices, but I have nothing great enough to give it as a useless gift."

As classes resume in October, Beauvoir is preparing for the sociology exam and teaching the psychology section of Mercier's *baccalauréat* philos-ophy class at Neuilly. In her diary, Beauvoir writes of a new friend, Maurice de Gandillac, who will figure prominently in her future, and declares the end of her relationship with Jacques, writing on October 17: "Jacques . . . was the first to take my hand to lead me into these roads where he has not followed me. I no longer love Jacques. . . . No, I will never love again." The diary's final entry, dated October 21, proclaims her autonomy: "I am not looking for anything. I have my strength within me. I love and keep myself; I give myself without losing anything. I don't need anybody!" But a marginal notation dated 1929, adjacent to the August 1 diary entry, indicates that the Claudelien dream of love remains at the diary's end. The August 1 diary entry reads: "An instant in the Luxembourg Gardens, . . . I found myself with an empty heart and knowing that *the one who would fulfill everything* doesn't exist." Written in the margin opposite this last phrase is "*Sartre—1929.*"

NOTES

1. For more analysis of Beauvoir's early philosophy in her 1927 diary, see Simons, *Beauvoir and "The Second Sex,"* 185–243.

2. See Farrington, *French Secondary Schools,* on the unique role of the philosophy class (292) and the difficulty of the *bac* exam (143–45). According to Farrington, an average of only 54 percent of those students who took both parts of the exam in 1902–8 passed.

3. Beauvoir, *Mémoires d'une jeune fille rangée* [Memoirs of a Dutiful Daughter], 219; my translation. Hereafter cited parenthetically in the text as *Mémoires.*

4. See Farrington, *French Secondary Schools,* 134, on the eight-hours-per-week standard philosophy class.

5. For further discussion of Beauvoir's work in philosophy at the Cours Désir, see Simons and Peters, "Introduction."

6. "In 1913–14, for the first time, two women candidates received doctorates from the *Faculté des Lettres* in Paris. . . . The second, Mlle Zanta, defended her thesis on the following subjects: 'The Renewal of stoicism in the sixteenth century' (Principal thesis), and 'The Sixteenth-century French translation of the manual of Epictetus by André de Rivaudeau' (Complementary thesis). She . . . received her doctorate with mention of *Très honorable.*" Charrier, *L'évolution intellectuelle féminine,* 213.

7. See Farrington, *French Secondary Schools,* 314–15.

8. Charrier, *L'évolution intellectuelle féminine,* 134.

9. Ibid., 135–36. See Offen, "The Second Sex and the Baccalauréat," 266, 272 n. 66, 280, on the support for girls' pursuit of the *bac* by Cécile Brunschvicg, a member of the Conseil national [des femmes françaises] (National Council of Frenchwomen) and leader of the Union nationale pour le suffrage des femmes (National Union for Women's Suffrage), and by her husband, Léon Brunschvicg, the Sorbonne philosophy professor who would later direct Beauvoir's *diplôme.* Cécile Brunschvicg would later serve as undersecretary of state for education in the 1936 Blum cabinet.

In a 1977 book, Françoise Mayeur discusses the role of women with the *agrégation* degree working in 1920 for assimilation of women's education with that of men. Mayeur notes that "Henri Bergson himself, according to *La Revue universitaire,* had 'shown himself to be in favor of a single philosophy *agrégation.*' He immediately asked that 'young women be given as professors women teachers with a true philosophical culture and not merely a *baccalauréat* coach (*préparatrices au baccalauréat*)." Mayeur, *L'enseignement secondaire des jeunes filles,* 431 n. 10.

10. Offen, "The Second Sex and the Baccalauréat," 277. On the idea of a "dowry substitute," Offen writes, "Indeed, in the turn-of-the-century literature on girls' education, one practical argument stands out from all the rest: formal education . . . would provide an undowried daughter with economic security in the event she did not marry; it was, in effect, a dowry substitute." Ibid., 262.

11. Offen writes of Bérard's actions, "In early 1924 Bérard announced [in a January speech published in March, 1924] his intention to carry out the reform of girls' secondary education, also by decree. In May, following the electoral victory of the Cartel des Gauches and before leaving the ministry, Bérard acted, again by fiat, to extend the classical *bac* program to girls. He issued a second decree, a 'reform in extremis,' that extended the girls' program from five to six years and inaugurated a new curricular option in the girls' *lycées* to prepare girls for

the newly reformed *bac*. It was to be introduced one year at a time over the next six years, so that the complete program would not be in place until 1931. In his report [to the Conseil supérieur de l'instruction publique] the minister emphasized that only one section of the girls' curriculum would lead to the bac." Ibid., 281.

12. Charrier, *L'évolution intellectuelle féminine*, 137.

13. Offen, "The Second Sex and the Baccalauréat," 281 ("triumph"). On the feminist debate over identity versus assimilation, Mayeur writes, "In 1921, Jeanne P. Crouzet willingly entitled her Bulletin in *La Revue universitaire*: 'Towards Identity' or 'Towards Identification.' . . . Indeed, to anyone observing the growing number of young women taking the *baccalauréat* after attending *lycée*, identification with masculine education seemed by far the most logical solution." Mayeur, *L'enseignement secondaire des jeunes filles*, 422.

14. "M. Gustave Cohen, professor at the Faculté des Lettres in Paris, said in 1930, 'If you asked me to name the greatest revolution that we have witnessed in our time, since the war, I would not say the fashion of short haircuts or short skirts, but the invasion of the University by women. While extremely rare thirty years ago in my youth, first they constituted one third of the students, then one half, then two thirds, to the point that we wonder in dismay if, after having been our mistresses [*maîtresses*] in the olden days, are they now going to become our masters?' [Trans.: Note the double entendre on the French word 'mistress' (*maîtresse*), which can also mean woman teacher]." G. Cohen, "La femme au xvii siècle" [Women in the Seventeenth Century], *Les Nouvelles Littéraires*, January 4 1930; quoted in Charrier, *L'évolution intellectuelle féminine*, 149. Charrier corrects Cohen's numbers: "The total number of female students at the *Faculté des Lettres* in Paris, in 1928–29 . . . constituted a bit less than half of the total number of students." Charrier, *L'évolution intellectuelle féminine*, 155.

15. Offen, "The Second Sex and the Baccalauréat," 284, 285.

16. Mayeur quotes a letter written by parents of students to the minister of education in December 1922 "where the parents asked that we return to the characteristics of what used to be a finishing school diploma, far removed from any practical goals, . . . but at the same time demanding an 'insurance for the future.'" *L'enseignement secondaire des jeunes filles*, 428.

17. In contrast to Beauvoir, Simone Weil, who also passed her *bac* exam in June 1925, enrolled that fall in the preparatory class at the once all-male *lycée* Henri-IV for the entrance exam for the prestigious École normale supérieure, which had also been opened to women. See Petrement, *La vie de Simone Weil*, 60–61: "In October [1925], she began the ENS preparatory class at Henri-IV. The students call this grade '*la cagne*' (or '*la khâgne*,' as they spell it in lighthearted grandiloquence). Starting the year before, girls were admitted. . . . Simone [Weil] wanted to go to the *École Normale Supérieure* on rue d'Ulm, and she especially wanted to hear Alain" (61).

18. Beauvoir writes: "My parents cited examples for me of 'remarkably intelligent' girls who nevertheless shone brightly in the drawing room. That irritated me because I knew that their case had nothing in common with mine. . . . This year I was preparing *certificats* in literature, Latin, and general mathematics, and I was learning Greek. . . . But precisely in order to impose such an effort upon myself with gaiety of heart, it was necessary that my studies did not represent a minor part [*un à-coté*] of my life but my life itself." *Mémoires*, 248.

19. See Bauer, *Simone de Beauvoir*, for a very interesting analysis of Beauvoir's question, "What is a woman?" in the context of Descartes's question, "What is a man?"

20. Jeanne Mercier (1896–1991), called Mlle Lambert in *Mémoires,* one of the first women to earn the *agrégation* degree in philosophy, was a member of a Third Order religious community, Communauté Saint-François-Xavier, founded by Madeleine Daniélou. By 1935 Mercier was *directrice* (director) of the École normale libre de Neuilly. Her publications include a review of books by Bergson and Maurice Blondel: "Deux livres sur la pensée" [Two Books on Thought]; and two articles on Blondel, "Remarques sur *L'Action,* t.I: *Le problème des causes secondes et le pur agir*" [The Problem of Secondary Causes and the Pure Act], and "La philosophie de Maurice Blondel." For more information about Mercier, see also Léna, "Jeanne Mercier, lectrice de Maurice Blondel."

21. Requirements for a *license* in philosophy included exams in Latin translation, history of philosophy, general philosophy, psychology, logic and scientific method, and ethics and sociology. Farrington, *French Secondary Schools,* 362.

22. See *Mémoires,* 286, on Beauvoir's visit to Lourdes, but with no mention of her proposal to achieve an equilibrium between the duties to self and others.

23. See Bergson, *Essai sur les données immédiates de la conscience,* trans. F. L. Pogson, *Time and Free Will.*

24. See Holveck, *Simone de Beauvoir's Philosophy of Lived Experience,* on Beauvoir's literary methodology; and Simons, "Bergson's Influence on Beauvoir's Philosophical Methodology," for a discussion of Bergson's influence.

25. Beauvoir, *Le deuxième sexe,* 1:352; my translation. Hereafter cited parenthetically in the text as *DS.*

26. See Mercier, "Le ver dans le fruit: A propos de l'oeuvre de M. J.-P. Sartre" [The Worm in the Fruit: Regarding the Work of Jean-Paul Sartre], 249. For a reference to Mercier's article, see Merleau-Ponty's "The Battle over Existentialism."

27. The phrase translated here as "lucid modesty" is translated as "clear-sighted modesty" in *The Second Sex,* trans. Parshley, 728.

28. For a discussion of Beauvoir's philosophy in *She Came to Stay,* see Merleau-Ponty's 1945 article "Metaphysics and the Novel."

29. See Baruzi, *Saint Jean de la Croix,* xxiii, xxiv, xxvi. Baruzi refers to Husserl's phenomenology and method of reduction in his December 1926 inaugural lecture at the Collège de France, "Le problème du salut dans la pensée religieuse de Leibniz" [The Problem of Salvation in the Religious Thought of Leibniz], 123. For further discussion of Baruzi, Husserl, and Beauvoir, see Simons, *Beauvoir and "The Second Sex,"* 197–202.

30. In her 1960 autobiography, Beauvoir describes her enthusiasm for "the richness of phenomenology" but credits Sartre with introducing it to her in the early 1930s. See Beauvoir, *La force de l'âge,* 231, 157, 215. Although Beauvoir's 1927 diary makes no mention of phenomenology or Husserl, given her close work with Baruzi in 1927, it is possible that she misrepresented the date of her introduction to phenomenology just as she did her early interest in philosophy and that her early descriptive philosophical methodology might reflect the influence of not only Bergson but also Husserlean phenomenology. Herbert Spiegelberg, in his history of the phenomenological movement, credits Bergson's philosophy as an important factor favoring the reception of phenomenology in France and reports that Husserl's reaction to first hearing of Bergson's philosophy of intuition in 1911 was to proclaim, "We are the true Bergsonians." Spiegelberg, *The Phenomenological Movement,* 428. See also, Heinämaa, "Simone de Beauvoir's Phenomenology of Sexual Difference."

31. For further discussion of the question of influence, see Fullbrook and Fullbrook,

Simone de Beauvoir and Jean-Paul Sartre, 97–127, and E. Fullbrook, "*She Came to Stay* and *Being and Nothingness.*"

32. See Lahr, *Manuel de philosophie,* 789. The passage on Hegel begins: "According to Hegel, everything starts from the self, which creates itself in positing itself, and in that very instant creates the non-self. The self *posits itself,* that is the thesis, but at the same time it *opposes* the non-self, this is the *antithesis,* and in that very way he *identifies* with it, this is the *synthesis*" (ibid.).

33. Bergoffen, *The Philosophy of Simone de Beauvoir,* 182.

34. See Kruks, *Situation and Human Existence,* 83–112, and *Retrieving Experience,* 27–51; for additional discussion of the concept of situation in Beauvoir and Sartre, see Simons, *Beauvoir and "The Second Sex,"* 41–54, and "L'indépendance de la pensée philosophique."

35. See *Mémoires,* 359, for a similar account of the conversation with Jacques.

Diary of a Philosophy Student

Volume 1, 1926–27

Second Notebook

August 6–December 2, 1926

Nothing is more cowardly than to violate a secret when nobody is there to defend it. I have always suffered horribly from every indiscretion, but if someone, anyone, reads these pages, I will never forgive him. He will thus be doing a bad and ugly deed.

Please respect this warning despite its ridiculous solemnity.

Second notebook (Stopped December 1926)[1]

Everything that happens to me is so important!
(J. Rivière)[2]

You say that you do not want to give me pain and suffering,
But it is that which I expect from you and that is my role.
(Claudel)[3]

What good are they, these complications of the heart? If a single life that moves the other men comes out of them, we will be justified.
Ramuz[4]

"2nd Notebook" appears at the top of the manuscript in Beauvoir's hand. The first notebook for this diary is apparently lost.

I suffer, the other suffers, and there is no traveled land.
Between her and me, no word and no hand.
Claudel[5]

The opposite opinion of all imposes itself on sensitive hearts.
But Philippe takes delight in impossible things.
Claudel[6]

a) He whom I enclose with my name is weeping in this dungeon. I am
ever busy building this wall all around; and as this wall goes up into the
sky day by day I lose sight of my true being in its dark shadow.
b) If it is not my portion to meet thee in this my life then let me ever
feel that I have missed thy sight—let me not forget for a moment, let me
carry the pangs of this sorrow in my dreams and in my wakeful hours.
Tagore[7]

And besides, not even you could understand
for I am far from you and you are far from me.
Jammes[8]

Am I loved? Do I love?
Did I love? I don't know.
I know that I am never weary
Of feeling tenderness for myself.
Mauriac[9]

The value of human beings is measured by their capacity to suffer
voluntarily.
L. Bloy[10]

All beloved beings
Are vases of venom that we drink with our eyes closed.
Baudelaire[11]

Friday, August 6

What sudden disgust at all intellectual and sentimental elegance before the
invalids from Lourdes! What are our moral sorrows next to this physical
distress? I was ashamed of all of it, and only a life that was a complete gift
of oneself, a total self-abnegation, seemed possible to me. I believe that I
was wrong. I was ashamed of living, but since life has been given to me, it is
my duty to live it, and in the best possible way. This magnificent saying by
Ramuz is the moral justification for what I momentarily believed to be futility and egoism. Yes, I must cultivate these nuances of my self [*mon moi*] and
out of respect for the treasure deposited in myself and for others. Too easy,

the absolute gift, which seems like a moral suicide to me. I know that "the limit in giving is to give without measure." I do not give enough; I know it too, and all desire for personal pleasure [*jouissance*] must be annihilated. But the power to suffer, never diminish it; to kill a sorrowful and subtle inner life with action appears to me to be cowardice, and in giving themselves I want simultaneously for people to reserve themselves, not for them to annihilate the consciousness of themselves in order to serve others. On the contrary, if they refine it, they will serve everything just as well. Thy neighbor won't suffer, but only the soul that will not find consolation in its devotion. We have two categories of very distinct duties, and the people whom I admire are precisely those incapable of sacrificing any. Very difficult, because the withdrawal into oneself turns readily into selfishness [*égoïsme*], and moreover, when people come out of themselves, it is quite rare for them not to come out too much and not to diminish themselves. Achieving this equilibrium is what I am proposing.[12]

Stick to this plan for living established since long ago. I used my entire being to work it out; I can therefore have faith in it. My being completely suits *me*. Yes, this choice leaves intact my admiration for other positions taken in life. Yes, I borrow other elements to enrich my own position, but I must not lose heart in front of an archetype [*type*] that is perhaps more beautiful, but not for me. No hollow idealism. Enthusiasm only has value if it results in something, without which it is only a useless expense of energy. There are a thousand ways to serve. Don't try to make mine conform to another. It is more fruitful to enlarge the one that I have chosen.

What austere joy in this certainty of being an independent being in the most metaphysical sense, which has a meaning whatever the contingencies may be: chances to exhibit one's activity, happiness, pain, opinion and affection for others. In this completely stark conception I find equilibrium and there alone, when I am fully aware and in full possession of myself.

But that is my life's philosophy; that is not my life itself . . .

Practically, it is necessary while I live my life, instead of philosophizing about it, to have faith in these truths that reflection has revealed to me, and to have the morale [*courage*] to act in consequence. Because of this hostility against the part of me that I alone esteem, I must be very firm and must not let reproaches instill doubt in me. Try to appear uncomplicated [*limpide*]? I'd like to, but I fear that the price to pay would be perpetual denial; and then, when one plays a character, doesn't something from that character remain? Let's try, I'll surely find out. I have no desire to be understood, admired, pitied, or even known; that's already to my advantage. Besides, here I have enough freedom and solitude to be able to get a grip on myself again after some sacrificed hours. Above all, I am not alone, I am certain that I am not alone.

What a difference there is between the moral sorrow that comes from the fear of losing acquired or hoped-for happiness [*bonheur*], and the one that is above happiness, which is made of scorn, of the refusal of all joy [*joie*]. I was right, happiness is a decidedly dangerous thing because one lets oneself be absorbed by it. Little by little one comes to consider it as a goal, the center of existence, by neglecting the rest. Alissa, Alissa, I admire your courage![13] Without saying "no" like you, would that I knew and accepted that there are much greater things, and would that I became attached to them first. All the same, what sweetness . . .

✳ ✳ ✳

> The enormous burden on me of these things that I cannot manage to give.*
> Claudel[14]

> To accept solitude
> It is to resign oneself to living.†
> (Mauriac)[15]

August 7

Profound moments of pure bitterness! It escapes me now that I want to reason it out, this so intense life of this morning. To think that there is no way I can remember it, and when I possess it, it seems to me to be the only truth! It is the soul facing the real, alas! and this is why these moments of lucidity are those of great suffering, and of suffering that one senses is useless because it is outside of daily life. Péguy says, "That's what hell is," useless suffering; and that is why my distress sought ways to use it: illusion![16] A work? I am not strong enough, and besides the deepest part of oneself is not revealed there. A love? On this plane souls cannot reach one another, in the pains that result from it, in daily sorrows probably, and even very deeply so, but how can an affinity [*sympathie*] be established between that which is my pure and incommunicable self and another being since even my present self

---

* This quotation is on the facing verso, next to the words "August 7" and to the sentence "It's the soul facing the real alas!"

† This quotation is written on the facing verso, across from "and then? oh: Mauriac's expression, so true."

no longer even understands it? I would say, as I now tell myself, "I felt hurt." And then? Oh! Mauriac's expression is so true in one sense, also speaking metaphysically: the essential solitude of beings, and even of moments of a being.

Because of that, the soul seeks refuge in life, not outer life . . . but the other type of life in short. Since in this second mode I had achieved [*atteint*] a great intimacy, I believed that I had found absolute life. This morning I really saw that I had been wrong to recognize the taste of former tears. How I hated then all that had deceived me, and the best because it had deceived me even more. To think that a look, a smile, even less, suffice to make one forget such intense moments; when life is so great and noble, to think that the impulses [*mouvements*] of my soul depend on such little things. And so now I am wondering again if the difference that I am establishing is not artificial, but it is difficult to judge the first state sanely when I am in the second of these two states; strange splitting of the personality, not in succession, but in depth—in sum, one life that plays itself out on the plane of the absolute, another on that of the relative—in the one, being appears in its unity, its nudity and its sterility (Paul Valéry); in the other it grasps itself only as a thousand exterior elements: action, passion.[17] To consider it coldly, speculatively, the first state appears absurd, but to live it! It seems on the contrary that all that one gives to the other is wasted. It is not on the intellectual plane that this conflict breaks out, and it is with my intelligence that I want to settle it. If I were to speak of it to someone else—someone capable of not taking me for a madwoman—what I would want to talk about could be imagined [*se représenter*] only intellectually. Thus, only personal experience is valid, and the experience of others is not mine.

The slight—and even the great—annoyances are really insignificant next to this distressing problem. It is all the same a consolation to tell oneself that at all costs, there is at least something absolutely impenetrable about this, since people do not want to respect the secret of the rest of myself. However, I suffer intensely from feeling even the most superficial part of myself endlessly violated; I much pity the affection that pretends to express itself in this way. You are right, Barrès, to say that a feeling or a thought bruised by unfamiliar [*étrangères*] hands loses its worth—regardless of the dearness of this hand.[18]

I am trying to delude myself here. If I were to put my life in order on this paper, would it be more useful? The elapsed minute is really lost. If I had the mummies for all these dead "selves" [*ces mois morts*] what good would it really do?[19] And besides, I have already felt this; it is impossible. I can allow myself only an analysis, an intellectual view; and what remains of feeling [*sentiment*], of certainty, of life? Nothing, absolutely nothing. Moreover, I am too modest even to write about my private difficulties; I fear mistreating them with words, more particularly that it is absolutely useless since reflection and meditation have nothing to do with pure sentiment. Why then? To give me the daily certainty that I am living, to affirm more strongly to myself the existence of this being in me that I alone know. This is also a certain discipline of thought, on days when I have the courage to think.

Curious thing to rediscover the taste of last year's emotions with my soul of today. My intellectual raptures! I would be incapable of resuscitating them. Philosophy is so indifferent to me! My brain can no longer be roused to action. I hear far more imperious voices.*

August 9

Could I have already during this year explored my entire soul, and is there no longer anything in me that interests me? Such indifference, such great disgust, is such lassitude natural or the proof that I am incurably mediocre? It is in solitude that being shows its worth.

* * *

But yesterday I left full of intoxication
Is it a vain hope that my heart does caress?
A vain hope, sweet and false companion
Oh no! isn't this right? isn't no right?
    Verlaine[20]

This inner brother whom you are not yet
    Régnier[21]

I. [T]he word with well-defined outlines, the brutal word, which stores up the stable, common, and consequently impersonal element in the impressions of humanity, suppresses, or at least masks the delicate and fugitive impressions of our individual consciousness.† (. . .) This suppression of the immediate consciousness is nowhere so striking as in the case of our feelings. A violent love or a deep melancholy invades our soul: there are a thousand diverse elements that dissolve into and perme-

---

* From "Philosophy" through "voices" is highlighted by two vertical lines drawn adjacent to this passage, in the margin of the manuscript. Throughout these footnotes, the term "highlighted" means that Beauvoir drew horizontal or vertical lines near passages in her diary for emphasis.

† This long quotation from Bergson is written on the verso pages facing the entries for August 12 and 13.

ate one another without any precise outlines, without the least tendency to externalize themselves in relation to one another; hence their originality. We distort them as soon as we distinguish a numerical multiplicity in their confused mass: what will it be, then, when we set them out, isolated from one another, in this (. . .) medium that may be called either time or space, (. . .)? A moment ago each of them was borrowing an indefinable color from its surroundings: now we have it colorless, and ready to receive a name. (. . .) Hence, we are now standing in the presence of our own shadow: we believe that we have analyzed our feeling, while we have really replaced it by a juxtaposition of inert states that can be translated into words, and each of which constitutes the common element, the consequently impersonal residue, of the impressions felt in a given case by an entire society. (. . .) Now, if a bold novelist, tearing aside the cleverly woven web of our conventional self, shows us under this appearance of logic a fundamental absurdity, under this juxtaposition of simple states an infinite permeation of a thousand different impressions that have already ceased to be the instant they are named, we commend him for having known us better than we knew ourselves. This is not the case, however, and by the very fact that he spreads out our feeling in a homogenous time, and expresses its elements in words, he in his turn is only offering us its shadow: but he has arranged this shadow in such a way as to make us suspect the extraordinary and illogical nature of the object that projects it; he has made us reflect by giving outward expression to something of that contradiction, that interpenetration, which constitutes the very essence of the elements expressed.

[Bergson][22]

II. [O]ur perceptions, sensations, emotions and ideas present themselves under two aspects: the one clear and precise, but impersonal; the other confused, infinitely mobile, and inexpressible, because language cannot grasp it without determining its mobility or adapting it into its common-place form without making it into public property.

[Bergson][23]

III. A second self is formed that obscures the first, a self whose existence is made up of distinct moments and whose moments are separated from one another and easily expressed in words.

[Bergson][24]

IV. The opinions to which we most strongly adhere are those of which we should find it most difficult to give an account in words, and the very reasons by which we justify them are not those that have determined [*déterminés*] us to adopt them. In a certain sense we have adopted them without any reason, for what makes them valuable in our eyes is that they match the color of all our other ideas, and that from the very first we have seen in them something of ourselves. Hence they do not take in our minds that common-looking form that they will assume as soon as we try to give expression to them in words; and, although they bear the same name in other minds, they are no longer at all the same thing. (. . .) an idea that is truly ours fills our entire self. Not all our ideas, however, are thus incorporated in the mass of our states of consciousness. Many float on the surface, like dead leaves on the water of a pond. (. . .) Hence we must not be surprised if only those ideas that least belong to us can be adequately expressed in words.

    [Bergson][25]

V. Within the fundamental self is formed a parasitic self that continually encroaches upon the other. Many live like this, and die without having known true freedom. (. . .) [W]e most often perceive by refraction through space, that our states of consciousness solidify into words, and that our living and concrete self thus gets covered with an outer crust of clean-cut psychological states, which are clearly delineated, separated from one another and consequently fixed.

    [Bergson][26]

VI. [T]here are two different "selves," one of which is, as it were, the external projection of the other, its spatial and, so to speak, social representation. We reach the former by deep reflection, which leads us to grasp our inner states as living beings, constantly in the process of forming, as states not amenable to measure, which penetrate one another and of which the succession in duration has nothing in common with a juxtaposition in homogeneous space. But the moments at which we again thus grasp ourselves are rare, and that is why we are rarely free. Most of the time we live outside ourselves, hardly perceiving anything of ourselves [*notre moi*] but our own colorless ghost, a shadow that pure duration projects into homogeneous space. Hence our existence unfolds in space rather than in time; we live for the external world rather than for ourselves; we speak rather than think; we "are acted" rather than act. To act freely is to recover possession of self, and to get back into pure duration.

    [Bergson][27]

VII. In place of an inner life whose successive phases, each unique of its kind, are incommensurable with language, we get a self that can be artificially reconstructed . . .

    [Bergson][28]

VIII. What makes hope such an intense pleasure is the fact that the future, which we dispose of to our liking, appears to us at the same time under a multitude of equally possible attractive forms. Even if the most desired of these is realized, it will be necessary to sacrifice the others, and we shall have lost a great deal. The idea of the future, pregnant with infinite possibilities [*possibles*], is thus more fruitful than the future itself, and this is why we find more charm in hope than in possession, in dreams than in reality.

[Bergson][29]

IX. [I]n cases of extreme joy, our perceptions and memories become tinged with an indefinable quality, comparable to a heat or a light, so new that at certain moments, as we take stock of our self, we feel almost an astonishment at being.

[Bergson][30]

X. [W]e might ask ourselves whether nature is beautiful otherwise than through the fortunate meeting of certain processes of our art, and whether, in a certain sense, art does not precede nature.

[Bergson][31]

[A]rt aims at imprinting feelings within us rather than expressing them; it suggests them to us, and willingly dispenses with the imitation of nature when it finds some more efficacious means.

[Bergson][32]

XI. True pity consists less in fearing suffering than in desiring it. A faint desire that we should hardly wish to see realized and that we form in spite of ourselves, as if Nature were committing some great injustice and it were necessary to remove all hint of complicity with her.[33]

Bergson (*Les donnés immédiates de la conscience*)

August 12

There was moral fatigue, there was physical exhaustion caused by the excessive heat. What joy today to find myself once again lucid and with a great gentleness deep within myself. I will not refuse it. Perhaps it is not an illusion, and then if I am mistaken, what does it matter? It is so cowardly to hold oneself back endlessly out of fear of suffering if one moves forward too much. I will suffer; that is all. I will be strong enough. Besides I have such confidence! Evidently when I reason things out, when I reflect with tranquility, I have doubts, but there are minutes . . . It is strange, these two beings in me: one so level-headed, capable of judgment and all in all quite self-possessed, the other the exact opposite, ridiculous and whom I prefer so much to the first!

To think also that in certain respects I am so complicated and all the same different from many others, and that in this respect it is so much the same for everything.

61

The differences between the intellectually known thing and the one that you feel. The past sometimes becomes so present that it is almost hallucinatory. A little more and I would stretch out my hand to touch the object that I am thinking of, and the memory is even more poignant than the reality itself was, probably because mixed with its sweetness is the regret that it is a lost moment. Then, because you have the time to examine and to savor slowly each incident, and especially because this entirely inner resurrection is not troubled by anything from the outside. They are sufficient for me, these memories from the year gone by, without any hope for the future, without any dream, that which was is enough for me. That could have not been! But it was.

I cannot believe that this will no longer be. Alas! there are so many other things that I would have wanted to prolong. In my notes from that year, there is above all this anxiety [*angoisse*] of knowing that the lived minute is going to disappear forever.[34] I have known the remorse of no longer crying over their disappearance; and yet, it was from knowing that I would not be crying today that I used to cry then. Life is a perpetual renewal. That is what I cannot get used to, and I am very wrong because I believe myself to be diminished. I am losing confidence in myself, whereas, in reality I am evolving very normally. At the same time, I am wearing myself out in continuing with what no longer is, instead of walking courageously towards the new. It is because I have felt the value of old emotions. First, much of this value came from their very novelty, and then, if I abandon myself frankly to the current impulses [*mouvements actuels*] of my soul, who is to say that I will not find just as great a richness? I remember one of Cocteau's pages on masterpieces and his aesthetics of the tightrope. That could be carried over perfectly into moral life.[35]

Of course, it would not be about forgetting, or even about keeping dead memories, but one must resolve to keep alive in oneself only that which is useful. It seems that there is more generosity in remaining faithful to everything—guilty faithfulness. One must not love the self of yesterday more than the self of tomorrow. I know that it seems to be a renunciation to continue to walk, only with more riches in one's arms, but stopping would be futile.

Yes, I attained moments of greater exultation, a more complete inner plenitude, but there is a sort of law of rhythm in it. The important thing is that in reality the general level be upraised, and to attain this average, it was indeed necessary to surpass it. Enthusiasm, wonder, they are all very good, but what counts is to continue the effort, once begun, in periods of drought. This does not preclude seeking to awaken a new passion [*élan*], to climb even higher, but one must not regret the first passion [*élan primitif*], which might be inferior overall to the current state. Thus, good-bye forever, my beautiful year with which a new stage of my existence started. I am preciously conserving the treasure that you brought me, but to you, who were something quite different from this treasure, and even more beautiful, good-bye.

Do not take pleasure—serve. The first thing was more logical. Why prefer the second? I remember after one evening last year, a discouragement that I could not justify. I was irritated because, out of great intellectual stupidity, I wanted my emotions to agree with my ideas (I was so filled with wonder at having ideas!). It is the same problem today, and it is more serious. Simple question of aesthetics? Certainly, it is by my taste (an instant analogous to the one that draws me toward the beautiful, despite all reasoning) that I feel moved toward devotion more than toward egoism; but isn't there anything else? Personally, yes. First, there is a liking for beings. For this I do not need a foundation; it is a necessity for me to love them and work for them just as it is to think. But why attach any value to this liking, which is what I do when, regarding others, I scorn the sensualist? Superior form of life—personal taste. Is it truly a sufficient ethic? If I had to teach it, I dare say not, but it is quite sufficient for me.[36]

Certainly, I am very individualistic, but is this incompatible with the devotion and disinterested love of others? It seems to me that there is one part of me that is made to be given away, another that is made to be kept and cultivated. The second part is valid in itself and guarantees the value of the other.

I have given up making this vacation the fruitful period that I promised myself during the year. I must rest, and I have felt that this is more than a cowardly pretext. And then I am devoured by too great an impatience.

August 13

Beautiful moment of glorified life. If I were an artist I would paint this hour "where already the shadows are descending higher . . ." No longer an analysis, but a rich and magnificent synthesis, the physical joy of being and of being eighteen, the intoxication of this sun and of this dazzling sky already announcing the contemplative night and warm affections. I almost regretted it. But what made the unique beauty of these moments [*instants*]? Was it not in fact the painful hours that I felt underlying this intense happiness?

63

Recompense, encouragement. But I am not dreaming of a life made only of such minutes.

I also slightly regretted not more intently savoring the sweetness of the country. I know too well the joys that it can bring me; it is even a too-often-read book and one that no longer moves me. Other years I realized union with nature. I asked its secret of every hour and every corner of the meadow. I would only be able to repeat these emotions. My goodness [*Mon Dieu*]! I have sought them, loved them. I really put my soul in all of these landscapes! But for that reason, my too familiar pleasure is exhausted. And then, I do not have a mind [*esprit*] that is open enough. Finally, I do not live each moment for itself. It is when I was not familiar with him that I applied this precept from Gide; precisely because of what it revealed to me, I surpassed it; and I care about achieving unity in my life, no longer about lazily letting myself be guided by circumstances.

Gide! He probably does a lot of harm as everybody maintains, and Massis's article has in fact convinced me.[37] But me, I owe everything to him! Can't a doctrine that is bad in itself contain some excellent directions? There are questions to which you could give a thousand different answers, and whatever you respond, if you lead me to seek an answer that suits me, I will be very grateful to you. *L'enfant prodigue* [The Return of the Prodigal] especially and *Les nourritures terrestres* [Fruits of the Earth].[38] I don't know, but this immorality itself seems to me to be more moral than a certain indifference. And as for influence, there are poisons that are also beneficial remedies. Besides, I would prefer the risk of poisoning myself to that of having the certitude of dying of starvation, even more so because there are antidotes.

It is, I dare say, doing nothing that gives me this great desire to work. I stave it off by making plans. First, I want to take energetic care [*m'occuper*] of the Équipes Sociales.[39] I know that there will undoubtedly be a lot of disappointments, but what joy if one succeeds in doing a little good. I would like to speak with them about moral philosophy or give them the taste for good literature. At any rate, develop in these girls a critical mind. Intellectual pleasures are so beautiful when one knows how to tie intelligence to life. More than a pleasure, a support, a transfiguration of existence. Mauriac's expression about the people who wander in the crowded streets struck me

Without ever a verse singing in their memory.

It is much like that; to know that another has felt like you; to know one's emotion better, thanks to him, to idealize it. There are even writers (Claudel) who bring something better than an affinity: a response and a sense of calm. For example, the admirable "St. Louis" in the *Feuilles de saints* [Leaves of Saints]. All of my efforts aim to reveal these joys, and if I do not succeed, at the least my friendship will not be lost. I have received a lot; I want to give a lot in return. This will be an indirect way to give in return. And as for the number, if we reached but a single soul, it would still be a lot. What I like in this work is that it is from an individual point of view; it does not propose any other goal than each being in particular. I will have to write here the result of my first attempts, to compare them with my hopes.

For myself also I will work. Philosophy? Finally I will perhaps find new reasons to like it. They are so far from me, these discussions that remain in a vacuum.[40] Above all, I must not abandon everything for my studies. It is so exciting to live in communion with the men of my time who think. And I so like my era for the intensity of its inner life, its disinterest, also, its intellectual and artistic asceticism, the union of a healthy realism and a desire for perfection.[41]

To seek the ideal not by raising oneself above the common condition, but by deepening the breadth alone of the mediocre life is healthier and more fruitful because it is based on simple reality, because it excludes nothing. And then there is an elegant refinement in transfiguring the vulgar rather than creating a different ideal from start to finish. *Do the same thing, for other reasons.* On a great number of points it is a formula that I cherish. First, it excludes all silly vanity. My complexities are known by me alone. It is the pleasure of splitting in two [*dédoublement*] that Barrès talks about: irony, secret pride, what better way to mock the "barbarians" than to let them believe that you resemble them; more seriously, an acute feeling of independence and personal dignity from acting for oneself alone. Then prejudice and acquired habits hardly survive without some reason for being, which is most often lost in such a way that people act out of habit. I can therefore scorn their act because of its intention, not because of the act's matter itself. I will scorn them if they displease me. If I like them, I have the sweet pleasure of being in communion with them and of seeing my refinement meet their ignorance. And at the same time I keep the independence of my mind, my sincerity, my desire for depth.

Here I am far from my plans for reading at the beginning of the school year.

August 16

My first great intellectual rapture since the reading of *Eupalinos*.[42] Whereas in reading other philosophers I have the impression of witnessing more or less logical constructions, here finally it is palpable reality that I touch, and I find life anew.

Not only myself, but art, and the truths suggested by the poets, and everything, after all, that has formed my study this year is magnificently explained. Simply an appeal to intuition, some dissociations of ideas by going more deeply into them, in short, the method that I spontaneously applied when I wanted to know myself and the thorniest problems fade. So many things in the 180 pages of *Données immédiates de la conscience* [Time and Free Will] by Bergson.[43]

First, I want to point out the pleasure of being able to establish the connection between [*rapprocher*] an artist, a poet, and a philosopher. I thought about Barrès in terms of language, about Tagore in terms of the two forms of the self, about Alain-Fournier, etc. What one encountered by chance, the other explains scientifically. There is a joyous astonishment in noting that these mysteries of the soul suggested by the artist have more than a subjective existence, and reciprocally that the abstract formulas of philosophy begin to live when they are clarified by quotes that resituate them in the current of individual consciousness.

Maybe a little bit of disappointment all the same. What I like in the discoveries of a Barrès, of a Rivière, is their purely individual and, consequently, mysterious appearance, which awakens an echo in me. It's true, but without taking on a universal value because of it. It is rather an unforeseen resemblance and one whose unexpectedness itself charms me. With Bergson, these impressions lose their adventurous character. They are explained intellectually whereas, by the artist, they are suggested by a feeling of affinity; they are accompanied by my own soul-searching.[44] In summation, Bergson explains the sentence with which Barrès explains me to myself. Thus Barrès says, "Why words, this brutal precision that mistreats our complexity?" Upon reading this sentence, I understand so well what I had already guessed, that my words damage the feelings that they intend to define; satisfaction to see someone adequately explain and define a rather confused idea that becomes precise and gains even more strength in me, and then satisfaction to see someone share one of my ideas; the sentence comes into my life; I assimilate it. Bergson tells him, "The brutal word suppresses or at least masks the delicate and fugitive impressions of our individual consciousness." For this sentence to please me, I must go through Barrès. Just as it is, it is first too general, scientific and not "written for me"; and then, it explains the observed fact whereas Barrès makes an observation in an elegant formula. It causes the intelligence to intervene in a region of the self that likes to remain obscure and unconscious. In summary, it is philosophy; Barrès is life. Hence, the very different effect that these sentences, appearing to differ in form alone, have produced on me. Still the difference, pointed out precisely by Bergson, between the idea that remains on the surface and the one that penetrates and incorporates itself into my being. I could have done the same comparison with Tagore. In summary, the writer pleases me when he rediscovers life, the philosopher when he rediscovers the writer who will serve as an intermediary with life. (I can serve as an intermediary. There is no need for a real writer; the virtual writer suffices.)

What really thrilled me was the analysis of the two aspects of the self; it is truly tremendous. This duality so often observed between the being that I am within myself and the being seen from outside, not deformed, seen exactly by me, having become an observer, between the true being considered from the exterior or the interior. That's this duality in a nutshell. This distinction that I had made between Balzac's psychology and that of Fromentin appears similarly clear to me. Balzac sees man in time-space, such as it is defined in quote V. Fromentin sees being in pure duration—it is not because one is an analyst and the other not. It would be fascinating to study the psychology of the great novelists in the light of Bergson. Nobody has better than he, not even Valéry in his study on Proust (*Variété*) [Variety], defined the art of the modern novelist, I mean of the type of Fromentin, Rivière, Gide, or Arland. To characterize them, I would say analysts, but *Manon Lescaut, La Princesse de Clèves* are analyses and it is not at all the same thing.[45] Now I would call them rather intuitive or bergsonian. Pure analysis is foolishness. Garric was perfectly right, although he did not say it along the same lines, I believe.[46] Bergson demonstrates it, and I have felt it a thousand times when trying to resolve a feeling or an emotion in its elements. I am surprised to feel that they are so rich and to find that they are so poor; the richness was in the synthesis. (Quotation 1)

* * *

This "heavy heart" from our adolescence, hang it somewhere in ex-voto. Forget it, so that another spring will gush forth [*jaillisse*] in us from farther away, a more secret water, more contained, richer, also more bitter.
Mauriac[47]

How sweet these roses would smell if he hadn't already breathed their odor.

Claudel[48]

August 17

Darn the people who come to bother you when you are so very tranquil. Oh, social life! All the more so because by dint of making concessions to others one manages to make them to oneself. Fortunately I just read some intelligent books that changed me; I have absorbed so many silly things. There is this exquisite play by Sarment, *Je suis trop grand pour moi* [I Am Too Big for Me]. Poor Tiburce, why are you more courageous in thought than in action, and why do you have the cowardice to take pleasure in a dream that you would not have the strength to live?[49] There is *Le maître de son coeur* [The Master of His Heart] by Raynal; love is, after all, such an important thing. I was astonished by the violence of this struggle; it is certainly not the love of children anymore but of mature beings for whom loving is the sole reason for being. I barely understand this mediocre love without friendship that remains too irrelevant to life.[50]

It seems to me that love should not make all else disappear but should simply tint it with new nuances; I would like a love that accompanies me through life, not that absorbs all my life. In *La jeune fille au jardin* [The Young Girl in the Garden] by Miomandre, I appreciated a pretty and sentimental irony, especially in the final pages; but these heroes are too instinctive to interest me truly.[51] I know that Jammes's young girls are also instinctive but Jammes is Jammes. I much preferred Barbey's *Le coeur gros* [The Heavy Heart]; there are astute analyses and even two or three truly moving sentences, but the book is neither worthy of its title nor of Mauriac's epigraph that suggested it.[52] I am so moved when I dream that I too will become a woman. Until the age of eighteen I was only a child. I have appreciated the joys of adolescence only for a year, not even, and soon—three, four, five years, perhaps less, I will have to put in *ex-voto*, this heavy heart from adolescence. Twenty years, even ten years from now, what will I think of my worries of today? I believe that I will like them, but they will be foreign to me. I will have chosen. I will have attained equilibrium. My being will be limited by my accomplished acts and pronounced words. I will no longer be "available" [*disponible*].[53] The wall erected around my true self will have become thicker every day, and I will have sacrificed so many things! I have faith in these words by Mauriac, "I am courageous before life." But how

painful it will be when I will have to say "my good-byes to adolescence."[54]
This unique moment of youth is so beautiful, probably the most painful,
and the most tormented, but new and rich; this discovery of the treasure
that one carries within and the permission to contemplate it without yet
using it up; the right for a while to keep everything, to try everything, not to
stop and choose. And then, so much intensity in sorrows as in joys; so many
uncertainties, beloved even when they torture you; the hesitations, the
enthusiasms [élans], of this "heavy heart" that suffers, but knows itself to
be young and cherishes the wounds by which its existence is more certainly
revealed. To be young! Oh! I would not have wanted a youth full of illusions
that would have been only a continuation of my childhood, the youth of
young girls from yesteryear for whom the age for all novelties brought love,
and even then a love synonymous, for them, with happiness. I passionately
wished to be a young man because of the suffering that I knew young men
experienced. I am more familiar with them now, perhaps because of my
inevitably more concentrated and more solitary life, and I cherish my youth
and those who revealed it to me.

How savagely I like solitude, not moral solitude that must be accepted but
has always torn apart even those who proudly adorned themselves with it,
but material solitude, which alone permits you to rediscover the company
of real or imaginary cherished beings, and the presence of oneself. To talk
to others is to become similar to them, to give oneself up [s'abdiquer], to
diminish oneself, especially when one must watch oneself with care. And
people really don't know how to make the most of the presence of those
with whom they could speak soul to soul; the best of oneself does not dare
express itself. Despite everything, the habit of being banal spoils what could
be so beautiful. So many sentences lovingly prepared that I did not dare let
out, and I knew however that they would reverberate, so many others that
come to mind afterwards, and that one is irritated for not having said. I
once had the courage to be ridiculous; I do not understand how I dared at
certain moments; at others it seemed perfectly natural to me. It should be
natural. Likewise, it sometimes seems grotesque to me to take oneself seriously like this, but everything is so serious, and everything that touches me
is so important, as Rivière says.

How astounded I am all the same to be so insensitive to these modes of
nature that used to move me so! It is stormy and sad. Well! From time to
time the idea of a possibility of being affected by it vaguely crosses my mind,
a memory rather of the effect produced on me by such a landscape in yesteryear, that is all. Deliberately, I would enter into communion with nature,

and I used to pity those who hadn't experienced the delights of living in harmony with it; now I live outside of it [*en dehors d'elle*]. It is only because I sometimes know how to raise myself above it that I do not pity myself. But did it ever bring anything comparable to my evening yesterday?

Since I forgot my Bergson, how about if I went back to my plans for the beginning of the school year? First, whatever the cost, continue this notebook.

Work, and work a lot; with ardor even, and pleasure if possible, without fear of being too intellectual: there is no longer any danger . . .

Take care of the Équipes Sociales as I decided.

Read, not enormously if I do not have the time, but read the *necessary* books whatever the cost. As much as possible, every week I will have to skim through some journals: *La Revue des jeunes, La Revue universelle, La NRF, Les Études,* maybe others.[55]

Finish Verlaine. Read Mallarmé, Rimbaud, Laforgue, Moréas. All that I can find by Claudel, Gide, Arland, Valéry Larbaud, Jammes.[56]

Continue, perhaps, Ramuz, Maurois, Conrad, Kipling, Joyce, Tagore, Maurras, Montherlant, Ghéon, Dorgelès, Mauriac.[57]

Tackle Arnoux, Fabre (*Rabevel*), Giraudoux,

Wilde, Whitman, Blake, Dostoyevsky, Tolstoi, Romain Rolland.[58]

André Chénier, Leconte de Lisle.[59]

All the Paul Valéry possible.

Inform myself about Max Jacob. Apollinaire.

some surrealists.[60]

Maurice du Plessys. Thérive. Chadourne.

Cahiers de la république des lettres.

Anna de Noailles (*Les éblouissements*) [The Dazzling Sights] Paul Drouot.[61]

✳ ✳ ✳

Joy, which was our profound reason for being and our great secret
In the eyes of a living person to see once more that this is true.
And to draw from human eyes the very lesson explained to them.
    Claudel, *Feuilles de saints*[62]

And the same for us, will this love not serve anyone only because it is
    great, because it is within us the same thing as life.✳

✳ This entire quotation from Claudel appears on the facing verso opposite the August 19 entry, across from the fifth paragraph, which starts, "There is one thing that . . ."

For us to give it to another and to feel this waking heart between our arms and these eyes which little by little recognize us with an immense joy! Claudel[63]

August 19

I reread these pages, and I am astonished to find in them an image of me so different from myself. This is because the most indestructible part of my soul remains voluntarily in the shadows; what good does it do to write what one feels so intensely? Yet if I keep this notebook, if I reread it later when I am old and probably dried up, I must remember that there was something else during this vacation. Later. What will I be? A teacher who will correct inept homework and will have a passion for the value of knowledge or other problems of the same significance? I am afraid of this: acceptance and resignation. Yes, I want that life, but on the condition of always, always suffering through it, not imprisoning myself in it out of cowardice; Tagore's expression (p. 1.b1). A beautiful life ... The greatness of forming little souls, of giving oneself to one's profession and to one's work, of cultivating one's intelligence and devoting oneself to others, of producing, of growing. Evidently, I still see myself saying: "I do not want happiness!" How many times did I repeat that this year. I have only to reread just the other day (p. 1).

All the same, there are moments when all that is fruitful, that is good, seems so empty. Now that I am writing I know that my life will have as much value and fruitfulness without happiness, maybe more. But this morning I wasn't using reason and it seemed to me so very hard. To feel eighteen years old, to know where happiness lies, and to tell yourself that you will probably never ever attain it; how colorless everything appeared. Fortunately, there are moments when I cannot believe that I will not attain it. If I had confidence in myself, this would be legitimate, but it is from the circumstances themselves that I expect something, or rather from each circumstance taken separately. I never believe in the realization of a hope, and I always see myself deprived of what I desire; but when I envisage life as a whole, I cannot think that it will be cruel to me.*

To think that in the middle of so many multiple impressions, one must maintain an impassive exterior. It annoys me a bit when after a day of tears, someone congratulates me for having slept well because I feel more forcefully the distance that separates one being from another being, but there is

---

* The last two lines of this paragraph are highlighted in brown ink in the manuscript.

such a burning irritation to feel that someone suspects something. In fact, I should be indifferent to all of this. Why worry about it? It is, I believe, an impression analogous to the one that one feels across from a distorting mirror, the rediscovery of features that are really yours but altered awfully, the impulses [*mouvements*] of the soul that one does not really understand oneself, those that one doesn't dare to admit to oneself, those that one loves and those that make you suffer. To see them and to know how to appreciate them in brutal sentences, brutal because they are too simplistic, because they isolate the elements from their entirety where they can only take on their worth. It is also a bit analogous to what I feel upon hearing that a very beloved work is appreciated with equal dogmatism [*catégoriquement*] and speed when I have studied its nuances at length, and I suffer from perhaps not having understood it in its entirety. When I myself am hesitant and uncertain, I do not like, whether it concerns me or another, to see someone acting rigid [*absolu*] and sure of himself, ignoring difficulties, not even close to suspecting the true worth of what he is talking about.

That is why you have to put people off the track. In general, it doesn't work too badly, and I like those around me enough to give the impression of being as they desire me. But I am only a woman, sometimes nervous and irritable like a silly little girl, and a single mistake comes along to compromise everything, for example, that idiotic excitement the other night. My will [*la volonté*] relaxes, I get a need to show myself as I am. I manage to triumph over myself, because I have seen that my attempts at sincerity have had pitiful results; but sometimes I show, at least, that I am perhaps not what people believe me to be. So much solicitude surrounds me; my affection, like my irritation, turns against me. I must learn to control myself better.

There is one thing that is terrible: we are at the same point, one of us stays in place, and the other abruptly advances with an extraordinary speed. How astonished he will be not to find the first by his side; whose fault is it? His alone; and since he cannot go back, may he resign himself to this strange dissonance.

There are moments when it is very simple: a memory or a desire and the soul is full. Everything in it suffers or is happy, the entire being occupied with a sorrow or a joy withdraws from itself; life has its reason for being. There are moments when one controls this simplicity, when one cannot completely abandon oneself to it, when a sensation of awful emptiness accompanies either the suffering or the joy that gets lost in this nothingness. So one judges, and even if one judges that such a feeling was good, as a result of one's appreciation, one denies that it has an absolute value. One accepts it and one chooses it, but without illusions. It then happens that these two modes merge: the memory of the judgment one made about it the day before is introduced into the intensity of the invading feeling, and the longing for hours when, due to excessive sorrow or joy, one did not reason seeps into lucid judgment and reasonable choice.

Am I not altering the best of my emotions with this mania for analysis, in conformity with what Bergson says? I don't believe so. It is less an effort to see clearly than to exhaust completely each mood [*état d'âme*], also to rise above what I feel at the time, more particularly to grasp what constitutes its specific originality, and thus only to live unique minutes, not to know the odious taste of the already seen and the already felt.[64] And it alters nothing of the sincerity of my emotions, especially because a lot of them escape me. I respect the emotions whose beauty resides in simplicity itself because they are the most intense.

Never have I felt so deeply, so spontaneously even, as since I have been examining my soul, and why should this be surprising? I can rid it of mediocre feelings, and it is thus free for the others to display themselves.

* * *

Superior need has its object, the desire which is more necessary than life.*
    Claudel[65]

Ah, there would not be any desire around us, and this mouth on our
    mouth in the dark,
And this certainty so strangely around us aside from all relationships with
    our worth and our power,
If only this being who says that he feels good forever in our arms and who
    never again wants to tear himself away,
From the heart of his cause in God with us were to ask us for something
    other than eternity! . . .
"The joy that is elsewhere than my heart," says someone, "do you still find
    it desirable?"
"Your prison, wouldn't you care about it still, O stupid, if it weren't me
    who had made it intolerable for you?" [Claudel][66]

And myself, it is not this beautiful body that bends and this tear-filled
    smile that I ask you for,
But something so fully given that it would be forever impossible for me to
    return it!
Are we staying the same? Did we get closer to each other in vain?

---

* This quotation is on the facing verso, across from the last line of the fourth paragraph of the August 21 entry, which begins, "It is the incarnation of an ideal . . ."

And since I have placed my hand on you, and you, will you leave me
whole?

This blow you dealt me was enough for me!

Those eyes through which you watched me for a second, I will never see
them again in this world!

Ah, it is yourself for a second, it suffices, with this trembling, whom I
touched without any mediator!

Do you believe that henceforth from where I am there is a way you could
be foreign to me?

O my kingdom! These flowers and the fruits that you gave me over time,
do you believe I still need them?

For you to be my kingdom forever, will it always be necessary to have the
morning Spring on my face?

O my wordless homeland in my arms, if you steal away for a moment, will
I ever be deaf enough for you to be silenced?

Far from you, my fortune, will this exile suffice for you not to exist any
longer?

If it were so simple to escape you, would it be worth the pain of being a
woman?

Is it only my body you want, or rather is it not my soul?

And don't you say that beyond perceptible things, your right in my heart

Is this place where time is of no use and separation is impossible?

What was only the naïve appetite has now become study and free choice,
and honor and oath, and reasonable will.

This kiss while the spirit is sleeping, in its place is longstanding insatiable
desire

For a very difficult paradise that is lacking, and that interests the entire
being.

It is not by chance that I love you, but from justice and necessity.

If I were not living first, do you now feel that you could not live or move?

What I was made to bring you, you could not have received from another.

Open your eyes, cherished sister, and recognize me!

Take and don't conserve anything, and seize [saisir] what was made
eternally to be your prey.

This great and terrible gift of love that does not go without dilacerations.

What was most hidden in us becomes manifest.

O my immortal male companion! O my morning star in my arms!

The love between us was too great for it to find satisfaction here below.

It is not by such a short path that one attains our being.

And you gave me your joy. But won't you let me know your thirst?

Will you deny me the desert? And all these years,

Won't you let me try what it is to be without life?

So that my soul can spring forth with tears and my flame will burst with
blood?

Could anything have made this wound as profound as your withdrawal?
Claudel (*Feuilles de saints*)[67]

The Spring, once wonderful, has lost its ardor,*
Baudelaire[68]

Superior to all personal joy and the same thing in him as birth,
God deposited in every man the profound duty of obedience.
And that is why it is called "egoistic," this voiceless calling that all his life is
spent trying to understand and that leaves him no repose!
For it is not for himself that he was born, but for some other higher
design.
These routes that appear so beautiful to us, that is what forbids them to us
and what intervenes just at the right moment.
There is this thing in us that pushes us and requires, and suggests, and
prays and refuses,
and that doesn't want to, and that tells us that someone other than us
could not accomplish it!
There is only one way to have found one's place; it is to have arrived where
literally one can no longer move away.
The only thing that sets a king free is to have both hands tied.
The only thing that releases one from Justice, is to be love's captive!
What is more necessary than oneself, there is only one victory, which is to
obligate it to be the strongest forever!
Claudel (*Feuilles de saints*)[69]

August 21

Already a month since I left Paris. For two weeks I've been here. I love having the right to spend these long afternoons in idle meditation. On days of spleen, it is hard because nothing comes along to divert you.[70] But on days of calm lucidity, what healthy relaxation! Finally to be able to exhaust all of my feelings without being hurried by work or annoyed by an importunate presence, not to stifle anything any longer, but to abandon oneself to emotions' caprice. If only I had books; I mean some of those books that are friends and masters! In fact, maybe this solitude, rendered more complete by their absence, is good for me to rediscover my true personality and my confidence in myself. My equilibrium, a bit compromised by the tense lifestyle at Cauterets, has returned, equilibrium or "reasonable disequilibrium," but at any rate what I myself mean by this word.[71]

---

* This Baudelaire quotation is on the facing verso, opposite the eighth paragraph of the August 21 entry, about marriage.

The letter received yesterday really made me notice the gap. I like my girl-friends just as much, even better perhaps, but I feel so much older, absorbed by such different preoccupations. And since they address themselves to the one they imagine me still to be, it seemed to me for an instant that my two selves were side by side. I saw their differences as if I had been placed across from two images.

Besides, at moments I have a memory of my past self that is a veritable identification; I do not know what one calls that memory; it is not an affective memory. During some seconds, barely, I relive not only a desire from the past, but the entire mood from which this desire was born, veritable flashback so brief that it is ungraspable.

What is the feeling the most suited to strengthening and testing a soul? I believe that it is still love. But there are so many kinds! There is love for a being one scorns; I can barely imagine it. There is also an unrestrained and uncontrollable passion: that of Phèdre.[72] I do not believe that it can have any moral value. There is the passion for a superior being, which is only a great desire to give without soul-searching, the need not to be loved by the one we love but simply to resemble him, to work for him, to have a little place in his heart. Such a love can be accompanied by a lot of suffering, but it is a great security. It is the incarnation of an ideal, it is the goal and the reason for being finally found, a fixed point, a solid base like a religious belief would be.

There is love for a being whose worth is about equal to your own, and it is the most difficult, perhaps the most fruitful. It is not a subordination, and it leaves the one who loves the care of seeking his own directions, of leading an independent, individual life. It in itself does not have an absolute principle of greatness. One must have the courage to struggle against it sometimes, to struggle for it also, because there are things that one must prefer to it, and one must prefer it to many others. One must know how to recognize that it is only that, and yet give oneself to it as though it were much more than that; to keep one's freedom of judgment and one's will; to alienate one's heart. It is there that one must accomplish the marvel of giving yet reserving oneself, without giving less because one reserves oneself, without reserving oneself less because one gives oneself. With love one will know sorrow, and the soul will be able to measure simultaneously its generosity before suffering and its force of resistance in despondency. One will know happiness also much more difficult to bear. One will know solitude, because one will reach out instinctively toward the impossible union of souls, and one will note the absurdity of the effort. It will be necessary to have a never-ending faith in the value of the one whom you love and know only with this faith because he is different from oneself; one must love him in this very difference without seeing it as an inferiority, which would be unjust for the other, or as a superiority, which would be unjust for oneself. If the soul comes out victorious from this perpetual struggle, these ambushes and these trials, it will then be fortified, and expanded, capable of a great happiness, and worthy of a long suffering.

There are several things that I hate about love: the abandonment of all of oneself that is a simple cowardice because a being is never an end, because evidently duty is all the same above love, and because duty forbids the alienation of one's liberty. I do not consider it a question of dignity, but of morals. I would willingly consent to all sacrifices for a being I loved, but I would not want to exist only through him (the sentimental blackmail that pushes women especially to see the one they love as a being responsible for sharing the burden of their soul that they are too weak to carry) . . . I know that at moments of dejection, you are sometimes taken with a great desire to cry out its pain to a soul friend, to see in dear eyes one's own reflection. This is loving oneself and loving in the other, the love he has for you. True love, is Goethe's expression: "I love you; does that concern you?"[73] Of course the confidences, the feeling of a mutual intelligence, are one of the sweet pleasures of love, because one does not always give, because it is also good to receive. But if one joyously accepts to receive, if one even has the right to ask sometimes, it is the giving that remains essential.

Nor would I like a being who would always be superior to his love, because it would be proof that his passion is not great enough if it never overwhelms him. I would scorn him for showing himself to be inferior to his passion because this would be a mark of his particular weakness. I would not want him always to reason because a great passion is primarily instinctive; or for him never to reason, because man must know how to raise himself above his instincts. I would want him to unite the lucidity of the hero of *Aimée* with the simplicity of *Le grand Meaulnes* [The Wanderer], or an elegy by Jammes, to join with the spontaneity of *Almaïde d'Etremont*, the painful reflection of Alissa.[74] A beautiful passion is more difficult and even more rare, I believe, than a beautiful work. Of the male and female lovers I know, none, I think, satisfies me fully. Alissa, Monique, Dominique, Philippe from *Le jardin de Bérénice*, the lovers in *Aimée*, *Clara d'Ellébeuse*, or *Le grand Meaulnes*.[75] The former perhaps more than the others; there are as many different beings as there are positions on love. The essential point in fact is to love and to be sincere. But love is such a serious thing, even for those who never love.

And marriage. Maybe one day I will get married. If it is not probable, it is at least possible. In any case, it is the greatest happiness that I could encounter in this life. It is the greatest happiness, I think, that any woman, any man, could expect in life, to marry the person he loves. What in the world is that happiness? When one reflects without passion, it seems so formidable. Not happiness—that is another question (for me exhausted by *Monique*)—but marriage.[76] Two beings love each other; I accept that they have tested each other, that they know each other very well. And then? They are between twenty and twenty-three, their entire life ahead of them. They are going to continue their life, side by side, but outwardly far from one another, and this, whatever their love may be, if they evolve in parallel, is perfect. But what if their routes separate? During this precise point of their life they realize an admirable harmony. Where will they be tomorrow? I well know, that if absorbed by life's brutality, their most inner being will perhaps lose its resiliency [*se figera*]. They will see their desires, their emotions, attenuated, their inner existence slowed down. Are they going to found their happiness on this diminution? And even, if at the moment they leave, confident and in love, each of them has the courage not to ask ever for his own happiness, at least he cannot accept the idea that the other would not be happy. I represent the happiness of the one that I love. I know that I am less than the need he has for me. I know that I do not have the right to give him an image he likes in place of me, or to be really unfaithful to what I am. I do not engage only my life, I also engage his; and each of us has only a single life. When one is resolved not to cheat, not to take a memory of love for love, an indifferent tranquility for happiness, what a fearsome weight one accepts to carry, and I would fear precisely the later acceptance of a lie, the witnessing of the decrepitude of my love.

This is a great audacity; its greatness comes from its very boldness. There is, next to the fear of doing oneself a lot of harm, the hope of doing oneself a lot of good. I believe that one would have to place oneself above happiness, not only for oneself, but also for the other, resign oneself to giving only what one can give, knowing that it is little, but something all the same; and because it is something, accept that it is little. One must love enough so that *little* applied to this being one loves takes on an immense value. Do not claim to lose oneself in the other, simply walk side by side, mutually helping each other a little. One must also be sure that if love disappears, a very great affection will remain, an affection that would be an awful thing if one wanted to pass it off as love, but which will form a still very sweet bond once one has confessed it.

For that, one must have a great faith in the person one loves, a very great love, and marriage can then be a great and beautiful thing.

* * *

> For it is truly, Lord, best witness in the world
> That we might give to you of human dignity,
> This ardent sob that calls onward from age to age
> And comes to die in meeting your eternity!
> Baudelaire[77]

August 23

Why this crisis the day before yesterday? Impression of dejection, of fatality, of despair, evidently all of it is in this brutal sorrow, in large part irrational, devoid of any sort of beauty. There are tears that are very sweet, neither joy, nor suffering, but a great surge [*élan*] from the soul moved by this very outburst [*élan*]. There are tears of irritation that flow due to some annoyances or nervous relaxation, irritation or distress that sometimes bring a physical relief, and over which one still keeps some control. There are those that one sheds apart from any crisis, any excitation, without any particular reason, because the bitterness of life is suddenly discovered, because one penetrates further into pure reality. They accompany all the more intense ways of feeling and all revelations had by oneself or found in a good book. They hurt a lot because one does not know what to hang on to, because they are an emotional form of the observation not of a passing unhappiness, but of a painful truth inherent to life itself that cannot cease being without absurdity for which one recognizes the necessity. These tears neither of revolt, nor of powerless resignation translate less an emotion than a cold intellectual operation—they are of great value because the soul, not the body cries them, because they indicate my being's interest in great problems, because they are almost impersonal. Indeed they are not accompanied by a soul-searching full of pity for myself (and pitiful from cowardice). Questions of joy and sadness remain aside. When a work causes such tears to flow, I am sure that it is a great work that captivates me neither with facile sentimentalism nor a flashiness without value. Jammes, Claudel, *Le grand Meaulnes,* thus made me cry from overwhelmed admiration. It is perhaps in this way that one reaches the height of disinterest and that is why I like for one to have a liking for tears, for those tears, I mean, that far from discouraging and weakening, bathe and strengthen the soul. Hence, it emerges more eager to live, to act, and to admire because these tears are born from the truth; and in the true alone one rediscovers the zest and the reasons for living.

However Valéry has said, "the real in its pure state instantly stops the heart"?[78] Yes, but he also showed that the truth of life is not the real in its pure state. That truth, I believe, one knows better precisely when one has glimpsed the real behind it and suffered from having noticed it. Besides, what is the real? What is life? Which prevails over the other? Life surely. But life is not an illusion that opposes the real; it is a reality of a different order.

First, what is behind these words: the real, life? The self in its pure state and the living self, I think, but these are still just words since the individual is one. Rather, two different manners of envisaging the self according to whether one considers it in its isolation or mixed with sensations, feelings, and intellections through which it apprehends *the other*—evidently, the first is not a simple negative concept. Both are equally. The first is; the second lives.

At the first reading, Baudelaire astonished me rather than moving me. Now I like him, not with the same abandon as Verlaine, but very deeply. Some of those poems do not have any precise meaning for you for a long time, and then suddenly they become clearer, and henceforth impossible to forget. There are also verses that detach themselves and seemingly come to meet you. He is a "strong" poet; not possible to take these verses to adapt them to my own thoughts, one must follow him; he is definitely leading, but he is also suggesting an entire world.

* * *

Fifteen long days still and more than six weeks
Already! Certainly, among human feelings of anxiety,
The most painful anxiety is the one of being far away. (. . .)
Draw from the morose infinity of thoughts
Something to awaken you, tired hopes
And don't take anything from it but the bland and the bitter!
Verlaine (*La Bonne Chanson*) [The Good Song][79]

and also
The lonely soul is heartsick with this dreary boredom. (Verlaine)[80]

In a street in the heart of a dream city,
It will be like when one has already lived
One instant at the same time very vague and very sharp . . .
Oh! this sun among the fog that lifts!
Oh this cry on the sea, this voice in the woods!

> This will be like when one is ignorant of causes
> An awakening after many metempsychoses:
> Things will be more the same than in the past.*
> > Verlaine[81]

and

> The things that I love do not love each other.
> > Ramuz

September 6

Return from La Grillère.[82] It seems to me that I am rediscovering myself. Too many insignificant readings and no less insignificant conversations, a horrible night of solitude and anxiety, some regrets from past stays, without an effort to revive them, and always in me this same desire, near me this same presence, that is the assessment of these days. I have three weeks ahead of me; impossible that they will continue in the same way. Too bad. I will hear reproaches, reflections that offend me, but I must live a little bit for me. From one concession to another, we come to all forms of cowardice. I clearly see that to seem entirely transparent [*limpide*], I would indeed have to be so. I no longer worry about how I appear. Yesterday, read a lecture by Cocteau.[83] It really sounded like him with his profound seriousness veiled by a veneer of gaiety, his solid good sense, his very sincere simplicity. When I first approached him, I discovered in him new and ingenious views, some amusing strokes of inspiration [*trouvailles*]. Now I admire him, and I like him. I admire him for his disdain for public opinion; that he seeks neither to flatter nor to annoy, thanks to a rare sincerity; for his faith in the work that is his, a faith founded not on a foolish pride, but on the consciousness of efforts he has accomplished and on his remarkable critical mind; for the depth of his views, novel without being paradoxical; and whose soundness I was always obligated to recognize, even when they first shocked me; his theory on masterpieces, "a masterpiece: a masterpiece is, period," his entire aesthetic had a indisputable value; and then too this art of gathering together in a very small formula a truth rich with a thousand consequences.

I like him for the ardor that he puts into his efforts, the union of his private life and his artistic life; for the profound seriousness that he brings to his admirations, his ideas, to his life, while rejecting academic seriousness;

---

* This quotation from Verlaine is written in the manuscript on the facing verso, across from the passage in the September 6 entry where Beauvoir imagines the types of stories that she would like to write, beginning, "I have fun imagining stories . . ."

the gravity that almost always serves to veil a nothingness. I also like him for certain words he has said:

"It hurts me to be a man, do you understand . . ."[84]

"Don't be too intelligent . . ."[85]

"So does the beloved . . ."[86]

the impression of the morning, heavy with the approaching day . . .

the fever from having cried too much and the advice "saturate your life with it . . ."[87]

I like him because he has felt all the lassitude, the nostalgia, the disgust, and with an admirable sobriety, exactly expressed them.

Oh, this distaste for life sometimes that is not up to our standards, this ache from being a man, how intensely I have felt it, just the other day, even this morning!

> The blue sky, the fields green and joyous,
> a very soft breeze passing by,
> the penetrating and bitter sweetness of nature that offers itself
> on the ground, a little thing that suffers with closed eyes,
> because all of this beauty overwhelms it, at once too
> great and too slim, because its soul is too heavy,
> because the soul desires it does not know what although it knows that it
> will not attain it,
> and because it knows especially that this desire will soon leave it.[88]

Or else very simply, one walks and one chats; suddenly without a reason the vanity of all this appears

> something, God, which is not vanity?
> what? what?
> all of the nothingness of life and the insanity of hope in this brief
> disillusionment.[89]

I really envy Cocteau for having known how to express all of that! Sometimes an irresistible need runs through me (just like Cocteau) for a work in which my soul would sketch itself out. I feel within myself so many things to say! But I do not dare. I am afraid of things already said; what appears to me to be necessary for a moment will soon seem vain. If I truly have something to say, I will know it for sure one day. In three years I will see. From here on in, better to let my soul mature slowly; my ideas become more mine.*

I believe that I have, in the midst of many others, two big faults that come

---

* This paragraph referring to Cocteau was highlighted in brown ink in the text.

from a common source. First, I am almost incapable of total sincerity in experiencing [*éprouver*] any impression. I must first judge its value, and I judge it very often according to someone else. Then too, I have a great mistrust of myself. In everyday life it is already very pronounced. Faced with even a mediocre lecture or homework assignment, it often seems to me that I would not know how to do as much, whereas I can do much better. Some minds, recognized afterwards as ordinary enough, seem to me to contain a thousand treasures unknown by mine. Now instructed by numerous experiences, my reason is on guard against this illusion, but the tendency is there. Psychologically it is very easily explicable. From what others reveal to me, I imagine an entire world that they possess hidden within themselves, whereas it is all of themselves that they have given me, and all that I believed to be the mark of something else is rather poor in itself. With myself, I do not have these surprises. I have decided [*fixée*] once and for all on my worth. It is a deplorable tendency because it keeps me from daring, daring to speak, daring to think, daring to write. I look for approval, for support in those I admire, contrary to Gide's precepts, "What I like about you, Nathanaël, is what is different from me," and because of Cocteau.[90]

I have fun imagining stories that I would like to see written by someone who would have a soul similar to mine, but who would know how to express it better. Here are some of them:

A young girl would be passionately in love without being able to actualize [*réaliser*] it. She would suffer greatly. In the midst of her suffering, consolation would come to her from another very tender love that she would refuse, although she had forgotten the first, because she wants to be faithful to herself. Then she would live sadly, but after all, she would live. She would notice that as a result, a self very different from the one that had passionately loved and suffered was substituting itself for the first. Since she would not be able to consent to this renunciation of heroic and exalted minutes, she would kill herself. Or, she would lead a low and crazy life so there would no longer be anything in common between her dream and it: two completely different beings, a brisk wrench, and not a slow and cowardly agony made up of bursts of enthusiasm and abandon.

Or again, a young girl who saves herself for a long time for a magnificent love made of mutual admiration and moral independence, who meets this love—and little by little falls short of her dream. Through complacency, she becomes the beloved; she loses her self-love and her self-esteem. She cries this out to him one day, and he consoles her for it. He himself is also weak. They seek to fool themselves with a profound affection, which is neverthe-

83

less banal and bruised for so being, and a hatred is born within their love. And evoking the beautiful dream, had and shattered, they separate to keep it intact.

What I would really like to depict is the one who cannot live because she sees the deception of love, the deception of life, because liberated, she cannot use her freedom because she seeks the real and not life.

And also the struggle between a soul who would like *to be* and who must resign itself to appearing, and the others, the victory of the barbarians over a soul too weak to hold out against them. For example, the journal of a young girl who would be engaged to be married, who wouldn't love but who would believe that she loved because people would tell her that she loved, and who would suspect, at moments, this deception, who would attempt to escape from the marriage, but who would marry.

I should try, if only to put down [*fixer*] my scattered ideas. Only one must know how not to say everything that one has to say at once, how not to use all these riches and how to accentuate favorably the ones used.

* * *

It is impossible to convey the life-sensation of any given epoch of one's existence,—that which makes its truth, its meaning—its subtle and penetrating essence. It is impossible. We live, as we dream—alone."
(Conrad—*Heart of Darkness*)[91]

September 7

For the first time last night, equilibrium and harmony, not in exaltation and enthusiasm but in a reflective silence. Everything that struggles within me, according to Ramuz's expression, found its natural place yesterday. It did not seem to me that these three weeks would be too long. For an instant this frantic regret went away, and with neither bitterness nor extreme sweetness, I savored its presence in peace. Is it because of having had the idea for this written work? However, I know that this is probably passing childishness, because at heart it is not why I was made. What does it matter? I want to work on it, if only to affirm my will. What better thing do I have to do here?

"It's starting to go better," said Mama; an expression that made me smile and hurt me a bit, like usually when I hear someone comment on my acts with an appreciation that misunderstands them. Go on! His advice is bearing its fruit: without being false, manage to give an impression of limpidity, a new debt contracted vis-à-vis him.[92] Only in the depths of my self, the desire for him to know the truth, very vain since he probably no longer remembers having said these words to me. Besides I am in those periods when I realize Barrès's "free man"; I am perfectly enough for myself, but if my need for the other is less strong, my affection for him remains intact.[93]

Vis-à-vis "barbarians" as Barrès says, my position tends toward its equilibrium; I am not deluding myself. I must always be watchful if I want to hold my own, continue to show myself to them in the light that pleases them more, but inwardly affirm my independence more and more. At this moment, it is especially in terms of this that I must find my emotional balance. How unfortunate to have to waste one's energy, uniquely to hold one's own; but after all, life requires it!

I have departed a bit from my rigorous asceticism. I allow myself more pleasures; it is really not at all necessary to refuse everything. This year I exaggerated a bit, I believe, because I had to disengage myself from things that I liked too much. This year! Every time that I relive it, I feel a new emotion. How I love it! Once again I see the great events: the lecture that overwhelmed me and armed me with generous resolutions, my relentless work and my scorn for all joys, the long hours devoted to feverish study at the Sorbonne library, Neuilly, and my cheerful walk toward the classes that fascinated me.[94] Then, *Le grand Meaulnes* at the Institut catholique, in the library where I could not cry as I wanted; that was one of the first beautiful days.[95] Long hours linked to this reading where I tried to focus [*fixer*] on my soul, filled with wonder at the discovery of inner life, crushed by the violence with which it had grabbed hold of me. I discovered Gide, Péguy, Claudel: the anguished readings at St. Geneviève where I would have liked to be alone to cry out my admiration or my pain, where all of this was stifling me, and then the revelation of *Aimée,* in the Luxembourg Gardens during a beautiful vacation day, minute of unique exaltation, plenitude of joy never rediscovered—a thousand other things: the Latin and math classes, (one especially), where I arrived in the grip of a private distress, and where I had to pretend to focus my attention again—conversations, a closeness more precious than anything, that I would give anything to rediscover.[96] The return trips from Neuilly, the evening, by metro or on foot, Champs-Elysées Avenue—many other memories, but I cannot resuscitate the color of my life, its painful and unique flavor during this period that I felt slipping away, that slipped away. I relive it, every hour bulging with memories, riches, more fruitful than the rest of my life altogether. My goodbyes to Paris at the end, my *two* so different good-byes, one feverish and in tears, the other so sweet, with a sweetness that I am still experiencing. And it is the past! When I compare it to my life of today! But that does not matter. What matters is that back in Paris my life be as rich, as full as last year. How can I do this? Will it, want it, will it again. Hold out my hands so as to lose nothing, open my soul, work, love.

September 9

Why was I so annoyed, so annoyed yesterday about going to spend the day with the Brugers? It was so beautiful out when I got up, at that cool time of the day that I adore. Once again I became fully conscious of myself and the value of my minutes. I would have liked to work on my little story. I felt that it could be a magnificent day of inner life, exactly the same rage as on certain Saturdays when I was supposed to go to tennis. Irritation: my throat constricted to the point of being physically painful; tears that are going to escape; I remember Cauterets, I don't want such moments when one employs all one's energy to control oneself, and the tiniest word hurts! A reflection on my face and their gentle mockery almost bring on the crisis; it is unbearable that they do not understand anything. I have noticed, at those moments, that all the thoughts most likely to accentuate the distress briskly reappear, very simple psychological phenomenon. I am then in the state that those thoughts have very often caused in me. By association, the thoughts themselves are revived; then it becomes terrible. I live such moments uniquely in the present, and the feeling of this useless suffering overwhelms me. Yet the tears shed this year are my most beautiful and most profound memories. Upon my arrival at the Brugers, the things happening before my eyes, the words said, nothing gets through to me. At such moments, you understand the idealist doctrines perfectly; all these people *are* not truly, simply phenomena; and then everything clears up.[97] I am absent from myself, banal and empty day from which even regret has disappeared.

Very amusing and instructive, my attempt at a novel. It is the only way to understand truly the difficulties an author comes up against. First, my heroine is so present to me that I believe she is present for everyone, and it is false. One must not only conceive her, but also make her understood. And then such an idea that for me is the result of many experiences, behind which I see a world, has no other meaning than its literal meaning for some other person. That is why everything loses its color when one writes, because it is isolated.

September 10

Little time to give to this notebook; it doesn't matter since I express it elsewhere. Idea for a novel that one could call "Experiences": the master, oneself, books, love, and after having asked everything of everyone, (the plot, too) cloaks itself in an elegant deception. But of what interest are these things which are not necessary? I am very persuaded that everything that happens to me is very important to me, but to me alone. Is it not for me alone that I write?

Beautiful pages by Bergson on the joy of creation.

Words, in books, that strike you and that are retained from the first reading on. One does not understand them, but one knows that they are rich with possibility and indeed, for a long while after sometimes, when one takes a turn at the mood [*état d'âme*] that the author was in and that he condensed in a short sentence, this short sentence appears immense, and a great sympathy (in the etymological sense) unites you to its author. I conclude from this that when one writes, one must not seek to be understood right away; the first tendency is to want to say everything; but as Cocteau says, what is interesting is what one reads between the lines.[98] A work is a big notebook full of white pages, with only a short sentence at the bottom of each page; each person inscribes what he wants in it. If the unique sentence is truly a sincere synthesis, the author will not have to worry. Its reader, sooner or later, will find in himself the development that it carries within it. The more a verse, a formula, expresses and suggests in a condensed form, the more beautiful it is. The two formulas, perhaps, at least of the ones that I have present with me, are these verses by Cocteau and Verlaine.

> It hurts me to be a man, do you understand?
> [Cocteau][99]

> The lonely soul is heartsick with this dreary boredom.
> [Verlaine][100]

A beautiful page by Bergson on the art of writing, which is the art of communicating the rhythm of his thought; precisely because one cannot say everything, it is imperative that the written sentences, the signposts, force readers to fill up the page as they themselves would have filled it up.[101] When one composes a scene (I am thinking of Balzac), one sees it first inwardly, and then one translates one's vision on paper. The translation must be such that the reading recomposes the vision exactly as the author conceived it. The irritating thing, when one is clumsy, is that one feels the reader will not reconstitute it, and so, a thought, which in itself has perhaps much value, will not have any for him. That is why a work does not exist if it is not well written. No matter what one says, if a work exists, from this alone I am certain that it is well written, more or less according to whether the meaning establishes more or less value, but indeed it exists. Besides, a work is not well written if it doesn't have any basic value, because it is not writing well to say everything when one has nothing to say. There is no art for communicating thought where there isn't any thought. A novel like Dostoyevsky's evidently leaves a lot of pages blank; but a minutely detailed psychological novel, in my opinion, also leaves a lot of them. *Aimée,* according to this viewpoint, is a marvel of art.

If one does not succeed in writing well, one will not succeed in *anything;* not anything, even vis-à-vis oneself because one cannot objectify one's place. And that is why I am almost certain that I will never succeed in anything, although I am also certain of the value of some of my reactions, thoughts, and emotions. But I must try, because I will only be sure of my uselessness [*nullité*] after trying and because this point is important enough that I want to clarify it.

Am I proud? Yes, in the sense that I love myself passionately, that I am interested in me, and that I am sure of wanting something, in other words, to be a unique and interesting form of life; but every being is a unique and interesting form of life. What is lacking for almost all is to be conscious of it, whether it be simply by soul-searching (Barrès, Gide . . .), or implicitly, by acts in which one expresses one's originality (Péguy). I think that to be *someone,* this consciousness, admitted or not, is indispensable. Now, is this truly pride? The observation of an evident thing is not pride. I am happy to be what I am. Is that pride? Obviously, I prefer myself because for myself nothing is as important as me. I owe me to me. This I believe in accordance with Barrès, but for me this completely moral position does not seem different from that of the Christian who *must* prefer the salvation of his soul to the salvation of others. Pride, for me, is to judge oneself preferable, which I do not do.* There are many forms of life that seem to me to be preferable to mine, many beings whom I admire and place above myself. I must admit that there are many that I place below me, for which I am wrong. I have the right to love them less, not to judge them as lesser, in the same way that I prefer a rose to an ant, without being able to say that a rose is superior to an

---

* From the beginning of this paragraph up to this point, Beauvoir highlighted the passage in brown ink on the facing verso. The last line of the paragraph is also highlighted.

ant, which is, on the contrary, false from many points of view. In short, I am really not much of anything, but I am me.

The image grows dimmer. I lose the exact notion of what he is. He becomes a construction of my mind. At moments the memory is precise enough for me to confront reality, and I then notice that I had gotten too far away from it. Very exactly: my former state of mind in relationship to him is no longer present in me. Because of this, he is at an immense distance. In *Aimée,* the hero loses his head because he can no longer situate her in space. This is much more terrible. I cannot situate him in me, and as my position in him has always been unknown by me, I do not have anything to hold onto, just as an aviator lost in the fog knows well that the earth exists, but at what distance? I am going to go home; it will be as if this vacation had not existed. I will have to go back to two months ago. Oh! I who had advanced so far! Perhaps I will even have to go much further back, and it is this thought that hurts me. And impossible to imagine anything; I am lost in a desert!

How annoying it is to see coldly written here ideas that are life, sorrow or joy for me. It is because I hurt too much to lose all of this, but I also lose it when I write an essay with a rested mind; when literature and philosophy come to help me. With reflection, I go beyond [*dépasser*] the present moment. Perhaps I put each thing in its place, but its specific character is not having a place, and being *everything* at the moment in which it *is*. Afterwards, it is only a small piece of my life.

September 14

I know now that I would be capable of seeing this work through to the end, but the effort is so useless! I myself am useless! Nothing about me matters to me any longer. Alone in me is this desire more necessary than life. Yesterday, in this barely familiar countryside, that I chose on purpose to avoid the assault of memories from a dead past, I believed myself to be so far from everything, so near and so far from him! Anxiety of *knowing* that the future will not give me what [I] ask of it.* The countryside was really beautiful upon my return, like a thing that one sees for the first time. This morning, memories give me peace, tranquil security . . . and yet I do not even know what my face looks like in the mind of those who think of me. For others,

---

* Beauvoir actually wrote in this sentence, "Angoisse de *savoir* que l'avenir ne me donnera pas ce que lui demande," which would translate literally as "Anxiety of knowing that the future will not give me what he is asking." But it seems more probable in context that Beauvoir simply left out the "I" (*je*) before the verb "ask" (*demande*).

what am I? Can one guess my veritable being behind the words that I have said? One never knows a being, since even if one knows all the elements in him, the unique manner in which the synthesis is formed is perceived only by the being himself, and it is this alone that matters. But one could know an exact symbol for him. How does the symbol for me look? And the place that it occupies? Wait . . .

* * *

I have such pity for myself that the pity of others no longer reaches me.
(Jean Sarment)[102]

How can this perversity be defined? I didn't like happiness.

Is it really that? Better to say: I loved my heart, I loved everything that it invented to feel. I believed in it too much. I used to await its modifications with too much curiosity; I desired too strongly for it to undergo them.

Which ones? All of them. If a woman whose beauty made every head turn passed near me, I would not content myself with desiring her like everyone. I was happy to desire her. I congratulated myself on that ardent wave that would go through me.

All those troubles that had assaulted me since childhood, and that I described, I probably would have been cured of them long ago, if only I could have wished to be cured. But they were too necessary to me; despite the powerlessness into which they plunged me, I found too much charm in their depths. I languished as soon as their return was delayed; I was afraid that my suffering and disorders would be finished forever.

Jacques Rivière (*Aimée*)[103]

September 16

Have read *Le mariage d'Hamlet* [Hamlet's Marriage] by Jean Sarment. Always the same indecisive and charming hero who suffers from not being what he is. A very beautiful passage where he defines what love must be, "Acceptance without discussion." Without discussion, says it all. If I truly love a being, I must never say, "If only he did not have this fault . . . if only he were like this." I must not deny in him what shocks or hurts me. He is that way. This fault is him as well as this quality; it is the flip side of one of his qualities, and inseparable from them, thus, as precious as them. This trait, which appears bizarre to me, has its logical place and is comprehensible in him; I do not understand it, only because I am judging from the outside. I love or I do not love, but if I love, let it be without reserve. I must have confidence in the one I love. I can make a mistake and poorly place my confidence. It is a risk to take. The day on which I am sure of my error, I will take myself back. In the meantime, once I have shown faith [*fait un acte de foi*] in him, I must continue to believe. If one of his acts is bad, he remains no less himself. It would be cowardly to take myself back.[104] This act will make me withdraw only if it shows me for certain that I had faith not in the being himself, but in an illusion of my mind. Evidently, there are risks, but that is precisely the beauty of love. To love just what one understands, what one knows, what is the same as you, what merit is there in that? To blind oneself to keep one's dream, again what merit is there in that? Behind all of that, there is a fundamental cowardice before suffering and a need for security that paralyzes and belittles.

Basically, love is a very extraordinary thing: the opinion of one being among billions of others, and his affection and his presence alone have value for you! Claudel explains it splendidly in his "St. Louis."

I am rereading *Aimée;* I feel closer and closer to Rivière; his horror of the happiness in which the soul falls asleep, his taste for fervent and painful experiences. Don't I also have this fear of not feeling, of not living enough, this coming year? I cherish last year for all the pains that it brought me. Oh! What if I fell asleep in the middle of my philosophy books, from the banality of life! I do not want to . . . If happiness does not come, I am afraid of becoming resigned, afraid that life will not carry me along . . . if happiness comes, I am afraid that it will numb me. I would want a happiness accompanied by pain, a happiness that would be only a pain shared. . . .

And so these last few days, I have felt the peaceful security of life. The other evening, from above the chestnut grove, in front of this magnificent pink and calm countryside, profound joy was simple! The joy of those country folk who were singing and whistling . . . healthy life, without complications, great sympathy for this happy life, and the harmony in me. It is because at these moments, I prefer myself. The others are only a part of my life, and I am right, for that is what they truly are. During minutes of anxiety I prefer others, and I place all of my reason for being outside of myself. Often waking up in the morning, this morning for example, with an indefinable emptiness, it is especially when I think about the end of the beautiful dream that I feel this emptiness, impossible and absurd dream, dream to which at present I prefer another, and that I regret like a dear past that will never be again . . . dream that was not absurd, while I would have accepted to live it. I should no longer suffer from it, since I have deliberately refused it. On the contrary, when it reappears, I have a vague remorse . . . the remorse of not having kept some contradictions within me, of sacrificing one possibility [*possible*] to another possibility [*possible*], perhaps less beautiful . . . remorse for living, for clarifying my life. However, it is necessary . . . but can't one regret the inevitable? More precisely I have this idea, that if the other dream also disappears, what will remain? Another, ah no! I would be too disheartened . . . at least *not before a long time, a long time when I will be completely other.** But my current life depends on this dream that I have in me, and that doesn't only depend on me . . .

I am anxious to rediscover another atmosphere far from this inner ordinariness [*vulgarité*] dragging down my soul. *Aimée* this morning plunged me back into this exquisite subtle and profound life. Am I going to rediscover what I expect?

Oh, isn't my life the most beautiful work that I could accomplish! Yes, I will always stay me for me, me.

* * *

> And your profound love which watches over my soul
> like a poor person's breath on a poor flame.†
> Jammes[105]

September 25

So weary at the announcement of all of this pain, heavy with regrets, desires, and remorse that will have to be reloaded onto my shoulders in a profound solitude! Last night, these last few days, the realization of my life was sufficient for me, I was daydreaming more about my work, about what I can produce, than about my veritable being; it is so much more consoling and easier! But once again, I hear this calling mentioned by Claudel, "And that is why this calling that all his life is spent trying to understand without a voice and that does not leave him any respite, is called egoistic!"[106]

Oh! this profound necessity in me not to be what others desire me to be but what I am—it would be cowardly for me to steal away—cowardly to lie. But I am so weak that I desperately wish for one who understands. I am "the free man" who suffices to himself alone, but all the same, to read in a friendly glance that one is right . . .

---

* On the facing verso, to the left and beside this sentence, is written in brown ink, "(And if the time has come? September 1929)."

† This quotation by Jammes is on the facing verso opposite the paragraph starting, "I believed last year."

And then once again this desire, more necessary than oneself and incompatible with everything. I love too dearly to free myself from the sorrow that it brings me, and yet I am afraid of having to drag it sadly along all during this year again. Nothingness of anyone who is not he, struggle to act anyway. If I were asking him only for happiness; it's for something so much stronger.

And so I am afraid of this long-awaited return; I so fear banality and the insufficiency of what will be. I cannot imagine anything; it seems impossible to me that anything will start the same way again. And I fear all differences.

I believed last year that it was sufficient to have acquired, and I see that the great difficulty is to conserve, to maintain. I do not dare even to dare to hope to enrich myself; holding on will perhaps exceed my force.

I can either walk forward and forget everything, happy with work, books, and action, and I will then see every effort bear its fruit, the result correspond to the work and smiles around me . . . I can desperately hang on to the secret life that surpasses work, effort, and the entire exterior of myself; and I will again know tears, sterility, and struggle. I think that I will have the courage; I want to have it.

* * *

And when you have read me, throw this book away—and go out.* May it have given you the desire to go out—to go out from wherever you may be, from your town, from your family, from your room, from your thoughts. [. . .] May my book teach you to care more for yourself than for it—and then more for all the rest than for yourself.[107]

A poignant existence, Nathaniel, rather than tranquility.[108]

Nathaniel, I will teach you fervour.

Our acts are attached to us as its glimmer is to phosphorous. They consume us, it is true, but they make our splendour. And if our souls have been of any worth, it is because they have burnt more ardently than some others.[109]

There are strange possibilities in every man. The present would be pregnant with all futures, if it had not been already informed [*projetait*] with its history by the past. But alas, a one and only past can offer us no more than a one and only future, which it casts [*projette*] before us like an infinite bridge over space.[110]

---

* This quotation starts on the verso page facing the September 26 entry, opposite the line beginning, "Do like Rivière . . ."

Never long, Nathaniel, to taste the waters of the past.

Never seek, Nathaniel, to find again the past in the future. Seize from every moment its unique novelty and never prepare your joys—or else believe that in its proper place another joy will be there to surprise you.

Oh, why have you not understood that all happiness is a chance encounter and at every moment stands beside you like a beggar by the roadside. Woe betide you if you say your happiness is dead because you had not imagined it in that form—and because you will only accept a happiness in conformity with your principles and wishes ... for each thing has a *special and different* value.[111]

Nathaniel, never stay with what is like you. Never *stay* anywhere. When your surroundings have taken on your likeness, or you yourself have grown like your surroundings, they have ceased to profit you. You must leave them. There is no greater danger for you than your own family, your own room, your own past ...[112]

    A. Gide (*Les nourritures terrestres*)

September 26

Vacation over, much different from those of other years. I did not seek as in the past to take pleasure in this nature that I congratulate myself for having known so well how to love. There were feverish days, especially at the beginning; stupidly resigned days; tranquil days; but throughout all these experiences I acquired the certainty that events and the external life no longer have any influence on me. I am strong enough to control them. I always redirected my thought toward the same objects; my life was probably less ardent in this solitude than in Paris. But all the same, I conserved just about everything that I could keep, and I am ready to start the year over on really different bases than those of last October.

I have an awful fear of falling back into my former stupidity. Right away, I am going to reread the notes from 1925 and some books from those who helped me. I will reaccustom myself to the intense meditation from which I have slightly departed. I will write in this notebook.

But most of all do not incessantly want to rediscover past days in the days to come. This period of transformation and initiation had an ardent beauty that I will probably never know again. I do not want to try to revive it with a vain exaltation; rather a sincere platitude than false enthusiasms [*élans*].

Accept and love all pains, *all.* Accept also the intoxicating joys, but not the banal satisfactions.

Work. Read. Affirm my opinions, seek to know and to think more; intellectually there remains a lot to do ... But above all, apply myself to *feeling*. (Easy!)

Struggle, even if all help abandons me. Consent to all blames.

(For that, I do not think that I will ever have the courage).

Do not sacrifice the deeper things, even if I have remorse; I would have even more afterwards.

Take care of other souls. I so like the souls whom I encounter; such a great desire to help them.

Don't let myself be paralyzed by admiration, but admire and make the most of it.

If great happiness wanders by, know how to face it; if great suffering, don't seek to skirt it; loyally drain out all of the bitterness; reorganize my life to make room for it.

Do like Rivière "Let nothing go by without risking something, even ridicule."

Besides, nothing is ridiculous for those who truly understand. Practical advice: don't believe that everybody attaches the same importance to things as I, and don't build a novel on an allusion, a case of negligence, or a word in the air.

Under *no circumstances:* Once you have formed an opinion and taken sides, in spite of everything, hold to it. Faith and confidence.

September 28

Journey that is only a great, joyous, enthusiastic movement [*élan*] toward the opening of this year. And then this morning, already extremely weary awakening, this too familiar awakening on a day one knows will be dreary. What good is it? Uselessness of even the smallest effort. And dull evening too similar to the past when, in memory of the year gone by, I seem to be reliving all of the year to come with a sickening similarity ... work, boredom [*ennui*], daily mediocrity.[113] There is in the gray light and the languid atmosphere of these last hours all that I have loved and that disgusts me to tears because it is already too familiar. Everything that I love from the past makes me sick when I project it into the future! Immense boredom from which no book, no show can distract me.

I desired this return. Since my departure I have been waiting for it; only yesterday I hoped it would be joyful. It was atrocious. So much closer and still just as far away; no longer any material obstacles and thus the ethical obstacles really loom up fearsome on the cleared ground!

"Ah, it is truly too sad! Ah! It is truly ending too badly!" . . . Even now the contemplative minutes that I generally like, I detest for so resembling others: others already lived, especially others that I have yet to live. I have had enough of incessantly starting over; so many possibilities [*possibles*], and implacable life always drags me onto the same paths. "Closed homes, shut doors . . ."[114] Ah! I lack courage before this coming year, which I *saw* today, will bring me nothing new, whereas my dream adorned it with a vague beauty that I could believe to be possible, far from Paris.

And especially, especially! . . . During vacation I knew only my desire, and today I saw that it would not be fulfilled! . . . Or rather, I saw that I would desire infinitely more than I believed! I see what I am going to receive and what I imagined myself reaching for, and I know that it is nothing in comparison with my need. Even more eager for this joy so ridiculously disproportionate to the one without which I can no longer live . . .

Such great discouragement. And especially, knowing that all year I will have this millstone around my neck and the even heavier fear of being brutally freed from it.

Literature disgusts me; even the books that are not literature can do nothing for me . . . vain attempt at Mallarmé, Jammes . . . work neither—oh! the Sorbonne, St. Geneviève, Neuilly!—myself neither, sleep![115] And a feeling of fatality, I cannot do anything; life carries me along. I have never obtained anything from it by force; I will never take anything from it that it does not consent to give me. How sincerely at such moments one wishes to die! . . . And then life is too ridiculous; yes truly too much with the staircase and the red carpet at the end of this great and absorbing sorrow. And tomorrow, to which I will really have to consent at the end of today.

To console myself at very fleeting moments, I imagine what I wish for tomorrow to bring me, but I know that it will not happen that way; and if it happens thus, what afterwards? Joy two months ago: how I laughed on the Champs-Elysées—nothing has changed and distress at present! It is because I continued to live during these two months . . .

Sleep!

* * *

I saw the things from last year returning . . .
Why hasn't my heart always been alone?
I wouldn't have this awful emptiness [*vide*] in the depth of my being . . .[116]

My God, since my poor heart is swollen like a grape,
and soon must burst and die in pain,
if this must be, O God, ignore my suffering soul . . .[117]

Thou giveth, and thou taketh away,
but then the loss is terrible; one feels its passing
deep in one's heart, frightening as a fearful wind.[118]

Nothing is left to me, O Lord, but sorrow
and the persuasion that I am nothing
but the unconscious echo of my fragile soul
like a bunch of heather with its leaves falling.
I have read and I've smiled; I have written and I've smiled.
I have thought and smiled and wept and I also smiled
knowing the world is impossible for happiness;
and I wept sometimes when I wanted to smile.[119]
    Jammes

September 29

And I did not rediscover the rare flavor this book had the first day I read it;
it spoke only to my intelligence whereas before it had led me into a new and
magnificent world. No matter, I understood better this time; I myself will
not apply what he said in the search for happiness. I do not want a happiness different from today's dream. I refuse; I hate the joy and the moments
that are precious to him, but I myself also want to go out, to seek, risk, and
love indiscriminately, in order to make my soul ardent and rich. Fervor!
Fervor! Ah! A poignant existence![120]

By Jammes among other wonders are the "Prière pour demander une
étoile" [Prayer for the Gift of a Star] and the "Prière pour louer Dieu" [Prayer
in Praise of God].

Moreover, I care so little about all of that! I can barely reread, and I can't
read anything for the first time anymore. What are all these books next to
my suffering! I know the advice on pride and resignation that they can give
me, but also that my hurt is too deep for anything to do anything about it. I
have known tears, many tears, but like just a while ago, never. I cried over a
happiness that was impossible and that I had always known as such. I cried
out of doubt over a possible happiness, but I had not yet cried over the brutal and absurd disappearance of a very near possibility [possible]—certainty
that it will not be whereas so easily it could have been. I can say that I had
the taste of nothingness in my mouth, complete darkness, not even the hope
of a glimmer of light. Oh, this weighty year to come! Never will I have the

courage to live through it, and I will not die yet. What then? Half of the time prostrate like today remaining passive, immobile under the waves of suffering; the other half, hanging on, like at this moment, to the vaguest hope, and with death in my soul, living nevertheless. I understood suicide a little while ago. If I had been certain that all my days would be like this one, I would not have known how to do anything but desire to die. What? Reasons to live are absent. If I rediscover them one day, it is because I will no longer be me, and there is no affection in me for this being that I will be. So?

Especially awful loneliness! A soul, no matter which one near mine . . . And this return tonight when I will be so alone, while I will appear to be surrounded by these beings I love and who love me and who hurt me so! . . . It is because they do not know; I am hurt by their ignorance, which makes them suffer a little because of me, and me, a lot, because of them. But I *can* not speak; besides, they would be just as ignorant . . . I admire people for daring to pronounce words and to give orders when they ignore what strange and terrible repercussions these words and orders can have on a soul. I think back to my childhood sorrows. Wasn't it already a little bit like that? Ah! Don't you ever respect the unknown soul? You do not know how you hurt it, even when you claim to touch it delicately.

Struggle! This morning when I saw such clear hostility, I was almost relieved to be able to take sides; now I am too weary. All that this struggle has already cost me! I *must* start over. Gide, Barrès will be of no help to me; I no longer have any pride; I no longer have anything. I am powerless, beaten, and I do not notice any resources around me. If there were any, I wouldn't even know how to use them.

Wait! But when will the waiting be over? Besides, I cannot wait any longer; today is today, more than the eve of tomorrow. Be free, finally, free to think, to act, to love. Moral dependence is more awful than any strict self-restraint [*retenue*], leaving me only the leisure to cry, and this time there is no longer any sensual pleasure in my tears. Too well known, I have exhausted all of their tasty bitterness. It's bland. It's sickening.

And then all of this is ridiculously disproportionate; I know that my entire destiny will not play itself out in an hour, but this morning, did those words involve [*engageaient*] only an hour? I suffer first from having lost a dear dream and then from the near certainty that all the other dreams like this one are going to vanish [*s'anéantir*]. During two months I held out my arms to these days, and now that nothing more puts distance between me and my desire, an obstacle—always the same one, oh! I hate it sometimes—has risen up against me. Unconsciousness or ignorant will? At least, I have understood how much I was sure that my desire, if it was realized, would not be disappointed, and I am not actually waiting for anything definite, nothing but what I will receive—what I would have received.

A little bit of peace comes with reasoning; before hostility a secret complicity is born, known by me alone. Maybe I am going to know the joy of the total gift that nothing can repay. (Goethe! Goethe!) But what if one does not use reason? And isn't this obscure prescience more sure than anything I tell myself in order to rediscover the courage simply to get up and walk? Where? Anywhere? The same solitude is everywhere. Ah! I am only a woman after all, and I have been well able to give up happiness sometimes; but I can also desperately desire it. And besides, much [more] than my happiness is at stake.

Dare! Want and will! I am letting my destiny carry me away. Ah! Risk everything rather than accepting to lose without a struggle; I live for that alone.

Not later than Sunday. I have had enough of being a coward.

October 2

I will never abandon this absurd habit of imagining a drama in every word that I hear! Thursday . . . feverish indecision; I felt how little I cared about confronting my dream with the truth. After an hour of anxious hesitation, I left almost without regret for not having seen him. I was once again captivated by life; yesterday too, this morning . . . compared to the first days of my arrival! Ah! It's because next to love, there is life, stronger than anything and in spite of everything, carrying me away. Another being can be only a bit like family, but I still remain apart from him, independent, intact. This will not be different!

I don't have the zest to start over with everything the same. I am more and more sickened by this similarity. Something else . . . but what?

And I no longer find any goal in my life. I have had enough of books. Shall I write myself? I reread my pitiful attempts, impossible. And then I am so persuaded that I will never be able to put myself entirely into my acts, that what I am infinitely surpasses all that I could do, that all acts seem to me to be equally indifferent. I would consent to becoming a cook at the moment. What does it matter, after all?

What have I done with my fervor from last year? with my energetic resolutions? Maybe I should act anyway during this dry spell . . . and then after all I will have to die one day, and it will all be erased. So what is the point?

October 3

All of the fever is gone. Good or bad, I don't know, but it took away all of my power to live. Every minute invaded by a hallucinating presence and such a suffering. There is now in me only my habitual tenderness, greater perhaps, more absorbing than ever, but I can walk through life with it instead of staying nailed down, immobile, with an overwhelming weight on my shoulders. The tenderness is more sweet than sad, made from a bit of hope, a lot of gratefulness, and especially the joy of feeling such a pure and strong sentiment. I am happy that an object worthy of the gift of my soul exists—oh, imperfect probably!—but of a noble essence even in its flaws. I am happy to have known his affection, that he was something for me and me for him; it is very much the same—at the moment—as my great childhood friendship.[121] Only I know less well the place that I occupy in a life very different from mine, very independent from me. Strange, but I believe I never worried about this. I do not doubt his friendship. I am not asking if it is or could be something else; everything is so natural and so sincere between us. My alternatives of joy or sorrow do not come from that. I am even surprised that I don't desire to know more about what I am for him. Am I therefore not acknowledging that I am certain of being a lot? Oh! Less than he is for me of course; not a heavy burden that encumbers life, not a presence filling every minute, but maybe an affinity (in depressed hours, a memory reading a book, a vague possibility [*possible*]). I am sad, and sometimes atrociously so when I contemplate the abyss between our two souls. I am joyous when I simply look at what I have from him.* Thus, this evening his memory invaded me entirely with a plenitude that he maybe never had. I am surprised to dare finally to write this, but it has become such a reality for me . . . and then it excuses me tonight for resembling those young girls of former days who wrote in their journals.

Childhood affection, friendship for my part rather great and mixed with a bit of spite—so indifferent—regret too for an affection that maybe, I thought, could be born between us. After all, I knew that I was superior to what he believed about me—what's more I was far from him. Last year, he said, "We were chatting about *La musique intérieure* [Inner Music] by Maurras," and I daydreamed that it could truly have been so.[122] And I started to become familiar with these things—books, ideas, inner feelings of anxiety;

---

* From approximately "but maybe an affinity"" to "what I have from him," this page is highlighted in brown ink in the facing verso margin.

and he started to meet with me again and again.* One dinner at the house, at the table he spoke of Gide, and nicely—without mocking them—of my studies; after dinner he recalled our former friendship: J. Verne, Schmitt's fairytales—I felt something coming back to life—I went to bed with a great hope of rediscovered friendship—hope that was totally realized.[123]

Car ride whose every detail I relive: his arrival; place de la Concorde we spoke about Gide and Cocteau with whom I was already a bit familiar; avenue des Champs-Elysées about my study plans; in Longchamp he told me, "One can be a very good person even with a college degree"; the rest was laughter and happiness, among the best hours of my life. I dared to say to him, "You must come more often." He laughed, but felt that it was serious. Tennis that I had to abandon immediately to walk home, so alone and crying over my overly perfect joy, which was already in the past. What distress!

An evening when papa wasn't there; he showed me some books; rather vague memory, I know only that he was delighted about it.

At his house, he lent me *Aimée*, *L'immoraliste* [The Immoralist], *De l'angélus* [From the Angelus]; he wasn't at home; prepared books and a note on the table, "Simone, take these books or others that you like." I waited for him. "I prefer to come see you when you're alone."[124] Rather insignificant.

Dinner. I didn't believe that we would be able to chat; on the contrary. "It is chic to like *Aimée*," and "I cried over Jammes." Papa said, "I'm bored." Was it that night that as H. said, "You are going to irritate him . . ." he said, "but nothing would give me more pleasure"?[125]

About all of that I was joyous, but I did not yet give myself over to it. I was afraid of what ended up happening, of a great obstruction in my life. I was afraid of playing my part alone. Then on the other hand, I was absorbed.

Other memories: evening with the three of us—Papa and Mama at the theater and him staying, preferring me to my parents!!! . . . He read some Verlaine, some passages in *Le jardin de Bérénice*. He told me, "It is in hearing works read by people who love them that we learn to love them."† Unforgettable evening . . . ("Throughout the summers, waited" . . .) So many others that hurry in: at his house, I arrive early; he reads me Mallarmé, "Apparition" [Apparition] and "Une dentelle" [A Piece of Lace] . . .[126] "It is maybe not very suitable"; somebody rings, "darn!" Ah! how nicely he said

---

* From the following sentence, beginning "One dinner at the house," to "*Le Jardin de Bérénice*," six paragraphs later, the text is highlighted in brown ink in the facing verso margin.

† From this sentence, beginning with "He told me, 'It is in hearing works read by people . . . ,'" through the paragraph starting "Departure finally too present," the manuscript is highlighted in brown ink.

that. Discussion on Cocteau, and between us an exquisite complicity—we had exchanged only a few words precisely on this subject "that I do not understand." And his confidence about his overly sentimental sister—also unforgettable.

Another dinner. His whole family is there, back to the dining room; I am seated. Standing he reads me a preface by Cocteau. He left us; his mother spoke of him.

Afternoon doing errands.[127] Ever-growing closeness to each other; my impressions of Barrès; his way of understanding friendship—"humble life . . ." surprises and shocks me a bit; I reflect, he is right—talks to me of *Étienne* and of *L'immoraliste,* for which my parents reproached him.[128] "When a work is worth the trouble," he said, and, "All the same, I introduced you to some beautiful things." A lot of seriousness, return in the tramway, often silence. To have had him for such a long time and feel that he wasn't bored with me.

And again, I was at his house; he wasn't there. Vexed wait. When I saw him again, so spontaneously, "Oh, my dear, forgive me . . ."[129]

Reading of Cocteau in the galerie, he explains to me, you are getting the benefit of all the work that I have done . . .

After a dinner at the house, he drives me to his house to get an article and some books, *Erewhon, Monique.* In the car, "I don't like girls," a semi-confidence on the milieu, how well he understands . . . Barrès, Bastia . . . very important.[130]

At his house again for dinner. We talk about *Monique* in front of Mama, and he brings me to his room to wash my hands, "My private complications; its frightening how complicated I am." Profound complicity again . . .

Before the departure, discusses *Orphée* with Papa, talks to me about his play; on the balcony we are alone for a few minutes.[131]

Departure finally, too present and too dear for me to write about it. I dared to thank him in a letter; so often I had wanted to, and then I did not know how to say it.

All his words, his intonations, his gestures, I have retained them, and I can revive them with exactitude. I have the certainty that he has forgotten everything. Why? I am perhaps mistaken. In any case, it almost doesn't matter. Tomorrow he will be in Paris. Will I see him again soon? I have always found him just as I wished him to be, although every time I was prepared to be disappointed, won't this change?

I believed that I no longer had any fervor; it's because now I have focused it on a single being.

* * *

My daydreaming liking to make me a martyr
Gets skillfully drunk on the perfume of sadness
That even without regret and without heartbreak, leaves
The harvesting of a dream to the heart that stole it.
    Mallarmé[132]

October 5

"I needed tonight, oh my beloved, oh self, to become a god again."[133] And
it is true that after the great painful prostration of the last few days, my life
resumed. Avid for things and beings, I went into the streets. But me, me, I
had not pulled myself together again; I was the prey of a thousand diverse
sentiments. I was not in control.

Yesterday after a reading frenzy, I knew the ecstasy discussed by Barrès in
chapter VI of "L'oeil des barbares." In front of the Luxembourg Garden's
red trees, and that light from the sunset appearing to be a palpable fog,
I rediscovered, in reading that book, or simply in marveling as I walked
through the garden, the great intoxication of being me. My love had not
left; I felt it present, profoundly real and important, but it no longer had the
sovereign sweetness of the other night, or the bitterness. I was in control of
it. It was no longer all of me, but an event in my life, which does not mean at
all that it was less strong, but that I was living on the plane of the absolute.

After the visit to my aunt, one hour of magnificent exaltation. I no longer
ask the streets for an entertaining spectacle. Faces are no longer possibilities
[*possibles*] to which I attach an attractive expression. There is me; there is the
rest of the world whose life gives rhythm to my own—illuminated streets,
noise from vehicles, the bustling activity of passers-by. I cross through all of
it, alone, face-to-face with my soul. I no longer have the desire for any other,
and others do not even exist for me except as adversaries. I do not need to
introduce anyone into this secret garden from which I scoff at the "barbarians." The quays, the Tuileries gardens where the street lamps shed such a
magical and mysterious light onto the somber branches, the whiteness of
the statues, the glimpsed shadows, and this fountain singing at night . . . and
always me and my magnificent intoxication, beyond happiness and pain.
With a strange intensity, I felt the self's continuity. "Why words" . . . and a
conviction engaging the entire being is indeed intellectually inexplicable,
but I who moan daily about denying yesterday, I who have suffered to see
the last school year come to a close, who envisage with horror a future in

which I will no longer be the same, I understood that I was mistaken, that this self which is neither my body, nor my ideas, nor even my emotions, but which lives behind all of that; I understood that I would always possess this self and even despite all the variations of my being. And already the year gone by and already my present love were no longer anything but events in which my most profound self was playing. And I gathered all of the past together to offer it to that self, allowing it all of the future as well. And I swore a magnificent fidelity to it without fearing "the barbarians," without burdening myself with prejudices and shyness. O my self, I will be sincere, sincere to you, completely sincere. I will not hesitate before a thought or an emotion on the pretense that something or someone will contest its value. My time will be burdened by my studies; I will be busy; I will admire; I will love, but of nothing will I be a slave, neither of a group, nor of a being. Nothing will modify my true self, and I will not refuse to give my heart away—if it were not yet given—but I will raise myself higher. And thus I have returned, having rediscovered the god in myself. And I would have wanted to cry out, "I look like a young girl who does one thing or another; but within me I carry a god."

And now, in this class where a part of my life will go by, far from all exaltation, I feel supremely detached from intellectual influences, from occupations that I will have, from the very friendships that I will cultivate.

I no longer know the need to express myself in a work, or to reveal [*livrer*] my soul in an affection; they were cowardly concessions to the barbarians.[134] This does not mean that I scorn action and love, but I respect them for other, more noble reasons, not to unburden myself of this self for which I will know how to suffice, for which I alone can do something.

And what gratitude when I think that it is to him that I owe such feelings! It seems to me that in detaching myself from him—in certain ways—I make myself more worthy of him; I get closer to him. Horror of all sentimentality, but sensitivity loved.

Ah! Barrès! In the last two chapters yesterday I found everything explained and especially the coldness of the soul, "this sorry and crushing queen who sits on the heart of the fanatics who have abused the inner life," who, wanting to transform the soul into the absolute, lose enthusiasm for the absolute.[135] And all of the rest! The exact description of these feelings of disgust where the disgust itself is only a memory, where one seeks a master, where one is empty, alone, sterile. And also the enthusiasm of being, despite infirmities, of being a god!

I was disappointed when I reread Gide because he is too avid for joy, too close to the earth. I was more enthused than the first time by Barrès, who is so high, so far from vain contingencies! What does my life matter; I am not my life.

Have read *Écrit sur l'eau* [Written on Water] by Miomandre; same strengths and weaknesses as in the *Le jeune fille au jardin* [The Young Girl in the Garden]. Duhamel does not write; there are ideas in the *Possession du monde* [In Sight of the Promised Land], but barely personal and expressed in a hopeless style. The chapter on the apostolate is, however, not bad.[136]

October 6

I got caught up again in philosophy last night (brilliant exposé on the *true* greatness of the history of philosophy—I will come back to this). This morning and until 4 o'clock I worked with pleasure, settled back, it seems into my life. "It's been 8 days," thought I, reviewing my anxiety already past, and everything had returned to normal.

Abruptly I saw him. Was it him? I would swear that it was his habitual smile, a cigarette, a happy look. Oh! Such a shock! And impossible from then on to think or to work, but once again such fever, then such incomprehensible prostration that resembles nothing that I could have ever imagined, need to speak to him and horror at the idea that I could truly have him in front of me. Tonight I told myself that he might come, but I did not desire it—on the contrary—banality of the words that we will say, and that he might be in this apartment so naturally, that his body might be there, whereas my thoughts make him [*laisse de lui*] only a soul. This is what I felt upon seeing him again. I think that there was the ordinary anxiety of knowing him to be so different, so far, living outside of my mind, where without realizing it, I was pretending to imprison him. His joy also caused me an awful pain. Most certainly, he wasn't thinking of me, and he was perfectly content. I am wrong about this point because first, one minute of happy relaxation does not lead one's entire inner life into a joyous tonality; and then, just because I am sad for him is no reason for him to be blue also. But upon reflection I believe that what truly overwhelmed me was simply to see him. The other day in front of his door I felt a terrible fright at the idea that he might appear before me; today, too, just upon catching sight of him. He has such an intense life within me that his life from the outside startles me like an awful alarm clock.

Now I know that he lives, that he is at home. I can imagine his acts; I do not suffer from them because his acts are of no value to me, but when I think that I am going to see him . . .

It is not fear of a disappointment, of confronting reality with dreams, etc. when I speak of banality; it is not that either. It is the unanalyzable, but with an implacable clarity when I feel it. He is no longer a material being; I see him in the past. I imagine him in the future as the future. If this future transforms itself into the present, if I think ahead to this moment in the future that I contemplate from afar, I draw back in fear. I cannot wait to come out of this type of enchantment. When we have chatted, when he has once again become a familiar being, this will probably be the end of this strange spell that paralyses me.

I no longer feel like confiding in him, nor having him confide in me, nor of chatting about literature . . . I must have a communion as intense as the one that I savor in my memories.

And then when I have seen him, I experience this horrible emptiness, this regret that it is already past . . . I know how I suffered last year and that it will start over, and yet what is even more overwhelming, I do not see how I will rediscover a state of mind such that I could suffer or take joy in his presence—his presence, something almost supernatural, incomprehensible. I do not even desire, no, for him to become familiar to me again; his friendship can no longer do anything for me. I no longer understand. I know that he is not on the same plane as me, that for him his existence is completely natural. I am in the grip of a disproportion, of an error in perspective, of a disequilibrium, and yet I am lucid and calm. I am in control of myself at this very minute. One might say that there is an abyss, something like the efforts that people make during their dreams to open their eyes, however I am not sleeping. I have just worked reasonably well. Besides all of this week I have had great hours of cold tranquility, and always this kind of feeling of which I was absolutely ignorant and which astonishes me because I really do not see any explanation for it.

Finally, I saw that I now know, in the midst of the greatest inner turmoil, how to maintain the appearance of serenity and without forgetting my pain!

October 7

Magnificent day. I found Zaza again! All last year and during this vacation, I believed that she was far, very far from me. And there she was infinitely close by and now we are going to be true friends. Oh! What a beautiful meaning this word has! Never have we spoken so, and I was not even hoping that it could happen—but why, too, never believe in happiness. She too suffers from her milieu. She knows the same sense of modesty and the same worries. Let us bring our two solitudes together! Boulevard St. Germain—the Seine that resembles an etching—the Tuileries that I discovered by night the other day. So much seriousness and depth, with so much naturalness. Something has truly been born between us.

And the joy of feeling that I was the one who introduced her to many of the things to which he had introduced me. It was infinitely sweet to me when she told me that I had made her experience modern literature and asked me who had revealed it to me. I feel that *Le grand Meaulnes* or *Aimée* correspond to something so deep within her, and that through me, it is to him that she is in debt.[137] This combination appears to me as admirably harmonious. When I had left her, I experienced one of the most beautiful hours of my life, my love and my friendship both greater from their union. Zaza was dearer to me for carrying a reflection of *his* ideas, and I better understood my happiness at having *him,* from the quasi desire that Zaza had shown, and from what I had been able to do for her, thanks to him. Inexpressible. One of my most beautiful sentimental emotions since reading *Aimée.*

October 8

I didn't believe that it could be so beautiful . . . He came yesterday, and I was overjoyed that he came so quickly. This morning upon going to find him, I was preparing myself to feel anew the delicious camaraderie that had enchanted me—at the end of which perhaps is love. He gave me something so much more painful and magnificent, not camaraderie—not love. No, tonight I know that never—this time I am no longer going to say, unless I change a lot—never will I love anyone else, but what one calls "love" between us seems henceforth just as impossible to me. Everything is swept away: my fears of no longer pleasing him, my jealousy, my insane feelings of anxiety, and also, the very sweet joys of his presence. Of all of this I am ashamed, since he lifted me higher, far above passion. I have dreamed of this exactly: two suffering together.* Thus, I am his true friend [*amie*], and in "the hot and lonely afternoons" he often thought of me. This letter! . . . If I did not

---

* The next three sentences are highlighted in brown ink in the left margin of the page.

have it here, I would not believe it to be possible. He is worth so much more than me! I probably have more courage to face life, but maybe because at the moment, I have let myself be put to sleep by my love. And him, what does he have? For one thing, he knew how to write such a letter. I can, I want to do something for him; and first, rise up with a renewed fervor to the arid summits of the inner life where he calls me, suffer, and then write him. I am going to tear up the second page and start it over with more care; and I will not seek to please him, but I will be sincere, sincere even when this sincerity should detach him from me. I will not think of myself, but of him.

This still appears so incredible to me: my painful appeals were thus heard. And it was on the days when I dreamed that his soul was facing mine that I was right . . . I no longer have anything to say, only to reread his letter; I am crazy. I will be worthy of him.

October 9

I did not tear up my letter; I think that I will not tear it up. What remains for me to tell him, I will surely have the time in the year ahead . . . I would want for him to reread certain pages by Valéry on "the real in its pure state"; about the boredom with living that he depicts. I would not want to leave through any lie, sentimental illusions, intellectual illusions, or intoxication over acts. Only there is perhaps more in this rich synthesis that is life than in all the arguments that we could make about it: dissect a tennis game, and each gesture seems devoid of interest; play, and you will feel a pleasure that the analysis does not explain.

Another thing, you say that you no longer have pride. I believe in effect that we do not have the right to scorn anyone, and I hate the arrogance of comparison; but I also don't like the distrust of self that is born from a confrontation with others. When I judge myself, I make the rest of the world an abstraction, and don't you believe that there is a veritable intoxication in feeling like "an irreplaceable being" as Gide says—irreplaceable regardless of your value, simply because of your individual temperament [caractère]. I often marvel at being a unique form of life in the world, and that is why I would say willingly with Rivière, "Everything that touches me is so important."[138] This idea is one of the ones that I care about the most because I attach a veritable *moral* value to it.

Maybe you do not desire strongly enough to get out of the "mess." There would not be too many disadvantages in staying there forever. The great danger is that when faced with life, one day exhausted and weary, you will adopt the first position to come by, an out, whatever it may be, and very probably it will be an ordinary lie to which you will have recourse . . .

You understand, you told me too much and not enough about it. I cannot stay with this burden of your pain on my shoulders. You must bring me a way to struggle against it—not joy, not peace; I don't seek that either for you or me, but simply for a point of support in order not to give way . . . and to dare more.

Maybe I should say words of faith to you. Alas! For quite some time already, I no longer regret not being able to pronounce *them*.

I would like to ask your forgiveness for all that has been selfish in my love; I often wanted to be loved more than to love. That is definitely over. I understand the great renunciation of love that Rivière mentions in *Aimée* and its heartbreaking sweetness.[139]

I am so happy that you put these words at the head of your letter, "does that concern you?" that I so often also repeated myself.[140] I repeat the phrases from "St. Louis," and this beautiful expression from Claudel too, "and if you had had to bring me joy, was it worthwhile for me to learn to suffer?"[141] Thank you for not bringing me joy.

Monday I will leave my letter at his house, without having rewritten it probably; and why should I prefer today's self to yesterday's?

I was able to work in spite of everything, but reading keeps me from thinking about him. I fear the sadness of the night to come.

October 12

Last night, what a magnificent synthesis! Simply because I had seen that for this young girl I could be something, a very pure joy was born in me. While I was walking down the avenue of the Champs-Elysées, I was singing a great hymn of thanks to all those who have made me what I am, and I was ecstatically preparing myself to spread my soul around me. I have such a feel for souls, and it is so easy to reach them. It suffices simply to look for them; of all those for whom I wanted to do good, none has ever withdrawn.

It's to you, Garric, that I owe this, I told myself, this great thirst for giving of myself that is in me, this sweetness that I feel tonight. All that you have been, all that you still are to me! In the school hallways, I remembered with sad regret my anxious expectation of last year, when you were going to come, speak, and instill in me such fruitful words. From simply seeing you, I understood the beauty of a life in sympathy with all men, and I have since sought to communicate with each of them all that I possessed within me. Last year, I owed to you so much fever, and ardor, and yesterday, this equilibrium, this sovereign and peaceful, but inebriating plenitude. Like fire, that simply by being, carries a beneficial warmth, by simply saying, I can do much, much good. To know that! I was full of pride; I admit it, but such a pure pride that I do not believe it to be reproachable. I loved myself for possessing within me that which attracts others to me; I loved myself for being such that people love me. Not out of vanity, but out of liking [*sympathie*] for others, I would have liked someone other than me who would have been for them what I am myself. I loved myself by way of a delightful detour! ... I took a healthy pleasure in this luxury that surrounded me; it too had its place in the synthesis that I realized. I did not desire these cars or this jewelry, but I congratulated myself that others could possess them. And I enjoyed my intelligence because I know that these scholarly successes allow me to get closer to other souls through intelligence and give me some qualities of assurance, decisiveness, and judgment, I dare say external, but nevertheless useful. I would grasp with such strength the link that attaches my individual self to the human community. Yes, this highly disinterested *culte du moi* [self-worship], from which I ask only personal satisfaction, really has value, such that even on the outside it is a good action.[142] Thus, this walk is not only a magnificent personal pleasure; it fills me with energies that will *be of service.* Everything calms down and is justified once the social point of view is found.

But precisely, it is only possible on the condition of not directly aiming for it. Because there are a lot of consolations, I was sometimes tempted to subordinate everything to others. And for this, I must thank you Jacques, who gave me a liking for these painful and sterile analyses. If it's useful, it is good, and when I observe it, I am flooded with peace. Yet one must be faithful to oneself without thinking that one will never use oneself—*for* oneself. Similarly, a scientist cultivates an abstract science for the pure joy of knowing; so much the better if it finds applications, that is not what he seeks in it.

I am going to take stock of my life now. The beings who have given me something before now, I thank them: Mr. Strowski a bit, a bit Mlle Mercier, a lot Garric, a lot Jacques—and Zaza, too, in the past.[143] Now, who are those with [*par*] whom I can do something:

Henriette (leave her alone, wait for the moment, speak a little)

Jacqueline (I wrote to her right away; I must give her what she expects of me; I would have to lend her some books, shake her up)

Zaza (more closeness [*intimité*], lots of affection, books, and ideas, confidences)—

110

F. Leroy (I made her happy yesterday, offer her my friendship, lend her books)

I would have to try to speak to M. Lardillon, A. M. Malingret (the former doesn't need anyone). There is L. Darnis, but I cannot approach her; and then she seems to have great inner help.

In Neuilly, at the Sorbonne, be more and more open and direct; drop all those for whom I can do nothing and who can do nothing for me; and give myself very completely to others.

While these resolutions, these bursts [élans] of thanks or of offers kept me occupied with a grave happiness, your face, Jacques, even though I didn't exactly focus my thoughts on it, never stopped smiling at me. For you, too, I had tried everything that I could for the moment—at the risk of displeasing you; and the idea that I exist for you filled me with joy. I feel that our affection has attained a peak; there is no longer any place for desire, not even for the regret of no longer having any desire since everything is so perfect. I am stopping, and I am looking at the ground beneath my feet to know better how far I have risen.

Delicious childhood friendship, by a marvelous refinement, it loosened its grip bit by bit and for me, you became almost like a stranger; however, I sometimes had the regret that you were not more. Renewed companionship, that I remembered the other day with intoxication (p. 31).[144] And then, during this vacation, because I believed that it would start over again just the same and because I suffered from it, love. I probably never wished for a word of tenderness, but after all, I was living selfishly towards him. I dared to cry over impossible dreams of the future (which was a way of declaring that they were possible). I prepared the words that would have to be said to him, what I expected from him, the disappointments that I would have from it all. But always, as I returned to his door or came across him in his car, I founded my disappointments and my desires, my jealousies, and my bitter anxiety on this fact that his life was absolutely distinct from me.[145] I have but to reread what I was writing just the sixth of October, exterior facts: only his image and the words that we said were important to me. I mean I did not think that anything more could be, and I felt all the more cruelly the insufficiency of all that which had been very satisfactory last year. I said during that vacation, "What is painful is that one of us is staying in place while the other is moving ahead." I was mistaken; we were both moving ahead. While I was desperately sobbing because he was so far away on September 13, he was writing me that admirable letter.

As a result, love has gone with what it contains that is selfish, pitiful, exclusive, and unbalanced [*déséquilibré*] when it is founded on doubt, worry, and hopelessness. What he gave to me is really a point of arrival; yesterday I felt this affection to be so high, so pure, so disinterested at last: no longer me, him. It occupies me entirely, but without overwhelming me or suppressing all life within me; it circulates in my blood. It did not settle heavily on my shoulders. What is beautiful, peaceful, and definitive is there because we finally walk in truth. I know that he knows what he is to me. And he is nothing more than what he knows himself to be. He limits himself (whereas my suffering came from treating him as a casual friend [*camarade*] and having a treasure of unused affection at his disposal), and I know what I am for him, surely, with confidence, while I used to fear that we had only a very superficial [*extérieure*] friendship. I believe that he can suffer or be soothed by me, as I can by him. In the greatest sense of the word, we are friends.

Since he seems to offer it to me, I would like for us to penetrate more and more deeply into each other's soul, and that is why I wrote to him. It does not appear to me that we can go back; at least, I will make every effort to guard against it; and we no longer have to move forward. We have arrived.

Very sincerely, a reciprocal love appears possible later, but it does not appear to me to be any less possible for it never to exist because I will give my soul completely to him without reserving anything mysteriously attractive. I would be incapable of acting otherwise because first, for me, no other feeling seems preferable to the one that currently unites us and second, I can be inspired only by that feeling alone, not by a hypothetical future.

When Mama smiles and seems to presume that I dream, as she does, about a precise conclusion, it annoys me tremendously. There is nothing to expect; there is nothing to conclude. She is wrong to cherish a hope for the future at the present time. The present is magnificent in the present.

So many words that I presumed were difficult to say, prepared detours, things that I wanted to make him understand. He understood everything. Everything is simple, natural, especially sincere, very sincere.

When we say male friend, female friend, it means everything; we know that there is nothing more, but we know also what an immense thing these words represent.

(I wrote him my ideas on the indifference of acts: one must be very sure of one's strength in order to allow oneself not to wield it; one is wrong about possibilities [*possibles*]; one can affirm their existence only if they translate it into the real. No intellectual deceit.

an irreplaceable being . . .

I would have wanted for him to understand the depth of my friendship, but at the same time for him to find a true intellectual aid).

* * *

The beggar within me lifted his emaciated hand toward the starless sky and shouted his famished cry into the ear of the night.
[Tagore][146]

October 14

I would want for him to be there and for us to cry desperately, desperately together . . . What better things remain for us to do? We have attained a peak. For my part, I have experienced a unique hour; I no longer expect anything. We no longer have anything to do but cry. It would probably have been better not to see him again, ever, and to cry over this magnificent memory for the rest of my life.

Now . . .

Now the joy of past conversations has gone. Nothing from these banal words can satisfy me. I liked them for the more intimate accent they sometimes conveyed. They gave me everything. Ah! I am so hurt . . . In this gay autumn morning, in these very beautiful Luxembourg Gardens, what a taste of death is in my mouth! Truly, this life will not end!

Painful, painful evening where his mask too hermetically concealed his face; I should be all the more happy that he shared his private life with me. There are many other things that I should . . . I should not regret having surrendered totally, having been exposed, powerless [démunie], to his blows since, at least in guaranteeing my defeat, I made sure that I would not make him suffer. That is all that counts. I should have confidence in his friendship, that he promised me, and not insult him with this doubt. I should, but I very much have the right to cry if I am hurt.

Feverish night; I plunged into sleep, to save myself, to save myself from this invasive suffering that I *recognized.* The shadows of the night aggravated it even more. And this morning, these foreign preoccupations, and Mama who doesn't know, who doesn't understand, who insists upon speaking of him. This disgust . . . I would want to vomit, vomit my heart . . .[147]

What have I done to suffer like this? This is the way I always challenge happiness. It obeyed me; it did not come, and now I am so weary that I almost beckon [appeler] it. Ah! Little soul who gets irritated by the pain that you did not choose!

It is also because I thought all of that was finished: fever; anxiety; despondency; diminution of my entire self; and this hatred for him at times, him the adversary, the enemy who too fiercely imposes himself upon me. I am not mad at him for hurting me so; he cannot do otherwise. How could the thorns of a rose not sting. People love roses. They pick them even if their fingers remain painfully wounded.

At least he is not suffering over me like I am over him! It is because I am thinking of myself that I am hurt and have regrets. And now, I don't know when I will see him . . . I do not know what he thinks of me. From any point of view, I am alone, far away in a desert where nothing allows me to find my bearings.

About all of that, I can truly say, "Does that concern you?" for in this despair I alone am playing my role.[148]

It is so easy to get rid of these letters we send. He will read it when I am not there, no reason to be shy. We are going away . . . When we find each other again, the letter will have found its way. It looms up implacable; we can no longer suppress it. I know that this letter can only distance him from me. I knew it when I wrote it, but I also knew that it would surely keep him from suffering because of me. And then it is useless to make myself better than I am. This morning I regretted having written it, having shown my poverty and my weakness, having stripped myself of all resources [*m'être démunie*]. And I am a little less hurt, not from exaltation over a consented sacrifice, but because last night's brutal image is disappearing, because once again his soul seems more related to mine.

Ah! Painful mystery. Battles, wounds, can't an affection live without them? I had dreamed so. I must resign myself; for me, every friendship will be a bloody struggle. As a child, how I suffered already from one word, from one look from Zaza; I believed that I wasn't loved; I incessantly feared bothering her; I was already familiar with feverish martyrdoms . . . less than today certainly; there is no comparison. But this tendency was already within me to see a drama in each word, to take everything too seriously.

Oh my friend, I have a great need for tenderness this morning![149] I would like not to be afraid of you, not to be shy, but straightforward [*simple*], so straightforward. I dread the first time that I will see you alone and the embarrassment that will be between us. Out of all the gold cups that I have voluntarily thrown out, there have not been any that I have cried over so painfully.[150] It is all of our straightforward companionship that has shattered within me, and my dreams of love, to leave room for something that is grimmer, more bitter, and so great and heavy that I am frightened by it.* I no longer know the pleasure of hearing and seeing you; I must have your entire soul (I am not asking you to weigh it down with mine). I carry my suffering; I carry yours, and I do not even know if you are not getting irritated to see me take your burden on my shoulders. You see, that is what is killing me.

If I were to reason things out lucidly, I would say, yesterday he was as always, a little crazier perhaps, but it is, I dare say, to hide my embarrassment. He did not say anything very private to me, but it is often thus; and there was a dual reason. He spoke very nicely of Thérive, of Laforgue, of Montherlant.[151] One thousand times already I have imagined the worst, and always the truth was shown to be contrary to my illusions [*rêveries*] and brought me happiness. It will probably still be that way; wait with confidence.

Yes, but to feel that we are so distant again, and that he can very well do without me, and especially not to know *when* I will see him again. And then I am afraid of seeing him again. I have dismissed the possibility of banal words; as in *Aimée*, we will only be able to speak about essential things, and that intimidates and frightens me.

I must very simply go find him, with or without a pretense. *Without* would be even better; control myself and speak to him as if it were about a very natural thing . . . Let's see, if I do not go, we will stand our ground, me without knowing, he . . . if I go, I might rediscover the same friendship as the other day, but I might also bother him, burden him. Me, the people whom I love don't ever bother me, and then even if I bother him, so what? I alone suffer from it . . .

The thing is that I think that we can no longer move forward. Maybe rereading this letter will give me confidence, but what will I do so that my heart does not beat too strongly when I ring his doorbell?

I have such a need to know what he thinks of me! I recall a bit of sweetness from our precious complicity. And the shame of having doubted him; I will repeat to myself, he is my friend.

What would have happened the other day if I had cried. He was as moved as I, as flushed, as embarrassed. But why didn't he make a date with us? Shouldn't I wait for him instead? Why must we delve into serious things that touch him so deeply? I accept him as he is. I will know how to prefer him to myself, but I know how much I will suffer from it again because I

---

* Beauvoir first wrote "amitié" (friendship) in the manuscript and then crossed it out and wrote "camaraderie" (companionship).

have too much pride, in the *moral* sense of the word, to submit or diminish my soul, and because despite my esteem and my affection, my *self* affronts his without having the weakness [*lâcheté*] to become absorbed. Because once the exact union of our beings ceases, each takes back its independence, its integrity.

I think too much; I should let myself go toward my friendship: seek happiness, complicate nothing, not invent suffering for myself. But I have committed [*engagé*] all of myself to this adventure, and now it is my life.

(And I understand today the great hatreds of love, the irremediable pride, the passionate ruptures, the mutual tortures; without a lot of tenderness and pity, every love would be like this ... In me, such impulses [*mouvements*] will always be repressed because he showed himself to me as weak and sad, because he did not try to show off, because softly and sweetly we complained to each other ... Ah!

Sweetness, sweetness, sweetness!)

So weary, so alone, I would almost consent to weeping before him.

But all of that, Jacques, you will always be ignorant of it.

"Does that concern you?"[152]

But you are not mad at me; you are my friend, right, right?

> "And if you had to give me joy, was it worth the trouble for me to learn sadness?"[153]
>
> All the same, today I do not have the strength to say, "Thank you."

I am tired of everything, and it no longer even amuses me to be tired. Only a single thing amuses me: to go home and to sing "Dolorosa" while I feel like crying.[154] And then I feel even more like crying when I realize that I have no reason to feel like it.

I like Barnabooth; I would like to meet him and make him read these notes.[155] If I did not have to work stupidly, I would like to intensify my disgust with his.

I will never know how to live; as soon as I have something beautiful, I ruin it. When I don't have anything, I am bored. I turn everything into dramas; I am perfectly ridiculous in my own eyes.

There are forty people around me who work and who are not thinking about anything, I am going to make the forty-first.

I do not have more perseverance in my dislikes than in my enthusiasms; that is what discourages me.*

---

* The quotation by Tagore that now appears before the October 14 entry was placed by Beauvoir on the facing verso, opposite this line of text in the manuscript.

There is a single lifestyle that tempts me: to withdraw into a very beautiful country where I would spend my days listening to the confidences of sad people whom I would never see again. Happy people are decidedly too numerous on this earth, and they are too dumb. I like them only if they are children because then they are building up their strength for the great sorrows. To think that when I was young, happiness seemed so easy to me. Marriage with someone whom one loves . . . books . . . beautiful weather.

At all costs, I will go to see him one of these days. Mama will undoubtedly try to hide her smile again (I love him too much at the moment; that embarrasses me too. My heart is too burdened, and it is nevertheless completely empty.) She believes that I enjoy [*me plaît*] Jacques's company, funny kind of enjoyment [*plaisir*]. In fact, she can believe anything that she wants; it is all the same to me because it is not true.

I feel like complaining!

October 15

I am rereading my notes from the year. Oh! What letters by Rivière, what nothingness, what a taste for death; and what a will to avoid ever denying oneself, to risk, to lead a pitiless life! Me too, I must have a pitiless life . . .

I will go to his home tomorrow. I want to suffer.

I am always rereading, abandoned too much the discipline of Garric-Péguy. I must reread Péguy.[156] I would have to have a bit of heroism and get out of myself. But I love myself so much! Ah, to rediscover all of my longings of six months ago—already! Perhaps I was better then, more mystical and more ardent, farther from the earth, more truly above happiness, especially more simple. Now I am complicated and sorrowful, more sensitive and more profound I believe, but with less youth and less enthusiasm [*élan*]. I am old! I have lived so much already this year! More than in all the rest of my life. I discovered a lot of things, but I explored many others . . .

And then from this divine life where I moved about truly as a free man higher than love, intelligence, and daily problems, I fell back to earth. Maybe I let fewer things escape; I go more in depth, but I no longer get lost. I esteem myself a bit less; I love myself more perhaps. And I have so much pity for myself.*

Certain things that I discovered in the past (first notebook: p. 13 and 14) are so familiar to me today![157] I am astonished not to have always known

---

* The sentences "I esteem myself a bit less; I love myself more perhaps. And I have so much pity for myself" are highlighted in brown ink in the margin of the facing verso in the manuscript.

them. I believed that I had always lived with these ideas. Alas! These discoveries that I made—my life itself has such an absolute value—how poor they seem in rereading them! There is in them only a slim intellectual residue of my past very rich *self*, this self that wanted to reconcile its tendencies from Barrès and its tendencies from Péguy. Now, I have definitely taken sides, as I wrote to J.; but "my life is completely empty inside of me."

On April 7, I wrote: Impossible to take Cocteau seriously. Ah! I mourn that beautiful time of intoxication that will never come again. The awakening! The now worn-out ideas then so new; the strange and marvelous appearance of life! Better formed judgment; sides taken; my barely awakened youth is already leaving. All within six months! Alone, my heart invents new experiences . . . I already have a past of almost one year. It seems to me tonight that I am forty years old.

April 9 I was taking stock of my life and I clarified my ideas. Except that every sentence would now have an infinity of underlying meanings, I would now write the same profession of faith; there would be more nuances and complexities in my thought, but for different and more complex reasons, I am still at the same point. Everything is more, infinitely more nuanced, and thus I see that I seriously gained some depth all the same; in particular, I have less courage, less will, and I would even delete "fruitful life." I am no longer asking for my life to be anything at all; it is already different enough that it is.

Ah! How proudly and bitterly I was set against the barbarians. Externally I was wrong; one has to resemble everyone else, but with a much more noble inner attitude. Is it this sentimental crisis that is draining me? Maybe, but despite everything, this weakness does not seem vile to me because it is familiar, accepted, controlled and especially because of the rare sorrows that it brings to me, and because of my great renunciation (see what I wrote p. 28).[158] Yes, she left this year; the one who is coming is other, but what a struggle too! I do not fear emptiness or blandness; on the contrary, I do fear an excess of fever and of suffering, and that I will not be able to carry through to the end.

Did I write p. 31?[159] This liking for nothingness was not habitual for me, and I considered it to be an ordeal to combat. Today I take pleasure in my disgust; no, not pleasure, but I gorge myself on its bitterness; and I grant it a profound value because it is no longer an accident, alas! I am seeking less to elude suffering through heroism.

Crying does not astonish me like before; I have realized my independence. Yes, I have been faithful to what I expected from myself. Precisely, from myself, as from Jacques, I no longer have to expect anything; I have obtained everything.

So?

I foresaw things precisely (p. 32); the bonds are renewed.[160] Do I regret it? No, it is good this way.

I was seeking a result; I believed my efforts to be useful. I no longer have any goal, and I feel the sterility of being. However, I believe that it is beautiful to be fruitlessly [*stérilement*].

Oh! These words by Barrès that I only jotted down before (p. 34) and that now I am living. "Mortal pleasure."[161] I did not understand Barrès as at present.*

My great worry was to defend myself against the barbarians; that is done. In fact, it was still the period of effort against myself and the others. And now that nothing in me is distracted by these struggles any longer . . .

Alas! I can reread page 40, "Anything rather than coldness and discouragement." I was right, I believe. I had to chase them away, these familiar and exhausting companions. I said, "The work is so vast . . ." But the work is accomplished. What should I do? Start another one (? . . .)

A beautiful life . . . surpassing oneself [*se dépasser soi-même*] . . . I must seriously reflect upon these things.

Ah! Claudel and what he said about love, "everything, always" (p. 47–48, first notebook). "Ah! let it stay a bit in the distance." . . . I reread these quotes and it is all of my soul that repeats them. Peace descends. Claudel always brings me answers.

"There is this need in man above all which is to escape happiness!"[162]

All right.† Ah! I esteem myself for having written this page; I am proud to think it again. I count on myself alone, and in friendship I would never seek support. Probably what I wrote then has another source of energy than my complaints of these days, but I was less unhappy. If I moan, at least I am not unworthy of my courageous self from the month of June. Yes, after all, despite everything, I fully ratify what I wrote then. And what follows (p. 63). It is really still the self of today that is speaking. And especially p. 64.[163] It really is that, my great affection.

Finished my reading. Let's conclude.

First, I used to write in this notebook with less abandon than today, and

---

* From "I was seeking a result," at the start of the previous paragraph, through "I did not understand Barrès as at present," the text is highlighted in brown ink in the margin of the facing verso of the manuscript.

† Beauvoir wrote "All right" in English herself.

the echoes of my suffering, however real they may be, only come to me muffled. What I said then, I would repeat today. My *ideas* have not changed. What has changed are the circumstances of my inner life. I have less confidence, less enthusiasm. Voluntarily, I make a bigger place for *the other*. I am more sincere; I analyze better. I prefer the real to intoxication. I am rediscovering my faith in myself, and equilibrium in independence, but I care about it less than before. I no longer want to be so abstract.

That's good. I am here; he is there. The supple and solid bond of written letters. Distinct but fraternal, our two *selves*. No exaltation; not even sweetness. Something strong. To know that he is simply.

October 16

I regret that I didn't see J. just now, after this reading of Rivière that gave me such a clear consciousness of myself. At the moment, I am no longer intimidated because my judgment is more precious to me than his own. I would dare to impose my differences on him. I am very content with this written letter because of a sentence by Rivière on the necessity of a brutal frankness before coming to profound sincerity.

Little tenderness; the desire for an intellectual commerce of exact analysis perfectly exclusive of all love; in reality, to me, he is not very present. But when once again I will feel the immense sweetness and the fearful anxiety of my affection, I must *dare* as I would dare today; I must enter forcefully into his soul.

We are very different; sentences from his letter sing within me ... Only I must be careful that my present very intellectual and lucid self is not all of me, and remembering my tears, before yesterday, in the Luxembourg Gardens, I must not define myself by what I am at this minute (fortunately!).

Resolutely pushing away any desire of fidelity to a dead self, any desire to trace a beautiful picture of myself, here the time has come for finally seeking the truth about myself, in comparing myself to him.

Overall, he appears to me to be more preoccupied with moral questions, and I with psychological questions. My most profound liking is a liking for meticulous analysis; I am more attached to myself than to the life that I lead. I do not worry, as he does, over choices; my rules are rather definitively set [*posée*]. Until now, I sought exultation first. Now, because the time has come where that exultation would be artificial, I am no longer going to be attached to anything but absolute sincerity.

It is perhaps more sentimental; however, I have known many fevers and tears ... I have only to reread; yes, but in suffering I kept my taste for seeing clearly.

I believe that I worry more than him about not losing anything in life, an unimaginable seriousness before the least of circumstances; I reject all pleasures out of fear of spoiling something within me. It seems to me that he attaches less importance to himself; he has something more spontaneous, younger and at the same time, weaker perhaps: I see that he *feels* more strongly these doubts, these disgusts. In fact, I know him very little; I imagine that his sensitivity is much finer and more delicate than mine (and that is why I esteem that he is worth more than me). I certainly have some sensitivity and even a lot, but different. I would be capable of more depth and fidelity than he perhaps, but he is more refined, more nuanced, more scrupulous. What I adore is his timidity; he puts on an ironic or flippant mask by which I myself am sometimes tricked. (And for that I am mad at myself; I know that if he came in laughing, his gaiety would make me perhaps doubtful, but with me he has always shown himself maskless, and not ironic, oh no. I should not fear him; I am surely the stronger.) In this reserve, this modesty, and this fear of displeasing I see one of the most attractive traits of his character.

He is an artist; I am not.

More exercised intelligence, more sure of itself than mine.

What disconcerts me are certain traits that appear to me to be a bit artificial: a liking for formulas, enthusiasms which are too great for their objects, somewhat affected disdains. There is often incomprehension from me about this (he gives only very little of himself), also, a desire to deceive himself. I do not know if he has ever attained perfect sincerity toward himself.

In short, according to the very little that I know about him, he surpasses me a) by a finer intelligence, b) by a much richer sensitivity, c) by a thousand nuances of his self having an incomparable intellectual and moral distinction.*

Me, I am more serious (I believe). I live a harsher, less relaxed life, even in sadness; I love [*aime*] myself more than he loves [*aime*] himself.

(Jacqueline came and interrupted this analysis; disappointment; too different; she is very pious and understands nothing of my complications—give her my sympathy. And then reinvasion; strangely detached like on certain nights in the past; everything appears to me as attenuated, deafened, dreamlike. In the middle of my room, alone; a great tenderness again; and the

---

* From "What disconcerts me," in the previous paragraph, to "moral distinction," the passage is highlighted in brown ink in the right and left margins.

peaceful certitude of never attaining happiness. A dream, my sentimental life; all of it happens in my imagination, and my imagination is found translated into reality . . . as a jumble. I am a bit tired . . . especially weary from not being left alone. Mama claims [*prétend*] to understand more and more and understands less and less; to see myself through her eyes is so strange for me. Confidence in J. I only have to wait, to dare. He is my friend.)

Without comparing now and with more nuances, I would like to figure out how to define myself more precisely. I hesitate just as I am about to sketch my portrait because this cold intellectual sketch will be so different from the living reality that I am! (A while ago, in front of the mirror, I liked my grave face for its applied seriousness under two somber plaits.) I do not have a lot of esteem for myself, especially since I have read those admirable letters by Rivière and Fournier; I still lack a perpetually fresh depth and richness. But I love [*aime*] myself so much, for my strength and for my weaknesses. (To think that I almost missed this affection that clutters up my life and deprives me of my perfect possession of self; it is through this, on the contrary, that I will be able to test my possibilities for suffering, for renunciation, for audacity, for weakness. The only thing is that I must not abdicate any of myself for him; I desire for him to know me and not for him to love [*aimer*] me—except when I am too sad and cowardly.)

Me in October 1926

Eighteen years, nine months, but only nine months of reflective life; only nine months, but weighing heavily like long years. Intellectual, sentimental, numerous and intense experiences; minutely detailed analyses; positions taken on life (others, me, etc.).

What I discover in myself first is a seriousness, an austere and implacable seriousness, for which I do not understand the reason, but to which I subject myself like to a mysterious and crushing necessity. I never thought of discussing it. Even when it bothers me I cannot hate it; it is myself. It is what controls my life. And first it prohibits me from that which is not essential. I have girlfriends who are worth as much as me and who know certain pleasures; the idea that one could refuse them would not even occur to them: tennis, swimming, theater, gatherings. What is so natural to them offends me when I find it in them. "How can they?" I think. For very little I would accuse them of frivolity, and when I reflect, I really feel that I am not basing my refusal of pleasure on any moral reason. Simply I am not *able* to give myself up to pleasure.

I carry this refusal in all the words that I say, and that is why I don't speak much. To say useless words makes me suffer like a diminution; at length I weigh each word as well as each act: before going to see a friend, writing a letter, etc. I have to deliberate slowly. I hate conversations precisely because they take me off guard and do not permit me to translate my profound sentiments very exactly. People sometimes believe that my reserve is disdainful; it originates on the contrary out of my respect for others. I am ashamed to give them what I do not consider important (and they ask me for that alone).

Alone face-to-face with myself or in my relationships with others, I am incapable of indifferent gestures; I must engage if not my entire self, at least an entire part of myself.

I am astounded that everyone is not like me, and I suffer from it; I suffer from it first because they do not understand the profound significance of all that I express. They forget one word that I have said or treat lightly one step that I have taken, and before pronouncing the word, or taking the step, I had hesitated for a long time, painfully deliberated. And then, it so happens that in judging them in terms of myself, I grant the same value to their gestures that they would have had for me if I had made them. I therefore try to reconstruct the psychological state from which they have emerged, to foresee for them the possible consequences, and I invent a thousand agonizing dramas that reality dispels into smoke.

Indeed, I have this infirmity of not being able to make do with what I receive or await the future patiently; I seek to penetrate what has not been revealed to me. I invent with an ingenious despair the least desired futures; or rather, I envisage all of them one after the other, but always looking at the one that satisfies me the least as though it is infinitely more probable. And the time when it is before my eyes, I suffer from it as from a certitude; I do not tell myself "maybe," but I reconstitute the present and believe in this reconstitution as an established fact . . . even if it means soon reconstructing on other bases. I am totally lacking in peace and confidence; I cannot *close* a *matter* once and for all. Thus, I should be completely sure of Jacques's friendship. Every day I call it back into question; every day I take up a new aspect of the problem and I turn it over in my head all day long. The most curious thing is that I do not proceed logically at all, basing my suppositions on solid psychological givens. I have the idea of a possibility [*possible*], and without trying to find if it is the least in the world justified, I become attached [*m'attache*] to it. Thus, about everything and nothing, I manage to create a thousand worries for myself: to forget, to wait—words that have no meaning for me. Many people know how to put aside a thought or a feeling any time when they cannot get anything out of it and how to take it, intact, out of the corner where they had let it sleep when once again this can be useful. Impossible. Faced with a closed box, instead of attending to other business while tranquilly awaiting the moment when I will be given the key, I take it in my hands and turn it over and over feverishly, knowing quite well, however, that these vain movements will not reveal the contents to me. It is a great waste of strength that would I dare say be useful elsewhere. Only it assures my ideas perhaps, and especially my affections of a depth and a continuity, that others do not possess; even in books I have rarely encountered a fidelity such as the one that I discover in myself, a fidelity of every minute. Nothing ever sleeps in me; nothing needs to wake up. Everything maintains a life of an extraordinary intensity; in particular, everything remains *present* for me, on the sentimental order, as well as on the intellectual order. I believe that it is simultaneously my most essential and most distinctive trait. It explains my memory—of books, of beings, of events, to which I attached importance. It is to this that I owe just about all the worth that I have, and it is this also that deprives me of spontaneity, whims, and unconcern. I am always burdened by myself and others.

This is thus how I manage to exhaust everything, to consider everything from all angles; by dint of dragging it in my wake, I manage to know all the aspects, to enrich them, to transform them. And I am astounded to observe all the variations that they underwent while reality remained approximately the same.

I believe that this is a tendency that brings me a lot of pain and fatigue, but it is also my greatest claim to honor. I do not consider it to be at all indispensable to every interesting being; I imagine exquisite natures that would not possess it, but me without it, I would be nothing.

It makes me very different because I believe truly that it has a strength in me that it has in very few other people, even among the most reflective.

I owe the continuity of my life to it and the letting go of so few important things (on the moral, psychological, sentimental, and intellectual levels).

In particular, I attach an extraordinary importance to myself; I take with absolute seriousness every idea, every emotion that I feel; I would have to have a whole supply of them to satiate myself. I chew them over and over again until they are perfectly assimilated to myself, and then they no longer have any life, any flavor; I must have others, new ones, original ones, which [illegible] as long as they are still foreign to me but with which I can no longer stand not being familiarized . . . and so on to infinity.

124

This concentration, this reflection on myself allows me to control my life energetically. I have hours of enthusiasm during which "transformed again into a god," I glide above the earth, but even in dry spells, I know how to take a hold of myself and keep myself as an entirety in my hand. I am often conscious that I am enough for myself. And I do not mean to say that I am ignorant of passionate longings [élans], frantic appeals, the great disgusts of solitude, oh, no! My sentimental life is ardent, profound, painful because of its intensity; it has happened that I have *preferred* others to myself! I am not saying esteemed them more: there are a great many people that I esteem more than myself. There is one whom I learned to love more, in the profound sense of loving. It is such a reversal of all values that I am surprised about it myself, my dear self, to be so unfaithful to you; it is true however. I do not find this either better or worse. It pleases me only to be capable of it despite the passion that I have for myself. Thus, my feelings participate in this seriousness, this fever that I bring to everything. However—except of course during still rather frequent hours of weakness—I do not ask them to unburden me of myself or to give me a new reason to live. I sometimes attain a true coldness [sécheresse] in this proud joy of feeling at the very heart of suffering that after all I do not need anyone to bear it. One must not be confused. I am not, not at all selfish in my affections; I would consent to all sacrifices for the happiness of the other, even to that of not being loved by him; truly, I completely contradict this stupid verse,

> To love, for a woman, means that one loves her . . .
> [Cocteau][164]

I am pleased to love without being loved; I desire only to give. But precisely, I have very little need to receive, to hang on to someone else, hence, a certain hardness (purely intellectual).* In reality, there are in me two very different moments [instants]: the one in which I simply suffer and love—the one in which I no longer suffer, in which I still love but in knowing it and controlling it. I cannot reduce them; in the first case my sensitivity alone is at stake. (However, even in my pain, I keep a lot of my dignity. I accept. I understand. I say, "Does that concern you?" I do not have the impression that he can do anything to me, but that I am torturing myself because of him.) In the second case, I go voluntarily to him; always, I remain conscious of this independence of the self. Will I say that I think my feelings? It would not

---

* From "I am pleased" through "(purely intellectual)," the manuscript is highlighted in brown ink in the right margin.

always be true; there are days when I make do with feeling. Rather, I do not come out of myself in love. I attract it to me more than I go to it; even when I relinquish myself [*je me renonce*], my self is still the center around which I organize my affection. Otherwise, I would not have consciousness of having relinquished myself. Once again, this does not deprive me either of passion or of tenderness; because of it the other is not less loved. This deprives me only of tasting the sweetness of love, of the great annihilation. (I have had this experience certain evenings, but very rarely.) It must be beautiful to be able to love while forgetting the self [*dans l'oubli de soi*] (by renunciation and forgetfulness, because one can relinquish oneself without forgetting oneself), with more resignation than harshness.

I make up for this with depth, seriousness, continuity (not an hour goes by without my thinking of the one I love: Z., G., or J.), and with the sincerity of my abnegation.[165] But evidently, I cannot love as someone who would not be me would love . . .

I have such a sense of modesty about my sensitivity, and it is something so painful and bitter that some believe that I do not have a lot. There is especially the fact that I cannot spread it about; I can love only what I prefer, and that is inevitable since a passion installed in me absorbs everything. I give myself entirely to it; I transfer everything to it. My affection is wildly, jealously exclusive. Naturally, I love very few people. (I love all souls, and passionately, but for them, not for me, with a love that takes nothing from me.) Voluntarily, before a greater love I sacrifice all others (Zaza). It would seem to me like betrayal not to reserve everything for the one that I have chosen. (Because I do not call love being interested in others and seeking to do them good, but only walking through life with my eyes fixed on them; and I cannot look at two people at once.)

Easily I open myself up; easily I offer my sympathy, but without committing myself [*m'engager*]. I give, oh! yes, but I give objects that I detach from myself and not myself.

Intellectually, I have experienced intoxications of thought, to the point of madness. Now I am no longer mildly interested in anything but ideas that I elaborate painfully with all of my being; the successes of others, I admire them, but rather coldly (yet there is Bergson and Valéry). My ideas, I suffer at moments from no longer being able to use them, express them, or clarify them. There is, in this, a part of me that exists only when it defines itself (in opposition to the other); maybe left to myself I would attach some importance to this. But there are so many things that entice me! I am tempted to write, to speak ... But my studies and my successes no longer mean any-thing to me.*

When I catch myself attributing importance to my thought or my act, I have a vague impulse to be joyful about it. And then the nothingness of that also appears to me.

I am tired of this analysis; I will study myself on other points.

October 17

Was at the Équipes. Good work to be done. But the placidness of these young girls discourages me. There is nothing in life that I can adapt myself to; I must resign myself to adapting everything to me. Egoism? No. Respect for myself.

Jacques is far away. Does he exist?†

* * *

Oh! life is too sad, incurably sad!
[Laforgue][166]

O Beloved! There is no longer time, my heart is breaking
And too much to hold a grudge against you, I have sobbed so,
You see, that the spleen of summer nights alone is sweet to me,
Long nights where all is fresh like a great dream ...
[Laforgue][167]

O vast convocation, magnificent suns.
[Laforgue][168]

O banal rancor of our human farce!
[Laforgue][169]

... broken hearts came
For these unknown evils
For which nothing, nothing is consolation.
[Laforgue][170]

Stars! I do not want to die! I have genius!
Ah! *to become nothing irrevocably again!*
[Laforgue][171]

---

* From "But there" to the end of this paragraph, the passage is highlighted in the right margin.
† In the manuscript, the following poetry was on the facing verso, next to the ninth paragraph of the entry called "Me in October 1926," starting "It makes me very different." This poetry by Laforgue ends on the page opposite the end of the October 17 entry.

But we have only one corner of immense deserts . . .
    [Laforgue][172]

Because it is an Enigma at least! I wait! I wait!
Nothing! I listen to the hours falling away drop by drop . . .
    [Laforgue][173]

And all the unknown and humble who silently bled! . . .
    [Laforgue][174]

And nothing remains! O marble Venus, vain etchings!
Insane Hegelian brain! sweet consoling songs!
Belfries of filigree woven, upspringing, consumed!
Books which held man's useless victories!
All that was born of your children's wrath,
All that was once your filth and your transient splendor,
O Earth, has become like a dream, a noble dream.
Go on sleep; it's over now. Eternally sleep.
    [Laforgue][175]

In those days, the great tragic bouquet of Life!
The doleful violets of disillusions,
The completely gray horizons of the followed rut.
And the infernal tones, of our corruptions!
    [Laforgue][176]

The illusion, more doleful in its macabre uproar—
    [Laforgue][177]

I splash the setting suns with tragic red spots
I throb from exile in the heart of the stars,
My spleen whips the great traveling clouds.
    [Laforgue][178]

Oh! it is finished, finished!
. At length the wind moans
All is yellow and wheezing, the days have gone by,
The Earth has done its time; its back can no longer take it.
And its poor children, lanky, bald, and pale
From having too often meditated eternal problems
Shivering and stooped under the weight of scarves
In the yellow and dying gas of the foggy boulevards
With a mute and empty eye, contemplate their absinthe.
    [Laforgue][179]

October 18

Have read Laforgue. Intense emotion. Never encountered anything as profoundly heartrending. Oh, the vanity of everything in this bus that was taking me to an insipid Greek class! I know very well that you are there, my poor friend, but what can you do for me, and me for you? I am only me; you are only you; and it is everything else that each of us seeks! At the most, all we can do for a while is to limit each other to our mutual desire—that is what people call love, but even if we forget them, will our other aspirations be less profound? Would we not be angry with each other about this limit? You see, I am not putting your friendship into question, but we are each as alone as if the other were not thinking of him. Of course, on those weary and relaxed evenings when the soul is no longer seeking anything but forgetfulness and illusion, I think that I am this illusion for you, and you for me. But when painfully we have consciousness of ourselves, we know well that another pitiful soul like our own would not know how to bring us consolation.*

There was a time when to possess the other's soul was the secret goal of all of my dreams; it seemed to me that in annexing it to my own, I would bring about a marvelous new peaceful domain without problems [*ennuis*]. At present, I no longer have this desire; the mystery that others carry within them no longer moves me (and a couple of months ago it was still a veritable obsession: reading things in the wake of Garric and Jacques, anxious conversation with my female companions; now I only seek to penetrate into others to help them, but I no longer experience this urgent necessity).

The mystery of my soul no longer exists for me either; I am no longer walking in the shadows, and this cold clarity that floods all of my inner life does not permit me to trust [*espérer en*] vaguely in some unexplored recess. I know my poverty; I know the poverty of other souls, even the richest since their riches are finite. I no longer have any illusions about beings. As long as I imagined inexhaustible and magnificent resources, I advanced with confidence and joy on a voyage of discovery that, I thought, was never supposed to finish; I no longer have anything to define. I am face to face with my awfully destitute self.†

It is not from pride that I scorn love; if it comes, I will welcome it of course; only I have such consciousness of its powerlessness. Because of this life that I have in his heart and he in mine, has anything changed? It is per-

---

* The final three sentences in this paragraph are highlighted in the margin of the facing verso.

† In this last paragraph, the passage from "I know my poverty" through the words "I advanced" is highlighted in the right margin of the facing verso.

haps from having cried too much that this drought [*sécheresse*] has come to me. But that does not keep me from loving him. Only what? How will that get us any further? I have never felt this so clearly as today. Besides, I am detached from everything; the real in the pure state cannot truly be lived, and at the moment, no intoxication has seized hold of me.

Tagore moves me for all the infinity that he brings to passion, to life; he transforms it into a complicated drama that plays itself out in a marvelous region, well above my despairing analyses.[180] All that is religious in his appeals, his joys, his sorrows . . . For him everything has a meaning, nothing is vain or sterile; nothing crawls along humbly on earth . . . And yet an admirable knowledge of the human heart, of these problems of the inner life that make me withdraw into myself, he transports them into a superior sphere where he moves; they are no longer facts of experiences, but the entire soul expresses itself in them with its shady abysses and contradictions. If I were less sleepy, I would like to study this more. I will copy only a couple of pieces in which I rediscover the cry from my heart.

This complaint by Laforgue to the Beloved!

(My equilibrium despite everything and my love of this so sad life and this dupery perhaps . . .)

October 20

Mama believes that she is making me immensely happy by sending me to Jacques's house. Every time that I come back from his house, I feel more down in the dumps; if only I were able to think that he felt a bit less blue! He said thank you to me in a tone so brief and hushed that tomorrow surely I will no longer believe that I heard it, but I know that it meant [*signifiait*] a lot. I did well to write to him since my letter made him happy. I am quite certain that I am torturing only myself.

This feeling that I have for him is so strange! He told me that there was something embarrassing about our relationship. Would this be a scruple for him? Does he fear that I understand "love" when he says "friendship"? I understood so well only a little while ago on boulevard St. Michel that I know deep down that I mean little to him! I am not "the great adventure" or "the ideal"; I cannot give him anything infinite . . . Myself, when he spoke to me of his silly life of this summer, how little *jealous* I was, to a degree that astonishes me. I envisaged the *worst* with absolute detachment.* (Besides, I

---

* From the beginning of the October 20, 1926, entry through the word "detachment," the manuscript is highlighted in the right margin of the facing verso.

do not believe this.) "Does that concern me?" He is himself, I am me. Only we are friends; there you have it.

Oh! I am far from the passionate waiting at his door or the tears of this vacation! All that I asked for then was his affection. I have it; and it is no longer important to me (I understand me); it is important to me that he makes use of mine.

It is the most beautiful thing in my life, later I dare say one of my purest and richest memories. I must be aware of this with exactitude . . .

This friendship for me is the opposite of love, almost a way of destroying it; today, he stripped it of all of its mystery, all of its slightly distant prestige. Disheveled like his suit, his soul showed itself to me, and I would be at a loss for words to say how grateful I am to him for this awful frankness that deprives me of adorning him in ideal love. He cannot give me any higher sign of his esteem and of his affection than to show himself to me as he is. It is candid; it is decent; it is humble and courageous. If he loved me—if he desired for me to love him—he would only have to let himself be seen briefly like he did last year, but he treats me loyally, as a friend. Thus, instead of undergoing the humiliation of loving my dreams through him, I know this bitter affection for a being whom I see as is, in all of his weakness and human poverty.* And me, I did the same thing by writing to him and coming to see him; I chased away all coquetry and all desire for his love—but I deserve less credit for it because to show weaknesses is less difficult for a woman than for a man.

From all of that comes a very complex feeling that is altered in one sense or another as soon as I have gone a rather long time without seeing him, simultaneously sorrowful and peaceful, rather harsh, hardly consoling but which, all the same, is my great current reason to live. My mania for analysis is going to ruin it without being able to evoke its unique flavor; I feel that in a few months, already, it will no longer be the same.

There is a sweetness in being something for him and in making him happy with my presence—the sensation of a definitive thing between us and thus strongly limited—at the same time an obscure rancor and a sincere gratefulness that he does not know how to bring me any joy, the bitter consciousness of my powerlessness, a lot of pity, affection, and also this idea that he is going to continue on his route, and me on mine and that this marvelous closeness will perhaps not even last one year . . .

I am facing life without illusions; at fifteen, I believed in the ideal, strong,

---

* From "today," in the first sentence of this paragraph, through the words "of his weakness and human poverty," the manuscript is highlighted in the margin.

balanced being who would dominate me with his intelligence and his love. I was even tempted last year to incarnate him . . . I know that this being does not exist; there are only men. I cannot lean *definitively* on anyone because every man—Jacques—is like me.* There is only the possibility [*possible*] of a great compassion.

It is so different from what I anticipated last year; it is better; it is more worthy, free of pride like in that ridiculous "wonderful companionship" that daydreams depict, not mutual admiration. And that is perhaps what bothers me; I do not admire him. But it is also what proves how deeply I have penetrated into him. I remember last year having felt hopelessly—I even wrote it down—the great dupery that there is at the base of all admiration. (I used to say love because then I thought love = admiration.) When I reach into the depths of myself, behind acts and words, there is nothing, nothing to admire, said I; I'll say it again. And in the depths of J as in the depths of myself, I find nothing, nothing to admire (which does not stop me from doing us justice but . . .).

Indeed, he is the one who is right. Everything can be demonstrated; one can find reasons for everything. This does not keep me from preferring one life to another. He tells me that he admires a beautiful work of art without seeking why; the painter has the right to trace such and such a line as I to commit such and such an act. It doesn't keep the work from being indifferently beautiful or ugly; the same goes for my life. It is perhaps a question of success, of genius in life as in artistic composition, and truly, it presents at least an equal interest. Propose this idea to him . . .

A security to rediscover in him the profound seriousness that I sometimes doubt; and this simplicity in our relationship, he too attaches importance to this . . .

Perhaps true passion is inseparable from jealousy; me, if I encountered Yvonne de Galais I would send her to him.[181]

Need for nothing more. We have attained, I repeat, the definitive point. After this confirmation, I think that there will be no more storms like the other day.

October 23

Oh! Days of the past! Only two years! Already two years! Books devoured in the solitude of this great leather armchair, a playground for shadows from

---

* From the words "a lot of pity," in the previous paragraph, to this point, the manuscript is highlighted in the right margin of the facing verso.

the fire in the hearth . . . and quiet dreams; this ardent view, confident in life of which I was ignorant. I remember the feel of it; I recall for a minute my serene and lonely soul of that winter . . . How I have aged! It is unlimited life that was opening before me, that cruelly closes itself off today. Two narrow paths, you must at all costs advance down one of the two, and the one is so off-putting that only a single one remains . . . and so many lands all around where I will never set foot! Here everything is becoming precise and inexorable; here my life is already decided, and I have only one life!

Last night everything was expected and charming: his laughter, his steady conversation, and the great fun together. I went to bed joyful; I woke up regretting my joy; I cannot manage to like joy!*

A little while ago in the cold streets, I wandered, prey to a great despair, the despair of not being able to escape this happiness! Oh! This is of no importance, not even for literature, but I really have to explain myself frankly. He wants to get married; if it is not with me, I will be very unhappy. If it is with me, it is evidently happiness. And I am afraid, and the sorrowful life is waiting for me, even though I know that I will choose the other. Oh! To see him, and me, not alone any longer. (So there are only two souls relying on each other without worrying about tomorrow, in the great sweetness of the present friendship.) But resituated in life, in the world, it is terribly painful to me!†

I am perhaps mistaken—and I almost manage to wish for this great disappointment—but everything pushes me toward his residence. Mama and Papa, ah yes! with a serenity and a security that revolt me and tear me apart; he himself, it seems to me; my own heart. I feel that I cannot resist, that I am fatally heading toward this end [*terme*], and I would have so wanted to linger in an imprecise affection. Can't we thus, for all of our lives, remain what we are for each other without creating tighter bonds? Sometimes, yes, I wish for a still closer intimacy. But I am horrified by everything that will have to be sacrificed and that it will be inevitable! For I am not free, I can choose only him. Happiness, life is him! Oh! Happiness and life, which were supposed to be *everything*. How I must love you in order not to hate you!‡

I am not thinking about him at the moment, but about me, about me for whom I feel pity, and whom I want to defend against what life imposes on her!

---

* From the start of the previous paragraph through the first sentence of this one, the passage is highlighted in brown ink in the margin.

† This paragraph is highlighted in the margin, from "but I really have to explain myself frankly" through "it is terribly painful to me!"

‡ This paragraph is highlighted in the margin, from "and that it will be inevitable" through "not to hate you!"

We are so different! He is essentially an artist; enjoying beautiful things is enough for him. Beauty brings him a plenitude. He loves happiness; he accepts luxury and the easy life. Me, I have to have a devouring life! I live with a great disgust for myself because for a month now my intellectual and moral avarice has become less intense. I need to act, to exert myself, to *realize.* I am used to a strong work discipline. I have to have a goal to attain, a task to fulfill. I will never be able to be satisfied with what satisfies him or then out of complacence I will deceive myself, and preferring his esteem and his affection to my own I will internally scorn myself—I will perhaps hold this against him.*

Only yesterday, chatting with Mademoiselle Mercier, I felt in myself so many riches that I wanted to put to use! On the intellectual order, in terms of action, I can do so much! This life that I dreamed about last year! Perhaps I dreamed about it because I was wrong to place myself on the outside and not on the inside to look at it.† It is internally that it appeared superior to me and my generous enthusiasm [*élan*] was, I believe, a simple desire to be able to admire myself as I used to admire the other. I no longer desire to admire myself, but I would not know how to stop having esteem for myself. Do I have the right to withdraw with this great burden of things that have been entrusted to me in order for me to give them away? Consecrate myself to him, that's fine. But is this exclusive preference not a form of egoism? I must for me, despite everything, keep *myself* and my ardor and the sense of my worth and of my duty. But I feel that I am absorbed by him, that I will cowardly accept not to look for anything beyond happiness and that I will find a thousand good reasons to justify myself! And I know that there does not exist a being who suits my being better than he! I know that if I do not marry him, I will never marry anyone; this would be better, I believe! But it would be so empty, so implacably sad that I would not have the strength to do much of anything either. My life, no matter what I do, will be useless. I will not respond to the calls heard; I will not realize the rich promises of my youth. Already, we see that my fervor has weakened! I no longer have any horizon but him; I no longer desire anything—barely him; I know neither how to want, nor to love. And he is so cruelly imposes himself upon me!

Maybe I am exaggerating; maybe it is only about holding my own [*me maintenir*]. He will probably accept the demands of my nature—besides, I

---

* This paragraph is highlighted in the right margin of the facing verso, from "We are so different" through "I need to act, to exert myself."

† This paragraph is highlighted in the margin, from the beginning to "look at it."

will frankly warn him about them—perhaps it would already be very good after all to be happy . . .*

Why would I have an empty life by his side? I am *able* not to have it. I am also able to have it. I must know how to control the first moments of my happiness, in other words, never consent to being unhappy with myself. For him evidently—supposing he loves me, and it also distresses me not to understand what could really attract him to me—the question is not being asked; he will simply introduce me into his life, but nothing will be changed. As for me, I am gambling all of myself! Very simply I will expose my scruples to him. I will explain how important it is to me and, hopefully, he will know how to judge from my point of view, not his. But why am I incapable of enthusiastic dreams? Why is it only in desire, in regret, or in pity that I experience great bursts [*élans*] of tenderness?

I have complete confidence in him and in his profound worth.† What scares me at times is my powerlessness to satisfy him. I am only me, only me. Oh, I hate myself. At other times it is the fear of sacrificing my own worth to his—apart from all questions of pride; I have no pride, especially before him. There is an incomparable charm in the secret and painful [complicity?] which is between us, and mixed with this open camaraderie. I live hours that I would have never dared to dream; the future is taking shape towards a radiant day . . . however.

I am not writing down tonight's great silent overflow of emotion by the fireside, the joyous and tender waves that strike are invading me.

October 24

Last night, obstinately seated in the calm darkness, there were a lot of things I understood. I am made for a life of struggle, effort, and suffering. Very young, I brought a passionate seriousness to my games; older, I liked only the triumph of conquering difficulties. There was a time when I had the idea of turning everything into joy; now I no longer manage to be interested in my own happiness; to act, to give myself, to waste nothing, and to brace myself against life, that is what suits me.‡ But if I am strong, won't I be strong

---

* From "And I know that there does not exist a being who," the twelfth sentence of the previous paragraph, through "all to be happy," the text is highlighted in brown ink in the right margin of the facing verso.

† From "Why is it only," in the previous paragraph, through "profound worth," the text is highlighted in the margin.

‡ From the second sentence in this paragraph, beginning "I am made," through "suits me," the text is highlighted in the right margin of the facing verso.

enough to carry happiness and good fortune? Offering my arms to the penetrating heat, I wondered why I am so repelled by these simple and complete pleasures? It's good that I have accepted pain, but don't I know how to accept joy? I, who so much like lucidity and truth, isn't there something fundamentally false in my taste for austerity? Why refuse everything, turn everything into suffering? It is not that I like to complain—I do not pity myself; it is not that I am basing this on any moral law. This tendency comes perhaps from the fact that up until now my most beautiful enthusiasms were painful whereas I have barely experienced only mundane [*vulgaires*] pleasures ... However, there was the reading of *Aimée* ... the serene nights in the Luxembourg Gardens ... All of it depends on the quality of the joy and the pain. I must be strong enough to withstand not exerting my strength.

I am not made for luxury. Exactly what I must have would be the most complete moral independence reconciled with the minimum of well-being, not to owe anything to money or to circumstances, to create my life for me alone. I am not saying that it would be better; I am saying that it is exactly what would suit me. But I love him ...*

Why did he pronounce those shameful words of marriage?[182] I had succeeded so well in forbidding myself to think about it! I so much liked this present free from the threat of all future ... But once again this bugaboo [*épouvantail*] retreats into the distance and with it, his face, too. How little I need him sometimes; how little I need anyone. It is at such moments in general that I write, and that is why this notebook is so different from myself.

I am starting to like intellectual work again. Peaceful equilibrium; perhaps Zaza is going to come; I feel like confiding in her ... Jacques, Zaza ... there are moments when I am happy. Don't I have the right to be after all?

* * *

In this world, there are only two tragedies. One is not getting what one wants, and the other is getting it. The last is much the worst; the last is a real tragedy.†
O. Wilde[183]

---

* From "I am not made" through "I love him," the text is highlighted in brown ink in the right margin of the facing verso.

† In the manuscript this quotation by Wilde is written on the facing verso, across from the paragraph starting, "To think that she is dead," in the October 27 entry.

October 27

Isn't this it, the great, great happiness, I wondered, the day before yesterday? Not exultant joy, but this grave resignation to life, the sweetness of a certainty? I believe that this is it . . .

Now, in looking, in trying the other forms of life possible for me, it is perhaps the one that first revolted me by its apparent easiness (October 23) that appears to me as the most legitimate and the best. Besides, I must notice that almost without exception all that comes to me from Jacques strikes me unpleasantly as a game or a cowardice, as a lack of seriousness (there I've hit the nail on the head). As soon as I think it over, I am firmly convinced of it, I cannot think otherwise. And here, it is not (as I said the other day) that I am absorbed in him.* I am rediscovering for myself the truths that he pointed out to me; I am not going down the same paths to do so, nor do I use these truths for the same ends. I simply understand.

There is action . . . I am going to take care of the Équipes Sociales. What that meant to me last year! No life seemed even possible to me next to Garric's! (All the same, there was that unavowed, weighty disillusion the day of that walk.) Now, I see a reduction in this overly consoling gift. Besides, it has always been my idea, since I have always supported Barrès. But I did not feel this idea so strongly until I myself got involved [*je me suis engagée moi-même*] . . . Of course, I am going to do my best and wholeheartedly, I will be happy to do good for beings upon whom I can act, but I do not want to experience the fever of action or the satisfied enthusiasm. I do not want anything to do with this soothing intoxication based on illusion. I will keep all my power for suffering intact. There is intellectual work. In the first logic class, I regretted no longer knowing such exhilaration of thought. That is decidedly finished; indeed, there are some things that interest me . . . but is it so superior to know and to discuss empty questions? I want the value of knowledge to be important, but my heart is much more interesting . . . I cannot take pleasure (this year) in this busy life that I have chosen (whereas not having a spare minute was my great joy last winter); I congratulate myself for having replaced the trivialities [*futilités*] with personal and social work, but it appears to me to be only superior, not of a completely different nature.† On this point, I make a clean break with last year. What I want to

---

* The foregoing three sentences, from "Besides, I must notice" through "absorbed in him," are highlighted in brown ink in the right margin of the facing verso.

† From "I cannot take pleasure" through "of a completely different nature," the passage is highlighted in the right margin of the facing verso.

rediscover is the profound inner life that sustained me before; what I want to cultivate is this great new affection. Except for the rare minutes when I raise myself up so high that I completely control myself, sensitivity included (when I again become a god, oh my beloved, oh self), every time that I need you less, my friend, is because I am worth less, because I lose myself.

Need you, I do not mean need to see you really, but need to feel your soul very close to mine.

When the soul is banally satisfied, it almost fears a more ardent plenitude. It must sometimes accept this near-indifference (because a perpetual fervor would fruitlessly use up new strength), but deep in the heart of this desire's abatement, may the soul knows itself to be capable of better, may it wait; may it know its state as temporary [*comme provisoire son état*]. So strange this alternation of moments when you are almost everything and of those when you do not currently exist! And yet, my heart is strangely faithful.

To think that she is dead, she, who read Lamartine in a dark blue net dress by the dimly lit window and who laughed so overflowing with the joy of living and of being in control (I used to try to serve soup with a ladle full of holes).[184] To think that I used to love so to talk interminably, to pour out my feelings, to joke! I was so eager to take pleasure in everything, not to lose anything of scattered pleasures! To think the girl from last year who had resolved all problems with a passionate admiration is dead, too! The one who believed she was making a sacrifice with renunciation, not knowing that the most painful and the most meritorious and the only legitimate act is to accept. The imperious need to be herself and to live her life were not yet tormenting her . . .

The one who cloaked beings with such a beautiful veil of illusion! I knew that I would not rediscover you, my beautiful year! So here I am awfully lucid and positive. Well! So be it. I agree to it. I will not try to revive my dead soul. But I will bring as much meticulous ardor into my coldness as in the past. No, I cannot waste anything of myself. I cannot live each day as it comes (maybe because I am not weary enough). I do not know the name of what I rise up against; I cannot justify [*je ne raisonne pas*] this rule inscribed within me . . .

I myself do not believe that everything leads back to the metaphysical problem. Probably one can uphold everything and say about everything, "What good is that?" But it is a fact that there is a voice in me that speaks imperiously. I can well understand that one might deny it any value, but there is really something more in it than in all the rational judgments that I could make about it.

(Deep down, I who am so intellectual, am I really not just simply instinctual? There is one curious thing; I put reason into my feelings and my spontaneity into my ideas.)

I conceive of *ethics* somewhat like a scientific hypothesis, like a *symbolic representation.* I choose—or rather, an unprovable postulate is imposed upon me that I agree to consider as true, and on it I build the most logical and solid system that I can. There are many postulates from which to choose. The criterion—strictly personal—is a certain degree of evidence; of most importance is not to make mistakes in the consequences that one draws from it (neither in thought, nor in act). Will we say that these ethics are illusory since they are not the only ones possible?[185] But Euclid's geometry is not illusory on the pretext that one can construct geometries outside of Euclid's postulate; it has a practical value (in the most scientific sense of the word) and a representative value. Or, for example, the atomic theory. Everything is happening as if . . . The scientists [*savants*] know very well that it is purely representative and treat it as if it expressed an objective reality. No serious scientist dreams of reproaching science for being only symbolic.*

I feel this so strongly! And if I say it to someone, it will not have any meaning for him! A conclusion is never entirely separate from the path that leads to it.

A marvel, these *Intentions* by Wilde![186]

Jacques is set on wanting to build in the absolute. He should closely study Kant. He will never get anywhere this way . . . unless he rediscovers a deep faith . . . or he sinks into an indifferent resignation.

October 29

I take back everything; I give up all faithfulness. I would like to read *Les nourritures terrestres;* I would like to live! I am going to live . . . I am giving myself up; I am letting everything collapse, and I will start over again with something else. I am no longer paying attention to moral values; I am no longer seeking to do something. I want to be, *to be.* My beloved self, on an evening of exaltation, I promised you I would love you well. Oh, how passionately I desired to keep that promise this morning crossing the Luxembourg Gardens as they burst with signs of spring! We are going to have a good time! I am no longer analyzing. I am no longer reflecting; I am

---

* This entire paragraph was highlighted in the margin, through "symbolic."

packing up sentimental and intellectual complications. I am setting my life adrift; I want to see what will happen. Oh, curiosities are being born in me too! I lived magnificently last year, without a doubt, with enthusiasm and asceticism; I lived a purely intellectual life; I created a god within myself.* And now I know this by heart; I have exhausted the bitter flavor of these renunciations; this existence is insipid. I take it all back. I am unfaithful. Likewise, it was pure madness to declare at eighteen that my mind was made up forever. I must live several lives before making a choice. It will be necessary soon enough to limit myself, to diminish myself! I want to get out of myself, to know people and their existence. I want to collect marvelous days of relaxation, joy, or tears. A splendid adventure is being offered to me; I am engaging myself in it. Since yesterday I have been living in the unreal and the real, without understanding, without searching. Already once again the Sorbonne, the cold philosophical discourses fall heavily onto my shoulders. Surely I will know how to free myself [*me dégager*] and continue my strange dream all year long. What will come of it? I do not know. Much disgust I dare say, some disillusion, some heartbreaks, whatever. The present is here in its unforeseen beauty. I do not have the right to let it get away! . . .

All day yesterday! And first this evening chez Lipp where encountering Jacques burdened my heart with an excessively heavy weight; my voice was strained.[187] My tears in the night because of this love for me that I believe to have felt in him, perhaps wrongly so, perhaps not, [and it?] oppressed me. I couldn't wait to shower him with all of my tenderness; I was giving way to his. I was feverish, I was afraid, I was happy.

And then, no, it isn't that at all, while perhaps being basically that, and that is what made the charm of the afternoon spent at his house ambiguous, painful and unreal, with a very rare originality! And first, from hearing him speak before me so freely, being there, the silent and accepted witness of *his whole life.* It proves that either he is oddly confident, or oddly indifferent, not to my affection, but to my opinion, such very simple and brutal frankness, that he found perfectly natural.† And me, torn between my affection, my prejudices, my imaginings and the facts, between my instincts and my reasoning, I was frightened by the unknown. He seemed to me to be completely separate from me, moving in a sphere that was completely other . . . I don't know; I am not analyzing . . . I know that it was sweet for me to be admitted into his intimate circle, treated like a male friend, to let myself

---

* The next six sentences are very hard to read in the manuscript; the ink got wet and ran.

† From "And first" through "in my opinion," the text is highlighted in brown ink in the right margin of the facing verso.

relax on the couch, not to say anything. I know it was painful for me not to be more for him than a male friend and to participate less in his life. I know everything was distant, relaxed; I did not have the courage to speak, nor the desire to say anything, nor to think. I know I was at the end of my rope when he left me alone. Absolutely insane crying jag: the joy of being there, as I never before would have believed I could be, alone, him knowing it; the anxiety of the street where I would have to find myself again; my love that I had not been able to say; my indecision, everything in fact . . . sensation of exhaustion and that, even with him present, I would remain there prostrate, sobbing. And thus no courage to escape.*

And then his return. Immediately on another level, more affectation, more money questions, plus that atmosphere of partying and waste that I sensed, once again the belief that it was finished, and that it was not taking anything away from him morally. He promised to introduce me to Delrive.[188] I have a grudge against him for this influence that he has on Jacques. If I do not find him charming, and especially if I do not understand him, I will detest him. What was exquisite was to be treated first with complete casualness, like one whose friendship is so sure that it needs no special consideration and then afterwards with this affectionate nuance of complete warmth, of communion, of comprehension that makes me more than just a casual friend. Indeed, he also said we were achieving something unique. We are as if our tenderness were a thing so certain that we can act in apparent ignorance of it. And then the coming of friends and the useless tranquil chat afterwards. And then our return together, and the thanks we said to each other before. Boulevard Raspail, Foujita's white painting that was so beautiful, so beautiful and Jacques beside me speaking to me so simply of himself.[189] I find him strangely humble and easily accessible. After having been disconcerted and irritated by his complexities, I am surprised that he agrees that [I] understand him perfectly;† I am surprised that he seeks neither to intrigue me nor to win my admiration. Truly, I doubt what I might be for him. Obviously, I am sure that he likes me a lot, that he is happy to see me. I am sure of being more than a good friend, and that is why I am surprised by his absence of all concern about his moral coquetry, especially since he does not pretend at all to treat me like a simple casual friend, and since he never wastes an occasion to say something nice to me. After all, it is useless

---

* From "I know that it was sweet," halfway through this paragraph, to this point, the text is highlighted in brown ink in the right margin of the facing verso.

† From "And then the coming of friends" through "he agrees that [I] understand him perfectly," the manuscript is highlighted in brown ink in the right margin of the facing verso.

to seek to determine the character of this friendship; it is even better than I hoped because it has a very solid, although difficult and rare, equilibrium. There is nothing to say; I have entered *his life,* not only his soul. I am aware [*au courant*] of everything (and that is why after having spent one afternoon by his side in this gallery, I understand and justify everything). I know his friends; he promised to introduce me to others; we will go out together etc.*
I myself believed I would remain a bit of an outsider; what expanded horizons! What a new way to conceive of life! I am making contact with concrete things; I am discovering unsuspected worlds. My conception of existence is becoming less rigid—it is even being destroyed.

I will abandon myself to this influence; first, I have no fear of influences: I will come away from them *myself* and enriched just as I came away from Garric's influence. And then, I have neither the strength nor the desire to resist; this cold-heartedness [*sécheresse*] and this feeling of helplessness [*désarroi*] could last no longer. I was trying to prolong a past, to reconcile irreconcilabilities. I am going to live something else that, even if absolutely it is inferior to what I lived last year, is better in terms of interest, simply because it is other . . . "Nathanaël, you will stop nowhere."[190] Yes, I will stop, but not yet so young, not on the threshold of such an enchanting palace. For all of this, very simple in reality, is unreal, prodigious; perhaps because Jacques is simply a center whose idealism reaches out over everything that he touches.

It is no longer the time to discuss it. He can do anything at present; no matter how much I might suffer atrociously, I would not take it away from my affection for him. It is truly *him* that I love, not his acts, not his ideas, even less an image that I would create of them. I desire passionately for him to be *good* so that my reason is reconciled with my heart, but . . .

And even today I do not care. Let him be what he wants; it is sufficient that he is.

(And that perhaps this evening, I will rediscover the energy of the other day, my need to exert myself, all that which is so profound in me . . . Well! I will respond to this need when I feel it; I will respond from day to day to all of my needs . . .

But at least I really *understood* this state of mind from having lived it. When I no longer understand it, remember this and do not condemn it.)

And then what does it matter: I am completely involved in the great joy of our friendship.

---

* From "After all, it is useless" to "we will go out together, etc.," the manuscript is highlighted in the right margin of the facing verso.

* * *

All the passionate ardor that I give to everything that presents itself on my route, you yourself use to push away what encumbers yours. The ardor that I exert haphazardly, you use to classify, to put into order . . .
[Fournier][191]

October 31

So many things to write at this end of the month!*

All day yesterday. Correspondence Fournier-Rivière. Projects. Adding finishing touches.†

I saw him again, as I expected, with some indifference because there are so many things between us that a few hours spent together no longer have anything but a sweetness of habit (when we are not alone). Is it this short insignificant poem he read to me? I learned with such a surprised joy that he was its author because my heart had so spontaneously desired to like the one that he had written. (I will have to ask him for it.) A universal soft-heartedness, like the one in the bus the other day upon reading Laforgue, seized me. Why did these words that unceasingly chanted over and over in me, "Awaited / Throughout the summers . . ." make me cry softly in the metro?[192] I had so much pity for all the men and the dreams that they will not live! In this rain, in these lonely streets of Neuilly, how I sobbed bitterly, without knowing why, barely thinking of him, with an immense desire to collapse into a friendly armchair, tears from a too heavy heart that is breaking, but with some hope and perhaps sweet pleasure underlying my distress!‡ And this sadness in front of these wet benches, "We can no longer sit down; all the benches are wet."[193] The damp dead leaves also seem to ask for my pity . . . I note this, because after all, it is part of my life, but cannot evoke the odor of these tranquil streets that merged with my tears.

This morning, on the contrary, in the rain and the wind, the Luxembourg Gardens gave me a thrill; they were empty as if only I were truly supposed to have the gift of taking pleasure in this wet autumn and converting it to passion.

---

* The quotation from Fournier that appears above this October 31 entry is written in the manuscript on the facing verso, opposite the sentence, "Submerged by the ordinariness . . . ," in the paragraph starting, "So the day before yesterday."

† The next paragraph is highlighted in brown ink in the right margin of the facing page, up through the quotation beginning with the word "Awaited."

‡ From approximately "And this sadness," at the start of the next sentence, through "merged with my tears," at the end of the paragraph, the text is highlighted in brown ink in the right margin of the facing verso.

A revelation, an immense help was this book already almost known and whose first half I feverishly devoured. I must finish it and then reread it and repeatedly meditate on all of its pages. No longer dead people like Gide or Barrès; a living example of fever, of ardor, and of beauty. There are things about me I have understood. There are words I would want to have written. There are some I have almost written. There are others I have so often thought! Through their lives, I have seen mine emerge, and desires, hopes, and promises were afloat in every corner of this room, deliciously overwhelming me.

Which do I prefer? The letters by Fournier on the whole have more abandon and emotion, are even written more on the spur of the moment, but some of the ones by Rivière (especially at the end of the first volume) on Claudel, which are perfectly good, surpass all that Fournier was able to write. Then again, no. But they have a deeper meaning for me. I love Rivière as I love myself, with severity and lucidity, with security, with the same intimacy. I love F. as I love Zaza or Jacques—with more pleasure and abandon, but without this harsh and exclusive character of my affection for Rivière. Fournier satisfies me much more; in a sense I prefer him, and a lot . . . but as one might prefer others to oneself.

I am not studying these letters; I am not copying excerpts. I am only trying to draw out my first impression and what these letters have brought to me personally:

A taste for life, a passionate desire to live that was already slowly awakening, a desire simply *to live* without moral considerations, without efforts to use, to realize, and in particular, without wanting to limit myself with a doctrine, a precise rule. Oh, what did I almost deprive myself of last year in claiming to establish an ideal for myself and in cutting out that which did not correspond to it. Don't cut out anything. Accept everything without even trying to reconcile things; it will be reconciled by the very fact that I live!

So the day before yesterday on the Champs-Elysées, I had a great desire for abandon, for easy life. I had escaped from those surroundings that no longer expressed anything; but without passion, in search rather for easy pleasure. And now I want to turn every minute into a poignant adoration! Submerged by the ordinariness of life and of beings, I did not understand that in becoming human again, I was still not giving up feverish urges, or life that we create ourselves from start to finish instead of being subjected to it! From understanding this, joy and ardor reawoke in me.

Yes, according to the opposition indicated by Fournier, instead of applying myself to clear my path, I am going to try with all of my strength to fill it;

instead of concentrating my life in myself, I too am going to stretch out my arms in order to seize everything. (If I let myself go, I would reread, I would copy, but I want to wait for a great lonely evening of tender warmth. The first book in a long time that gave me such a feeling of intoxication . . .) Last year, I painfully discovered and conquered my self; this was a great and magnificent work. I hold it firmly in hand, and it no longer suffices to dig more deeply. I have to go to things, pile up emotions, joys, sorrows, and perhaps classify less, analyze less, although I myself am as methodical and lucidly passionate, and especially, according to the nuance indicated by Fournier, to let myself be more taken by the moment, "to sacrifice a conversation with a friend in order to continue a conversation with someone who does not matter."[194] I need new foods to assimilate.

I want *to read,* something I no longer do, read like last year while writing down excerpts and getting excited. I want *to love* each being more and more, and the more and more numerous the beings. I want *to taste* the evenings and the rain and the sad mornings; and the colors, and the perfumes; to refuse nothing, no more forms of life to realize, no more sacrifices, *to be.*

(And in this wave of ardor that uplifted me danced his dear image; I would have wanted to be under [*subir*] the influence of these great enthusiasms [*élans*] by his side. I spoke to him, "I am sure, after having lucidly reflected, without taking my affection into account, that a work of art in which you would truly put all of yourself, with despair and perseverance and faith, and as if responding to a necessary calling [*appel*], would be something very beautiful." Me, I have judged myself. I have a certain intellectual power, a serious intelligence that sees profoundly, but no original sensitivity . . . rather no, I am still reserving judgment. For the moment at least I am capable only of living. But he *can;* he has the necessary leisure time. With that, he must do something.)*

I have to have an entire day of serious reflection in the company of Fournier and Rivière to really perfect everything that I write as it flows onto the paper. Maybe I am wrong to write here too often and too many of my impressions of the moment. Here is what I would have to do: each day to jot down all those little things that the example of Fournier convinced me to write, although they are less important to me than to him—to make a note of the passing fluctuations of my self, to jot down everything. Once a week (or every two weeks) to summarize it, to sort it out, to reason it out without allowing myself any approximations, as if I were explaining to someone else.

---

* The last three sentences in this paragraph are highlighted in brown ink in the right margin of the facing verso.

And now, appraisal of this month of October: a) what it gave to me, b) what I got out of it.

a) In order to know what it gave to me, I could evidently reread what I wrote. But what interests me is the memory that I have of it. The central point is very clearly the story of my friendship with Jacques (and I am all the more at ease to write it because I am going to spend two weeks without seeing him again. This comes just at the right time; I didn't dare repeat my visits; I would not have voluntarily wanted to distance myself from him). In the beginning, fever, passion, impossibility of doing anything.* I thought it was impossible to respond to this need for something else that dwarfed and overcame [anéantie] me—this need is typified by expectations on a bench in the little Luxembourg Gardens in the splendor of the beginning of fall. And the feelings of loathing in the morning before the day I would have to live through anyway.

And then, his friendship very sorrowfully accepted (a unique day, that nothing will bring back, when he gave me his letter, and I did not yet see how this ideal affection would play itself out in life).

And then, struggles with myself because of the anticipated future. Doubts, the impression that this excessively beautiful thing was going to crumble suddenly to the ground, and that we could not live it.

Finally, without any more mental reservations, the admirably comforting experience of this friendship transported into life—and it is epitomized in a beautiful painting by Foujita, at seven o'clock in the evening with a rare sweetness in the air and a touching simplicity in him.

And tonight it is a peaceful and happy confidence.†

Zaza was also more closely rediscovered during a beautiful walk one evening in the Tuileries Gardens, in a metro coming back from Neuilly.

Intellectual life without ardor. I am just interested enough to look like I am interested enough. In Neuilly, some friendships were formed, walks in the vestibule with F. Leroy, who expects something from me.

These cold lecture halls count very little in my life this year; went to philosophy class, observed that Mlle Mercier had a very pretty and intelligent smile and elegant attitudes, that sometimes kept me from following her thoughts.

Vague contact with the Équipes Sociales that does nothing for me.

---

* The rest of this paragraph and the first half of the next are highlighted in the right margin of the facing verso.

† These last two paragraphs, starting with "Finally" and ending with "confidence," are highlighted in brown ink in the right margin of the facing verso.

146

Readings: rather insignificant and very poorly done. *Les Poésies* [Poems] by Mallarmé was too rapidly skimmed, liked *Barnabooth* a lot and *La Corbeille de fruits* [Fruit-gathering] by Tagore.[195] The great revelation was Laforgue's verses, which I want to continue and reread. I am irritated with such dry readings. I am going to intoxicate myself with poetry during this month of November: Verlaine, Laforgue, Rimbaud.[196]

Very discouraging inner life. This excessively lonely vacation stripped of all support exhausted me. And then I don't want to accept the necessity of starting everything over again, when I used to believe that everything was definitive. I spent my time being irritated that I could not resuscitate the past instead of employing myself to create a magnificent present. Only my sentimental emotions were intense. (Nevertheless, walk in the Tuileries Gardens alone with Barrès and the return on the avenue of the Champs-Elysées in a magnificent synthesis.)

b) Larger conception of life; desire for something else. Renewal of all of myself. I involuntarily cleaned out all the obsolete parts of myself that I had not shed before vacation.

Strong with acquired riches, I head toward another path from which I can better profit.

I acquired knowledge of myself, still rather incomplete, but accurate in terms of the essential points. I must continue this study.

The evening

A bit tired, I am stopping. I note only: true intoxication before this continued book in which I recognize myself more and more, and I recognize him, desire to read it with him, to talk to him about it.

At the cinema, in *Vanina,* the vision of the bride, very tiny by the open door, white silhouette of an incomparable purity with a thin face barely visible in the mirror ... extraordinary beauty of two arms hanging onto a door and reaching out with a heavy white form. She has her back to the audience, her black hair on her silver dress, more beautiful than the minute before when we saw her face. Very beautiful too stretched out on the ground, slumped over the foot of the altar in the distance. In the dark stairwell, a dress which ends up disappearing. I also like two faces on a balcony, the great glass galleries where very little men are filled with trepidation.[197]

Rien que les heures [Nothing but the Hours] is full of charming details.[198] I appreciated certain qualities of tact and sobriety—the barely visible disgust of the woman who immediately smiles at the sailor with a smile *that is not sorrowful.* At the very beginning, her walk as she leaves, with her shoulders a bit tense, is of a more poignant psychology than any commentary. The weary attitude of the newspaper woman at the end of the day; it is so much like that, not even a sigh, a pause containing all the bitterness of exhausting work that will have to be picked up again tomorrow.

There is a scene where we see only the feet of someone getting out of a car, and a big doll that falls into the river. It is already forgotten when it looms up sorrowful and comes to fall flat on its face on the edge of the sidewalk with an abandonment of a weary body. There is the breathtaking fair (parade of blues and reds at top speed), the man and the woman who are sleeping, a candle on a table, at night, when the sergeants of the city pass by looking quite little in the big streets, and the death of the newspaper woman, a marvel!

I would have wanted to analyze this film; I am not an expert in this area. I believe it has great value. Only rapid, touching scenes replayed themselves before my eyes.

I am going to rediscover Fournier and Rivière.

This incessant need to compare yesterday to today is extraordinary! I reread my notes from the end of vacation, and now I want to see how I conformed to them (p. 26).[199]

"I have an awful fear." No, there is no danger. I only oriented myself in a totally different direction than the one that I was taking; indeed, I preferred the "sincere platitude," and new springs have gushed forth.

"Consent to all blames; for that I do not think that I will ever have the courage." Yes, I would have it. I love him more while admiring him less; I admire him better while admiring him less, and I would want for him to know me instead of desiring for him to approve of me. (Maybe I say that because I *know* that there is no longer room in his affection for blame that would weaken the affection.) Our friendship is strong enough to withstand frankness.

"If great happiness wanders by, know how to face it."
I repeat these words today.

"Nothing is ridiculous." It is because of having applied this idea that a joy was born.[200]

Ah! Gide! Gide, some of whose quotes I read, to see that after having adored them, then scorned them; I am going to live the *Nourritures terrestres!*

Reread Gide. My enthusiasm is reborn.

November 1

I am rereading my notes from vacation. Oh! How I relive these sorrowful days! And how I love them for having prepared me for this day. Everything was realized so much as I desired that I cannot believe it is true! In particular, September 16, "I would want a happiness accompanied by pain, a happiness that would be only a pain shared." Exactly that.

How painful this solitary struggle against the barbarians was without books and without friends! I handled it pretty well overall, but at the price of how many tears!* Now this question is taken care of; externally I resemble everyone, and nobody worries anymore. However, I suffered during the month of October like never last year. But I know how to say reassuring things and laugh with a heavy heart, and appear to be interested in what does not exist for me. Above all I know how to do all of this truly without losing any of myself in it. I have such support elsewhere, right?

Program for two weeks (Wednesday 3 to Wednesday 17)

Wednesday 3: Go to Cérès's, the Sorbonne (vague morning)

    afternoon: work at least 4 hours on my essay [*dissertation*], reading[201]

    evening: Rivière, Fournier

Thursday 4: morning: essay

    afternoon: reading at Ste. G., essay (Liard, Russel)[202]

    evening: reading

Friday: busy, evening of notes

Saturday: morning: essay

    afternoon: essay and visit to the Louvre

    evening of reading.

Sunday: morning: essay; afternoon at M. Boulenger's house[203]

    evening of reading.

Monday: work on *Les penseurs grecs* [The Greek Thinkers], essay.[204]

    evening of reading.

Tuesday: morning: essay; evening reading.

Wednesday: morning: reading, afternoon: essay and study of Aristotle (or logic)

    evening of rest.

Thursday: Arsenal Library, morning, and afternoon: (Greek translation?)

    evening in Belleville†

---

* From the next sentence, starting with "Now this question," through the end of the paragraph, the text is highlighted in the right margin of the facing verso.

† Here Beauvoir had written "evening of essay [*dissertation*]" but then crossed out "of essay" to write "in Belleville."

Friday: something planned
Saturday: morning: readings—(Greek translation?)
    afternoon: essay and Aristotle, evening: reading (Greek translation?)
Sunday: reading, notes, rest, *prep for Greek class*
Monday 15: study of Aristotle, evening: reading (or essay if not finished)
Tuesday 16: essay or reading of Aristotle
    evening: essay (or reading if it is finished)

Work: a completely finished essay
    books on logic for each class
Greek—read Zeller, Gomperz, Caird, Brochard, Croiset[205]
(without taking notes)
Readings: if possible Rimbaud, Laforgue, Verlaine.
Painting: Louvre, maybe the Luxembourg Gardens, reproductions by Picasso, Foujita
And especially *make room for everything unforeseen!*

∗ ∗ ∗

Art never expresses anything but itself. It has an independent life, just as Thought has, and develops purely on its own lines. It is not necessarily realistic in an age of realism, nor spiritual in an age of faith. So far from being the creation of its time, it is usually in direct opposition to it, and the only history that it preserves for us is the history of its own progress. Sometimes it returns upon its footsteps, and revives some antique form, as happened in the archaistic movement of late Greek Art (. . .) At other times it entirely anticipates its age, and produces in one century work that it takes another century to understand, to appreciate and to enjoy. In no case does it reproduce its age. . . .

(. . .) All bad art comes from returning to Life and Nature, and elevating them into ideals. Life and Nature may sometimes be used as part of Art's rough material, but before they are of any real service to art they must be translated into artistic conventions. The moment Art surrenders its imaginative medium it surrenders everything. . . . The only beautiful things are the things that do not concern us. (. . .) Life goes faster than Realism, but Romanticism is always in front of Life.

Life imitates Art far more than Art imitates Life. This results not merely from Life's imitative instinct, but from the fact that the self-conscious aim of Life is to find expression, and that Art offers it certain beautiful forms through which it may realise that energy.

It follows (. . .) that external Nature also imitates Art. The only effects that she can show us are effects that we have already seen through poetry, or in paintings. This is the secret of Nature's charm, as well as the explanation of Nature's weakness.

[Oscar Wilde][206]

So little do ordinary people understand what thought really is, that they seem to imagine that, when they have said that a theory is dangerous, they have pronounced its condemnations, whereas it is only such theories that have any true intellectual value. An idea that is not dangerous is unworthy of being called an idea at all.

[Oscar Wilde][207]

You have told me that it is more difficult to talk about a thing than to do it, and that to do nothing at all is the most difficult thing in the world; you have told me that all Art is immoral, and all thought dangerous; that criticism is more creative than creation, and that the highest criticism is that which reveals in the work of Art what the artist had not put there; that it is exactly because a man cannot do a thing that he is the proper judge of it; and that the true critic is unfair, insincere, and not rational. My friend, you are a dreamer.

—Yes, I am a dreamer. For a dreamer is one who can only find his way by moonlight, and his punishment is that he sees the dawn before the rest of the world.

[Oscar Wilde][208]

A steady course of Balzac reduces our living friends to shadows, and our acquaintances to the shadows of shades.

[Oscar Wilde][209]

This young dandy sought to be somebody, rather than to do something.

[Oscar Wilde][210]

Education is an admirable thing, but it is well to remember from time to time that nothing that is worth knowing can be taught. Through the parted curtains of the window I see the moon like a clipped piece of silver. Like gilded bees the stars cluster round her. The sky is a hard hollow sapphire. Let us go out into the night. Thought is wonderful, but adventure is more wonderful still.

[Oscar Wilde][211]

Action indeed is always easy, and when presented to us in its most aggravated, because most continuous form, which I take to be that of real industry, becomes simply the refuge of people who have nothing whatsoever to do. No, Ernest, don't talk about action. It is a blind thing dependent on external influences, and moved by an impulse of whose nature it is unconscious. It is a thing incomplete in its essence, because limited by accident and ignorant of its direction, being always at variance with its aim. Its basis is the lack of imagination. It is the last resource of those who know not how to dream.

[Oscar Wilde][212]

It is sometimes said that the tragedy of an artist's life is that he cannot realise his ideal. But the true tragedy that dogs the steps of most artists is that they realise their ideal too absolutely. For, when the ideal is realised, it is robbed of its wonder and its mystery, and becomes simply a new starting-point for an ideal that is other than itself.

[Oscar Wilde][213]

Life cheats us with shadows, like a puppet-master. We ask it for pleasure. It gives it to us, with bitterness and disappointment in its train. We come across some noble grief that we think will lend the purple dignity of tragedy to our days, but it passes away from us, and things less noble take its place, and on some grey windy dawn, or odorous eve of silence and of silver, we find ourselves looking with callous wonder, or dull heart of stone, at the tress of gold-flecked hair that we had once so wildly worshiped and so madly killed.

[Oscar Wilde][214]

The sure way of knowing nothing about life is to try to make oneself useful.[215]

Wilde (*Intentions*)

November 2

Another day of vacation, and then I will work according to the established schedule, reserving precise hours for study and passionately living all the others. This doesn't mean to let everything go and end up flunking, but means even less to make my studies the center of my life as I did last year.

Yesterday afternoon with Zaza I rediscovered the warm atmosphere of the street of Varennes as it appeared to me at twelve years of age. True closeness and affection, but she is too small all the same for this great confidence; I do not sense anything within her that calls for such a confidence. I am afraid of ruining my secret in confiding it, even to her. This other friendship is so much greater!

Raspail Boulevard at 7:00 in the evening next to invisible Jacques whose presence I did not desire; happiness that meets suffering. I do not see the difference existing between the two, since both always end in tears. Oh! Breathtaking Paris evenings lit up by street lamps, wonderful existences that barely touch mine and with which, with all of my strength, I am in union. Subdued exaltation without desire or fear.

Peaceful evening with Rivière-Fournier-Jacques until midnight. Dreams, one, for example: him feeling an irresistible need to write to me. That was true for the time it appeared necessary to me.

A little while ago, I was painfully irritated upon seeing those who don't understand and who bully those who surpass them. Self-satisfaction! But I would have liked to cry out how humble you are, my friend, and as for me, how little I esteem myself! Indeed, we know the price of our worries, of our complexities, but our worth! You yourself doubt yours in which I have faith, and we know that even if we were worthy, we would still be such poor things. Faced with "barbarians," I rediscover the internal pride of not resembling them when their rudeness makes me suffer; but alone, in the absolute, what excessively great discouragement even I feel at times! I love and esteem you but do not take pride in you, and have no admiration for you. As great as the worth of a man may be, I know that he is only a man. I can offer him only my pity, and if he thinks he doesn't need my pity, then he will have my scorn. Pity, not for his sufferings (I am rather hard on others because I am enormously so on myself), pity for his insufficiency!

I have a headache; I am sleepy. I cannot write anything sensible. But I know for one minute I passionately desired to have you near me, the only one beside whom I feel true *reality*, what life has that is most concrete, only exists in our souls. Next to others, even Zaza, I always have to transpose; my inner life appears to superimpose itself on what people pompously call Life: a luxury, an aside. With you (like with Fournier, Rivière), this life is the center of all. It is on its plane that we naturally move about, and we simply hook the rest on to it.

Have read *Paludes* [Marshlands] and *Le voyage d'Urien* [Urien's Voyage].[216] Find the time to speak of it. Afternoon of laziness at home with my open books that cannot interest me. I am intoxicated by Rivière and Fournier, but I do not have enough leisure time to deal with them today.

Intentions by Wilde. Profound truths in the guise of paradox. With stylistic differences that all the same do not allow comparison, this genre of criticism reminds me a lot of "Le rappel à l'ordre" [Order Considered as Anarchy] by Cocteau.[217] It is thought out less strongly, but more closely to life; each sentence seems to be the summary of painful experiences. And even in a translation, these dialogues conserve a character of poetic conversation; irony, which doesn't take itself very seriously and which artfully seems to disappear; always contained enthusiasms, even in pages that are sumptuous poems (not really sumptuous because of such sobriety even in enthusiasm and abundance).

In the dialogue on "The Decay of Lying," this idea develops that nature imitates art and not art nature; rather banal in fact, but transformed into a delicious certainty.[218] He himself summarizes his aesthetics in the final pages.

So far, I know three great critics:

Cocteau, Gide, Wilde.

Criticism and art. Importance of criticism that is a new creation. To speak to Art and not to Life.

Joy of leaving this fire and going out into the rain and the night with my dear self currently intoxicated with itself because it is itself and because for someone, over there, it means something . . .

* * *

[O]ur pride was heightened by this resistance, and underneath the splendor of our cloaks we felt welling in our hearts a fatiguing desire for glorious actions.
   [Gide][219]

And we thought of great sails, of departure; but having wished in vain for so long and under such monotonous circumstances, now that nothing prevented us from departing, we felt so weary, so disturbed, so serious about the solemnity of our tasks, so fatigued by everything, that for twelve more days we remained on the big island, sitting on the beach and facing the sea, speechless, pensive, sensing the uncertainty and excessive immensity of our wills.
   [Gide][220]

We felt that we had come almost to the end of our voyage; we still felt strong enough, however, to climb up the frozen wall, suspecting all the while that our goal lay beyond but not knowing what it was. And now that we had done everything possible to attain it, we found it almost useless to know it.
   [Gide][221]

We no longer felt the desire to return to see the regions where flowers bloomed more profusely; this would have been the past with no surprises. One does not travel backward and downward toward life. If we had known first that this was what we had come to see, perhaps we would not have started down the path; that is why we gave thanks to God for having hidden the goal from us and for having withheld it from us until our efforts to attain it had given us some joy, sole and sure; and we also thanked God that our great suffering had made us hope for a more splendid end.

We would have wanted indeed to invent anew some frail and pious hope; having satisfied our pride and feeling that the fulfillment of our destinies no longer depended on us, we now waited for the things around us to become a little more faithful to us.

Kneeling still, we probed the black water for the reflection of the heaven of which *I* dream.[222]

A. Gide (*Le Voyage d'Urien*)

My thought has been nothing but the unfolding of my life . . .

Great morbid effort of those who love each other to communicate their thoughts to each other. Great painful and vain effort (. . .). I believe unlimited affinity is alone capable of communicating this past life that produced thoughts, that is thoughts (. . .)

At the moment I am thinking of someone who always goes to the end of the current movement without worrying about the future, someone who does not sacrifice anything for anything else, someone who misses a date with his friend to finish a captivating conversation with a person who doesn't matter. Toy of the passing minute.

[Fournier][223]

(. . .) this timidity made of tact and clairvoyance that all intelligent people have experienced.

[Fournier][224]

This reminds me of all of Brittany such as I have not seen it (. . .).[225]

Fournier

Now I want to live on, to reach out my arms, reach out my arms. Moreover, this will not be so that I will lose and then deliciously rediscover myself: it will be to move forward methodically and without weakness. I will act in order to complete the totality of what I must be, but I will do it with precision, directing my strength, and without scattering myself haphazardly.

[Rivière][226]

Isn't developing ourselves a good enough reason to be? Must we explain ourselves with something else? Isn't it sufficient to realize for oneself the admirable spectacle of man tearing himself away from the earth and raising his arms to the sky, of man gaining his serenity by dint of heartbreak? Life suffices for explaining life (. . .).

[Rivière][227]

Sorrow is a sign of life, and also joy, and terror, and exaltation. Everything is life. *And it is life that one must seek before happiness* (. . .).

[Rivière][228]

You think that everything is legitimate (in other words, beautiful) simply because it exists, and yet you suffer from the daily pettiness of the little things that surround you and in which you do not really have the strength to seek beauty. But there is no contradiction there unless you admit, with the common herd and the majority of mediocre doctrines, that one must not suffer (. . .) *One must not seek happiness!* Indeed, we have other things to do. To accept all things is not to decide not to suffer from them any longer. No, it is to want to love them even when they tear you apart because they have the holy privilege of existence.

　　[Rivière][229]

Let me know this word that I am, whose horrible effort I feel in myself.

　　[Rivière][230]

Is there a joy that is worth that of a precise view of life, without illusion, without pessimism? What other way is there to place oneself above a great acting force than to understand it in its becoming? This is not to reduce its passion; this is to submit it to a supreme clairvoyance.

　　Rivière[231]

November 3

It is nothing, but finally she had to come see what I was doing tonight! Oh, and that stupid card to Jacques when I would want . . . and this wearisome surveillance! To be alone, to be at peace!

A little while ago, I was coming back from the library in the monotony and the banality of what was last year my passionate life, when suddenly you loomed up. I vividly remembered your "thanks" and other words you said to me, "I do care . . ." and I could not believe it. This marvelous adventure is not true, is it? Jacques doesn't exist. I am inventing him; life could not be this good. Again I think about Wilde's profound words that I unfortunately did not write down because I hadn't lived them yet, everything that is not probable and is true, everything that life has given to us and in which we refuse to believe.

Tender evening . . . my friend, my brother.

I worry little about what he thinks; I can barely imagine it. Impression that we each play our part without hearing anything of the other's performance; nevertheless we find ourselves in unison.

A great desire simply for your presence—simply to assure myself that you are indeed real. But it is much more agreeable than if you were in Paris; because truly you cannot be there; it's the absence. In Paris, it is not the absence, and it is so rarely the presence.

Yesterday, upon seeing Garric, amazement that I was so far away already! While the bus doesn't come, I intently watch cars zoom by in the night

... I myself, I who infinitely surpass any work [*oeuvre*] within which I was intending to confine myself, or any being that I have wanted to serve, and to think that from one minute to the next this world that I avidly inhale could disappear! Someone else dies, and it is only one less being on earth; if it is myself, the world disappears. Banal idea in this peaceful office, but so overwhelming while I was feeling it.

These young girls are nice, but they do not really fit at all in my life! (I would like to know why there is still room in my life.) If I talk with them about serious questions, I am going to bore them; if they are coming to be entertained by me, they might as well go to the movies. I will like them well enough, but they are so useless to me! Still one could try to make them have a discussion once every two weeks on: the books they like, self-love, happiness—friendship etc., make an appeal to their thought processes and say serious words. I will meet with some success! But what isn't essential is so unimportant to me! And how can I create something necessary between them and me? I would be pleased to help *one* interesting or sorrowful personality, but to give them smiles and the banal friendship they can get from just anyone ... Fraternity, solidarity! Team spirit [*esprit équipe*]! I believed in all of that.

Now I no longer believe in slow and inevitable unions where one soul sorrowfully hangs on to another or in the discouraged silences of those who love each other too much to be of any help to one another.

Those to whom I give my friendship do not have any of me; they must take it from me.

I have no desire to do what someone other than myself can do, and I will never be an irreplaceable being for these girls.[232]

Very conscientiously I am going to take notes on them, prepare beautiful sentences, take them for walks. Disgust for giving them pleasures that I scorn.

Readings—I rapidly skimmed this short masterpiece called *Paludes,* the exact counterpart of *Nourritures terrestres.* Tityre-Nathanaël?[233] The two sides of life envisaged as they are offered in their tragic irony. Irony, irony! Whence is born this disconcerting and inevitable comedy that one cannot embrace without some mental reservation because the author appears to be mocking not only what causes your amusement, but also the very amusement itself. Nuance is, after all, this manner precisely of blurring with either false good faith or candid bad faith, the two planes on which existence unfolds. The life of thoughts and feelings transported into a world of colors and words, what a paradox! And what profound truth at its base under an apparent drollness! It could be unbearable; it is so short and of such a truly unexpected fancy that one isn't aware of the process.

In *Le voyage d'Urien* I rediscovered the passionately voluptuous Gide evoked by Rivière in a beautiful letter. Oh, such melancholy in the most ardent sensuality; such a manner of *thinking sensations,* of rediscovering in their essential simplicity the entire infinite complexity, and infinity, and mystery . . .

Last night I was shouting in the streets "Nathaniel, I will teach you fervor . . . a poignant existence, Nathaniel."[234]

Saw reproductions of Cézanne today (The card players, the harvesters, landscapes, bathers, Temptation of St. Anthony, portraits), of Matisse (less familiar, but I like them a lot). Rousseau (the sleeping bohemian, the party, I also like).

Saw some Toulouse-Lautrec, but I am beginning to be familiar with impressionism.[235]

Discovered that one could read *L'art vivant* [Living Art] at Picart bookstore; interesting. The Salon d'Automne opens on the fifth.[236]

At the moment, while literature disgusts me a bit, I begin to have a passion for painting. I have such a need to come out of myself, and in a book I cannot help looking for myself. In a painting I admire, I take pleasure; I forget myself. Purely intellectual joys and very outside of *Life.* Whereas in a book I almost always neglect Art for Life, I like Art only because it is not distinguishable from Life.

The *Moralités légendaires* [Moral Tales] sometimes shocked and sometimes delighted me.[237] No time, alas, to study them closely. I am noting that I adore "Pan et Syrinx."[238] I like "Hamlet" and "Persée et Andromède" [Perseus and Andromeda], but there is no comparison.[239]

But it is a very sad book that often grimaces in order not to cry. This is sometimes awful, sometimes sublime.

The beginning of "Pan," evocation of sunshine and joy . . . and the pursuit and the end and everything. For everything is in everything!

* * *

I no longer experience those mornings when, in opening the window of my little room to the beautiful weather, I would feel myself rise, grow, triumph, aspire, be torn apart by desire and passion. In a terribly expressive word, I am glum. Oh! My poor inner intoxications, the whirlwind of myself toward God, me in short, what I call myself, all of this is lost. And will I rediscover it? In a year won't I have forgotten to be excited, unlearned how to desire? Won't I have only an irremediable lassitude left? I am interrogating myself, and the impossibility of answering myself doubles my anxiety.

Rivière[240]

I am weary of wanting love and of wanting life. I take refuge in the middle of the images that are in myself.

[Fournier][241]

But today, I can no longer resign myself to that. What I call my love is more or less than that—and that is why I do not know if I must call it my love or myself.

Fournier[242]

Today I know too well what I am worth to worry about any affectation and to desire any praise. That is what gives me my strength (...)

I have everything, I have everything, I am powerful, I am god.

Such is my force.

[Rivière][243]

Why do I now sense within me this stupid human respect and the secret irony that my words do not betray but that gnaws away at the purity of my emotions?

After all, I am me. [244]

R. [Rivière]

To the beloved woman, one can only say, you brought me a part of the world's beauty, whereas one dreams about all beauties and all lives synthesized towards a single beauty, a single woman, a single life.

One resigns oneself to love as one resigns oneself to life.

[Fournier][245]

We recognize our brothers in those alone who will not have wanted to make happiness the goal of their existence.

F. [Fournier][246]

And yet, my desire must be exclaimed.

[Rivière][247]

November 4

Saw a painting by Foujita less beautiful than the one on Boulevard Raspail. Afternoon when my thoughts like my heart were incredibly light; joyous lucidity in work and near-exhilaration in thinking of him. In the evening, the beings in the fog appeared so isolated! And once again, thinking of him, I didn't understand; there is no necessary bond between him and me.

Whence comes this strength that unites us? Nothing necessary; I am—he is—an abyss. How is it that this hiatus is often filled?

Correspondence Fournier-Rivière—vol. 2

I am starting with volume 2 because Jacques has not yet read it.[248]

First, Fournier's initial letter on ecstatic and silent acceptance and life that one can neither reduce to formulas nor communicate. How can he be quoted? How can he be summarized? Fournier cannot be summarized or quoted . . . How I like him (p. 7 to 11)—page 12 is the opposition between Jacques and me, especially between what I was and what I am . . . but no, even now my pleasures are regulated and the unexpected is expected. I am very much like Rivière.[249]

Well, well! "Pan and Syrinx" that I was just reading last night; I felt it exactly as he did. His impressions of the painters . . .

What force in Rivière's letter on Claudel (p. 33 to 37) and his definition of him p. 36 that is so exactly myself . . .[250]

And to rediscover the questions that are so poignant for us in these young people of twenty years ago on the acceptance of life, and its vulgarity! What a lucid, admirable response Rivière gave (p. 89–90).[251]

(p. 92) on the rise of desire[252]

Rivière is so strong, he is so strong before life because he accepts to suffer and to face up to things; it is for that too that I am so self-sufficient, even in my desire, and behind this strength are such treasures of sensibility.

There are some simple words by Fournier that "steal my heart away" such as "I am going to write to you for an hour because I need to say certain things this morning before putting myself to work" and all of the letter where he speaks of She [Elle].[253] Rivière and the fleeing of desire (p. 118).[254] I have experienced almost exactly the same thing! And this too touched me (p. 127). Such delicacy, such respect in recognized and tried friendship.[255]

p. 160 to 163 on "a free spirit" very strong.[256]

And Fournier's heartrending letters, of such physical and intellectual misery, and feelings, especially p. 196.[257]

Rivière's strength (p. 213).[258] I too have experienced this; I experience it in facing barbarians.* Oh! Pleasure, self-intoxication. . . .

Description of maneuvers, more Gide than Gide himself.[259]

---

* In the manuscript, the quotations from Rivière and Fournier that Beauvoir mentions here are copied on the facing verso pages, starting opposite this sentence. In the translation, they appear immediately before the November 4 diary entry.

* * *

Consciousness that my purpose is other than joy has made itself so profound, so intimate, so intermingled with my substance that I have no idea of restraining my sorrow, of attenuating it with stoic considerations. I live my sorrow entirely with its cries, its starts, its protests, its obsecrations, its infinite subsidence. The idea that happiness is not my end gives me no consolation, no comfort, I do not use it as encouragement. This I know well, I feel it well; I no longer have a need to contemplate it. What I have to do is to develop my life according to its rectitude, to save nothing.

[Rivière][260]

A cooler place on the feverish pillow
A novel mirage at the bend of the path,
Crawling more crazily towards the happiness of lips
And opiums longer to dream. But tomorrow?
[Laforgue][261]

And may I be absolved for my sincere soul . . .
[Laforgue][262]

We can no longer sit down, all the benches are wet.
Believe me, it's really over until next year . . .
[Laforgue][263]

So, then, poor, pale, and sickly individual
Who only believes in Himself in his lost moments . . .
[Laforgue][264]

My body, O my sister, really aches in its beautiful soul . . .
[Laforgue][265]

O, coolness of the woods along the path.
[Laforgue][266]

Maniacs for happiness.
[Laforgue][267]

But neither wanted to take the first step,
Wanting too much to fall to their knees together.
[Laforgue][268]

Nobody expects me; I am not going to anyone's home;
I have only the friendship of hotel rooms!
[Laforgue][269]

Oh! if only one by Herself, one fine evening would come
No longer seeing anything but to drink from my lips or die! . . .

And I know perfectly that my destiny is limited
(Oh, I have already gotten so used to it)
To following you until you turn around,
And then to express you as you are!
Truly I don't contemplate the rest; I will wait
With tender feelings for my life made expressly,
To tell you only that I have wept for nights,
And that my sisters really fear that I will die from it.
I weep in every nook and cranny, I no longer savor anything;
Oh I wept so on Sunday in my prayer book!
You ask me why you and not another,
Ah, never mind, it's really you and not another.
I'm sure of this as of the senseless emptiness in my heart.
    [Laforgue][270]

November 5

I have so much more pity and indulgence for all beings! In times past, view-ing any mistake I would have a proud distance and the words "cowardice" or "baseness" would easily come to my lips. Is this because I myself am less rigid in facing up to life? Or have I understood that I am in great part not respon-sible for my virtue? Rather that. I am very lucky in life, but placed in other circumstances, wouldn't I also have been able to sink very low? I am such that in suffering, in deprivation, or effort, I find my joy. But what if I had been less strong? I understand many more things, many more lives; I am not only excusing what revolted me long ago, I am almost sympathizing with it.

What a good grip I have on myself tonight; I almost regret not being able to use the strength I feel in myself. Not fervor, or tenderness, or desire; I am not surpassing my self at the moment, but such plenitude in the possession of this self.

I contemplated the small role that our conscious will plays in our life. Around me almost all beings have docilely obeyed circumstances. How little I myself choose, how much life imposes itself upon me, *my* life to which after all I have to resign myself. However, I can say about one or two acts that they were truly willed: my letter . . .* The only problem is that I do not know exactly what role they have played in my destiny. I dare say my fate would have been the same. Yes, but I would not have had the illusion of having made it myself; it would therefore have been different.

On the role of happiness in life. I sincerely believe happiness alone is fruit-

---

* Beauvoir did not finish her sentence.

ful. Only in happiness (given, at least, inner peace) can one realize a work, act, be useful. Happiness is the time of realizations. But isn't to realize already to diminish oneself? Every word said, every act that you put yourself into, leaves you much poorer, smaller. The sole thing of worth is thought cultivated for itself, pain in which no one participates. Sorrow focuses you on yourself; it forces you to hang on to yourself. Its only reason for being is you.

What I think

I barely take interest in what I am anymore. However my self would not know how to be my only subject of study for eternity. I would like to put my thoughts in order. The trouble is that in two weeks they will have changed; it doesn't matter.

My thought is always reaching toward this triple problem that, for my age, is not only of theoretical interest, or practical interest, but of such an essential interest that the question of what is and what must be are the same: life—love—happiness.

Among these three terms, I see an irreducible opposition, and the difficulty is to know which to prefer to the other since I cannot reconcile them.

Life

Life is me. I split my existence into two parts: one for others, that I established [*fixée*] once and that I barely think of anymore, that mechanically follows its course. I nevertheless attach a lot of importance to it because I very intensely feel the bonds that unite me with all beings. And then there is a part for myself; I love myself because I alone love me, because I am an irreplaceable being, because I don't see anything better to do (such familiar ideas that I am not developing them).

Without any pride, I believe that people must live completely apart from the barbarians, live like them, but on another plane altogether—not worry about them: one will meet oneself or not with them; it doesn't matter. For my life, others' experiences can do nothing for me.

Do not seek *to use* your life; this is essential, and do not judge life from the outside—two closely linked points. It is because I am watching from the outside that I want to use. Everything has in itself its reason for being, or maybe doesn't have it, but after all, nothing has its reason for being outside of itself. My reason for being is not in my action, which could be that of another; it is in me or it isn't. My thoughts, my feelings, are useless [*ne servent à rien*]; when they are useful, it is by accident, and there again it is still not myself who is useful, a product of my mind at the very most, something external.

163

Life is a death of every minute, and without hope of resurrection; with the firm will, on the contrary, not to resuscitate. And it is heartrending, but it is very beautiful.

Every position toward life is acceptable; its value depends on the being adopting it. The life a man leads barely has importance; it is he himself who is important. In general, however, one can judge a man by his life, not by its intrinsic value, by its value as a sign. First, certain genres of life have an influence on the being who has chosen them and they diminish him. Second, life is very often an approximation of the man who lives *it*. Just because every position may be possible does not mean that there are not any preferable ones. In law, perhaps not, but in fact, yes. A life is beautiful as a work of art is beautiful although the existence of shapeless doodling is as legitimate as that of a beautiful painting. You must put genius into your life.

The position that I choose for myself is one of fervor, of clairvoyance, and ardor.

From others, I ask only one thing: for them to be aware of their lives and to control them, even when they accept to put up with them by the very fact that they know they are putting up with them.[271] I want to deal with conscious beings. Now is this a true superiority? But I can have esteem only for the beings who think their lives, not for those who only think, or for those who only live.

I have a passion for life, and I would like to have written Rivière's page on the holy privilege of existence.

Don't scorn. Don't admire. Understand; and love or hate.

Love

Love is the other—strange effect of perspective. Everything centers on a single being who has in himself [*en soi*] no reason to be chosen and to whom nothing necessary links you. I have already written how I've understood this.

Happiness

By this I mean ardent plenitude without *desire*—equilibrium and peace— an exaltation that isn't aware that it must come to an end.

Life and Love

"One resigns oneself to love as one resigns oneself to life."[272] Nothing to add. There is this painful struggle between the two because of all the limitations; love is the most rigid. It is not possible to bring back into love all of the life that infinitely overflows it, and yet, love would not know how to be a simple incident; it tends to absorb everything. What is beautiful is to maintain each in its place, to put all of one's life into love, to enrich life with love. But one must not sacrifice one to the other; one must above all not pretend to confuse them.

Happiness and Love

What horrifies me, when I think of the future, is that love could bring me happiness. At least, a certain happiness. What is so solemnly in me is I dare say happiness; rather no, it is precisely my full and richer life, not happiness as I defined it. I do not claim that one must love only with tears, but how could love be confused with happiness? Love that brings only part of the world's beauty—love that leaves apart two beings who would want to [illegible word] each other?[273] Love in short.

Happiness and Life

If it comes, take it—it is only worthwhile if it is life—it is absurd to refuse it, absurd to seek it.

Laforgue

I like this second volume less than the first. Yet, the verses that I am copying are so beautiful!

All of the poem "L'hiver qui vient" [The Coming Winter], and this one especially

"Ah! qu'une d'Elle-même . . .". [Oh! if only one by Herself . . .],
and the heartbreaking "Solo de lune [Moon Solo]," "Where at this hour is she?"[274]

These words that She [Elle] said to him, I also said them myself, one day, before his door.[275] I would no longer say them today. He is more and less than my destiny. Yet, I don't know; if I were nothing to him . . . but there have been days when I have said exactly those words.

November 6

Feeling the influence I have on H.[,] Z., others; feeling these lives that depend a bit on mine, these beings into whom I have put a bit of myself; feeling this power I have.[276] And having no need myself, of anyone, being so self-possessed and self-sufficient, no longer desiring, like last year, approval and advice. There is my strength! How strong I am!

And how I like to strip myself of this strength, to adorn my heavy heart with your absence . . . Do I *need* you? To be, probably not, but I cannot live without you . . .

Strength, thought, pride or doubt, how all of that disappears and melts away once you loom silently up by my side. Last night I reread your letter. This morning I desired with a great desire to see you again.

This world that I carry within me, in which you are the center, along with these beings similar to ourselves who are grouped around you and seen in part through you: Fournier, Rivière, Gide, Arland, Barrès, and the heroes of all books—and Zaza, and the others whom I do not know, and dreams, and feelings, and subtle sorrows . . . what partition separates this world from the other; what high wall of incomprehension, of indifference. Dearer than everything to me is the infinitesimal nuance of this life that is not a dream, that is not outside of banal life, that envelops and transfigures it on the contrary, that is *my* life.

Sometimes it seems to me that it is an other who is living this novel and that I am watching; splitting in two, amazed. And then other times, I really sense that I am the one living it.

Eight days without seeing you, and how many more?

And yet it is not from love, since I tense up awfully at the idea of any slightly tender gesture, since I cannot resign myself to your bringing me happiness.

But it is not an intellectual friendship either, because what is important is what I cannot write: the immense tenderness; the gentle tears; the great enthusiasm of the soul which no longer contemplates anything, which only sees one face again and again and evokes the sound of one voice.

November 7

Joy of going into rainy streets without recognizing anything, neither the long, long gates of the Luxembourg Gardens, nor the strange trees against the red sky, nor myself whom I take for another, looming up from the same past. For a year, I too have been enveloped everywhere in this world of mystery mentioned by Fournier, rather often in a *perceptible* form like last night, but especially . . . How does one explain this inner split, this life that does not know if it is lived or dreamed, this strange and unique beauty? I pity those who know only the uniform and lifeless face of existence.

I daydreamed; maybe love is deception and madness, but what pettiness to refuse to be deceived—or to accept to be on the condition of keeping clear consciousness of such deception. Be straightforward, give of oneself directly; I mean like a great indivisible thing where there is not one part that loves, another that watches this love with a smile—the same in admiration—in pain—in joy.

You were present last night with such intensity! Much more than the beings seated in the armchairs of this living room. This morning I think of you without desire or anxiety, or even tenderness. But after all I cannot stop thinking of you.

The Self

Marie-Louise's note overwhelmed me with joy, with remorse, and with pain, "you are lucky; you play a big role in a lot of people's lives"; lucky . . . yes, I find that very sweet.[277] But it is so heavy, too! They do not know—nobody, not even him—how much their pain weighs on my shoulders! Marie-Louise does not know that I cry upon thinking of her . . . how I love, this year! I don't know how to do anything anymore but love. I would like to be burdened by all people with all of their suffering. For that alone I am worthy; for that alone I am.

What I so joyously felt on the boulevard of the Champs-Elysées now affects me to the point of anxiety. I am afraid of all those who hang on to me and whom I will not be able to satisfy, and yet I am looking for still others, other lives to support with my own. Such a responsibility; such a load. I have such little need for these beings! Rather yes, I do need for them to need me.

But I feel sorrowful remorse, and I suffer from all anticipated remorse! Her, for example, she meant so little to me; I thought that maybe I didn't mean much to her. There was almost an anguished regret in the words that she said to me . . . to have a place in someone's life! But doesn't this necessitate making that person suffer! I do everything to keep those I love a lot from suffering due to me, and besides, since I love them, I keep the promises that I make to them (and yet I often cry when I feel so truly beneath the affection they have for me [after the evening at chez Lipp]). But those whom I do not truly love—I am really so mad at myself; all the pain that I cause them, that I will cause them despite everything, really hurts me. I would like to cry out to them forgive me, forgive me! Oh such slavery, such a burden of so much affection!

Yesterday, I said therein lies my strength. But therein is also my pain, and my duty, and all of my weakness. I will not be able to measure up; yes, I will, if I consent to wrenching myself apart.

This pain tonight combines with my great anxiety at leaving Jacques's house; they put so much faith in me! I cannot respond to these appeals from everywhere.

How sad she looked, Marie Louise! It is true; it is a lot for me to know such hurt! Oh, suffer, but not from emptiness in life. She was complaining about not knowing any genuine affection, (and to think that maybe mine was lacking for her), and then this very humble and lucid confession: I myself have no personality; I am nothing to anyone; nobody needs me.

Forgive me! Forgive me Henriette, F. Leroy, Zaza, and you Jacques (but less, because, you, I love you). The others whom I maybe do not know, forgive me!

I am going tomorrow morning to try to see her; I will tell her—(or Tuesday if I do not see her tomorrow)—"I was so happy to chat with you. I believed that you did not have any problems in your life," and reassure her of my great friendship. I will not be lying. I passionately love all those who suffer.

At all costs I will give Zaza my greatest trust; I owe it to her.

And you, you! I don't know. I am giving you everything, but then the others who ask me, won't I answer them?* You tell me "thanks," but it makes me happy to merit thanks from you; I am afraid I will no longer think of others whose thanks do not make me joyful ... a total abnegation where you are concerned, but this is a horrible selfishness because I love you. And then I cannot accept for you to suffer because of me! I would like to do so much, to be so much for you!

To imagine that a bit of your happiness is in my hands—(and sometimes a lot, I say to myself, and this burden then overwhelms me)!

But even so, I have great pity for those men and women whose life is not full of such anxiety and such sweetness.

(I did not know how to love before this year, since I was ignorant of the passionate desire to suffer horribly for those one loves.

Zaza, how close you are to me tonight, my friend.)

And you, if only I knew your feelings.

November 10

Last night, while G. was singing his ridiculously sentimental songs, I was looking at the photo of you at twelve, discovered in an old box. This verse by Baudelaire was tearfully crying in me:

---

* Instead of "répondrai" [will answer], Beauvoir had first written "demanderai" [will ask], but she crossed it out and wrote above it.

"But the green paradise of youthful loves."[278]

To think that so much ardent regret and memory could be contained in a single verse! Oh! Twelve-year-old Jacques who will never again return! I would have wanted to start my childhood over by your side. Our nineteen years are already so old! I contemplated our great childhood friendship, "we are married by love," and Jules Verne, and the old Charles, and such a very simple and carefree joy with no thought of yesterday or tomorrow, enemy of complications, an unmarred joy.[279] I dare say it is better for us to be separated long enough to meet each other again with all the wonder of a discovery, with the sweetness however of never having been strangers to each other and of having our lives as adolescents slightly merge from time to time. I am not sorry that we were not friends at fifteen; I am sorry that we are no longer fifteen. Oh! I used to feel such things so intensely, such a heavy past already, worries, feelings of disgust, and the brilliant, the new sparkle of childhood that was laughing in that photo. He no longer exists. I barely knew him, and I could have known him; it was he, your dead self, that I loved last night.

However, yesterday and today, I had two beautiful days of peace, not forgetfulness, or the tender and poignant memory. But to walk calmly under a clear sky toward an indifferent task saying it is not a thing that has been, or that will be, or that could be. It is a thing that is. If only I could, for just one hour, get a taste of this security, for those who know me, what deep confidence that would prove!

There are other hours, my friend, when I feel almost like crying in gratitude—no, the word hurts you—the great thanks that I owe you. Jacques, thank you. Whatever tomorrow may bring, thank you. One day I will really have to say these thanks to you.

It is not for your affection that I thank you. It is for being such that I can give you mine. Something immense; because I was able to put all of my soul into it, and because you've put, or at least I've found, all of yours there, too. Thank you for not having obligated me to leave anything of myself at the door of my heart. I do not know how to express all of this. Every novel seems realist to me if compared to my life; every soul seems simple if I compare it to my soul. You permitted my dream to remain the unique reality. What I call dream is not a hollow edifice looming up in the clouds; it is my profound life playing itself out in the most secret recesses of myself. The closer I get to you the more the ideal character of my existence is accentuated, but I manage to rediscover often in myself this unique nuance surrounding the least of your gestures. My best girlfriend is often in dissonance with this life of mine; the words I say do not find an echo in her, do not awaken a mysterious harmony. Near you, immediately.

You see, I have such pity for those who do not know. My girlfriends, for example, move in another sphere; they distinguish between the fanciful literature and life in the very effort they make to combine them. For me, the novel is my life—and what a subtle, sorrowful and happy, and tormented, what a magnificent novel . . . I don't know; aside from and above everything (although I care very solidly about everything). Belleville from where I am returning no longer exists—Greek class did not exist even while it was taking place—and yet I am attentive; I work, but none of it touches me. Very exactly, none of it *exists* for me . . .

You alone, and me.

The girls who have not found you glance around themselves to find someone of whom they will be able to dream; my dream was born with you—not because of you, with you, which is much better. And I can—I will be able to suffer. But thanks to you, this will not be mundane suffering. You saved me from the common herd (banal friendships—acts—studies).[280]

(But, I do not love you only for being my dream, you know; I love you especially for being you.)

I think that perhaps you are thinking of me.

I think it is splendid that there are no longer any possible misunderstandings between us—as far as we know—as far as we know the other knows.

And each one, however, keeps the great secret of his or her way of loving.

Do you often hate me? I hardly ever ask myself such questions, but a little while ago in front of a mirror I said to myself, "Perhaps for him all love—all of what's possible—resides in this face!" I ask your forgiveness for only being myself.

You are very far away.

No, you are quite close, my friend, my brother, since now I am crying from a senseless desire to see you again. Oh, don't say anything, don't look for anything, just simply be there, just be there . . . Neither joy, nor pain, nor your heart, nor anything . . . Your *presence*.

Two weeks ago, across from you, so close, so close . . . and alone tonight. Not your soul in front of my soul: your eyes—your laughter—you, you.

Two weeks are long, you know.

* * *

It is so tiring to have the same hope for a long time.
    [Jean Sarment][281]

—I never saw anyone suffer because of me.
—Would you have noticed it, Mama?
—Naturally.
—Good.
    [Jean Sarment][282]

Sometimes I have to go back to the old games that don't amuse me anymore.
    [Jean Sarment][283]

Words! they are a front one gives oneself.[284]
    Jean Sarment

Like a god with huge blue eyes and limbs of snow, the sea and sky lure to
    the marble terraces the throng of roses, young and strong.
    [Rimbaud][285]

The flowering sweetness of the stars and of the night and all the rest
    descends, opposite the knoll, like a basket—against our face, and makes
    the abyss perfumed and blue below.
    [Rimbaud][286]

DAWN
    I embraced the summer dawn.

    Nothing yet stirred on the face of the palaces.
The water was dead. The shadows still camped in
the woodland road. I walked, waking quick warm
breaths; and gems looked on, and wings rose without a sound.

    The first venture was, in a path already filled with
fresh, pale gleams, a flower who told me her name.

    I laughed at the . . . wasserfall that disheveled its hair
through the pines: on the silver summit I recognized
the goddess.

    Then, one by one, I lifted up her veils. In the
lane, waving my arms. Across the plain, where I
notified the cock. In the city, she fled among the
steeples and the domes; and running like a beggar
on the marble quays, I chased her.

Above the road near a laurel wood, I wrapped
her up in her gathered veils, and I felt a little her immense
body. Dawn and the child fell down at the edge of the wood.

Waking, it was noon.
[Rimbaud][287]

November 11

Salon d'Automne—impression that a lot of things escape me. I don't know much about painting, and I prefer directing my attention to a single painter to try to understand him well to dividing it among as many paintings as I can possibly take in with a sweeping glance. I observe, however, that I am beginning to grow accustomed to this, thanks to the reproductions with which I have become familiar; I will continue because each day I am more interested.

Very beautiful *Foujita:* a Negro drawn with an incomparable power, some *Pisarros* that I like a lot; a river, a corner of a field with a farm, beautiful harmonies in green, a technique I am too ignorant to define that I like anyway.[288]

Some by *Bakst;* there was one especially that I like, oppositions of green nuances, very beautiful contrasts of dark and light.[289]

A *Dunoyer de Segonzac:* trees in a storm, I like too.[290]

Gromaire: I am not familiar with this painter, but his brown-toned boats detained me and the woman, too, whom I understand less—rather straight lines but powerfully harmonious—equilibrium of tones and traits, which is a true intellectual satisfaction.[291]

Van Dongen: a woman in white; a Van Dongen—a bit artificial, and then it is always the same painting.[292]

Desvallières, I appreciate only moderately.[293]

Charles Guérin: Ah, that one really "stole my heart away" according to Barrès's expression—in this room I saw only this painting: a young girl playing the guitar, seated; on the wall an engraving; a table corner with a box or can of [illegible]*[294]

Rather: a harmony of red and gray on a bluish background, very clear and clean—a touching face—a simplicity of subject, of technique, of inspiration, a sincerity that deeply moved me. I would like to see other paintings by him.

---

* I deciphered this last expression as "boîte de conserve," which would translate as a "canned good." Sylvie Le Bon de Beauvoir found it to be illegible, and so I chose to maintain the ambiguity of "boite," which could be translated as "box" or "can."

I passed by the rest too quickly. I sometimes sensed, nevertheless, the presence of beautiful things.

Readings:

La couronne de carton [The Cardboard Crown] and *Le pêcheur d'ombres* [Rude Awakening] by Sarment—evidently it is always the same play and the same hero. But I really like this indecisive young man who trembles on the threshold of his dream, who has no hope of making it enter into his life, who, all the same, tries sometimes, who suffers. An echo of my own melancholy, and that is why I feel at home here; the scenes between Jean and Nelly are quite beautiful, in spite of this eventually rather aggravating tenderness that the man feels in front of the woman who is making him suffer. He is alone; even the one he loves does not understand him, or at least he does not feel understood; he remains above his love (Hamlet-Jean-Tiburce.)[295] He tries to cure himself with love. Poor him, love never solved the problem of life; it can only help to stand it.

I picked out some good expressions, but the charm of these dialogues consists especially in the words that are not spoken.

Les illuminations [Illuminations] by Rimbaud. This did not grab me like Laforgue. However, I really like certain prose poems a lot; I have never read sentences with such magnificent harmony, magnificent due to the rhythmic pressure combined with a great vagueness of thought (which is nevertheless expressed in a very precise vision).

Above all I like the piece entitled "Aube" [Dawn].

The Équipes Sociales. I will have to think about them again. Yesterday's impression: they will be absolutely nothing to my life. I am obligated to leave too many things at the door; intellectually, I can only give of a diminished self. My thoughts transformed for such excessively simple brains no longer interest me; they are no longer my thoughts. It is not very sincere, not very honest perhaps. As for true friendship, it's impossible; they are nothing to me, and in particular I have the impression that even if they like me, I will never be a necessary being for them. It is impossible to bring them up to my level; I have to descend to theirs; that bothers me.

Indeed, I have very much lost my team spirit. It's because there is so much more grandeur in a profound sentiment than in a vague and universal and fraternal affinity! Are these relationships that, despite everything, remain quite external, truly worthwhile? Companionship—reciprocal favors—chats, etc. yes, maybe, but it does not touch anything profound in being (except in particular cases—but a charitable work [*oeuvre*] does not take particular cases into account, at least it is not for them that it works). I really believed all this last year! I think I am now exaggerating to the opposite extreme. But this (surface) cordiality, this illusion about the value and the power of simple exchanged words, this joy of being together that keeps us from seeing how far we are apart, all of it hurts me.

It is a beautiful summer day for St. Martin's.[296] I was incredibly young this afternoon on the quays of the Seine; my thoughts wandered, the joy of life enveloped me, my dreams were imprecise enough not to embarrass me.

It has been two weeks since I have seen you, Jacques. You must have been very nice to me for me not to spend these days in feverish anxiety! At the moment, I think I could easily do without you. You are nothing to me, but a little while ago in the tramway I was telling myself I think you are perhaps thinking of me; and I have the right to think such a thing. I think maybe I brought you some joy, and I have the right to think such a thing. I remember your "thanks" full of emotion and the night of your exam, when you left us. As the car took you away, wasn't it because of having seen me that you were starting to enjoy life again? From where do I get the great happiness that would enable me to believe that that is true? I suffer from being a possible sorrow, but I also *know* that surely, on certain days I was also a great sweet pleasure. Jacques, who brought me the same bit of joy I brought him! So many tears shed, so much suffering voluntarily endured, such a strict severity toward myself. Thanks to that I do not feel completely unworthy of this magnificent privilege that falls to me. This vacation's heavy sobs earned your smile; how I would accept even harsher pains if I could be certain that yours would be diminished *thanks to me.* (This is not about disinterest and sacrifice; if disinterested, I would accept to suffer simply for you to be happy without worrying that I was the one making you happy. I am thinking rather about my own happiness, about the immense and pure happiness that floods me when I think that I have given you a few hours that were more pleasant.)

It is one thing that is . . . I have your letter in my drawer. I have some precious memories. Perhaps one day I will say this no longer is, but I will not be able to say I was mistaken, this never was.

And then, I will not have to say, this is no longer, right? This is not yet something that you can easily remove in this way. Everything that you said to me binds you, and especially this affection that you must feel for me since you said it.

To think that only six months ago I did not dare get involved, and I gave myself up totally—because in the depths of my heart I have this great hope that you will not hurt me. You have never hurt me; you have always said the word, and you have made the gesture needed by my poor soul. What I find sweet is to know that these slightly more tender words that I am telling you here, in themselves will not impede the great simplicity, the great sincerity of our loyal friendship. With less shyness, I am not saying anything to you that I have not already made you understand. There is no secret that I jealously keep; you know what you are to me. You know I know what I am to you.

Without too much impatience, I am waiting for your return.

November 13

Yesterday afternoon, leaving for Neuilly, I was astonished to savor a peace as simple as if I had been a carefree little girl: memory of him, who will probably soon come to rejuvenate my life, and my studies: a corner in my heart for this calm affection. It didn't last long; no, my poor girl, you must not believe you could so easily unburden yourself of your soul and your love. Know at least what the great demand is: everything, always. Everything, always; I cannot escape it. Why am I suffering? First, I doubted him; oh, doubt, the awful doubt that ruins all of my joys for me! I have the elements of a great happiness in my hands, and I have to turn them into tears! And not good tears; shameful tears, that disgust me while [I] shed them, and that I do not have the right to shed. No, I do not have the right to doubt you because I caught sight of your car at the door of D'Harcourt, or your affection because you have not yet come to see me. I do not have the right to think like yesterday, tonight, and this morning that I am no longer anything since you have rediscovered your life and your friends. I waited for your letter for a long time, and it was written . . . you explained everything to me; you said such truly affectionate words to me; I do not doubt your friendship. Perhaps today I am asking for more than friendship.

I was very proud that I didn't tremble upon spying your car; very proud of my indifference, that, I thought, guaranteed my happiness. And then, suddenly, from hearing your name pronounced by others, from having evoked you through what others know, while I was an outsider to all of it, the same senseless feverish anxiety caught hold of me just as it had upon my return from vacation.

I reasoned with myself; I chased away the awful doubt. And my pain got even stronger near the Sorbonne and in this library where I so intensely felt the awful distance between beings: such a sorrowful me, and such peaceful students. So absurd to be there, while you are very close by, very close. No

175

more doubt, but this painful observation that my love is not my life, even less yours. You had no reason to come so quickly, no reason, even if you loved me, not to laugh with your friends. And I myself have to go to Greek class and study Aristotle. I am bored; I feel bad, I feel bad, and especially from not knowing why I feel bad . . .

First some things were too good between us, and we will no longer find them, never again. Your mother is going to come and your sister. You have your friends; then the military service. Oh, my anxious letter, the chat in the gallery more than two weeks ago already, our two souls so close. Finished, finished . . .

And no matter how much we loved each other (I say *we*) we are, all the same, very distant, very alone; you cannot guess how many days my need for you becomes even more urgent. And I myself cannot go ring your doorbell to say I need to see you today. Why? Because it may very well be that at the same moment we will no longer be on the same plane. I want to believe that you need me, sometimes, but surely it is not always when I myself need you. When I feel like crying, you are perhaps inversely at peace. It is magnificent that so often our pains coincided; only, that does not mean that they have to coincide.

Oh! I must see you again, hear an affectionate word from your lips; maybe this pain will subside. Sometimes your presence suppresses all distances for days on end. But during such a long absence, I lose my head, I doubt, I no longer know. I really have your letter in my pocket; I am sure that you love me. But I would like to see you.

Jacques! Jacques! These cries that cannot reach you! In reality, you play no part in these senseless crises, whereas in the sorrowful or happy equilibrium of our friendship you are just where you belong, very near, very much yourself.

The more I have, the more I request, but one must never make requests. You shall give me what you want.

Oh, in the Luxembourg Gardens where the yellow dahlias were very pale on the very pale green of the lawns, under the very pale gray sky, how I bowed down my head, resigned, accepting. I would have to keep from thinking of myself. Only when I am hurt, I always address you because you are the only one who is so truly my friend. Zaza is my friend, but I have not given my entire self to her.

My friend. It is you I invoke against this very love that comes today to ruin my beautiful affection by introducing jealousy, demands, and doubts. It's the first time since my return to school, I assure you; it's physical, it's nervous. My friend, my very affection for you is so pure, so calm, even in my pain, and so disinterested and so consoling. One neglects friends a bit sometimes without having the friendship weaken; you can neglect me a bit.

Upon entering this church, I was in great distress; I cannot pretend to work this afternoon. I need to think of you—my home does not leave me to my thoughts, and yet I desire a warm home—(oh! gallery 143). I desire an affection: neither Zaza, nor Jacques today. Alone, wandering, especially alone with a great coldness in my heart as in the street and a desire for distress and abandonment.

The memory of your friendship comforted me. For you are not responsible for these chagrins that I create for myself. It is not your true self, but a figment of my imagination that is the object of this fever.

I am going to take a walk while thinking of you, while thinking of me, of myself, that I am completely employing in this adventure, with its riches, its nuances, its refinements, but also with all of its infirmities. For that reason, one must not be mad at me for my hours of weakness or my crazy imagination.

Oh, how I long to be happy!

Once again saw Rembrandt, Van Dyck, Franz Hals, Ruysdael, Ingres, Delacroix.

Discovered *Olympia, Portrait of Zola,* one of Whistler's portraits.

Liseuse [Female Reader] by Vermeer, some Corots especially *Une soirée* [An Evening]. I adore the Corot paintings.

Millet and Meissonnier are detestable. Rousseau mediocre. Corot! Corot!

And this beautiful Vermeer.[297]

Look at the elderly single lady who is pontificating, followed by young girls who believe that they like painting because they are taking notes! And the young man filled with wonder because smoke is coming out of the nostrils of a cow painted by a painter I don't know and who is atrocious: Troyon.[298]

Oh! Corot's pale greyish green mill! And his golden *Soir* [Evening] and *Ville d'Avray!* And all his simple tables.

Evening

If someone had predicted to me last year that one day when I was being sought by a lot of work I would cry over Laforgue at the booksellers on the quay and would wander through the halls of the Louvre, I think I would have choked in astonishment. I could not foresee such a sentimental crisis. Evidently it truly exists, this "need greater than its object" discussed by Claudel; it's not that I don't see Jacques as he is.[299] Only in hours of feverish anxiety, my desire no longer has any common measure with his veritable value. (Besides, what do I mean by his veritable value? The one he should normally have for me? All of it is very relative. It is impossible to seek the reason for the great impulses of the soul; it suffices to know they have a reason in themselves and not outside of themselves.) The Louvre calmed me down a bit by distracting my attention; I experienced some pleasant minutes when my suffering seemed truly legitimate to me, when I liked it because it gave me the certitude that what I am giving him truly and infinitely surpasses anything that he could hope for because he does not know. I would be the same with him even if I gave him a lot less, and I could very well be a little more sparing with my affection, but I have an excessive soul that gives itself completely once prudence no longer restrains it. To this extent, however, it is absolutely senseless. Now that I have taken hold of myself again—so well that he no longer means anything exact to me at the moment—I find myself to be absurd; only, it's easy to call oneself absurd after the fact! I must manage to depend on him less. If I really *willed* it, *wanted* it, I would be capable of it; I know it. So what good is willing or wanting it? I do not have any base pride.

Have read *The Picture of Dorian Gray*.[300] The idea is wonderful. The art of the dialogue incomparable, and what interesting theories on the influence, and the price of life, on the attitude to take; a lot of Wilde can be rediscovered in André Gide, especially this idea never to deny oneself, to go to the very depths of one's desire. One cannot be more deliciously immoral.

La vie unanime [The Unanimous Life] by Romains is a very powerful book.[301] I rediscovered a lot of familiar impressions in it; others were suggested to me. I especially admire the truly remarkable aptness of the vision and the impression; *that* is it in a nutshell. There is nothing to add; there is no other way to say it. Only, it is very abstract; it is the work of a gentlemen who never cries, as he puts it, and for whom all of life happens in his brain. It is not a friendly book.

(Oh, books are such good friends! Useless to open them, but how it does one good simply to look at them! Those who wrote them have also lived, and cried.)

This school in Neuilly is very interesting to study, directed by a woman whom I like for her great probity and her real moral as well as intellectual value, but who, I believe, is not capable of suffering because of others [*par autrui*]. Of these young girls, the ones happy with their studies alone are already comfortable with their worries and life, and blind to what they are leaving outside; others suffer from this false, too regimented existence without any contact with the real world.[302] The serious mistake is that they remain enclosed in a very narrow-minded circle. How can one walk with dreams in these corridors? How can one maintain a lofty inner life in the middle of all of these unfamiliar secret relationships? Certain girls read, but a book is a truly imperfect source of support. They lack a sense of responsibility; they never have to make a decision. They lack passionate friendships. They do not have the time; suffering loses its appeal for them.

To the Sorbonne, the students only bring their impersonal student personalities [*caractère*]; this doesn't fit in with my projects! The young girls barely interest me; the young people with whom it could be fruitful to chat scare me! Those I have heard chatting are so intellectually and morally rude! Impression of an awful mundaneness [*vulgarité*] that comes from the fact that there is no sign allowing one to recognize the true values, from the fact that they all show only what is most exterior, the most general, and thus, the most mediocre in themselves.[303]

Philosophy would be fascinating if there were no exam to prepare and if one could devote oneself to it in depth. But I am no longer intellectual enough. Yet, it interests me a lot.

Oh, my childhood photos! They made me cry last night. (Only a year ago, I never cried.) That little girl is now this sad and complicated big girl; poor little girl.

I care more and more about this notebook that is helping me to see clearly into myself—to reason out my chagrins a bit and to believe in them less as I write them—not to die completely. Only I should put some serious thought into them and not pour out my feelings with a great number of ellipses; at least I am perfectly sincere.

November 16—Tuesday

Sunday morning, for one or two hours, I experienced happiness. Don't talk, don't think, and in the peace and quiet, hear in one's own private world a dear voice, in the contemplation of the kitchen, in the middle of childish occupations, profoundly evoke a smile, a handshake full of complete affection.

Yesterday morning, blasphemous tears, awful depression when I was panic-stricken by my own voice, and now I am very far from that bad fever, no longer taking vain contingencies into account. Left to myself, many little things enter into my love: fears, regrets, desires for an immediate presence; they have their price, but after all, these are things that pass. The avenue du Bois with its blue sky and its beautiful sun brought me a kind of peace (oh, the scent of this autumn in the woods where baby carriages run over the red leaves!), but it is rather a despondent resignation that I try to escape with forgetfulness, shouting, Why limit my life to him when there are so many scattered beauties around me? This long chat with a mademoiselle Mercier previously unknown to me transported me to this region I will call "Claudelian" because as in Claudel's universe, life appears to be a necessary drama that infinitely surpasses the poor humans who live it. Will he come tomorrow or not, I don't know. I know this vagueness that goes through me passes infinitely over his head and mine. I know I can neither escape from my love, nor whittle it down to proportions that would allow it to be easily contained in my soul. I know I cannot act on this immense thing; Jacques cannot do anything either, and that is my way of controlling my love. Ah! Beyond the weaknesses of the being I love and my own, beyond the immediate need we have one for the other, beyond the suffering and the joy we can bring each other, beyond the words exchanged, the neglect, the misunderstandings, there is something which nothing can affect. And if he no longer loved me, I would love him still; and if he acted poorly, I would still be there. In my soul's mystical attraction [élan] to his, nothing about him can stop me anymore. At moments, he appears to me as only the pretense for a higher necessity to which I bow my head, and that is why this morning, the idea of a very possible discord between our two ways of thinking (since in the rhythm of life, it is evidently not always at the same instances that we attain the same altitudes), this idea, does not make me suffer. He is perhaps very far from me, maybe very banal, very far from soaring like me this morning. But I am experiencing eternal sentiments that do not address what he is today, or even what he is this year. And my love has no need of a response to be self-sufficient.

A great strength comes to me from feeling that my love is so immense because if I myself am timid, my shyness would not know how to impede the enthusiasm [élan] that propels me, because it will have to impose itself on him as it imposes itself on me. Thus I will not hesitate to go to find him very straightforwardly on Wednesday, November 24. Little does it matter to me if he doesn't come between now and then; on the contrary . . . let him guess the power that is within me. Even vis-à-vis him, I am proud of my love.

And this does not seem at all disproportionate to me because my exaltation does not have a single day's desire as its object, but concerns all of my life and his. This is what I had tried to make him understand. If I were expecting only happiness from him, I could do without him, but I need him in order to live. I would like for it to be reciprocal. I believe that, even if he does not suspect it, it is reciprocal; I feel things in myself that only I could give him. Oh, won't he come ask me for them? For the first time, I dare *to desire* a great, a necessary lifelong love; I dare *to demand* [*appeler*] a lifelong union, one of "these beautiful unions" described by Mademoiselle Mercier. Thanks to her, I dare because she gave me enough confidence in myself for me to judge myself perhaps worthy of receiving something greater than myself all the same. She also gave me back a faith that I used to have in the value of such demands, but that faith could not be valued without confirmation outside of myself. I am far from banal sentimentalities (that I do not scorn, moreover, because they are also found in the weakness and the sweet pleasure of life). I wanted to write at the beginning of this notebook, "This is nothing but the petty nastiness of living." No, there is something besides this petty nastiness.

Wednesday [November] 17

Ah! Mademoiselle Mercier understood; there is my strength! There is my value! Woke up this morning with such immense distaste for living, carried into my work such exhausting lassitude, and this evening found myself again lucid, courageous, with a good grip on myself.

How well she understood! A little while ago Zaza disappointed me, still overly committed to this automatism from which I freed myself, not yet getting her acts and her thoughts to coincide, not yet isolated and lofty. Mademoiselle Mercier was so close, so ardently desirous of understanding [*pénétrer*] my self, so intelligently sympathetic. Oh, how can I describe the darkness of her austere office, our two faces in the shadows and this ardent breath on my very weary soul! Upon arriving in class exhausted by tears, I really needed someone, but I wasn't hoping for that . . . that she would open her soul to me as well. The grave silences, the same seriousness in both of us, facing the same problems; her eyes brilliant with intelligence and behind her great strength and her encouraging words, an immense sorrow that she allowed me to sense, a bruise that she had transformed into a flame. I had misjudged her. She is one of these beings for whom the same questions (propriety, common sense, routine, etc.) don't exist and with whom I feel on equal footing because everything appears to them to be uniquely within, because they become attached to only the most essential part of the self.

What did she tell me? Things I had told myself, but my own approval had no value in my eyes because of this fear I had of trying to conform the truth to my desire, to my demands. She told me of the grandeur of love, this inspiration that passes over us, much higher than us, "understand, you see, understand," and that this need two people have for one another is really majestic, and their union is a really complete and beautiful thing, the most beautiful. And if one is truly designated, called [*appelée*] by a being, that is where one must go, and for the rest that one will not achieve, no matter. Save everything in principle, which is always possible—live in thought what one will not live in fact. (And this very touching question—perhaps very emotional, "Do you believe that a woman can have a normal life outside of marriage?" To hear such passionate tones from the mouth of the woman I believed to be purely intellectual!)

She told me that my weaknesses—these crying fits, these feelings of disgust—were valuable, that I am complete because I think my life, and at the same time, I live intensely; because after a day like today, I can have an evening of strength like tonight; and especially, after being so self-possessed tonight, I am capable of becoming weak and crazy again tomorrow. Know that one will always rediscover oneself, but even in knowing it, forget it so completely that one doubts, that one suffers, that one lives.

I needed someone who would understand *everything* as she did and who esteems me and loves me *for* what I am (not in spite of it). I needed it to start liking myself again.

Only, while showing me my riches, she increased my ardent desire for *him* to come take them—but also my strength to go carry them to him.

She assured me of the value of many dear ideas (on happiness—the gift of oneself—the necessity of using oneself—of freeing oneself); and these were not only words that she was saying; I definitely felt warmth from her entire soul.

And especially that she understood the grandeur of my love, the only one.

Yet, today was very weary. I felt how very brief my truly ardent youth had been; six months, now nothing limited in fact, but I am awfully limited in desire. Nothing has been achieved, but there is nothing left but to expect one achievement and to hope for one sole possibility [*possible*]. And it is true that at moments, in this living room, in front of *La politique* [Politics] by Aristotle, it is no longer an expectation, but an apprehension, as Gide says, "the earth waits for rain," "my soul waits for love."[304] An awful emptiness, how can I drag along for perhaps fifty more years of 365 days, or even two years? Boredom! Only comparable to the emptiness of vacation (La Grillère and the illustrations).[305] The joy of being more myself than last year no longer satisfies me. As a result of wanting to think one's life and always live more intensely, and load oneself down with thoughts, fears, and hopes, shoulders sometimes sag; what is great becomes heavy. One would like "to shrink all things to the measure of sweetness that they are for us," "Tired! Oh, so tired of living!" I wrote . . .

Sorbonne: A certain sweetness tonight in this lassitude, these weary voices, this discreet light, this whispering of peaceful and grave life cradles my soul—how strangely words are going to ring out so exterior to myself in a little while.

Where is dream? Where is life? Jacques—Zaza—me—Sorbonne—me—Jacques—me . . .
whirlwind where I lose myself—
and all those whom I will never know.

(And why so preciously gather together these small pieces of myself? Because in this awful emptiness, all I have left to keep myself busy is a certain curiosity vis-à-vis myself. I am going through a crisis, psychologically rather strange; it interests me—it soothes me.)

These young girls have brought me so much consolation that I am already very frankly attached to them and feel that I *can* do something for them. Chatting about literature interested them; intelligent, rather ardent and capable of knowing that Bordeaux has no talent.[306] Once again, false first impression. Garric is right; many points of contact.

It is because I have again felt this power of my self that, oh, without any pride, I am presently happy! I am finding a meaning for myself aside from him. My chat with Zaza gave me a pride in my opposition. All the same, I am not similar to any of the young girls I know because of more sincerity and more suffering. Truly, it is unbelievable how much I managed to suffer since the beginning of October, a suffering now lacking in novelty and last year's savor, and with a morose, overwhelming, and sometimes base sadness. (But out of this baseness, powers spring forth as she told me!) Indeed, almost all my sorrows come from him. There are in particular such cruelly sweet memories of being and of being memories. But that's life, and that will perhaps be happiness later. And I accept, I accept!

* * *

For stupidity is dreadful in this one respect, that it can resemble the deepest wisdom. When it opens its mouth, it gives itself away immediately; but where it remains hidden, where it resembles wisdom, is when it merely laughs.

Valéry Larbaud[307]

November 21—Sunday

Return to work and many thankless tasks knocked off in a couple of days. Thought about him with peace and indifference (physical, emotional, without tears or feverish anxiety), such a great tenderness, yesterday evening for example, and this regret of not being able to offer it all to him. I was happy to learn that he was on a trip; he was thus unable to come when he didn't come. Such confidence.

Interesting observation: I have had violent passions for ideas; a bit of this ardor was revived the day before yesterday. Why? Because of having chatted with an ardent metaphysician. Ideas in themselves hardly interest me anymore; I must see the beauty, the grandeur, that would be possible to attribute to these ideas, through the importance they have in the mind of someone who is profoundly in love with them. Besides, I think intellectual solitude weighs on many as it weighs on me.

At the Sorbonne, there is still this irritation in the presence of those beings whom I will never reach. And I no longer endow them with a mysterious prestige or desire to know their secret, but I would like to make use of them. I would like to expand my vision, to know, to come out of myself. Oh! Come out of myself and away from all those who are too much like me. It was a true pleasure to chat with the director of *L'Esprit* for a quarter of an hour.[308] Immediately I am imagining all that he could bring to me.

I found some pretty sentences in the books I study, and this also is a true little pleasure. Oh! simple pleasures, "the last refuge of complicated souls," how much I appreciate you.*

"fidelem si putaveris, faciès" [If you believe him to be faithful, you make him thus].[309]

"cum solitudinem faciunt, id pacem apellant . . ." [When they make solitude, they call (it) peace][310]

---

* In the manuscript, in the following sentences, Beauvoir had written Greek letters, which translate roughly as "illusion" or "deception," and two quotations in Latin, for which I have provided the Latin and an English translation.

184

and this formula for our friendship "absolute reciprocity and the identity of consciousness."[311]

This morning I absorbed this blue sky reflected by the Seine, I made it mine. Lightness of the air and of my heart, slow-moving and easy life.

And these metaphysical preoccupations that last night at dinner made me once again so perfectly absent—the banal surprise before the given—before what is, and could, it appears, not be. There is me; there are these motionless quays of the Seine. Why is something motionless? Why do I see? Why do I feel? Why this civilization, these houses, and not something else? How come them? How come me? Especially how come this adaptation between them and me? Oh, this problem of sensation and reason, of our relationships and those of the world! So absurd, so exasperating. According to what preestablished harmony, what chances, do I find myself in a sixth-floor flat on the street of Rennes, before a sheet of paper? Ah, this feeling of being someone's dream, hardly a possible, a point in infinity, a point knowing not where it is placed [posé], knowing nothing, understanding nothing! And then this certitude of a very simple, evident solution, that, nevertheless, for two thousand years men have been wracking their brains without managing to discover, like a magic trick that even a child could figure out; but nobody does.

It is not this banal idea, but the intensity with which I have experienced it that interests me, while just missing getting run over by a butcher's boy on a bike.*

Équipes Sociales—relaxing and friendly mediocrity.

Less fatigue—something less profoundly hopeless, but duller. It is time for reflection.

I did not know how to realize this passionate surrender to life whose sweetness I had tasted on the avenue of the Champs-Elysées. It is too contrary to myself. And then, this year, I cannot do what I want anymore with my life; I have to endure it (but I have accepted and chosen this apparent passivity).

I am living infinitely more than last year.

Obstinately in my books, I knew of true existence only very beautiful and strong, rare and intense minutes. Now I don't work much anymore; in particular, I no longer experience the obsessive worry of not losing any of my time or of myself. The strolls, the daydreams seem precious to me; life has value outside of its content. And to do nothing is to live. In living a lot,

---

* From "Ah, this feeling," in the previous paragraph, to "bike" at the end of this paragraph, the text is highlighted in the right margin of the facing verso.

bad or silly hours intermingle with exalted or painful hours, but at least I am living a lot.

There is one thing, the only, really, for which I love myself; it is for totally lacking what some call good sense, for being incapable of measuring an act by a rule arbitrarily established outside of myself. How can I put this? In the strongest sense of the words "to exist," for me nothing exists except what is profoundly felt by me. To think that I act uniquely on impulse would not be completely fair because my acts are thought out, but thought out entirely on the inside with complete originality, as if nobody before me had lived and every situation, every feeling, was virgin. It is extremely profound; it goes well beyond a banal disdain of conventions. It is a need for living only in the necessary.

How beautiful my life is, from novelty, sincerity, and necessity!

November 24—Wednesday

Boredom! Boredom!

The odor of coal in the morning and this same chocolate in these same bowls for how much more time? Oh, too sad awakening for all of this coming day. Distaste that I no longer even have the strength to elevate to the height of suffering. And these analyses bore me and I bore myself; my self and its brothers are no longer of interest to me. If only I could leave on a trip, have fun.* Oh, for very little I would ask the barbarians the secret of their happiness! Philosophy, what ridiculous irony; what do Kant and Maine de Biran matter to me, and the principle of causality is stupid.[312] Books bore me. What can I hang on to? To suffering? To walking in the streets again as I recite his letter to myself? I don't know; he is far away, very far. I have freed myself from him (for the time of his absence), and so everything is empty.

I gave everything, and yet this time it was not a gift I mastered; so much was given that I feel completely stripped when he is gone. My self has meaning only beside his. I can no longer live. It is madness, madness; I had even sworn to myself to keep myself always.

It's horrible not to have any desire for perfection or use anymore, horrible to try to sleep my life away until he makes life possible for me because I no longer expect anything except from him, whom I don't currently like, for whom I have no tenderness. And will I see him again? And when?

---

* This November 24 entry is highlighted in brown ink in the right margin of the facing verso, up to about this point in the manuscript.

I am bored! Such emptiness that does not even make me dizzy . . . such grayness, such drabness, all these hours that I am not *living*, that I try to evade.

Read Madame de Ségur last night.[313]

If I could only tell myself that this sorrow comes to me from him, but I can't at all. This disgust is born outside of him, on the contrary, and is the possible consolation on the horizon, the only thing keeping my boredom from turning into despair. For if I expected nothing from tomorrow, if I spread my boredom out across the future, what then? It is already so sickening; not even sickening, insipid.

It is not like last week, a great fatigue; nothing, this, it is nothingness. Never have I been so low. Oh, if there were a place where I would be sure of not meeting myself! Come out of myself . . . no longer any moral energy, no longer anything, nothing but a need to escape this common [*vulgaire*] boredom at all cost. For it is common, my inner life is common, and my pain and everything.*

If I were a young man I would live it up.

I try to make myself cry, to make this pain, only rising to the surface, spring forth, this pain that I feel possible, threatening, and that is my only distraction.† Oh, to get drunk on my tears! And then, no, I am going to translate some Greek.

Even I don't have pity for myself. Even I am not interested in me; my final refuge, my last friendship that I thought I could always count on is failing me. What should I do? And all the possibilities [*possibles*] in life that I come across in the streets. Is this going to last long?

Oh! I am so bored!

Evening

I took all of the future into my two hands today, and I made it into an intoxication; and from this intoxication surged a great happiness. And if this is what is called happiness, then there is nothing better to do in life than to make it happy.

I made the red sky and the yellow, translucent atmosphere fit into my more beautiful revived dream; and Notre Dame embodied all of this, my beautiful, sculpted daughter created for me. "I will never live through this

---

* This entire paragraph, starting "It is not," is highlighted in brown ink in the right margin of the facing verso.

† To about this point, this paragraph and the sentence before it are highlighted in brown ink in the right margin of the facing verso.

hour of my life again," I said, and what tipsiness to hold it thus, unique between my fingers.

The cathedral was so dark that one could not see the tears on the faces; the purple stained-glass windows, and the sound of the clock were a distant and enchanted decor, marvelous to find myself there. Who is myself? Where is there? In what magical country, at what unreal hour, that no clock would chime?

During one brief half-hour, I sobbed with such immense happiness that one life would not suffice to exclaim it. At the end, I did not know if it was truly joy or nerves or sorrow. That's how happiness is: tears that flow indefinitely, closed eyes that see all of life, and an ineffable blossoming as I knelt in the church.

And tell oneself afterwards, this is my life and mine alone, this is really happening to me, it so very wonderful! And yet it's true. Oh, it's marvelous to be eighteen and to have such capacity for joy and to anticipate as possible, as certain a future whose splendor makes me feel faint. Miracle of living!

This famous, discouraging book that I took out at S.G. [St. Geneviève] to distract my boredom with a bleak distaste made me tremble with hope because he is not like that, because my life, no matter what happens, will not be like that. And in a bedazzlement, I saw my life such as it will be. (Will it be? No matter. It is enough that I am sure of this, and I will keep being sure despite everything, even when I refuse to believe in it.) My life will be so beautiful! Such a beauty cannot not be realized, but how did I merit catching a glimpse of it? How was I chosen, from all the young girls, for such a youth? How come happiness knocked precisely at my door?

I saw, and I saw that it was good.

I saw him and myself seated side by side after the definitive acceptance; I saw us on life's threshold, each asking the other alone for all happiness. I saw us tremble before such a heavy responsibility; I saw us feverish and crying. And I trembled awfully in my entire being. And I saw that it was good.

We would have left all complications, and we were straightforward and serious before the supreme hour. And we were looking at each other like two strangers, and only our great friendship came to help us with our overly heavy love. Oh, dreams!

I know I am only one of innumerable possibilities [*possibles*]. But I know too that nobody will love you like I will love you; of this I am sure. I will not bring you everything, alas! But what I will bring you, I know that nobody else will be able to bring you. And I know that my life no longer has any meaning outside of you, and that by your side, it will suffice for it to be in order for it to be as it must. I have nothing else to expect. And this is why I was made to be your wife. (And I dare to write this word, without fearing tomorrow and its doubts; and I no longer envisage such a union only in the abstract, but I see myself at your house . . . ah!)

* * *

The reason, fool, she cries is that she's lived!
And that she lives! But what she most deplores,
What makes her tremble even to her knees,
Is that tomorrow she'll be living still!
Tomorrow, every day!—And so will we.
    [Baudelaire][314]

I have more memories than if I were a thousand years old.
    [Baudelaire][315]

How far away you are, perfumed paradise (. . . .)
But the green paradise of childish loves (. . . .)
The innocent paradise, full of furtive pleasures,
Is it already further away than India and than China?
Can we call it back with plaintive cries
And _____ it _____ once more with a silvery voice,
That innocent paradise full of furtive pleasure?[316]
    Baudelaire

Saturday, November 27

Thursday at the Sorbonne I had taken out a book by Spinoza; well beyond the texts, in partial sun, my thoughts went back to a month ago by his side.[317] Vague tears because of this very heavy thing that is perhaps not a torment, but so great that my heart is breaking, either from joy or sorrow, it doesn't know. In the hot and doleful library where students were whispering vaguely at the irritated end of a day, I had an irresistible need to read Baudelaire, who reminded me of similar oppressed evenings in the hotel room in Cauterets.[318] How profoundly this very poet entered into me on bleak days when I wasn't reading. No Thursday was as close to my heart, because of his very profound spleen without reason and especially because of the mournful music of his verses, this lamented, shattered, and voluptuous thing that at the same time lulled me gently, gently, all the while doubling the bitterness of my repressed tears once again.

    Oh! "Le balcon" [The Balcony]—"L'invitation au voyage" [Invitation to the Voyage]—"Harmonie du soir" [The Harmony of Evening]—"Vous êtes un beau ciel d'automne . . ." [You are a lovely autumn sky],—"A la très chère, à la très belle . . ." [To the dearest, to the most lovely], and all, all![319]

In the morning, childish emotion upon rereading Zaza's letters. Oh, it's because this idea haunts me; this idea that never, nevermore will I rediscover such feelings upon seeing her handwriting, my admiration, my agitation, and my preoccupations at fifteen years old! I cried stupidly in front of my drawer. More and more, it seems to me that I am burying an entire past; "I have more memories . . ."

And everything goes by so quickly! Again I see myself only two years ago; the future appeared to me to be infinite, at a vague distance, and it's here! I used to think about my friends' marriages. I would say this will show me that I am old . . . and I feel this by myself. I imagined that I would stay the same as at sixteen. And everything has changed so much!

If someone had predicted to me this closeness with Jacques, the books I read, the thoughts I have, I would never have wanted to believe it. I remember that I would often say it is not possible for one to write, to say, to think such things; everything outside of the customary automatism appeared impossible to me, and now . . .

Thursday after Baudelaire, I wandered at length on the quays of the Seine repeating sad verses to myself; the Seine was a true shadowy abyss, so calm, so unified, so tempting. I understood what is called dead waters. And I called him desperately, the one whom I believed to be far away, and I am still surprised to think that one hour later! . . . Tears that will be dried in a little while, storms soon calmed . . .

Yesterday resigned without desire. And then him, in the evening, so straightforward. I no longer have reason to doubt; everything is natural, simple, and yet a bit touching. And today a joy, that to avoid overwhelming me, will not elevate itself to happiness. What rest and relaxation in this confidence, this sentimental equilibrium! Tomorrow, I think that my turmoil will return, but with a peaceful certitude underneath.

These half-comical, half-serious allusions to my letter, and all the veiled tenderness in his simplest words. He used a pretty expression concerning J. Lemaître that Fournier treats as an idiot, "It makes one love to think so."[320] Right away, so close when I read Fournier-Rivière to him.*

Nevertheless, very little of all this anxiety and love and the sweetness of this long month has passed into this review. Whatever one does, the present

---

* This paragraph and the preceding one were highlighted in the right margin of the facing verso.

will never account for the past. My poor soul of yesterday is indeed deprived of all joy.

This too: in words I am only expressing today; to lie is to say the contrary of what one thinks at the moment one speaks, but isn't it also lying retrospectively to contradict what one meant and did not say? It bothers me to express only one moment of my being whereas all of them are of equal value; I arbitrarily cut out a piece of my inner life to present as something stable what incessantly contradicts itself. And then this idea: perhaps it is precisely our thoughts of yesterday that would have better corresponded to those that the other has today. Often, we would have passionately desired to make known yesterday's thoughts whereas we are not interested in those that we do reveal (experienced with Mademoiselle Mercier).

Always this feeling that my life, as people see it, is being played out on a plane so other than the one where I live! Augmented by the fact that J. is totally different according to whether he is or is not in a tête-à-tête. I am not suffering from that now (or almost not) because I no longer need to get closer to his private self. I have reached it; it suffices for me to observe that he is there, that he lives, to look at him and to know . . .

I have always considered the affection others have for me as a developing sentiment that I fear destroying through some blunder, and now I'm feeling a delicious sense of security, freedom, and an unknown lightness. I can do everything and say everything about myself. He loves me *myself,* not an ideal type I must resemble. As a child I never dared to impose myself on Zaza; I tortured myself to resemble what I thought she desired me to be. There are such loves, but they are pitiful. Of course, in the beginning, to keep him from getting lost on complicated paths that lead to the heart of being, one must take the other by the hand, guide him very carefully to avoid repelling him. But once he has arrived and accepted you, it suffices to reveal yourself in all sincerity.

Sunday, 28 November

Melancholy of these letters reread while waiting for a pretty pleasure very close by, with the verses from "Miracle" that bring tears to my eyes,

> in the ancient sun of these afternoons
> heavy with silence
> those who shed tears of love and tears of childhood.
> [Alain-Fournier][321]

191

Old words of affection to which life has inevitably made me unfaithful. Monsieur the *abbé*, Mlle Lejeune, Isabelle Galtier (and M. de Wendel to whom I vowed the suppressed violent passion of a little girl), Jacqueline . . . to feel this so far away. These letters from Zaza, where I today read such profound feeling, whereas despite everything I used to torture myself with doubts.

And to feel how far away this is, that everything is replaced with you from whom I have only two lines of writing that filled my heart with passion upon rereading them, and that had previously left me so indifferent!

Monday, November 29

I must first shout my exasperation! A scene for having been to see Zaza while it was such a necessary and beautiful thing! And she came in a little while ago when we were nicely chatting with Henriette and then wouldn't leave us alone![322] While I dream of a life in the middle of the only beings whom I love, made of simple pleasures and complicated sentiments, far from nagging, conventions, vain gestures and false words . . . and she airs her grievances to Papa, to Madame Lacoin, to anybody. I shouldn't write that . . . but really tonight the contrast is too great. . . .

And then, what does it matter? I am returning to my own life.

Yesterday, Zaza was very close in the living room while we spoke in hushed voices of Fournier-Rivière and evoked our childhood memories, even closer under the umbrella while I told her about Jacques, and she was so far from conventions; she understood so well, my girlfriend.

Claudy opened the door to me, and for forty-five minutes I told Jacques of my lethargy [*ennui*], which made us laugh outwardly, although we knew it was serious.* Marcel Arland brought us back together on the couch; I so much love to hear Jacques read. But above all, there was this expression that he said to me in reference to his novel, "It is much for you that I have done this."

Aunt Charles bothered us a lot, but what charming complicity, especially when she congratulated him on his gaiety and when he said that it was right to praise me for my equilibrium and my strength. It was as if he had shaken my hand very hard. I like Jean Delrive, barely glimpsed, for his slightly curt propriety, and for being so like everyone, although I know he resembles nobody. It was a lamentable failure, but I don't think back on it without pleasure.

---

* From the beginning of this paragraph through the next, which ends with "pleasure," the text is highlighted in the right margin of the facing verso.

And then awful evening at the restaurant with the weight of both of these encountered affections. It hurts me a lot to love so much. O, my friend, all this tenderness that I had wanted to give you that remains heavily in my hands! And yours that I feel so immense and that you also allow me only to glimpse. I nervously await the day I can get rid of all of this affection. But can one ever do this? Isn't the beauty of love not to declare it to each other? Only to know about it. And I know with so much sweetness "it is much for you that I have written this . . ."

Crying jag in my bed because of these affections not enough said and too passionately felt—chat with Poupette. I scare myself. Only one way out for me now. If I pass through it, something magnificent will be realized; if not, my life is cut off from the start. If Jacques died, I would perhaps not kill myself, but I would not live either. And it is all the more awful that there used to be other routes that could have led me less far than the path chosen, but that would have led me after all. And that won't open back up again. If the best escapes me, I will never be able to seek refuge in anything good. Anxiety: in the physical and moral sense of the word. And my feeling of helplessness and confusion is too great for me to accept a longer solitude. I will seek refuge at Zaza's house after lunch. How would I put it? How can I express her tenderness before my tears, her delicacy when she speaks to me of Jacques, understanding with so much simplicity and emotion, and the joy of speaking completely heart to heart, and of isolating ourselves from the world, and of *saying* our mutual affection. Zaza . . .

Coming back from Neuilly in the rain, what ineffable sweet pleasure swells my heart, my heavy heart.* (That is truly the right word tonight.) Such beautiful, such great, such *necessary* friendships! So Jacques, you were thinking of me on those black days when the act of confidence was difficult for me. You were writing this novel for me. You will write it. You love me . . . So Zaza, it was possible to confide completely in you. A wonderful feeling. And great despair not to be beside you and not to say to you and to hear you say all the concealed love that our hearts hold. To live there as lovers do, to live there as lovers do![323] How pretty life will be if Zaza finds, if *I* realize, and if we surround each other with mutual affections! I would like for Jacques and Zaza to know each other. She likes him so much already.

There you have it! A little while ago it was painful to be so far away, to be unable *to say;* now it is infinitely sweet to be so near, *to know* . . . I have also

---

* This paragraph is highlighted in the right margin of the facing verso, up through "To live there as lovers do!"

really understood that I could not be jealous of Jacques's friendships since mine has never been so immense as in my love's glow. "It is much for you that I have written this." And I have understood how Zaza loves me.

This evening is peaceful and sweet. Soon I will see them again. I have nothing to fear from them; the future might be charming. The present is magnificently full [*d'une magnifique plénitude*]. I don't care if I flunk. I believe that I am happy.

Tuesday, November 30

Exquisite daydreaming on this rainy morning, with a bit of fear, desire, and regret underlying my happy and tender peace ... A rather new internal landscape, made of a great, serious, and loving beauty; it is made of Zaza's smile and Jacques's glance (and then Poupette has her place there too).

November brought me a lot of things: an admirable book, this Fournier-Rivière correspondence, Mlle Mercier, Zaza infinitely dearer, and the awaited Jacques, and Poupette.

In particular I remember:

> an evening alone in the office with my book, strength, exaltation,
> a talk with Mlle Mercier in her dark office where love floated in the air,
> Sunday afternoon and yesterday afternoon with Zaza,
> Sunday at Jacques's house,
> and also gossiping with Poupette,
> Marie-Louise Lévesque one evening ...
> some rather agreeable evenings with the Équipes Sociales ...

But more than all, the avenue du Bois with a sunbeam on my tears and the wet autumn ... the quays where I would moan, where I would accept, where I was crazy ... walks insane with fever and sorrow ... and an immense happiness in somber Notre Dame.

The story of this month is an awful fatigue of all too great and heavy things, an unimaginable collapse, a neglect of my intelligence, of my pride, of everything. And then days of confidence, and then the boredom that is not even suffering, the emptiness, the blackness, the disgust. In the middle, Mademoiselle Mercier giving me back a bit of courage. And the end, hurried and magnificent; Jacques rediscovered very close by, Zaza, and this marvelous happiness.*

---

* This paragraph is highlighted in brown ink in the right margin of the facing verso, from its beginning to this point.

Where am I in all of this? I know that I am a lot to him, that he thought of me in times of solitude. All shyness left me; him, he is still my great tenderness. Now I would say yes without too much dread! Limiting my life no longer worries me; I am less attracted to what is difficult. A very simple life of affection, among chosen beings, in intelligent and easy occupations, without too many moral and social worries, tranquil love, a very absolute and confident passion, truly I ask for nothing beyond that; I no longer dream of harshness. The rare qualities that we possess can be used just as well to fabricate joy as sorrow. I am a bit weary of so many struggles and tears; I now believe happiness cannot truly be bad for me.

Zaza is splendidly my friend; I intimately associate her with my future dreams. I want her to be happy; I love her passionately after having often seen her rather far away. Abandoned shyness, great frankness, wildly happy, both of us.

The Équipes Sociales mean little to me; however I like these young girls, more intelligent than I first believed.

Relaxed inner life, made of sorrowful or tender dreams, some days of black drought [*sécheresse*], many days of strength and of inner recovery. At the moment, for the first time, I think, I no longer seriously contemplate observing my force; I only seriously contemplate that I am *very* loved, and that touches, troubles, and oppresses me sometimes, but sometimes too, like today, it gives me exquisite and infinite joy and felicity because it is like a long expected and not too unmerited recompense.[324] It justifies all of my torments; it gives a meaning to my life and to myself, to *all* of myself, since it is my *entire* self that one loves with my weaknesses and my complications . . . I don't know . . . it's infinite, it does me an immense good . . . I see the utility of being me; nothing appears lost to me . . . Their affection reaches out even to what they don't know . . .

Poupette has such an admiring trust . . .

Mademoiselle Mercier, who understands so well and who esteems . . .

The others whom I don't know well or love much, but whom I help (Équipes Sociales, Neuilly) and whose friendliness I know . . .

Zaza, for whom I am the only girlfriend: tenderness, compassion and such reciprocal affection . . .

Jacques . . . the future maybe, a bit of a dream . . . a support . . . maybe a love . . . "it is much for you that I have written this"—ah, yes, he loves me! . . .

So sweet, so sad . . . sweet for the hope, sad because he is not there . . . but it is indeed the taste of happiness, of a not too heavy and yet strong and great happiness . . .

What will December bring? This I think. A blossoming of my heart, something quite different from what I expected this year before my vacation. I used to want to make a very precise, very limited space for sentiment. And then he invaded everything; I live for memories, for hope, for love . . . and it is the most beautiful of lives.

* * *

> Before me are my lamp and paper;
> And behind me a troubled day
> Passed within me
> As I followed the hundred turns and tourneys of my thoughts . . .
> (. . .) And now, before this paper,
>> And now, here at home,
>> I am once more inside myself, smothering.
> (. . .) I am tired of interior doings!!
>> [Charles Vildrac]³²⁵

> Hoping for nothing, to sail through life,
> Is worth whatever pain be in it,
> Just to feel how good the sun is
> When it passes by
> Would you be aware how happy you were,
> If your happiness lasted more than an hour?
>> [Charles Vildrac]³²⁶

> I would want to vomit my day!
> I have its rancid taste in my mouth
> And my breast is abject   .
> With the foul air it endures.

> Into none of my gestures of this day,
> Which are my every-day gestures,
> Have I been able to put love.
>> [Charles Vildrac]³²⁷

> And it was then that he turned, as if to living,
> To knowing as many people as he could,
> To knowing them slowly and one at a time,
> By dwelling and talking with each of them
> When they were themselves, when they were alone.
> (. . .)
> His happiness was to share
> With each and every one of them,
> The secret memory of a single instant,

But of an instant magnified by such joy
That they could live in it night after night . . .
    [Charles Vildrac][328]

I entered into this time when memories
Suddenly start
To wound a little the heart that loves them
And holds them close and dwells on them
And is afraid of losing them.
(. . .)
And so there arose from memory
And came to snuggle up by my side,
The adolescent boys whom I had recently been,
And all the children I had been before;
Came one at a time, the tallest first,
And I lingered alone with each of them,
To meet with him and speak to him,
To seek his voice, to seek his eyes,
To find him in me whole again.
(. . .)
I don't want to leave even the most dormant
As if dead, in death, behind;
May there be no dead, O memory,
If one survivor remains!
Come all together and never be fewer,
Be more, with those who will come by;
If it happens that one shall stop and leave us,
I take an oath to bring him back persistently.[329]
    Vildrac (*Livre d'amour*) [A Book of Love]

But let us remember what life is. Can one ask for more than to be justified
    for one minute?
    Drieu de la Rochelle[330]

December 2—Thursday

I quite liked these very simple poems by Vildrac translating often felt trivial
or powerful emotions into an easy, slightly timid language that I read Tuesday evening during a boring Philosophy class.

Very beautiful piece entitled "Tristesse" [Dejection] and "Autre paysage" [Another Landscape], "Visite" [Visit], "En revenant" [On Returning], "Amitié," [A Friendship] and especially "Avec moi-même" [By Myself] and "En gloire" [Glory].[331]

197

Have read *L'Esprit.* There are two strangely beautiful articles by a certain Morhange.[332] Skimmed *Les feuilles libres, Nouvelle revue, Cahiers du mois* and Gide's *Si le grain ne meurt* [If It Die].[333] But I am barely fascinated with literature anymore.

In *Interrogation,* a truly beautiful sentence that I noted.[334]

This Tuesday evening was an unimaginable thing, with "Spinoza" in front of me, under the eyes of Mama and Henriette, who suspect nothing; what a simultaneously languid and ardent dream! In the middle, Zaza and Jacques, with Rivière and Fournier very near. Mauriac passed by, Mme Combemale, bruised and dreamy beings. I was so far away, in a very beautiful, very near, very vague world made of tears and voluptuous pleasures. How can I rediscover it? Childhood memories passed through it: my evenings in the office, the four of us who loved each other so much. Jacques in uniform, in Stanislas, when he looked so tall to me, and one day when we were going to the races together, the quay of the metro, papa so close to my heart, and the pleasure of being with Jacques; it is very far away.[335]

I didn't know that I had such a power for dreaming. Yesterday I managed to withdraw [*m'abstraire*] to such an extent that I no longer had any desires. I experienced this other side of life depicted by *Le grand Meaulnes.* Oh, if only one could remain in this enchanted kingdom! To do nothing is a voluptuous pleasure to me, even a necessity, because these minutes are more overflowing and richer with life than the others.

This morning, in the Luxembourg Gardens, I deliciously felt the harsh lucidity of this winter. My soul had emerged from the fog; I could see again with a marvelous clairvoyance the beginnings of our friendship at the moment when I was asking how to confide in him more intimately. Oh, how truly distant and happy I was all snug in my muff, crossing these gardens where my heart was so often broken! I worked well afterwards, and even this afternoon. Maybe it would be more beautiful to continue my regular and applied life than to wander off on adventures in my memories and my desires. Maybe. But it is so dull as soon as I can do without him.

I make an exception of last night, however, when the laughter and the friendship of these young girls healthily took me away from my little stories. I truly like them; there is a young and gay sympathy between us.

All the same, still this hurt from all the distance that separates us. See him, see him. When? And I have so many things to tell him.

At the library, in front of their stupid camaraderie, how I took pride in my love, in myself, in him, in *us.* We are not similar; we do not love each other similarly. I know very well that I never encountered and didn't even imagine something like what I am feeling.

Walk on the quays with Zaza, who came to get me at the library.

All these problems in life that add such a painful malaise to love, remember that love brings about all of life even today. Remember that, in sum, I sacrificed all of my desires; I no longer desire anything, no longer even a single work [*oeuvre*] of my own, and for him, very little, only that we love each other.

"And in the fallen darkness she sobbed, understanding confusedly that the lives of sensitive beings are voluptuous and sad things."[336]

Oh! how voluptuous and sad my life is!

NOTES

1. The 1926 diary is written in a green Librairie Classique Gibert notebook. "R103 354" is written on the inside cover for the cataloging purposes of the Bibliothèque Nationale de France. The 1927 diary is written in a thick gold Librairie Classique notebook with a red spine.

2. The source of the quotation by Rivière is unknown. My translation. Jacques Rivière (1886–1925) was a French author who founded the *Nouvelle Revue Française* (*NRF*). He exchanged a lengthy correspondence with his brother-in-law, Alain-Fournier, as well as with Claudel and Gide. His writings include the letters exchanged between him and Alain-Fournier, published in Rivière and Fournier, *Correspondance* (January 1905–July 1914); studies of Gide, Claudel, and Jammes, published as *Études* [Studies]; an account of his experiences as a prisoner during World War I, *L'Allemand* [The German Man]; a novel, *Aimée*; and notes about his thoughts on Catholicism, *A la trace de Dieu* [Tracing God].

Rivière's novel *Aimée* made quite an impression on Beauvoir, who referred to it several times in the 1926–27 diary as well as in *Mémoires d'une jeune fille rangée* (hereafter referred to simply as *Mémoires*). *Aimée* is the story of a young man named François, who although happily married to Marthe, his best female friend, falls madly and passionately in love with Aimée, the impossibly independent wife of his best male friend, Georges. François pursues Aimée throughout the entire novel but cannot bring himself to make a true pass at her due to his moral values and self-control. Upon learning that Aimée truly loves her husband but fears that he does not return her love, François realizes that true love means self-sacrifice and preferring the beloved to oneself, themes that are dear to Beauvoir in her diary and later novels. His realization causes him henceforth to devote all his energies to getting her husband to love her in return. Of interest to Beauvoir's development as a novelist is that all of Aimée's words, gestures, expressions, and actions are scrutinized much in the same way that Beauvoir's first novel, *L'invitée*, will analyze each of Xavière's moves and possible thoughts.

3. Paul Claudel (1868–1955) was heavily influenced by two major experiences: his discovery of his faith in God and of the French poet Rimbaud. A playwright, lyricist, and theoreti-

cian, Claudel also had a career as a foreign diplomat, which led him to spend considerable time in America (1893–95) and in the Far East (1895–1909). This quotation is from act 2 of *L'échange* [The Trade], 83, when Marthe learns that Louis Laine is leaving her. See also Claudel, *L'échange,* 69. Beauvoir may have chosen this quotation because it is quoted by Jacques Rivière in Rivière and Fournier, *Correspondance,* 1:322.

4. Source of quotation by Ramuz unknown; my translation. Charles Ferdinand Ramuz (1878–1947) was a Swiss-born regionalist author whose works include *Aline, La beauté sur la terre* [Beauty on Earth], and *Fête des vignerons* [Wine Grower's Feast]. His writing is noted for its mixture of the picturesque, tragedy, lyricism, sensuality, and mysticism. Certain of his works testify to his interest in man's destiny, his greatness, and his limitations when faced with nature or the supernatural. One sentence from his novel *Vie de Samuel Belet* [The Life of Samuel Belet] seems to figure in Beauvoir's diaries from 1926–30: "At any rate, one must live, and one must die while still living."

5. Claudel, "Ténèbres," 430, trans. Shipley, "Shadows," 72. Beauvoir must have been quoting from memory when she wrote down this and many other excerpts for she has taken certain liberties with the second line of this text. Her quotation reads, "Je souffre et l'autre souffre et il n'y a pas de chemin / Entre elle et moi, pas de parole, ni de main," as reflected by my modification of Shipley's translation. The original "Ténèbres" [Shadows], 430, by Claudel, shows, "Je souffre et l'autre souffre et il n'y a pas de chemin / Entre elle et moi, de l'autre à moi point de parole ni de main," the second line of which Shipley rightly translates as "Between her and me, from the other to me no word and no hand."

6. Claudel, "Saint Philippe," 415, my translation.

7. Rabindranath Tagore (Rabindranath Thakur) (1861–1941) was an Indian musician, painter, poet, and the author of more than one thousand poems and numerous novels, dramatic plays, and songs that had a great influence on modern literature in India. He won the Nobel Prize for Literature in 1913. Part "a" of the quotation is from section 29 of Tagore's *L'offrande lyrique,* which was originally written in English by Tagore and translated into French by André Gide. Part "b" is from section 79 of *L'offrande lyrique.* Beauvoir's quotation was from André Gide's French translation of Tagore's English translation of his own original Bengali text. See Tagore, *Gitanjali* [Song Offerings], 23, 78.

8. These lines are from Jammes, "Elégie troisième," trans. Alwyn as "Third Elegy," 32. Francis Jammes (1868–1938) was a French writer who initially benefited from the support of Mallarmé and Gide. His friendship with Paul Claudel inspired his return to Catholicism.

9. This quotation is from the last four lines of François Mauriac's "L'Etudiant—Départ II," *Les mains jointes* [The Student—Second Departure, with Clasped Hands], 336; my translation. François Mauriac (1885–1970) was a French novelist noted for his Catholicism, which seemingly influenced him to create somber worlds in which individuals were tortured by their lack of religious grace. The novels that might have influenced Beauvoir between 1926 and 1930 include *Le baiser au lépreux* [A Kiss for the Leper], *La chair et le sang* [Flesh and Blood] *Génitrix* [Génitrix], *Le désert de l'amour* [The Desert of Love], and *Thérèse Desqueyroux.* Beauvoir has taken slight liberties with the syntax of Mauriac's verses. Her version of the first line reads "Suis-je aimé? est-ce que j'aime?" [Am I loved? Do I love?] Mauriac's poem reads "M'aime-t-on? Est-ce j'aime" [Does someone love me? Do I love?]

10. Source of quotation is unknown. Léon Bloy (1846–1917) was a French writer noted for attacking naturalist schools and in particular Zola in "Je m'accuse." An ardent Catholic, he wrote fictional works, based on his autobiography, *Le désespéré* [The Hopeless One], and

La femme pauvre [The Woman Who Was Poor], in which he expressed his personal torments, fears, and spiritual illuminations. His writings include an apocalyptic diary in eight volumes that appears under a variety of titles, such as *Le mendiant ingrat* [The Ungrateful Beggar], *Mon journal* [My Diary], and *Le pèlerin de l'absolu* [Pilgrims of the Absolute]. He is sometimes considered a visionary.

11. This quotation is from Baudelaire, *Poésies diverses,* in an epistle sent to Sainte Beuve, number 25 in *Oeuvres complètes*; my translation. The first line of this poem reads, "Tous imberbes alors, sur les vieux bancs de chêne" (All beardless then, on old oak benches). I thank Wilson Baldridge for this reference. Charles Baudelaire (1821–67), sometimes considered to be the precursor of all modern poetry, stands at the apex of the romantic revolt.

12. Henceforth when I have used the word "selfishness" it translates *égoïsme,* and "selfish" translates *égoïste,* unless otherwise indicated. Hereafter, the words "achievement," "achieving," or forms of the verb "to achieve" translate the French noun *réalisation* or forms of the French verb *réaliser,* unless otherwise noted.

13. Alissa, the heroine in André Gide's novel *La porte étroite* [Strait Is the Gate], gives up love and marriage out of a sense of religious duty. Gide (1869–1951) was a French author noted for having a strict Protestant father and a rigid Catholic mother, which resulted in a religious crisis and a search for true morality that permeates much of his work. His most frequent themes include individualism, the sublime, literary creation, and homosexuality.

14. Claudel, "Sainte Thérèse," , 627; my translation.

15. Mauriac, "L'Etudiant—Départs II," 335; my translation.

16. Charles Péguy (1873–1914), a French socialist philosopher-poet fascinated by politics, founded the journal *Les Cahiers de la Quinzaine* in 1900. Like many others of his generation, he returned to Catholicism, in 1908, after having distanced himself from the church. He published such works as *Note sur M. Bergson et la philosophie bergsonienne* [Note on Mr. Bergson and Bergsonian Philosophy], *Notre jeunesse* [Temporal and Eternal], *Notre patrie* [Our Country], and others in free verse, such as *Le mystère de la charité de Jeanne d'Arc* [The Mystery of the Charity of Joan of Arc], a meditation on love and a work that made his concept of Hell renowned.

17. Paul Valéry (1871–1945), a French poet and novelist, was torn between intellectual narcissism and the detachment required to discern human possibilities. His crisis in Genoa one night in 1892 led him to abandon his first idols—love and poetry—and to distance himself from aestheticism and a search for pleasure. In their place, he glorified abstract reasoning.

18. Maurice Barrès (1862–1923), a symbolist French author, was sometimes viewed as a dreamy rebel. In works that postdate the ones Beauvoir mentions in this diary, Barrès is also sometimes viewed as paving the way for fascism because of his increasingly rigid right-wing views. In 1926 Beauvoir most often spoke of his *La trilogie du culte du moi* [Trilogy of Self-Worship], which was comprised of three different novels, *Sous l'oeil des barbares* [Under the Surveillance of Barbarians], *Un homme libre* [A Free Man], and *Le jardin de Bérénice* [The Garden of Bérénice]. To my knowledge, no published English translations exist for these works by Barrès.

19. "Ces mois morts" could also be translated as "these dead months," and such a translation is certainly evoked by Beauvoir's reference to time. However, her repeated mention of the self in the preceding paragraphs suggests that the translation "these dead selves" is more appropriate. "What good will it do?" (à quoi bon?) is a repeated question discussed in Jean Cocteau's *Le Potomak,* 110–12. Cocteau (1889–1963) was a prolific French playwright,

novelist, poet, essayist, and artist. Of his voluminous work, the writings that Beauvoir most likely read between 1926 and 1930 include *Thomas l'imposteur* [Thomas the Imposter], *Le grand écart* [The Great Gap], *Le Potomak, Les enfants terribles, Orphée, Plain-Chant, Opéra,* and *Le rappel à l'ordre* [A Call to Order]. The latter contains the four essays "Le coq et l'arlequin" [Cock and Harlequin], "Le secret professionnel" [The Professional Secret], "D'un ordre consideré comme une anarchie" [Order Considered as Anarchy] and "Picasso."

20. Verlaine, "La bonne chanson XIII," 150; my translation. Paul Verlaine (1844–96), a French poet and a contemporary of Rimbaud and Mallarmé, was especially known for his tumultuous affair with Rimbaud, for whom he left his wife and son in 1871. In July 1873 Verlaine shot and wounded Rimbaud, who was threatening to leave him. Verlaine was imprisoned until January 1875. From then on, he led a rather bizarre existence.

21. This quotation is an approximation of the last line of Henri de Régnier, "La main tentée" [The Tempted Hand], from *Tel qu'en songe* [As If Dreaming], in Henri de Régnier, *Poèmes 1887–1892,* 265; my translation. Régnier (1864–1936) was a French writer best known for his symbolist poetry.

22. Section I is from Bergson, *Essai sur les données immédiates de la conscience,* 98, trans. Pogson, *Time and Free Will* (hereafter *TFW*), 132. See Henri Bergson, *Time and Free Will,* trans. Pogson, 132–34. Translation modified to correspond to Beauvoir's quoting of text; ellipses enclosed by parentheses indicate that words were omitted by Beauvoir from Bergson's text. Henri Bergson (1859–1941) was a French philosopher who taught at the Collège de France from 1900 to 1914 and whose philosophical works won him the 1927 Nobel Prize for Literature. Hostile to Kant and to positivism, he argued for a conscious return to intuition and for a philosophy attentive to immediate experience. Bergson was very popular until World War II and influenced many French authors, including Henri Massis, Charles Péguy, and Marcel Proust, whose works Beauvoir refers to in 1926–27. The works by Bergson that Beauvoir might have read at this time include *Essai sur les données immédiates de la conscience* [Time and Free Will], *Matière et mémoire* [Matter and Memory], *Le rire* [Laughter], *Introduction à la métaphysique* [An Introduction to Metaphysics], *L'évolution créatrice* [Creative Evolution], *L'énergie spirituelle* [Mind-energy], *Durée et simultanéité* [Duration and Simultaneity], and a variety of lectures that were published.

23. Section II is from Bergson, *Essai,* 85, trans. Pogson, *TFW,* 129; my revised translation.

24. Section III is from Bergson, *Essai,* 91, trans. Pogson, *TFW,* 138; my revised translation.

25. Section IV is from Bergson, *Essai,* 89, trans. Pogson, *TFW,* 135–36; my revised translation.

26. Section V is from Bergson, *Essai,* 125, trans. Pogson, *TFW,* 166–67; my revised translation.

27. Section VI is from Bergson, *Essai,* 173, trans. Pogson, *TFW,* 231–32; my revised translation.

28. Section VII is from Bergson, *Essai,* 178, trans. Pogson, *TFW,* 237; my revised translation.

29. Section VIII is from Bergson, *Essai,* 7, trans. Pogson, *TFW,* 9–10; my revised translation.

30. Section IX is from Bergson, *Essai,* 8, trans. Pogson, *TFW,* 10; my revised translation.

31. Section X is from Bergson, *Essai,* 10, trans. Pogson, *TFW,* 14; my revised translation.

32. Second part of section X is from Bergson, *Essai,* 12, trans. Pogson, *TFW,* 16; my revised translation.

NOTES TO PAGES 61-66

33. Section XI is from Bergson, *Essai*, 14, trans. Pogson, *TFW*, 19; my revised translation.

34. The standard translation for *angoisse* is "anxiety," according to the *Vocabulaire Européen des philosophes*, and I have translated *angoisse* as "anxiety" throughout the text. In this diary Beauvoir never uses the French word *anxiété*, which would also translate as "anxiety."

35. See Cocteau, "D'un ordre considéré comme une anarchie," 67–86. For the passages on the tightrope in "D'un ordre considéré comme une anarchie," see pages 70, 83–85. Cocteau argues in these passages that one should have style instead of having *a* style. He claims that regardless of how one writes, there will always be critics who mock the writing for being too simple or too complicated because fresh beauty is invisible. Cocteau also talks about the tightrope in *Le Potomak*. In it, he compares the tightrope to something stretched over a void into which one can resist falling only by writing. Each word constitutes a careful step: "Il y a toujours sur le vide une corde raide. L'adresse consiste à marcher, comme sur des oeufs, sur la mort. Un mot d'écrit: un pas d'ôté à la chute" (257). [There is always a tightrope over the void. Skill consists in walking, as if on eggs, on death. One word written: one step removed from falling.] Two other passages in the essay "D'un ordre considéré comme une anarchie" are also of importance for Beauvoir. Cocteau believes that certain works move us, others uproot us, and still others force us to leave our homes (79). A masterpiece, he maintains, cannot appear to be a masterpiece. Its many faults are what make it a masterpiece (86). Overall, he thinks that in order to make a masterpiece, one must not worry about copying others. See also note 19.

36. I have translated the French expression *sans doute* as "I dare say" or "probably" throughout this diary. Beauvoir never uses the now popular French word *probablement*, which would also accurately translate as "probably."

37. Beauvoir refers to Massis, "André Gide ou l'immoralisme," in *Jugements*. Henri Massis (1886–1970), a French essayist, literary critic, and literary historian, was a student of both Alain (pseudonym of Emile-August Chartier; see notes 1, 124, and 146 in the 1927 diary) and Bergson (see note 22 in the 1926 diary), and he published on other authors dear to Beauvoir, such as Maurice Barrès (see note 18 in Beauvoir's 1926 diary). Originally considered to be a disciple of Bergson, Massis over time became increasingly nationalistic. See also note 59 in Beauvoir's 1927 diary.

38. Gide, *Le retour de l'enfant prodigue* and *Les nourritures terrestres*.

39. The expression "Équipes Sociales" literally translates as "Social Teams." It refers to study groups organized by a social service institute that was founded by the professor and philsopher Robert Garric to aid and educate the working classes in the eastern districts of Paris. Beauvoir volunteered to teach literature to young women for this institute. Her particular group was located in Belleville. See Beauvoir, *Mémoires*, 249–54, trans. Kirkup, *Memoirs of a Dutiful Daughter* (hereafter called *Memoirs*), 179–84; Francis and Gontier, *Simone de Beauvoir*, 51–52; and Bair, *Simone de Beauvoir*, 9.

40. I always use one of the English words "empty," "emptiness," "vacuum," or "void" to translate the French word *vide* throughout the 1926 and 1927 portion of Beauvoir's diary.

41. "Inner life" is the common translation in discussions of Barrès for the expression *la vie intérieure* found frequently in his works.

42. *Eupalinos, ou l'architecte* is a philosophical play by Paul Valéry.

43. See note 22, for Henri Bergson.

44. I have consistently used the English expression "soul-searching" to translate the French *retour sur soi-même* or *retour sur moi-même* throughout Beauvoir's 1926–27 diary.

45. Paul Valéry wrote *Variété* [Variety], in *Oeuvres*. Eugène Fromentin (1820–76), a French painter and writer, was most famous for his lucid analysis and depiction of emotions in his idealist novel *Dominique* (1863), about his adolescent love for an older Creole woman who marries someone else and then dies. Marcel Arland (1899–1986), a French author attracted to dadaism and surrealism, often collaborated on the journal *Nouvelle Revue Française* (see note 55). His writings manifest his interest in the complexities of the human soul. His works include *Monique, Terres étrangères* [Foreign Lands], *Étienne, La route obscure* [Dark Road], *Les âmes en peine* [Souls in Pain], *Étapes* [Stages], and *L'ordre* [Order]. In 1929 he won the Prix Goncourt for *L'ordre*. Abbé Prévost was the author of *Histoire du chevalier des Grieux et de Manon Lescaut* [The Story of Manon Lescaut and the Chevalier des Grieux]. Mme de La Fayette wrote *La Princesse de Clèves* [The Princess of Clèves].

46. Robert Garric was a professor, a philosopher, and the founder of the Équipes Sociales; see note 39.

47. Source of quotation by Mauriac unknown; my translation. For Mauriac, see note 9.

48. Claudel, "Saint Georges," 610; my translation.

49. Jean Sarment is the pseudonym for Jean Bellemère (1897–1976), French playwright, novelist, poet, and actor. He acted alongside Réjane and Louis Jouvet in the Sarah Bernhardt and Vieux-Colombier theaters. He is best known for his earliest plays, including *La couronne de carton* [The Cardboard Crown], *Le pêcheur d'ombres* [Rude Awakening], *Le mariage d'Hamlet* [Hamlet's Marriage], and *Je suis trop grand pour moi* [I Am Too Big for Myself].

50. "Irrelevent to life" translates *hors de la vie*. Paul Raynal's *Le maître de son coeur* [Master of His Heart] is the story of a love triangle among Simon, Henry, and Aline. Simon and Henry are best friends who have known Aline since childhood. Simon confesses his love for Aline first to Henry and then to her. Aline is at first surprised, then decides that she returns Simon's love. They seal their love with a kiss. When Aline sees Henry, she realizes that she loves him and he loves her, but neither admits it openly. Finally, Aline avows her feelings. Henry rejects her love because Simon is his best friend, whom he does not want to betray. Soon the three are back together and Aline and Simon are once again in love. As Henry is leaving for Italy, his goodbyes reveal special feelings for Aline, who suddenly proclaims that she was mistaken and that she truly loves Henry, not Simon. In horror, Simon shoots himself. As Simon dies, Henry repeats that he had not betrayed him, but Simon, perhaps, does not hear him and the play ends.

51. Francis de Miomandre (1880–1959), a French novelist, essayist, poet, moralist, philosopher, and translator of Spanish (especially of *Don Quixote*), received the 1908 Prix Goncourt for *Écrit sur de l'eau* [Written on Water].

52. Bernard Barbey's *Le coeur gros* [The Heavy Heart] is a coming-of-age story for the adolescent narrator and also the tale of a love triangle among three people. The narrator is in love with his older female friend Claude and greatly admires his older male friend Walt. Walt and Claude decide to marry. Once they marry, they no longer seem so happy together. The narrator admires Walt less, finds Claude less vibrant, and becomes jealous of his friends' interest in each other. He starts to plot how he can get closer to each of his friends. At the end, he and Claude have exchanged a sign of affection in front of Walt. As the book concludes, the narrator and Claude seek Walt to reassure him and to discover if he feels betrayed.

53. *Disponible* (available) is a word often used by Gide and especially stressed in *Les nourritures terrestres,* in which he indirectly defines it as something one can be only by giving up home, family, all places where one might rest, including continuing affections and

faithful love affairs, attachment to ideas, and anything that compromises justice. It is only if one is entirely available that one can embrace novelty. *Les nourritures terrestres*, 184.

54. "My good-byes to adolescence" is probably a reference to François Mauriac's second book, a long poem entitled *L'adieu à l'adolescence* [Good-bye to Adolescence].

55. *La Revue des Jeunes* was a journal founded in the 1920s to promote the study of the thought of Thomas Aquinas. *La Revue Universelle* was one of the most important nationalistic and Catholic journals after World War I. *La NRF* (Nouvelle Revue Française) was a journal founded in 1909 by André Gide, Jacques Copeau, and Jean Schlumberger, among others, who wanted their journal to emphasize aesthetic issues and to remain free of any political parties or moral schools of thought. *Les Études* (an abbreviated name for *Les Études Philosophiques*), a philosophical journal, was founded in 1926 by Gaston Berger.

56. For Verlaine, see note 20. Mallarmé (1842–98), a French poet sometimes considered as the master of symbolism in poetry, was noted for his exploration of the themes of nothingness, the difficulty of being, and absence. He became increasingly interested in depicting the effect produced by a thing as opposed to the thing itself. In her diary, Beauvoir speaks of Mallarmé's "L'après-midi d'un faune," a poem composed of 101 alexandrines that retrace the thoughts of a faun envisioning memories, dreams, and reality. Claude Debussy based his orchestral piece *Prélude à l'après-midi d'un faune* on this idea. Arthur Rimbaud (1854–91), a French poet, was noted for his revolutionary poetry considered to be a precursor of surrealism, his tumultuous love affair with Paul Verlaine, the phrase "Je est un autre" (I is another), and the notion that it is only through a "long, great, and sensible derailing of all the senses" that one can progress beyond individual consciousness and meet up with the profound self and cosmic unity. Jules Laforgue (1860–87), a French poet and contemporary of Gustave Kahn and Paul Bourget, published *Les complaintes* [The Complaints] and *L'imitation de Notre-Dame la lune* [The Imitation of Our Lady the Moon]. He is noted for poetry combining audacity and fantasy. Jean Moréas (1856–1910), a French poet of Greek origin, spent his childhood in Athens, traveled extensively in Europe, and came to settle in Paris in 1882. His involvement in the Symbolist movement led him to write *Les cantilènes* [Songs]. He eventually founded the "École Romane" [Roman School] with Charles Maurras and then produced *Le pèlerin passionnée* [The Passionate Pilgrim] and especially *Les stances* [Lyrical Poems], numerous meditations on life and the world. For Claudel, see notes 3, 5, and 6. For Gide, see note 13. For Arland, see note 45. Valéry Larbaud (1881–1957), a French author, traveled widely in Europe. His work dates from before 1935, when he became aphasic. At the time of writing her diaries during 1926–30, Beauvoir probably would have had access to the following of Larbaud's works: *Fermina Márquez* [Fermina Marquez], *A. O. Barnabooth* [A. O. Barnabooth: His Diary], *D'amants, heureux amants* [Of Lovers, Happy Lovers], *Enfantines* [Childish Things], and *Ce vice impuni* [This Unpunished Vice]. He is also noted for translating Spanish and English. Several of his poems touch on themes dear to Beauvoir in these 1926–30 notebooks. For example, he has poems entitled "Le masque" [Mask], "Le don de soi-même," [Gift of Oneself] and "Les borborygmes" [Stomach Rumbles] in the Pléiade collection. For Jammes, see note 8.

57. For Ramuz, see note 4. André Maurois (1885–1967), a French historian, novelist, essayist, and humorist, wrote of his war memories in *Les silences du Colonel Bramble* [The Silence of Colonel Bramble] and left several traditionally fanciful novels treating wisdom without illusions, for example, *Ni ange ni bête* [Neither Angel nor Beast] and *Climats* [The Climates of Love], which Beauvoir might have been reading during 1926–30. Beauvoir also mentions

Joseph Conrad (1857–1924), an English novelist of Polish origin; Rudyard Kipling (1865–1936), the English poet and novelist; and James Joyce (1882–1941), the Irish poet and novelist, who was best known for his novel *Ulysses* (1922). For Tagore, see note 7. Charles Maurras (1868–1952), a French politician and writer, was the author of *La musique intérieure* [Inner Music]. Henri de Montherlant (1896–1972), a French writer, was noted for his ideal of heroic life that excludes women. Henri Ghéon (1875–1944), a French playwright, was co-founder of the *Nouvelle Revue Française* (1909). Roland Dorgelès (1886–1973) was a French novelist known for his narratives on the bohemian life in Montmartre, on the war, and on life abroad. For Mauriac, see note 9.

58. Alexandre Arnoux (1884–1973) was a French novelist and poet. Lucien Fabre was the author of *Rabevel, ou le mal des ardents* [Rabevel, or the Ache of Passion], a novel that won the Prix Goncourt in 1923. Jean Giraudoux (1882–1944) was a French novelist and playwright. Oscar Wilde (1856–1900), an Irish author of various genres including poetry, essays, short stories, and novels, was best known for his numerous plays. He also won fame for his broad knowledge; his barbed and clever wit; his flamboyant dress, taste, and manners; and his penchant for glorifying beauty for itself. A good friend of Gide, Wilde spent the last few years of his life in France after having served two years in a British prison as punishment for his homosexual behavior. Walt Whitman (1819–92), the American poet and journalist, was best known for his *Leaves of Grass*. William Blake (1757–1827), English poet, painter, and engraver, was known for his hatred of repressive Christian ethics and religious dogma in general. Fyodor Dostoyevsky (1821–81) was a Russian novelist renowned for his fictional portrayals of the human being torn between the presence of evil and the search for God, the unconscious and the conscious mind. The Russian author Leo Tolstoi (1828–1910) wrote many novels, including *War and Peace* and *Anna Karenina*. Romain Rolland (1866–1944), a French writer, dreamed of a nonviolent hero who wanted to understand everything in order to love all.

59. André Chénier (1762–94) was a French poet noted for creating a new type of poetry combining a worship of art and sincere inspiration. Charles Leconte de Lisle (1818–94), also a French poet, was known for advocating objective poetry that would unite science and art and for depicting past civilizations and great religious myths.

60. The French poet Max Jacob (1876–1944) was considered to be a precursor of surrealism. His poetry collection entitled *Le cornet à dés* [Dice Cup] reveals a mind tormented by mysteries and a spirit torn between its own contradictions. Guillaume Apollinaire (1880–1918), another French poet, was considered to be an initiator of modern art in poetry.

61. Maurice du Plessys (1864–1924), a disciple of Moréas, was a French poet best known for his collection *Le feu sacré* [Sacred Fire]. André Thérive (1891–1967), the author of *Sans âme* [Without a Soul] and *Plaidoyer pour le naturalisme* [Plea for Naturalism], was cofounder of the populist movement in France in the 1930s, a movement that studies obscure souls and the lives of the poor forced to do routine work. Louis Chadourne (1890–1925), a French poet and novelist, was the author of the poetry collection *Accords* [Harmonies], containing poems treating the relationship between self, time, and happiness, and of the novel *L'inquiète adolescence* [Restless Adolescence]. *Cahiers de la république des lettre, des sciences et des arts* is a journal that sometimes explored women's societal roles. Anna de Noailles (1876–1933) was a French poet and novelist known for her exploration of such themes as the beauty of the world, light, and the French landscape, the ephemeral nature of time, the passing of youth, and the meaning of solitude and death. She was the author

of *Les éblouissements* [The Dazzling Sights]. Paul Drouot (1886–1915) was a French poet noted for his unfinished masterpiece published posthumously, *Eurydice deux fois perdue* [Eurydice Twice Lost].

62. Claudel, "A la mémoire de Georges Dumesnil," 603–4; my translation.

63. Claudel, "Saint Louis," 653–54; my translation.

64. I have consistently translated *état d'âme*, which literally means "state of the soul," as the more colloquial English word "mood" throughout Beauvoir's 1926–27 diary, unless otherwise indicated.

65. Claudel, "Sainte Thérèse," 625; my translation.

66. Claudel, "Saint Louis," 656; my translation.

67. Ibid., 654–56, my translation.

68. Baudelaire, "Le goût du néant," *Les Fleurs du Mal*, 77, trans. McGowan, "The Taste for Nothingness," *The Flowers of Evil*, 153. I have modified McGowan's translation to reflect the version of the line Beauvoir is quoting. In some French editions the last word of this verse would be translated as "scent."

69. Claudel, "Saint Louis," 658–59. I have provided a literal translation for Claudel's verse.

70. "Spleen," meaning a melancholy without apparent cause that is characterized by disgust with everything, is a popular term in the poetry of the French poets Alfred de Vigny, Charles Baudelaire, and Jules Laforgue. Beauvoir quotes both Baudelaire and Laforgue in her diary of 1926–30.

71. Cauterets is a village in the Pyrenees to which, according to Beauvoir's *Mémoires*, she had been invited by her aunt Marguerite and uncle Gaston on vacation. She spent her time going on endless excursions while longing to see Garric and her cousin Jacques. See *Mémoires*, 284–85; *Memoirs*, 205–6.

72. Phèdre, the female character from Greek mythology who falls madly in love with her stepson Hippolyte, declares her love to him, experiences the shame of his rejection, and then tells his father and her husband, Thésée, that Hippolyte tried to rape her. To avenge his honor, Thésée asks Poseidon, the god of the sea, to bring about Hippolyte's death. The story of Phèdre inspired fictional works by Sophocles, Euripides, Seneca, and the French authors Robert Garnier and Jean Racine.

73. This line by Goethe is also quoted in Jean Cocteau, *Thomas l'imposteur*, which includes the subtext in which a young girl in love, Henriette, attributes the silence of her beloved (Guillaume Thomas) to the idea that either he does not love her and flees from her or he loves her and is trying to extinguish a flame to which he dared not aspire. Beauvoir reacts similarly to Jacques's lack of attention in her diary. In her autobiography, Beauvoir recounts that Jacques quoted this line, "I love you; does that concern you?" before their separation for the summer and after he has flunked his law exams, and that she, believing that it might be his hidden declaration of love, wrote him a long letter overtly stating her love for him. See *Mémoires*, 283; *Memoirs* 205.

74. For *Aimée*, see note 2; Beauvoir refers also to *Le grand Meaulnes* by Alain-Fournier and *Almaïde d'Etremont*, by Jammes. Alissa is a character in Gide's novel *La porte étroite*.

75. Monique is the heroine of Marcel Arland's *Monique* (see note 76). Dominique is the adolescent hero in love with the older woman, Madeleine, in Fromentin's *Dominique*. Philippe is the hero from Maurice Barrès's *Le jardin de Bérénice*. Francis Jammes wrote *Clara d'Ellébeuse*.

76. Marcel Arland's *Monique* is a very strange novel about a young penniless girl who struggles (out of pride) against her love for Claude, a young, handsome, and rich gentleman who has fallen in love with her and wishes to marry her. Although she finally agrees, the novel ends with her internal battle against her love for him: "C'est fini, murmura Monique; je lui appartiens désormais. Une femme comme les autres" (202). [It's finished, murmured Monique; from now on I belong to him. A wife/woman like the others.] The last line of this same novel is "L'argent, la honte, la colère renaissaient en elle, et la préparaient à de nouveaux combats." [Money, shame, and anger were ignited within her, and prepared her for new battles.]

77. Charles Baudelaire, last stanza of "Les phares," *Les Fleurs du Mal,* 48, trans. McGowan, "The Beacons," *The Flowers of Evil,* 25. This poem is about painters and mentions Rubens, Leonardo da Vinci, Rembrandt, Michelangelo, Puget, Watteau, Goya, and Delacroix.

78. This same quotation appears later in Beauvoir's philosophical essay *Pyrrhus et Cinéas,* 25.

79. Verlaine, "La bonne chanson X," 148; my translation.

80. This is the beginning of the second stanza of Verlaine's poem "Langueur" [Apathy], 371. I have provided the closest literal translation found: MacIntyre, "Apathy," *French Symbolist Poetry,* 33. Norman R. Shapiro's translation reads, "A dense ennui sickens my soul, my sense"; see "Languor," *One Hundred and One Poems by Paul Verlaine,* 134.

81. Verlaine, "Kaléidoscope," 321; my translation.

82. La Grillère was a country residence with a large mansion and gardens, near Uzerche in the province of Limousin, where Beauvoir would spend parts of her summers with her aunt Hélène, her uncle Maurice, and her cousins Robert and Madeleine, who lived there year round. It was at La Grillère that Beauvoir developed much of her affinity with nature. See *Mémoires* 35–36; *Memoirs* 23–25.

83. Jean Cocteau's published essay was first a lecture entitled "D'un ordre considéré comme une anarchie," which was also an homage to his lover, Raymond Radiguet. See notes 19 and 35.

84. This quotation comes from Cocteau, "Tentative d'évasion" [Attempt to Escape], 59; my translation. Cocteau may have meant "man" (*homme*) in the universal sense of "human being," but I have chosen to reproduce the ambiguity of his wording.

85. This quotation is a repeated refrain in an untitled poem in Cocteau, *Le Potomak,* 110–12; my translation.

86. This quotation is a line from stanza 8 of Cocteau, "L'adieu aux fusiliers marins" [Farewell to the Marine Riflemen], 450; my translation.

87. These two lines seem to be Beauvoir's paraphrase of parts of Cocteau, *Le Potomak,* 152. The words she quotes are from Cocteau, *La Potomak,* 153.

88. This might be Beauvoir's own attempt at poetry. I have been unable to attribute it to any other author.

89. This too might be Beauvoir's own attempt at poetry. I have been unable to attribute it to any other author.

90. "What I like about you, Nathanaël, is what is different from me" is a quotation from Gide's *Les nourritures terrestres,* 248; my translation.

91. Conrad, *Heart of Darkness,* 2036. I have given the quotation as in the original English text, although Beauvoir quoted it in French. It is uncertain if the translation was her own or

from some unnamed edition. Her quotation rendered "its truth, its meaning" as simply "la réalité."

92. In *Mémoires*, Beauvoir attributes this advice to Jacques (281). This passage does not appear in the currently published English translation. Whenever Beauvoir mentions an unnamed "he" or "his" or "him" in the 1926 and 1927 entries of her diary, she most probably refers to Jacques Champigneulles, her slightly older cousin, who became her intellectual mentor during her adolescence and her first childhood sweetheart. Up until 1930, she still hoped to marry him.

93. Barrès's "free man" is the title of one of Barrès's books, *Un homme libre*, and concerns a man who has no prejudice, lives with intensity, and nourishes his soul with noble and precious emotions. Jacques Rivière discusses Barrès at length in his letter of September 26, 1905, to Henri Fournier, in Rivière and Fournier, *Correspondance*, vol. 1.

94. It is probable that the lecture referred to is the one by Garric that caused her to feel that everything in her life should be for a purpose and that she must serve others. See also *Mémoires* 250–51; *Mémoirs* 180–81.

95. As stated in my introductory essay, in 1925 Beauvoir's mother, believing that philosophy corrupted the soul, refused to allow her to study it. Instead, Beauvoir studied mathematics at the Institut Catholique in Paris. During the same time period, Beauvoir also pursued a *certificat* (a document certifying completion of a course of study for specialization) in classics at the Institut Sainte-Marie in Neuilly. In Beauvoir's time a *licence* (an undergraduate diploma) would normally require the completion of four *certificats*. Moi, *Simone de Beauvoir*, 50. At the Institut Sainte-Marie she met Mademoiselle Mercier, who encouraged her to return to her love of philosophy, and Robert Garric, whose lectures she continued to attend even after completing her certificate, and who motivated her to get involved with the Équipes Sociales. Mademoiselle Mercier (Mademoiselle Lambert in Beauvoir's *Mémoires*) is Jeanne Mercier (1896–1991), holder of the university *agrégation*, and a member of the Communauté Saint-François Xavier, founded in 1913 by Madeleine Daniélou, a philosophy teacher at the Institut Sainte-Marie in Neuilly. See Léna, "Jeanne Mercier, lectrice de Maurice Blondel." In 1926 Beauvoir was thus very familiar with the libraries and teachers at these schools and often returned for visits. *Mémoires* 233–34, 272–73, 282–83; *Mémoirs* 168–69, 197, 204.

96. St. Geneviève is a library in Paris. For *Aimée*, see note 2.

97. The French for "all these people *are* not truly, simply phenomena" is "tous ces gens ne *sont* pas vraiment, simplement des phénomènes." This might be interpreted to mean that all these people do not truly exist; they are simply phenomena. But I have chosen to reproduce the ambiguity of Beauvoir's phrasing.

98. The encouragement to read between the lines is seemingly also the message in Cocteau, "Tentative d'évasion," 46–68.

99. This line is from Cocteau, "Tentative d'évasion," 59; my translation. See note 84.

100. This is the beginning of stanza 2 of Verlaine's poem "Langueur," 371, trans. MacIntyre, "Apathy," 33. See note 80.

101. See Bergson's *Time and Free Will*, chapter 1, "Aesthetic Feelings," on rhythm in art and on the writer's trying to "enable us to experience what he cannot make us understand" (*TFW* 18, *Essai*, 13).

102. Approximation of quotation in act 3 of Jean Sarment, *Le mariage d'Hamlet*, wherein Hamlet learns that he is not noble but rather the bastard son of the stableman (20). The

original quotation reads: "Mais j'ai moi-même une telle pitié de moi-même que celle des autres ne m'atteint plus." [But I have such pity for myself that the pity of others no longer reaches me]; my translation.

103. Rivière, *Aimée*, 23; my translation. See also note 2.

104. This notion of taking oneself back seems to be a continuation of thoughts found in the entry of August 21, where Beauvoir writes that "one must accomplish the marvel of giving yet reserving oneself."

105. This is an approximation of the end of stanza 2 of Jammes, "Elégie huitième," 76. The original quotation reads, "Je pense à ton amour qui veille sur mon âme comme un souffle de pauvre à quelque pauvre flamme." [I think of your love which watches over my soul like a poor person's breath on some poor flame]; my translation.

106. Claudel, "Saint Louis," 659; my translation.

107. Gide, *Les nourritures terrestres*, 7, trans. Bussy, *Fruits of the Earth*, 13.

108. Gide, *Nourritures terrestres*, 156; my translation. For a less literal translation, see Bussy's translation in *Fruits of the Earth*, 19.

109. Gide, *Nourritures terrestres*, 156–57, trans. Bussy, *Fruits of the Earth*, 21.

110. Gide, *Nourritures terrestres*, 158, trans. Bussy, *Fruits of the Earth*, 22.

111. Gide, *Nourritures terrestres*, 167–68, trans. Bussy, *Fruits of the Earth*, 37–38.

112. Gide, *Nourritures terrestres*, 172, trans. Bussy, *Fruits of the Earth*, 42.

113. I have translated the French word *ennui* as "boredom," unless otherwise indicated in this diary.

114. Beauvoir gives "Closed homes, shut doors" as a quotation from Gide in *Mémoires*, 268; *Memoirs*, 194.

115. For St. Geneviève see note 96. Neuilly is where she goes to class at L'Institut de Sainte Marie.

116. Lines from Jammes, "J'ai vu revenir les choses . . . ," 310; my translation.

117. Lines from Jammes, "Prière pour que les autres aient le bonheur," 1:317, trans. Alwyn, "Prayer for the Happiness of Others," 7.

118. Lines from Jammes, "Prière pour demander une étoile," 1:318, trans. Alwyn, "Prayer for the Gift of a Star," 8.

119. Lines from Jammes, "Prière pour louer Dieu," 1:326–27, trans. Alwyn, "Prayer in Praise of God," 15. I have modified the translation to make it correspond more closely to Beauvoir's quotation in French.

120. "A poignant existence" is a quotation from Gide. See note 108.

121. "My great childhood friendship" most likely refers to Beauvoir's relationship with Elisabeth Lacoin (Zaza, or Elisabeth Mabille in Beauvoir's *Mémoires*), Beauvoir's first real school friend, who was her most beloved female friend from the time Zaza was eleven until her death in 1929. To understand Zaza's friendship with Beauvoir, see Lacoin, *Zaza*. One might also take Jacques to be the friend in question, given the nature of this paragraph in Beauvoir's diary, but there is little in her autobiographical presentation of Jacques to support this view, whereas her depiction of Zaza remains lyrical for many pages. See *Mémoires*, 125–31, 274–82; *Mémoirs*, 91–96, 198–204.

122. Maurras, *La musique intérieure*. See notes 56 and 57.

123. Jules Verne (1828–1905), the French author of plays, science fiction, comic operas, short stories, and novels, is best known for his novels concerning future inventions and

contemporary history. Louis Schmitt was the editor of *Contes choisis: Les frères Grimm* [Selected Fairytales: The Brothers Grimm].

124. For *Aimée,* see note 2. André Gide wrote *L'immoraliste* [The Immoralist]; see note 128. Francis Jammes was the author of *De l'angélus de l'aube à l'angélus du soir* [From the Angelus at Dawn to the Angelus at Night].

125. There is a play on words that is lost in English. The French verb for "to like" or "to love" is *aimer.* Jacques thus says, "It is chic d'aimer Aimée." H. is probably Hélène, Simone de Beauvoir's younger sister.

126. Mallarme, "Apparition," 74. "Une dentelle s'abolit" [A piece of lace is destroyed] are the first words of an untitled poem in Mallarmé, *Oeuvres complètes,* 74.

127. The French reads "Après-midi aux courses," which could also be translated as "Afternoon at the races." Without more of a context, the translation "Afternoon doing errands" seems more likely.

128. Marcel Arland wrote *Étienne.* André Gide's *L'immoraliste,* often considered to be autobiographical, examines the tormented conscience of Michel, who, having discovered a fierce need for absolute freedom from his wife, Marceline, has affairs with Arab boys, becomes fascinated with poverty and squalor, and alternates between wishing to escape from his wife and loving her more than ever, although chastely, as her illness brings her closer to death.

129. "My dear" translates the French term *mon petit,* which literally means "my little one," and whose gender is masculine, although it is used as a term of endearment for both males and females.

130. Samuel Butler's *Erewhon, or, Over the Range,* a novel translated from the original English by Valéry Larbaud, is a satire of religious and moral traditions endured by its author but placed in an imaginary society. The word "erewhon" is an anagram for "nowhere." Bastia is the pseudonym for the French playwright Jean Simoni, who wrote numerous vaudeville pieces in the early 1900s. *Monique* is a novel by Marcel Arland; see notes 45, 75, and 76.

131. *Orphée* was written by Jean Cocteau.

132. Mallarmé, "Apparition"; I have provided a literal translation. A more poetic translation is offered by Ludwig Lewisohn: "My thought in its strange, self-tormenting way / Felt all the subtle melancholy sting / Which, even without regret, the gathering/ Of any dream leaves in the dreamer's heart" (73).

133. This quotation is from chapter 6 of Barrès, *Sous l'oeil des barbares,* in *Romans et voyages,* 76. But either Beauvoir read another edition or she misremembered the quotation. The edition reads, "J'avais hâte de cette nuit, ô mon bien aimé, ô moi, pour redevenir un dieu." [I couldn't wait for tonight, O my beloved, O self, to become a god again]; my translation.

134. Barrès's theory concerning the barbarians states that we want to do certain things only because others in society give them value; see *Sous l'oeil des barbares.*

135. These quoted words are from chapter 7 of Barrès, *Sous l'oeil des barbares,* 84; my translation.

136. For Miomandre, see note 51. Georges Duhamel (1884–1966), poet, novelist, essayist, and playwright, wrote *La Possession du monde,* which won the 1919 Prix Goncourt and develops the theme of a modern humanism denouncing the excesses of a mechanical civilization.

137. For *Aimée*, see note 2. Alain-Fournier's *Le grand Meaulnes* is the story of Meaulnes, the heroic adolescent adventurer who falls in love at first sight with Yvonne de Galais, eventually marries her, gets her pregnant, and then decides that he must leave her in search of a greater good, that of reuniting a former love with her beloved. As in Beauvoir's diary, recurring themes of this novel are that love involves suffering, that some men are adventurers, and that if a man truly loves a woman she might believe that it is her duty to make his happiness, but she will ultimately learn that she is nothing more than a "poor woman like the others" (*Le grand Meaulnes*, 283); my translation.

138. On Rivière, see note 2.

139. For *Aimée*, see note 2.

140. "Does that concern you" is another reference to Cocteau. See Beauvoir's August 21, 1926, entry. See also note 73.

141. This phrase is an approximation of a quotation from Fausta in Claudel, "Cantique du coeur dur" [Song of the Hardhearted], 363; my translation.

142. The original French for this and the previous lines reads, "Je saisissais avec une telle force le lien qui rattache mon moi individuel à la communauté humaine; oui, ce 'culte du moi' si désintéressé auquel je ne demande que des satisfactions personnelles, il a vraiment une valeur telle que même au dehors il est une bonne action." "Le culte du moi" is the movement attributed to Maurice Barrès in which the most important thing is to cultivate one's ego and to be true to oneself. In its most extreme form, his doctrine implies that all those who are not the self are barbarians. See also note 18. This concept is commonly translated as "self-worship," "egoism," or "ego cultivation," or simply rendered in French as "le culte du moi."

143. Mr. Strowski (Fortunat Strowski in *Mémoires*, 242; *Memoirs*, 173–74) was a literature professor at the Sorbonne and noted for his work on Montaigne and Pascal. For Zaza, see note 121.

144. The page 31 referred to by Beauvoir corresponds to her diary entry of October 3, 1926.

145. The French sentence, "Mais toujours je fondais mes désespoirs et mes désirs, mes jalousies, mon angoisse amère au retour à sa porte ou en le croisant dans son auto, sur ce fait que sa vie était absolument distincte de moi," could also be accurately translated as follows: "But always, as I returned to his door or came across him in his car, I would dissolve my disappointments, my desires, my jealousies, and my bitter anxiety, on this fact that his life was absolutely distinct from me."

146. Tagore, *Fruit-gathering*, section 26, 110. The original English text is by Tagore. The French version quoted by Beauvoir is Gide's translation.

147. "I would want to vomit, vomit my heart" evokes the line from the poem that she will quote on December 2, 1926, by Vildrac: "I would want to vomit my day."

148. The reference is once again to Cocteau. See entry of August 21, 1926, and note 73.

149. It is clear from the French that Beauvoir is addressing a male, most probably her cousin, Jacques, the only male whom Beauvoir refers to by her use of the informal French "you" ("tu" or "toi") in her 1926–30 diary.

150. This is probably a reference to the "King of Thulé," a song from *Faust*, by Goethe, which was translated into French by Gérard de Nerval (my English translation):

Il était un roi de Thulé [There was a king of Thulé]
A qui son amante fidèle [To whom his faithful lover]

Légua, comme souvenir d'elle, [Bequeathed, in her memory,]
Une coupe d'or ciselé. [A chiseled gold cup.]

C'était un trésor plein de charmes [It was a treasure full of charms]
Où son amour se conservait: [Where her love was kept:]
A chaque fois qu'il y buvait [Every time he drank from it]
Ses yeux se remplissaient de larmes. [His eyes filled with tears.]

Voyant ses derniers jours venir, [Seeing his last days upon him,]
Il divisa son héritage, [He divided his inheritance,]
Mais il excepta du partage [But he left out of the division]
La coupe, son cher souvenir. [The cup, his dear souvenir.]

Il fit à la table royale [To the royal table, he invited]
Asseoir les barons dans sa tour; [The barons to sit in his tower;]
Debout et rangée alentour, [Standing and lined up around them,]
Brillait sa noblesse loyale. [Shone his loyal nobility.]

Sous le balcon grondait la mer. [Under the balcony roared the sea.]
Le vieux roi se lève en silence, [The old king rises in silence,]
Il boit,—frissonne, et sa main lance [He drinks,—he shivers, and his hand tosses]
La coupe d'or au flot amer! [The cup of gold to the bitter waves!]

Il la vit tourner dans l'eau noire, [He saw it turning in the black water,]
La vague en s'ouvrant fit un pli, [The wave, opening, won a prize,]
Le roi pencha son front pâli . . . [The king inclined his pale forehead]
Jamais on ne le vit plus boire. [Never again was he seen to drink.]

151. See note 56 for Laforgue. See note 57 for Montherlant. See note 61 for André Thérive.

152. This line by Goethe is also quoted in Jean Cocteau, *Thomas l'imposteur.* See note 73 and diary entry for August 21, 1926, for the first reference to this quotation.

153. This line is an approximation of one of Fausta's lines in Claudel, "Cantique du coeur dur": "And if you had to give me joy, was it worth the trouble to learn suffering?" (363).

154. This probably refers to a 1925 popular fox-trot song, E. Dumont's "Dolorosa," sung to music by F. L. Benech. Dolorosa is a femme fatale who is mysterious, mocking, more seductive than all others, and who will only cause pain to those who love her. I have provided the words to the first verse below with my English translation of each line.

C'est à Paris, il est minuit, on chante, on rit [It's in Paris, it's midnight, we are singing, we are laughing]
Bouquets de fleurs! Propos charmeurs! Femmes jolies! [Flower bouquets! Winning words! Pretty women!]
Voici Manon [Here is Manon]
Aux cheveux blonds [With blond hair]
Voici Mimi [Here is Mimi]
Qui nous sourit [Who smiles at us]
Mais d'où viens-tu, belle inconnue aux yeux moqueurs, [But where are you from, beautiful stranger with the mocking eyes,]

Ecoute-moi, l'amour est roi, à toi, mon Coeur, [Listen to me, love is king, to you,
   my Heart,]
Laissez-la donc, [So leave her alone,]
S'écrie Manon, [Manon cries out,]
Si vous saviez quel est son nom! [If only you knew her name!]
DOLOROSA
C'est la femme des douleurs . . . [She is the woman of sorrows]
DOLOROSA!
Son baiser porte malheur . . . [Her kiss brings bad luck]
Prends garde à toi, [Look out for yourself,]
Si tu lui donnes ton Coeur, [If you give her your Heart,]
Car ce jour-là, [For on that day,]
Tu maudiras [You will curse]
DOLOROSA

155. Barnabooth is the main character of Valéry Larbaud's novel *A. O. Barnabooth, son journal intime.*

156. See note 16 for Péguy.

157. The whereabouts of Beauvoir's first notebook are currently unknown.

158. See self-analysis of September 28, 1926.

159. Corresponds to parts of the entry for October 3, 1926.

160. Corresponds to October 3, 1926 entry, from "Bérénice" to the end of the entry.

161. Corresponds to entry for October 5, 1926, from the end of the fourth paragraph, when she speaks of her heart, to the end of the paragraph on Barrès.

162. Claudel, "Ode jubilaire," 681; my translation.

163. Beauvoir's references to pages 63 and 64 pertain to earlier, currently undiscovered notebooks of her diary.

164. This is an approximation of a quotation from Cocteau, *Le Potomak,* 153.

165. It is most probable that "Z." stands for Zaza, "G." stands for Garric, and "J." stands for Jacques, as these are the three people having these initials whom Beauvoir has discussed in this diary in relationship to love.

166. This is the first line of the last stanza of Laforgue, "Soir de carnaval" [Night at the Carnaval], 14; my translation. *Le sanglot de la terre* was to be a volume of poems expressing metaphysical anxiety.

167. Four lines from Laforgue, "Spleen des nuits de juillet" [Spleen of July Nights], 18; my translation.

168. Laforgue, "Marche Funèbre," line 1 and refrain, 25, trans. Terry, "Funeral March," 19.

169. Laforgue, "Crépuscule de dimanche d'été" [Twilight on a Summer Sunday], line 3, 40; my translation.

170. Last three lines of Laforgue, "Petite chapelle" [Little Chapel], 45; my translation.

171. Last two lines of Laforgue, "Eclair de gouffre" [A Flash in the Abyss], 53. Beauvoir, not Laforgue, underlined these words; my translation.

172. Stanza 1, last line, of Laforgue, "Curiosités déplacées" [Displaced Curiosities], 24; my translation.

173. Stanza 3, lines 1–2, of Laforgue, "Curiosités déplacées," 24; my translation.

174. Line 56 of Laforgue, "Marche funèbre," 27, trans. Terry, "Funeral March," 23.

175. Entire stanza of Laforgue, "Marche funèbre," 28, trans. Terry, "Funeral March," 23.

176. Stanza 8 of Laforgue, "Rosace en vitrail" [Rosace in Stained Glass], in *Le sanglot de la terre*, 32; my translation.

177. Next to last line of Laforgue, "Rosace en vitrail," in *Le sanglot de la terre*, 33; my translation.

178. Stanza 2, lines 2–4, of Laforgue, "Hypertrophie" [Hypertrophy], in *Le sanglot de la terre*, 39; my translation.

179. Lines 16–23 of Laforgue, "Couchant d'hiver" [Winter Sunset], in *Le sanglot de la terre*, 43; my translation.

180. See note 7 for Tagore.

181. Yvonne de Quièvrecourt was the girl with whom Alain-Fournier fell in love at first sight although she spoke to him only once and married another. His memory of her inspired his fictional character Yvonne de Galais, the heroine, who incarnates the ideal wife, and who marries Augustin Meaulnes, the main character of the Alain-Fournier novel *Le grand Meaulnes* and also resulted in his volume of poems and essays entitled *Miracles* [Miracles].

182. There is an episode in Beauvoir's *Mémoires* that suggests that all Jacques said was that he would get married one day (296; *Memoirs* 214). It is not certain that this is all that really happened, since Beauvoir changed many of the details concerning Jacques as she wrote *Mémoires*. See Klaw, "Simone de Beauvoir, du journal intime."

183. Dumby to Lord Darlington in act 3 of Wilde, *Lady Windermere's Fan*, in *Complete Works of Oscar Wilde*, 417. See note 58 for Wilde.

184. Alphonse de Lamartine (1790–1869), French poet, writer, and statesman, was noted for his lyricism and poetry expressing the inner recesses of the soul.

185. "Will we say that these ethics are illusory since they are not the only ones possible?" appears in the French as "Dira-t-on que cette morale est illusoire, puisqu'elle n'est pas la seule possible?"

186. For Wilde, see note 58. *Intentions* is a collection of Wilde's essays in which he took on the role of a critic who was also an artist. He used dialogue between fictional characters in imaginary settings to present ideas on art and criticism. Wilde thus refuted the more popular notion that writers were either critics or artists, but not both.

187. Chez Lipp is Brasserie Lipp, a combination restaurant-bar in Saint-Germain des Prés, Paris.

188. Jean Delrive is Jacques's friend, known as Lucien Riaucourt in Beauvoir's *Mémoires*.

189. Tsuguharu Foujita (1886–1968) was a Japanese artist first known for painting in the cubist manner and later for mixing Oriental and European styles of painting. He also painted expressionist works and specialized in nudes. He moved to Paris in 1913 and became a French citizen in 1955.

190. This is a reference to Gide's *Les nourritures terrestres*; my translation.

191. Fournier to Rivière, March 21, 1906, in Rivière and Alain-Fournier, *Correspondance*, 1:208. All translations from this work are my own.

192. This same verse is in a poem by Alain-Fournier, Rivière to Fournier, September 20, 1905, in Rivière and Alain-Fournier, *Correspondance*, 1:61.

193. Stanza 2, line 1, of Laforgue, "L'hiver qui vient," 143; my translation. See also Dale, trans., "The Coming Winter," *Last Poems*, in *Poems*, 387.

194. This is an approximation of a quotation from Fournier to Rivière, March 21, 1906, in Rivière and Alain-Fournier, *Correspondance*, 1:208; my translation.

195. For *Barnabooth*, see note 155.

196. See notes 20 and 56 for Verlaine, Laforgue, and Rimbaud.

197. "*Vanina*" may refer to the German silent film *Vanina oder Die Galgenhochzeit* (1922), directed by Arthur von Gerlach. I thank Tom Zaniello for this information.

198. *Rien que les heures* was a 1926 silent film by Alberto Cavalcanti showing a surrealist view of life in Paris during a twenty-four-hour period. It is considered a landmark in the tradition of documentary film.

199. Beauvoir's reference to page 26 pertains to the diary entry of September 26, 1926.

200. In this and the three previous paragraphs, Beauvoir is quoting her entry of September 26, 1926.

201. The French word *dissertation* refers simply to an essay. It might be a final paper for a class or any other essay. I have consistently used "essay" throughout as a translation for the French word *dissertation,* unless otherwise indicated.

202. Liard and Russel are philosophers to be read for her thesis. Louis Liard (1846–1917) was a French author of several texts on various topics including geometry, teaching and ethics, logic, Descartes, and Positivism. By "Russel" perhaps she is referring to Bertrand Russell (1872–1970), philosopher, mathematician, and author of several books on topics such as geometry, Leibniz, mysticism and logic, and pacifism.

203. M. Boulenger is perhaps the friend from Cours Désir called Marguerite Boulanger by Deirdre Bair (*Simone de Beauvoir,* 77).

204. Beauvoir may be referring to *Les penseurs grecs avant Socrate, de Thalès à Prodicos,* edited and translated by Jean Voilquin (Paris: Garnier-Flammarion, 1968).

205. Beauvoir probably refers to Eduard Zeller, *Outlines of the History of Greek Philosophy* (1883); Th. Gomperz, *Les penseurs de la Grèce* [Greek Thinkers] (Paris, 1904–8). Beauvoir may have read one or more of numerous volumes by Edward Caird (1835–1908), author of several books on Kant and Hegel and a two-volume work uniting critical essays on Goethe, Rousseau, Carlyle, Dante, and Wordsworth with a discussion of Cartesianism (Descartes, Malbranche, and Spinoza) and metaphysics. Caird is especially noted for trying to show that the mind will always come back to a center of unity. Victor Brochard was the author of *Études de philosophie ancienne et de philosophie moderne* (Paris: F. Alcan, 1912) and *Les sceptiques grecs* (Paris: J. Vrin, 1887). Maurice Croiset and Alfred Croiset edited and translated many of Plato's texts in *Oeuvres complètes: Platon* (Paris: Les belles lettres, 1920).

206. Wilde, "The Decay of Lying," 54–56. In each quotation from Wilde throughout this translation, I have quoted the English as Beauvoir has quoted the French, although certain phrases or entire sentences are missing in the French without indication that something has been omitted.

207. Wilde, "The Critic as Artist," 187–88.

208. Ibid., 223–24.

209. Wilde, "The Decay of Lying," 18.

210. Wilde, "Pen, Pencil and Poison," 67.

211. Wilde, "The Critic as Artist," 115.

212. Ibid., 132–33.

213. Ibid., 152.

214. Ibid., 165–66.

215. Ibid., 184.

216. *Paludes* and *Le voyage d'Urien* were written by André Gide.

217. See notes 19 and 35 for Cocteau.

218. Wilde, "The Decay of Lying," 3–57.

219. Beauvoir's version differs slightly from the Pléiade version of this quotation, and I have modified Baskin's translation accordingly. The "resistance" refers to the men's resistance to the queen's charms. A beautiful queen has imprisoned twelve men in the hope of receiving their sexual favors, but they refuse to succumb to her charms. See Gide, *Le voyage d'Urien,* 34, trans. Baskin, *Urien's Voyage,* 47.

220. Gide, *Le voyage d'Urien,* 40, trans. Baskin, *Urien's Voyage,* 56. I have modified the translation to make it correspond more closely to the French quoted.

221. Gide, *Le voyage d'Urien,* 63, trans. Baskin, *Urien's Voyage,* 89. I have modified the translation to make it correspond more closely to the French quoted.

222. Although there are slight changes in verb tenses and vocabulary, Beauvoir's quotation approximates the version found in Gide, *Le voyage d'Urien,* 64, trans. Baskin, *Urien's Voyage,* 91. I have modified the translation to make it correspond to Beauvoir's rendition of Gide's text.

223. Fournier to Rivière, March 21, 1906, in Rivière and Alain-Fournier, *Correspondance,* 1:206–8.

224. Ibid., 1:210.

225. Fournier to Rivière, April 3, 1906, in Rivière and Alain-Fournier, *Correspondance,* 1:216.

226. Rivière to Fournier, April 5, 1906, in Rivière and Alain-Fournier, *Correspondance,* 1:223–24.

227. Ibid., 1:222.

228. Ibid., 1:223.

229. Rivière to Fournier, May 4, 1906, in Rivière and Alain-Fournier, *Correspondance,* 1:254.

230. Ibid., 1:256.

231. Rivière to Fournier, May 20, 1906, in Rivière and Alain-Fournier, *Correspondance,* 1:265.

232. This is a reference to Gide's irreplaceable being, which Beauvoir first discusses in her October 6, 1926, entry.

233. Tityre is the main protagonist of Gide's *Paludes;* Nathanaël, of Gide's *Nourritures terrestres.*

234. Another reference to Gide's *Nourritures terrestres.*

235. Paul Cézanne (1839–1906), a French painter, was influential in the development of abstraction in modern painting and was noted for simplifying forms to their basic geometric equivalents. Henri Matisse (1869–1954) was the French leader of the Fauvist movement in painting around 1900. Henri Rousseau (1844–1910), a French painter, was the archetype of the untutored artist and an innovator of Naïve art. Henri de Toulouse-Lautrec (1864–1901), French painter and lithographer, was known for his works depicting the music halls, circuses, brothels, and cabarets of Paris.

236. Librairie Picart was on the boulevard St. Michel (*Mémoires,* 324; *Memoirs,* 234). The first Salon d'Automne was organized in 1903 to exhibit the innovative developments in painting and sculpture eschewed by the more conservative official Paris Salon. After World War I, the artistic works most frequently displayed in the Salon d'Automne included those of the Montparnasse painters Marc Chagall, Amedeo Modigliani, and Georges Braque and the sculptors Constantin Brancusi, Aristide Maillol, Charles Despiau, and Ossip Zadkine. The

glassworks of René Lalique and the architectural designs of Le Corbusier also figured in the exhibitions.

237. Jules Laforgue's *Moralités légendaires* combines realism with the author's personal feelings about the ephemeral nature of life.

238. The exact title is "Pan et la Syrinx," in Laforgue, *Moralités légendaires*.

239. These titles stand for chapters or "contes" in Laforgue's *Moralités légendaires*.

240. Rivière to Fournier, June 4, 1906, in Rivière and Alain-Fournier, *Correspondance* 1:271.

241. Fournier to Rivière, August 15, 1906, Rivière and Alain-Fournier, *Correspondance*, 1:318.

242. Fournier to Rivière, August 22, 1906, in Rivière and Alain-Fournier, *Correspondance*, 1:322.

243. Rivière to Fournier, August 29, 1906, in Rivière and Alain-Fournier, *Correspondance*, 1:329.

244. Rivière to Fournier, October 7, 1906, in Rivière and Alain-Fournier, *Correspondance*, 1:355.

245. Fournier to Rivière, October 13, 1906, in Rivière and Alain-Fournier, *Correspondance*, 1:363.

246. Fournier to Rivière, October 15, 1906, *Correspondance*, 1:367.

247. Rivière to Fournier, December 3, 1906, in Rivière and Alain-Fournier, *Correspondance*, 1:405.

248. The letters by Rivière and Fournier referred to by Beauvoir as if in the second volume are in the first volume of the editions easily accessible today.

249. For Fournier's letter on acceptance and life, see Fournier to Rivière, December 9, 1905, in Rivière and Alain-Fournier, *Correspondance*, 1:121–24. For the opposition between two individuals, see Rivière to Fournier, January 13, 1906, in Rivière and Alain-Fournier, *Correspondance*, 1:130–31. For the tendency to regulate and foresee things, see ibid., 1:131–35.

250. Beauvoir is referring to Rivière to Fournier, February 1906, in Rivière and Alain-Fournier, *Correspondance*, 1:178–81, for the part on Claudel, and 1:185, for Rivière's definition of self: "Je me suis vu—en deux mots—comme un composé de deux êtres radicalement ennemis, l'un rationaliste et idéologue, l'autre mystique et passionné, et de leur conflit j'ai vu sortir toutes mes souffrances, toutes mes délicieuses souffrances." [In two words, I saw myself as a composite of two radically opposed beings, one rationalistic and idealistic, the other mystical and passionate, and I saw all of my suffering resulted from their conflict.]

251. She is probably referring to Fournier to Rivière, April 21, 1906, and Rivière to Fournier, May 4, 1906, in Rivière and Alain-Fournier, *Correspondance*, 1:245–46, and 1:254, respectively.

252. She is probably referring to Rivière to Fournier, May 4, 1906, Rivière and Alain-Fournier, *Correspondance*, 1:255–56.

253. Fournier to Rivière, May 27, 1906, in Rivière and Alain-Fournier, *Correspondance*, 1:267–70.

254. Rivière to Fournier, June 4, 1906, in Rivière and Alain-Fournier, *Correspondance*, 1:271.

255. She is probably referring to Rivière to Fournier, June 10, 1906, in Rivière and Alain-Fournier *Correspondance*, 1:279–80.

256. Rivière to Fournier, July 11, 1906, in Rivière and Alain-Fournier, *Correspondance,* 1:295–97. Rivière says, "Un esprit libre, c'est celui qui sait poser les problèmes sous une forme qui n'implique à l'avance aucune solution." [A free thinker is one who knows how to formulate problems in a way that does not imply any solution in advance.] Ibid., 1:295.

257. Fournier to Rivière, August 15 and 22, 1906, in Rivière and Alain-Fournier, *Correspondance,* 1:317–23.

258. Rivière to Fournier, August 28, 1906, in Rivière and Alain-Fournier, *Correspondance,* 1:327–29.

259. Rivière to Fournier, September 16–20, 1906, in Rivière and Alain-Fournier, *Correspondance,* 1:342–52.

260. Rivière to Fournier, December 6, 1906, in Rivière and Alain-Fournier, *Correspondance,* 1:409.

261. Beauvoir's quotations differ slightly from the original verses by Jules Laforgue: "Nobles et touchantes divagations sous la lune," *L'imitation de Notre-Dame La Lune,* in *Oeuvres complètes,* 1:268, and my translation reflects this. For a less literal translation of Laforgue's verses, see also Dale, trans., "Noble and Touching Digressions under the Moon," *The Imitation of Our Lady the Moon,* in *Poems,* 250–55.

262. Next to last line of last stanza of Laforgue, "Avis, je vous prie," *L'imitation de Notre-Dame La Lune,* in *Oeuvres complètes,* 1:275; my translation. See also Dale, trans., "Advise, I beg you," *The Imitation of Our Lady the Moon,* in *Poems,* 260–61.

263. Stanza 2, lines 1–2, Laforgue, "L'hiver qui vient," *Oeuvres complètes,* 2:143; my translation. See also Dale, trans., "The Coming Winter," *Last Poems,* in *Poems,* 387.

264. Line from stanza 3, Laforgue, "Dimanches III," *Oeuvres complètes,* 2:151; my translation. See also Dale, trans., "Sundays III," *Last Poems,* in *Poems,* 396–99.

265. Line from stanza 7, Laforgue, "Dimanches III," *Oeuvres complètes,* 2:151; my translation. See also Dale, trans., "Sundays III," *Last Poems,* in *Poems,* 399.

266. Line from stanza 5, Laforgue, "Solo de lune," *Oeuvres complètes,* 2:168; my translation. See also Dale, trans., "Moon Solo," *Last Poems,* in *Poems,* 415.

267. Stanza 8, line 1, Laforgue, "Solo de lune," *Oeuvres complètes,* 2:169; my translation. See also Dale, trans., "Moon Solo," *Last Poems,* in *Poems,* 417.

268. Lines from stanzas 3 and 9, Laforgue, "Solo de lune," *Oeuvres complètes,* 2:168; my translation. See also Dale, trans., "Moon Solo," *Last Poems,* in *Poems,* 415.

269. Lines from stanzas 11 and 12, Laforgue "Solo de lune," *Oeuvres complètes,* 2:170; my translation. See also Dale, trans., "Moon Solo," *Last Poems,* in *Poems,* 419.

270. "You ask me why you and not another," a line by Laforgue, is repeated throughout Beauvoir's diary. All of the verses, starting with the translation of the French verse, "Oh! If only one by Herself" [Ah! qu'une d'Elle-même] and extending through "emptiness in my heart," are from untitled poem 9 in Laforgue, *Oeuvres complètes,* 2:178; my translation. See also Dale, trans., untitled poem 9, *Last Poems,* in *Poems,* 427. The ellipses are repeated from Laforgue's original French.

271. The original French reads as follows: "Aux autres je ne demande qu'une chose: qu'ils se rendent compte de leur vie, qu'ils la dominent, même quand ils acceptent de la subir par le seul fait qu'ils savent qu'ils la subissent." This stresses that each individual has a unique life, by keeping "life" in the singular, which is standard usage for French. In English, such usage would not be grammatically acceptable. Beauvoir's thought here seemingly refers to her November 3 quotation of Rivière, "To accept all things is not to decide not to suffer from

them any longer. No, it is to want to love them even when they tear you apart because they have the holy privilege of existence." See note 229.

272. This quotation repeats the words of Fournier to Rivière, October 13, 1906. See note 245.

273. I read *punir* [to punish], whereas Sylvie Le Bon de Beauvoir finds this word in Beauvoir's manuscript illegible.

274. Laforgue, "Solo de lune," *Oeuvres complètes*, 2:168. See also Dale, trans., "Moon Solo," *Last Poems*, in *Poems*, 415.

275. Beauvoir is referring to the verses of "Ah! qu'une d'Elle-même . . ." by Jules Laforgue, which she quoted earlier, in which "Elle" tells her lover that he is the only thing of meaning in her life.

276. The initials H. and Z. most likely stand for Simone de Beauvoir's sister, Henriette-Hélène Bertrande de Beauvoir, whom she most often called Poupette or Hélène, and her best friend, Zaza, respectively.

277. This is most likely Marie-Louise Llévesque, one of Beauvoir's friends from Cours Désir, to whom she also refers in her diary entry of November 30, 1926. See Bair, *Simone de Beauvoir*, 77.

278. She refers to a verse from Baudelaire, "Moesta et Errabunda," 80, trans. McGowan, "Moesta et errabunda," 129.

279. For Jules Verne, see note 123.

280. "Mundane," "common," and "banal" are three context-specific translations in this sentence for the French word *vulgaire(s)*.

281. Sarment, *Le pêcheur d'ombres*, 264. This refers to the passage in which Mama speaks to René about her son, who is waiting for his books to be successful. All translations provided for this work are my own. See Keene and Foulke, trans., *Rude Awakening*, for the entire play in English translation.

282. Sarment, *Le Pêcheur d'ombres*, 264, in a passage in which Mama is discussing her life with René.

283. Ibid., 322.

284. Ibid., 326.

285. Rimbaud, "Fleurs," trans. Varèse, "Flowers," 85.

286. Rimbaud, "Mystique," trans. Varèse, "Mystic," 79.

287. Rimbaud "Aube," trans. Varèse, "Dawn," 81, 83, translation modified. In Beauvoir's transcription of the poem, the word "blond" is left out after "wasserfall," so I have also omitted this adjective from Varèse's translation.

288. Camille Pissarro (1830–1903) was a French impressionist painter who, with Georges Seurat and Paul Signac, eventually developed techniques regarded as neo-impressionist, using the claims of science to support a new style of painting light and color. A fervent anarchist, Pissarro attacked French bourgeois society in his album of anarchist drawings.

289. Leon Bakst (1866–1924) was a Russian artist influential in founding the Ballets Russes, where he became the artistic director. He was most noted for his stage designs. The Ballets Russes toured outside Russia from 1909 to 1929. The composer Igor Stravinsky, the artists Pablo Picasso and Henri Matisse, and the poet Jean Cocteau all participated in productions of the Russian ballet, which, breaking away from classical technique, were often considered erotic and even scandalous. Occasionally the performances caused riots in Paris.

290. André Dunoyer de Segonzac (1884–1974), a French painter, reacted somewhat against cubism and abstraction. He claimed a preference for classicism, landscapes, and the human form.

291. Marcel Gromaire (1892–1971) was a French expressionist artist who made his reputation with a painting entitled *La guerre* (1925).

292. Kees Van Dongen (1877–1968) was a Dutch Fauvist painter.

293. Georges-Olivier Desvallières (Paris 1861–1950) was a French painter with a liking for jewel-like colors, biblical history, Greek mythology, and the Italian masters of the fifteenth century.

294. Charles Guérin (1875–1939), a French impressionist painter, was noted for his unusual and unique use of color, his paintings of nude and vampish women, and his illustration of several works by Colette. In 1923 he was one of the founders of the Salon des Tuileries in Paris.

295. Hamlet, Jean, and Tiburce are all characters in the plays of Sarment.

296. The feast day of St. Martin's, which is celebrated on the eleventh day of the eleventh month of the year, honors one of the patron saints of France as well as his namesakes. It used to mark the end of the agrarian year and the beginning of harvesting.

297. Rembrandt (1606–69), the Dutch painter and portraitist, was noted for exploring the interplay between light and shadows. Anthony Van Dyck (1599–1641) was a Flemish Baroque painter specializing in portraits and noted for his brilliant use of color. The Dutch painter Franz Hals (1580–1666) was admired for his use of light and the freedom of his brushwork. *La bohémienne*, one of his most well known portraits, hangs in the Louvre. Jacob van Ruysdael (1628–82), a Dutch painter, etcher, and highly celebrated portrayer of landscapes, emphasized the darkness and splendor of nature and the insignificance of humankind within it. Jean-Auguste-Dominique Ingres (1780–1867), a French painter inspired in part by Raphael, was known for his linear, graceful portraits and for compositions revealing his unusual sensitivity. Eugène Delacroix (1798–1863) was a French painter influential in founding the Romantic school of painting and noted for preferring color and movement to line and static detail. Edouard Manet's painting *Olympia* (1865) caused an uproar because he chose to paint a real nude woman of his time (a courtesan) instead of modeling his figure on historical, mythical, or biblical prototypes. *Portait of Zola* is also by Manet (1832–83), who was scorned by the public at large and who was staunchly supported by Zola. As a sign of thanks, Manet painted him surrounded by accessories attesting to the controversy, including a reproduction of the *Olympia*. James Abbott McNeill Whistler (1834–1903), the American painter and etcher, was largely inspired by the realism of Corot and known for his delicate sense of color and design. Jan Vermeer van Delft (1632–75) was a Dutch genre painter known for his sensitivity in creating effects of light and color. Jean-François Millet (1814–75), a French painter of melancholy scenes of peasant labor, was considered a social realist. "Meissonnier" may refer to Juste-Aurèle Meissonnier (1695–1750), a French architect, designer, and occasional painter known for his Rococo style. Henri Rousseau (1844–1910), a self-taught French primitive painter, produced paintings that were consistently naïve and imaginative. Jean-Baptiste-Camille Corot (1796–1875) was a highly influential and widely copied French landscape painter especially gifted in celebrating the countryside and in delicately handling light.

298. Constant Troyon (1810–65), a French painter of the Barbizon school, was renowned for his portrayal of animals, especially cows, in landscapes.

299. The quotation Beauvoir gives is an approximation of a phrase from Claudel, "Sainte Thérèse," 625.

300. Oscar Wilde was the author of *The Picture of Dorian Gray.*

301. Jules Romains (Louis Farigoule) (1885–1972), a French writer and student of philosophy, became known as the chief exponent of unanimism, a literary theory positing a collective spirit or personality. This theory pervades his work *La vie unanime.*

302. These experiences were reworked in Beauvoir's fiction, for example, in the character Lisa in *Quand prime le spirituel,* 107–29.

303. An alternate interpretation of the word *vulgarité* would be "coarseness." Often used in literary circles and literature, *vulgarité* also means "mundaneness" or "ordinariness."

304. The phrases are from Gide, *Nourritures terrestres.*

305. For La Grillère, see note 82. *L'Illustration* is a French magazine with pictures that were often used to decorate the walls in the room that Beauvoir shared with her sister at La Grillère, the estate in southwest France where they visited their aunt, uncle, and cousins. See *Mémoires,* 104–8; *Memoirs,* 76–80.

306. Henry Bordeaux was a novelist.

307. Larbaud, *Fermina Marquez,* 397, trans. Hubert Gibbs, 56 (beginning of chapter 13).

308. *L'Esprit* was a French journal (1926–27) of the "Philosophies" group, consisting of Pierre Morhange, Paul-Yves Nizan, Georges Friedmann, Georges Politzer, Henri Lefebvre, and Norbert Guterman, who believed in rethinking Marxism and in linking the individual and the universal by the promotion of the idea that self-definition is based on one's actions in the world. The thoughts of Blaise Pascal, Benedict Spinoza, Friedrich Nietszche, and, above all, F. W. von Schelling and G. F. Hegel heavily influenced the group. Opponents of this group included Henri Bergson, Emmanuel Mounier, Louis Aragon, André Breton, Gabriel Marcel, André Gide, Hendrik de Man, and Victor Serge (Thorpe, review of *French Marxism between the Wars,* 1–3). See also Beauvoir, *Mémoires,* 326–27; *Memoirs,* 236–37.

309. Seneca, *Letters to Lucilius III,* sentence 3; I am indebted to Tamara O'Callaghan for this reference and its translation.

310. Tacitus, *Agricola,* 30.5; I thank Tamara O'Callaghan for this reference and its translation.

311. This idea of "absolute reciprocity and the identity of consciousness" comes from Hegel's notion of freedom, stating that for the conscious subject, to be free is to free the other. See Hegel, *Philosophie de l'esprit,* 431, 532.

312. The German philosopher Immanuel Kant (1724–1804) maintained that things beyond the realm of possible experience are noumena (things-in-themselves, such as God, freedom, and immortality) and are unknowable, although we presuppose their existence. Phenomena (objects of experience) can be perceived in sensibility, space, and time, but they can be understood only if they possess characteristics of causality and substance-structures of phenomenal experience. Maine de Biran (1766–1824) was a French philosopher who stressed the importance of inner consciousness of the self and who found the basis of morality in the consciousness of volitional activity.

313. Sophie Rostopchine, Countess of Ségur (1799–1874), was a French author known for writing children's stories with flat characters and conflicts between irrational impulses and goodness and good sense. Some psychoanalytic criticism of her works have recently viewed them as portraying sadomasochism in society. According to Beauvoir's autobiograhy, Mme

de Ségur's stories influenced her to view the body and sexuality as something dirty and shocking as a child. See Beauvoir, *Mémoires*, 113; *Memoirs*, 82.

314. Baudelaire, "Le Masque," *Les Fleurs du mal*, trans. McGowan, "The Mask," *Flowers of Evil*, 43.

315. This is the first verse of Baudelaire's "(LXXVI) Spleen," trans. Clark, 74. For a less literal translation, see McGowan, trans., *Flowers of Evil*, 147.

316. The verse with blanks normally reads, "Et l'animer encore d'une voix argentine" [and bring it alive once more with a silvery voice], but Beauvoir must have forgotten the "animer." "Moestra et Errabunda," trans. Clark, *Selected Poems*, 71–72. See also McGowan, trans., "The Mask," 131, for a less literal and more poetic English translation.

317. Baruch Spinoza (1632–77), the Dutch philosopher, believed in deduction, rationalism, and monism. He reworked Descartes to argue that mind and body are different parts of the same whole, which he referred to either as God or Nature. Spinoza also viewed "adequate ideas" as coherent and logical associations of physical experiences. Confused and contradictory experiences are improperly related to the totality of experience.

318. Cauterets is where Beauvoir spent her vacation, very unhappily, with her family in the Pyrenees, as noted in *Mémoires*. See note 71.

319. These are all poems from Baudelaire, *Les fleurs du mal*. The last two quotations are of the first lines of Baudelaire's poems "Causerie" [Conversation] and "Hymne" [Hymn], respectively.

320. Jules Lemaître (1853–1914), a French academic, poet, playwright, and essayist, was best known as an "impressionist" critic whose pieces were marked by a great breadth of knowledge and by irony. He was also known as a political pamphleteer of the Right.

321. Approximation of lines from Alain-Fournier, "A travers les étés," *Miracles*, 99; my translation.

322. Beauvoir again refers to her sister, Henriette-Hélène Bertrand de Beauvoir.

323. This line immediately evokes Baudelaire's poem "Invitation au voyage" [Invitation to the Voyage], cited earlier as part of *Les fleurs du mal*. It contains the same line, "Vivre ensemble" (To live together), that McGowan more freely translates according to its implication as "To live there as lovers do!" See McGowan, trans., *Flowers of Evil*, 109.

324. Sylvie Le Bon de Beauvoir deciphered *félicité* [felicity] where I deciphered *lucidité* (lucidity), but neither of us was certain of this word.

325. Charles Vildrac (1882–1971) was a French poet whose poetry opposed the decadent excesses of symbolism. His verse optimistically praises simple things such as friendship. *Livre d'amour*, which appeared for the first time in 1910, is considered by some to be Vildrac's masterpiece. The lines Beauvoir quotes are from Vildrac, "Commentaire," *Livre d'amour*, 14–17, trans. Bynner, "Commentary," *A Book of Love*, 5–7. I have modified all of Bynner's translations of the poems in Vildrac's *Livre d'amour* to make them correspond more closely to the French.

326. Verses from Vildrac, "Sans Espoir de Rien," *Livres d'amour*, 21, trans. Bynner, "Happy-go-lucky," *A Book of Love*, 15; translation modified.

327. Verses from Vildrac, "Tristesse," *Livre d'amour*, 42–43, trans. Bynner, "Dejection," *A Book of Love*, 37–38; translation modified.

328. Verses from Vildrac, "Gloire," *Livre d'amour*, 64, trans. Bynner, "Glory," *A Book of Love*, 59; translation modified.

329. Verses from Vildrac, "Avec moi-même," *Livre d'Amour*, 81–82, trans. Bynner, "By Myself," *A Book of Love*, 79–80; translation modified.

330. Drieu de la Rochelle, "A Vous Allemands" [To You Germans], 45; my translation. Pierre Drieu de la Rochelle (1893–1945) was a French writer heavily influenced by Nietzsche and very fond of the works of Shakespeare, Goethe, Schopenhauer, Dostoïevsky, Proudhon, Sorel, Barrès, Kipling, Péguy, Guénon, and Maurras. He is noted for his decadent thoughts and his pessimistic descriptions of the world as well as his far-right-wing beliefs, his fascism, and his eventual collaboration with Vichy.

331. Two of the titles of these poems are slightly different than Beauvoir remembers. They are called "Une amitié" and "Gloire," as their translations reflect. These title translations come from Vildrac, *A Book of Love*, trans. Bynner.

332. Pierre Morhange was editor of *L'Esprit* in 1926. See note 308.

333. *Les feuilles libres*, *Nouvelle revue*, and *Cahiers du mois* are all literary journals. André Gide's novel *Si le grain ne meurt* offers a complex and seemingly sincere autobiographical portrait of his life.

334. Beauvoir is referring to the last quotation in this 1926 diary, by Drieu de la Rochelle, from his first collection of poems, entitled *Interrogation*.

335. Stanislas is a school in Paris founded in the early nineteenth century that offers a curriculum ranging from middle school through college preparatory classes. See also *Mémoires*, 169–70; *Memoirs*, 121–22.

336. This is a line from the end of chapter 4 of Barrès's *Le jardin de Bérénice*, 308; my translation. This same line is also quoted in Rivière to Fournier, September 7, 1905, in Rivière and Fournier, *Correspondance*, 1:128.

Fourth Notebook

April 17–October 21, 1927

Who doesn't know whether courage is needed to love
as soon as one thinks.
    (Alain)[1]

Calm, calm, stay calm.
Experience the weight of a palm leaf
Supporting its abundance.
    (Valéry)[2]

We blow out a soap-bubble as long and as large as possible,
although with the perfect certainty that it will burst.
    (Schopenhauer)[3]

My only support is absolute despair.
    (Lagneau)[4]

"Fourth Notebook" appears at the top of this notebook in Beauvoir's handwriting. The third notebook for this diary is apparently lost.

The metaphysician is a mystic who restrains himself. It is perhaps not normal to philosophize.

Bergson[5]*

If the beings of a higher level do not raise themselves above the conservation of life in the struggle for existence, if they do nothing more than attain the same goal in an infinitely less simple way than those at a lower level, is this not a step backward rather than progress? The passionate thrust towards life and the complete emptiness of painfully conquered life constitute the most violent contradiction.

Eucken[6]

April 17

The years gone by can be held in the hollow of my hand. Will even one very light cinder remain of the one who I am today? Easter Sunday 1927! The vague memory of past holidays does not move me. Deep down, I barely like my childhood. Rarely do I glance behind the partition that brusquely appeared at the beginning of 1926 to split my life in two. It does not seem to me that any link attaches me to the little girl whom I was; although sometimes I am amused to find in her some of the traits of my face of today, more often I tell myself that from her, entirely other, was born my identical self at nineteen.

One of the wonders of the prime of youth is every year to feel richer and traveling towards this ideal type that sketches itself in the disclosure of time. Now, one must no longer talk of "getting bigger" but rather of getting older.

I would like to write a novel about a young girl who is so scared by her future forty-year-old face that she uses up all her energy in refusing to live. But of everything that I imagine, I know that nothing, alas, will cross the threshold of my brain, and yet I would have many things to say . . .†

I would like to rediscover a little bit of the interest that I used to have for myself. For two months, I think, I have cast off my presence with disgust. Hello! You can come back now. My desire for you is reborn.

---

* In the manuscript Beauvoir originally wrote "philosopher" instead of "mystic." It is crossed out with "mystic" written above it.

† This paragraph is highlighted with a vertical line in the margin of the manuscript. Throughout these footnotes, the term "highlighted" means that Beauvoir drew horizontal or vertical lines near passages in her diary for emphasis.

* * *

If our soul has trembled with happiness and sounded like a harp string just once, all eternity was needed to produce this one event—and in this single moment of affirmation all eternity was called good, redeemed, justified, and affirmed.

Nietzsche (*Volonté de puissance* [The Will to Power])[7]

All metaphysics is in the first person singular. All poetry too. The second person is still the first.

Louis Aragon[8]

Anything is better than false love, than desire mistaken for passion, than passion mistaken for acceptance. Anything is better than slowly to take up the old relationships, than to have a heart, little by little, turn away and become a stranger to you.

Claudel[9]

April 18—Easter Monday

Ah! I don't know if there is anything sadder than these too beautiful spring evenings. Last night, stretched out on my bed, I staved off my boredom with Mallarmé and Barrès. "L'après-midi d'un faune" transported me to the land of true beauty, the only one, with the land of love where the soul can find peace, and in Philippe's collapse, I rediscovered a little bit of pride for living.[10] Maybe in a little while I'll go find them again. Things cannot go on this way! What? Working without enjoyment, losing oneself at night in a heavy sleep, wandering without passion in streets that are even lonelier because they are so joyous in the sun, and finally, escaping from myself at the theater or the cinema! Keeping up a whirl of activity in order to stand life, whereas I could be living ardently, passionately!*

To Zaza, I wrote hopeful words: it's true, I know that happiness will come and that it will bring me peace. I agreed to live and said that I will know how to grow older. But how much more time? Nearly two years . . . Ah! Even suffering would be better than this indifference into which I have thrown myself.† My ardent love has been asleep for too long; I think about Jacques only to observe sadly what I will call his spiritual absence. Did the past

---

* The last few lines of this paragraph are highlighted with a vertical line in the margin of the manuscript.

† The passage from approximately, "Ah! Even suffering . . ." through "to forgive him," at the end of the next paragraph, is highlighted with a vertical line in the margin.

happen, or was all of that only a dream? My appeals to him, "our leisurely chats," this mystical union of our souls . . . do they no longer exist?

And all the rest: the masters whom I've read and loved, the hopes, the cries for life, the revolts, the expectations, and the offering of my entire self? Tears, stifled joys, ecstasies, and mournful depression, my life, in short, did I bid you adieu? Face of tenderness and beauty that I tried to create for myself . . . My photo looks back at me with this smile of reproach and pity that appears to foresee today and suffers from having to forgive him.

Coldness [*sécheresse*], "this sorry queen who sits on the heart of fanatics who abuse their inner life."[11]

What do I want? Peace. A calm and bourgeois life, a husband to love without fearing every minute that this love will bruise me. A vigilant love, attentive, alive, and passionate but not worried, waiting or painful enough to cry out for everything that it does not achieve. Children to care for and cherish, simple occupations and leisure without remorse. I want to achieve something. I am at the end of my search, the end of my complicated diversions. To have the force to love myself now, to adorn my soul, I must depend on the love of someone else.*

This emptiness in me . . . if only you would come to ask me to give you these riches that weigh so heavily, which encumber my soul without filling it. I am lonely to the point of anxiety today. My love reawakens from this distress with a great need to cry . . .

No, this exaltation itself does not last. In reality, I do not desire Jacques. I desire desiring him, and I know his mere presence will bring me this desire. But in this living room there is nobody but me, a young girl seated in front of a table who tries by writing to create, at least in herself, a passion that will keep her busy.

To console myself, I must glance at this self with the multiple faces that my friends' eyes reflect. I must also take account of my riches. The beings for whom I am something: Poupette, who tells me so often, "What would I do if I didn't have you?" She loves her big sister, who is so intelligent, sad, complicated, and pensive; her love comes from a profound admiration for what I am and a lot of thankfulness for what I bring to her. This image of myself is not displeasing—yes, I do a lot for her, and almost all the passion in her life comes to her through me. But do I love her as much as she loves me? And of what help is she to me? Yes, there is the pleasure that she needs me, and the joy of being able to seek refuge in this real tenderness when all

---

* This paragraph is highlighted in the margin.

else fails me, complicity at the same [time?], an ear to listen to what would take on too much importance if I did not say it. I like her a lot.

Zaza, "You have broken through my solitude." For her I am "the girl-friend" to whom one can say everything: "intelligent, open, lively," energetic despite my depressions, lucid and mistress of myself, ardor towards beings and things.[12] This image is also true and comforts me. To be what I am for a girl like Zaza would be worth the trouble of living, if the beauty of an image born of us were worth the trouble of living. (Maybe it is worth it.)[13] What she is for me: my confidant, my other self, the calm, wise, and so much better girlfriend [amie]! There is no other word. I "respect" her. Often I cried out passionate thanks to her, and I shed tears of tenderness. When I am nasty, like tonight, it seems to me that as for Poupette, yet less, I especially like a reflection of myself in her, a more indulgent and loving self, "so close to the self even in moments of tears," but coldheartedness is not any more lucid than passion.

Jacques: "the terrace of d'Harcourt is really empty since you no longer go there." I don't want to know anything else before he has told it to me, "Does that concern me?"[14] What is he for me? Everything—my only reason to live. When I am nasty, I can, at the most, notice his insufficiencies, cry out that I am stronger than he, but I do not dominate him. I cannot even be sure that I love him more than he loves me. Oh! You, so close and yet so far, the only one who, I feel, is like myself, elusive [insaisissable] and yet so easy to grasp, simultaneously the most "self" and the most "the other." I wait so impatiently for the day when you will no longer be "the other" or "self," but it will only and definitively be "us." On that day, I will be at the end of my journey. Amazing, here in the midst of thinking about you so calmly, a calm tenderness fills my heart. My very dear friend . . . I have a total confidence in you and in your love. I am sure of what you are and of what you are to me. But to be able to keep this confidence, I must ignore too many parts of you, these vague desires running through you, these quickly stifled bad or crazy aspirations, the vagueness that resides in every being. I see all of that; I refuse to ignore it on the pretense that the essential is stable. I see you in your total-ity, and it is in your totality that I love you. Just as I often worry and disgust myself without ceasing deep down to have faith in myself or to love myself above all, I do the same for all with whom I have succeeded in identifying in a way that I thought was unrealizable. So much so that often, when I want to judge you from the outside, I am unjust as I am for myself. If you were pres-ent, I would not be so scrupulously seeking how I love you; my tenderness can also be the simplest, Jacques, you know. I would want to chat with you.

Thérèse Marie: the only girlfriend, adorned with all perfections and so superior! How much of myself is in that image? Simply my spontaneity toward beings, my power for life, also a little: my tenderness and my dream. She is nothing to me.

My young girls from the Équipes Sociales: gaiety, life, intelligence and cordiality, images of the simplest ones in whom there is what's true, and I am happy about it. I am pleased, even if I am so withdrawn into myself, that I know how to be superficially outgoing. I am pleased to attract friendship spontaneously.

In Neuilly: some appreciate only my solemn intelligence, my facility for study. (Françoise Leroy) and others know me better for my critical mind, my occasional irritations, my easy camaraderie, and a slightly untidy side of myself, which rarely manifests itself.

And the Sorbonne: for G[eorgette] Lévy, I am a young girl with a strong personality whom she quickly took as her confidant. Like those who know me little, she is especially attracted to what is independent and self-important [*suffisant*] in me and allows me to dominate those weaker than I so easily.

Those who mean something to me aside from myself:

- Mademoiselle Mercier—she appreciates my intelligence, my ardor for life, and at the same time, the gravity of my thoughts, my scruples and my desires, my strength, which she sees lined with weaknesses that she cannot identify. She is the one who creates the most perfect, but not the most likable, picture of me—however, she knows me well. For me she is a brain and also a serious confidant. I like her for talking to me about me and for listening to me with all of her intelligence. I like that this intelligence is great enough to be worth the trouble of speaking.
- Mademoiselle Blomart: a young girl who is my peer and who is yet other. I like her for her differences from me, for being other, for being.
- Ch[arles]-H[enry] Barbier: the nicest and greatest intelligence that I have met, a young man who is *his* peer and who is different from *him*. His intellectual faith attracted me.
- Garric—of my ardent admiration, only gratefulness remains.

These are the only beings I have approached whose personalities impressed me. From afar I noticed with liking: Strowski, last year, to whom I owed a lot.[15] Baruzi attracts me this year with his scrupulous and profound faith, the intellectual ardor of his brilliant eyes, and his manner of living his thoughts to his fingertips; he possesses an inner life.[16]* Mr Brunschvicg is perhaps a man of worth, but for me = zero.[17] And that's all . . .

* * *

From the moment that we have something to say to each other, we are compelled to hold our peace (. . .) As gold and silver are weighed in pure water, so does the soul test its weight in silence, and the words that we let fall have no meaning apart from the silence that wraps them round. Maeterlinck[18]

April 20, Wednesday

"White twilights grow tepid underneath my head."[19]

Never better than today have I understood this verse of Mallarmé. I've just left a note at Jacques's house telling him that I will stop by to see him tomorrow; he won't be there. It tires me out to think of him.

The influence of the mental on the physical and reciprocally: Maine de Biran's journal and James's theory of emotions.[20] Why, at nothing more than the thought of him actually present am I filled with a physical malaise, a cold anxiety that keeps me from having lunch, and a desire to lie down, to weaken, to cry from lassitude? Turmoil before the closed door. This life that is unfolding behind it, isolated from mine—one move from my finger is going to make it enter mine. From such contact what unforeseen face will spring forth to frighten me? And him, how will he welcome such an intrusion? Admittedly, I move towards him with a much greater and confident simplicity than at the beginning of the year, as though he had pronounced these words that he has never said. But I can never manage not to feel this jolt that destroys my peace of mind [quiétude] "each time that his presence replaces my image of him." How easily I do without him, I who filled every minute of this winter with his name! But how much less I am worth in this fearful refusal.

Beautiful pages of Maeterlinck on silence.† I would like to understand how I am able to isolate myself like this from my dearest memories and my closest desires. I have often already felt this: no matter how agreeable an afternoon, or how moving a conversation, I attribute them to another. Like Jacques's very face, they come out of a fiction. I cannot bask in them; these are not *my* memories.

---

* There is a vertical line in the margin of the 1927 manuscript, next to this sentence on Baruzi.

† This sentences and the last two sentences of the previous paragraph are highlighted with a vertical line in the margin.

What did this year bring to me intellectually? A serious philosophical formation that perhaps accentuated even more my tendency to consider each thing in its aspect of totality, and that sharpened my (alas!) too penetrating critical mind and my desire for rigor and logic. Rather a manner of sorting my thoughts with the help of a useful vocabulary, and formulas that permit me to recognize myself more easily. I read just about everything essential and ran through most problems. Everywhere I observed only our inability to found anything in the order of knowledge as in the order of ethics.

In painting, I made progress. I learned to appreciate a beautiful painting in depth: Picasso, Braque, Foujita, Derain, impressionism, Seurat, Matisse, Cézanne, Picabia, M. Denis and I became familiar with many others.

Theater: *La comédie du bonheur* [The Comedy of Happiness] by Evreïnoff.[21] *Le grand large* [Outward Bound], *Le dilemme du docteur* [The Doctor's Dilemma] by Shaw.[22]

Cinema: jazz, etc.

(But often this desire to cry after the show!)

In literature: tackled ancient and foreign literatures, read piles of minor journals and modern authors of little renown. I am quite at ease with well-known names; my avidity and my curiosity are satisfied. But little solid nourishment. And besides, it is with a very intellectual friendship that I like books now.

My thought has not profoundly changed. Same liking for psychology and analysis, but no longer any faith or enthusiasm. Seen too many things, tried too many attitudes, understood too many positions, adopted too many ideas—relativity of everything, uselessness of everything. Much less strength, and desire for happiness—Stability [*sic*] and no longer uncertainty. I have gotten older but without any profound modifications. I have learned above all about love and all the problems it poses; I have also learned that one can resolve some problems only by not formulating [*poser*] them.

I would want, as in times of courage, to force myself to give a face to each of my days, to escape from this tranquil stupidity. What must be done? To want it. Barrès, help me! This face can be calm as well as painful, but my life must not be a shapeless mass of gray. I no longer live with love but as though trying to make it through a boring task.

I feel like seeing Zaza. I feel like loving Jacques.

(Later)

Courageous, calm, faithful . . . this is the piece of advice given to me by the sky, so peacefully blue, and the benevolent sun in the square de Cluny. My inner beauty! From an exaggerated worry about being sincere with myself, I really neglected it! I know that it has no absolute value. But could you prove to the painter that he was wrong to paint a painting? Futile [*vain*] work? No, because he loves it. It is true if I believe it, and it is good if I love it. But can arrogant people make the same claim? No, because they would first have to be capable of loving and believing. How can this inner beauty be attained? Not attained but lived. No moral preoccupation, simply the will to be always present to myself, not to flee from myself, not to stifle my voice. I have lived for a long time this way. Start again simply after this too lengthy rest. Love myself without passion but profoundly; trust in myself. Be as simple as this happy day of spring, not by closing my eyes, but by surpassing my scruples and my fears. Rich simplicity is not poverty. And I wish that he too could conquer it: give up being amused by his feelings of disgust, give up his feelings of disgust, and humbly accept happiness. Be completely true, both of us: in other words, grant more importance not to what we find interesting or worrisome, but to what despite everything is the most important. If these games were only cruel, okay so what, but in prolonging them too much, we would risk forgetting that they are only games.

Perhaps this brutal simplification will offend me tomorrow—games and these worries experienced to the point of tears? Are the barbarians right then? The barbarians will always be wrong. As Zarathustra says, "Even if you were to repeat my words, as they passed through your mouth, they would become false."[23] One does not have the right to say, "Pierre is alive" just because Pierre is alive; one must have acquired the right to say so (Spinoza).[24] Besides, to play is necessary. But one day one must put away even the most beloved doll.

(At the Luxembourg Gardens)

Marvelous hour whose beauty is constituted by the grace of this little girl in the violet hat jumping rope, by the greatness of the Spinozist theory on truth that I understand with delectation far from my books, which have been closed for some time, by my sudden love present in all of its simple truth. No intoxication, but rather great peace in my mind, my sensitivity, my soul, the presence of a certitude, the certitude of being.

Coming back up rue Racine, I was telling myself this conquered peace is only the shining sun. A similar sun shone on many sufferings. Oh, my vacation! I am not going to say that he does not have something to do with it. My body is also happy. A splendid synthesis: not a parade of riches, external to me, but rather consciousness of myself full and complete, of my life, and consciousness of him; not the thought of him, him in his most profound essence, in his greatest truth.

Here hours of morose hairsplitting are justified. Here my inner life is blossoming. Here one of those rare hours of beauty is being realized, even more rare for moving only a single being.

* * *

> Each must follow his own path, a path that he has not chosen and we do not even know where it leads us.
> Ramuz[25]

April 28, Friday

Quiet week with Madeleine in Paris.[26]* The big revelation was Madame Pitoëff in "Sainte Jeanne" [Saint Joan]; what a beautiful play and above all, what a great artist![27] This woman does not act; she lives, she creates. I lived off of it for three days, and I have preciously internalized it.[28] Living is still worth the trouble if there are joys of this quality to encounter, joys that are fully justified in themselves and demand nothing outside of themselves, a bit brief perhaps because of this, and which have worth only in the present but not as memories.

Sunday at Malmaison with my group of the Équipes Sociales. Saw G[eorgette] Lévy again and spoke on the social self and the pure self; amusing discussions: she is truly Jewish and is too fond of playing with words.[29] Returned to the Sorbonne with a certain pleasure.

Saw Jacques Thursday: agreeable chat. Little need to see him again: we are both calm; we will see each other again when we feel like it.

Saw Zaza again.

Have read *Âmes en peine* [Souls in Pain] by Arland and *Les cahiers* [The Notebooks] by Rilke.[30] It has been a long while since books have so moved me.

In the brilliant sunshine I felt the desire to take walks in muslin dresses completely soaked with my sweat, to stretch myself out in the grass without a thought, to take refuge in this sensual pleasure, in my body, which doesn't need to depend on anybody.

My strength has come back to me and a desire for well-chosen reading

---

* In the manuscript this sentence is highlighted with a vertical line in the margin next to it. In the third paragraph of this diary entry, Beauvoir also highlighted "Jacques" by placing a vertical line in the margin next to the sentence containing his name.

(especially Greek, English, and Russian literature) and for intelligent dis-tractions. I have peace. I live pleasantly, in a way that two years ago I would not have dared hope to live, and yet, I would give all of this up to be once again the wonderstruck child that I was a year ago.

Yesterday suddenly in a flash, at a street corner in Belleville, on this lovely evening in the inner suburbs where life seemed to have the same cordial simplicity as the fresh air that one breathes on doorsteps, a passion burst into my heart. I contemplated what a walk in this neighborhood and my task as one of the members of Équipes Sociales would have been for me if my enthusiasm had not already barely survived a year; I had so desired *this!* No, not *this* with today's soul; this with the possibility of adding the infinity of a love and a devotion to it. More strongly than ever I have understood how much my life is myself, how much only what I love has worth, and what I imagine is, and nothing is but that.

My past is behind me like a thing that has left me, something I can't do anything about anymore and that I watch with foreign eyes, something I don't share. The present that I experience today will not, I feel, give me a past. My life is so empty! Not an emptiness from which I suffer—my health is excellent—rather an emptiness that I observe as necessary, that I accept. Whether it be Zaza, Garric, Jacques; the Sorbonne or the Équipes Sociales, Péguy, or Gide, or Claudel, my childhood and adolescent passions were trembling and suppressed, and I was oppressed by their weight, tiny, *absorbed* by them. Now my self absorbs all of them; my feelings of happi-ness are reasonable and precise; the affections that I feel are not the center of my life; I can so easily do without them! They leave me feeling so lonely! Quite lonely! Not from the metaphysical solitude felt in the depths of love and translating itself as suffering; we must be two since we complain about remaining one. I am lonely from this solitude that excludes the other because one doesn't have any desire to destroy it for the other. Coldness [*sécheresse*]? No, it is accompanied by a great tenderness for Zaza and Poupette, for him also, but a tenderness that comes out of me to go to them without moving anything in me. Others can no longer be anything definitive and complete for me; the big renunciation that I dreamed about is impossible! They are only themselves like I am only me, and above all I do not need them.*

My love appears already like something past, not the dead past, like my passion from last year and this strange and magnificent life that I led, a past that will revive one day but with another face. I did not judge it severely or

---

* In the manuscript there is highlighting in the margin of this paragraph, near the words "Quite lonely" and the next sentence, and beside the last two sentences.

compare it to others;* I know that of the men whom I could know, he will always be the one whom I prefer; I do not love *him* less; rather, love has less value for me.† I am at peace: I know that it will become valuable again, but right now it seems so insignificant. Does a single being suffice to satisfy a soul? Rather no, it's not that; I am simply not hungry.

"Nathaniel: I will teach you fervor."[31] In reading Marcel Arland, a feeling came back to me, and it seemed that worthwhile tears could still be shed. Always this wrenching refrain: it is only that, only that, only that, poor child with the "ambiguous face," only that, poor woman tired "inside."[32] We barely sketch out the gestures of which we dream, and we are truly right since we like them only for their distance, their impossibility to be realized, "which, even without regret, the gathering of any dream leaves in the dreamer's heart."[33] Again, I evoke poignant souls. Life is poignant, and I understand Rilke with my entire astonished and fearful soul on so many evenings. Yet, one must see, one must know what it is; and out of lassitude I close my eyes so often! Ah, Rilke, teach me to taste each of these lukewarm seconds like something precious and unique!

Calm, yes, but a sort of calm that is not death. Have I already finished living? What if I must go on in this way, satisfied with my repose and my small pleasures? If there really is nothing else, what good is it all?‡

I would want, would want . . . what? Tears I think; it has been such a long time since I have cried!

I am rereading Barrès and I pity Philippe; I would not want to go to so much trouble to fabricate impoverished enthusiasms for myself.[34] It does not matter; Barrès's hard-heartedness and his precise sense of existence do me good. Gide is far away; I have exhausted his lesson.

So? Is it going to continue like this? What can I do about it? Work with interest, read with curiosity and with passion if the occasion arises, chat, take walks, go to the theater, vaguely dream, think precisely about objective things, come here more regularly to mark my intellectual progress and my discoveries, get upset when I can. Yes, yes, yes. What else? Analyzing myself amuses me, but I do not always dare to go to the end of my analyses.§ I will

---

* This paragraph is highlighted by a vertical line drawn in the margin, from "My love appears" to this point.

† The passage is highlighted by a vertical line drawn in the margin from this point through the end of the paragraph.

‡ This paragraph and the next one are highlighted by a vertical line drawn in the margin of the manuscript.

§ Up to this point, this paragraph is highlighted by a vertical line drawn in the margin of the manuscript.

still find the most resources in self-worship [*culte du moi*] at the moment because I sense my worth, and I am happy to have it (but have no desire to use it).

I like *La province* [The Province] by Mauriac. I like the grave and tormented adolescent boy who analyzed himself in the gardens of Bordeaux. I would like to know Arland, Mauriac . . . I say that, but I really feel that I know myself too well to be able to expect anything from anyone else. Oh, except intellectual pleasure, etc. but nothing profound. Rivière however, and Fournier? Yes, these men remain my friends in spite of everything.

Let's go do some Greek . . .

*　*　*

Beauty is eternal; this is why we men do not want old beauties. We want the beauty of the day, similar to that of other days and yet new, just as one woman does not resemble any other woman.

But it is impossible for there not to be something else. If there was absolutely not, at this moment, somewhere in the world, a fresh beauty in the process of being born, then I would drop dead because men live only if they are supported by the mind.

However, every which way I turn my eyes, I see nothing, neither to the east, nor to the west.

What if the last architect were dead? . . Our times are certainly strange, like the expression that passes over the face of the dying. A threat lurks about, tightens its circle, merges with our shadow, blows on our neck . . .
Drieu de la Rochelle (*Suite dans les idées* [Singleness of Purpose])[35]

That is simply what happened. The main thing was, being alive. That was the main thing.
[Rilke][36]

There are multitudes of people, but there are many more faces, because each person has several of them. There are people who wear the same face for years; naturally it wears out, gets dirty, splits at the seams, stretches like gloves worn during a long journey.
[Rilke][37]

You had your death inside you as a fruit has its core.
[Rilke][38]

They all had a death of their own.
[Rilke][39]

. . . For the memories themselves are not important. Only when they have changed into our very blood, into glance and gesture, and are nameless, no longer to be distinguished from ourselves—only then can it hap-

pen that in some very rare hour the first word of a poem arises in their midst.
[Rilke][40]

Is it possible to believe we could have a God without wearing him out?
[Rilke][41]

And with what comes, a whole tangle of confused memories arises, hanging from it like wet seaweed on a sunken object. Lives that you would never have known about bob to the surface and mingle with what really happened, and drive out a past that you thought you knew; for in what rises there is a new, rested strength, while what was always there is tired out from too much remembrance.
[Rilke][42]

I don't think there is such a thing as fulfillment [*accomplissement*], but there are wishes that endure, that last a whole lifetime, so that anyhow one couldn't wait for their fulfillment.
[Rilke][43]

. . . Vaguely foreseeing that life would be like that: full of truly strange things that are meant for one person alone and can never be spoken. What is certain is that gradually a sad and heavy pride arose in me. I pictured to myself how a person could walk around full of inner happenings and silent.
[Rilke][44]

What he wanted was that profound indifference of heart that sometimes, early in the morning, in the fields, seized him with such purity that he had to start running, in order to have no time or breath to be more than a weightless moment in which the morning becomes conscious of itself.

The secret of that life of his, which had never yet come into being, spread out before him. Involuntarily he left the footpath and went running across the fields, with outstretched arms, as if in this wide reach he would be able to master several directions at once.
[Rilke][45]

. . . And the house did the rest. Once you walked in to its full smell, most matters were already decided. A few details might still be changed; but on the whole you were already the person they thought you were; the person for whom they had long ago fashioned an existence, out of his small past and their own desires; the being—belonging to them all, who stood day and night under the influence of their love, between their hope and their mistrust, before their approval or their blame.
[Rilke][46]

... They have the best of it; they stay in the shadows, and on him alone falls, along with the light, all the shame of having a face.
[Rilke][47]

... Not until long afterward would he remember how thoroughly he had decided never to love, in order not to put anyone in the terrible position of being loved.
[Rilke][48]

... He was probably able to stay. For every day he recognized more clearly that their love, about which they were so vain and to which they secretly encouraged one another, had nothing to do with him ...
[Rilke][49]

... and already from far away you saw that this pleasure was good only for anyone else but you, that this was a completely foreign pleasure; so foreign that you did not even know what it could be used for.[50]
Rilke (*Cahiers de L.M.B.*)

Saturday, April 30

Oh! I love myself and I love my life. I just reread the pages written in this notebook, and combined with the recent reflections on myself, it all results in a marvelous drunkenness. How can I say it all?

Thursday, I discussed philosophy in a group with average students, who nevertheless had a (certain worth).* Yesterday Mlle Blomart and Zaza came over to have a snack with me, and we chatted at length. I had two conversations with Poupette in which I began to see myself more clearly. Finally, the sun shone these past two days, and I enjoyed studying Greek.

My strength! To sing it out I would want to have the enthusiastic pride of a Rivière. Yesterday in front of the door to the library, I was looking at the courtyard of the Sorbonne, and I discovered my strength, just as Cocteau says in the *Le secret professionnel* [The Professional Secret] that we suddenly discover things that are too habitual.[51] The students who were walking in the light seemed created by my mind. I felt life invade me completely. Memories of books, of beloved paintings came crowding back into my head. Like yesterday as I was lying down: it is I; *I* am at the center of this life, but useless, words cannot depict such certitude.

Life is beautiful from all of the beautiful paintings that men paint during

---

* Next to "(certain worth)," there is a marginal note in the brown ink of later years: "too certain!"

it, from the marvelous books that they write, and from the thoughts and the systems that they build. Life is beautiful because of the intelligent and sensitive beings who live there, the sun from hot days, and the chilliness of slightly gray mornings, beautiful from easy companionship and deeper friendships. It is beautiful from all of my wealth! I am so rich! Little girl from the school, Cours Désir, who did not suspect any of this; were eighteen months really enough for you to make such conquests?* So many verses sing in my head! So many paintings in the depths of my eyes, so much knowledge in my brain, and in my heart so many beings whom I am happy to know! And then there is me, me. It is ridiculous, I think, but after so many dislikes, and since I am certain to rediscover them tomorrow, can't I be joyous about rediscovering myself this way? Without exaltation, but with a serene certainty of myself that I learned to know last year. I love myself for having learned how to be so passionate, for "never letting anything go by without giving it some love and life," and especially for being so intelligent! I know that I am. I cannot get close to anyone without finding out that I more quickly understand and seize profound and unforeseen relationships. In Jacques alone do I find the same speed.

Only here is the thing! Cocteau certainly did say "don't be too intelligent," and Mademoiselle Blomart and Poupette plunged me into an abyss of reflection yesterday.[52] There are beings whom I esteem and like: Garric, Desfontaine, whom I do not know at all well but whom I imagine, and all of those who resemble them, even Mademoiselle Blomart, who are restless [*inquiets*], but who possess at least some convictions that they hang on to.[53] They build their lives on them, and on this solidly established plane, they have nothing to do but to let their lives blossom. When I woke up a little while ago, I felt how much I wanted on such gray mornings to get up hastily and walk, tranquil and ardent towards a peaceful task that I would believe to be useful and that I would only have to fulfill. Be a flame. Do good. Give of oneself. When she spoke to me about Bach, about her work, I felt ashamed for lacking certainty, for not having resolved the "how of living," for being egoistical, with a radical egoism that can be qualified only by whether I make it focus on those I love or directly on myself. Yes, I suffered last night from not being what they are, and which I could have been perhaps.

And at the same time, I said to myself what good will it do, what good will it do? I am really in a paradoxical situation; I feel my intelligence and the positive power that it could have; I would like to do something, and if

---

* There is a vertical line drawn in the margin, from "beautiful from easy companionship" through "eighteen months."

I daydream so often about Barbier or Baruzi, it is because I would like to have a passion for a philosophical work as they do. I feel capable of carrying it out successfully. I also sense my will, my power to act, and I would like to dedicate myself entirely to a work in which I believe. To do something would be an even greater joy for me because I know that I am capable of doing something very good. Only these very qualities that require to be of use also show me what an illusion it is to claim to be of use for anything. Is this Jacques's influence or is this my truest self? If I had loved Garric or Barbier, would I have attained a perfect equilibrium? Or would this critical mind have awoken anyway? Was it necessary to act first, and would I have not then had to ask myself the question why act?*

I think a lot right now about the beings I know, or rather about the ideas that these beings are for me, about their position on life, without worrying about whether it is truly theirs, but deducing it logically from their point of departure. I like them. I am happy about the differences that there are between them; at the same time I guard myself against them and accept quite readily not being them. But at the same time, to judge myself "objectively" I compare myself to them and questions form . . .

I sometimes happen to reproach Jacques, Jacques-idea, quite passionately for this inaction and skepticism . . . and yet I look upon him as the most intelligent one, and his position is mine. It is the only position that appears true to me.

Indeed, it is ridiculous to let myself be troubled again by the certainty of others. I cannot keep myself from envying them because it seems that in faith and happiness, there is something more complete than in doubt and restlessness. However I do indeed *know* that their God is not. The people for whom God is real without being able to satisfy me, I don't bother with them; those whose God could satisfy me even if I cannot believe in him, those are the people whom I envy when I say to myself: they are right. Right about what? About being able to keep their illusion? Foolishness. There is nothing to do but to love them and to rejoice in their difference from myself, but I must not desire to be as they are.

But me, what am I? My unity comes from neither any principle nor even any feeling to which I subordinate everything. This unity forms itself only in myself. I can neither define nor classify myself. This does not appeal to my taste for clarity, nevertheless I hate labels.

No, really; what I like more than anything is not ardent faith and the

---

* This entire paragraph was highlighted by a vertical line drawn in the margin.

noble but simple deed that nevertheless move me out of respectful admiration. It is exhausted enthusiasms [*élans*], searches, desires, especially ideas.
It is intelligence and criticism, lassitude, and defeat. It is the beings who
cannot let themselves be duped and who struggle to live in spite of their
lucidity. It certainly is Jacques whom I love and not another.[54]

I love the things and beings who can make me suffer the most. This refinement of sensitivity, this elegance of thought, these subtle complications, this
is what I love. Next to a soul who is reflective, intelligent but less hardheart-
edly in love with the naked truth, and more profoundly simple, I sometimes
feel inferior. On the contrary, if I get close to those who resemble me, I feel a
little bit of tender pity for those who don't know what we know and whose
greater peace is composed of less exigency or intelligence.

There is nothing in which I believe. This is the terrible thing that I must
acknowledge to myself. Not even in myself. I can love: life, action, Jacques,
my own perfection, and act according to my love: this is what allows me to
be lively and passionate. But I do not master love, and once it stops, I have
nothing to hang on to. I hate dilettantism; and logically, shouldn't I be led
to dilettantism? In what way am I so different [*loin*] from the skeptics that
I detest? And yet, I am very different [*loin*], because I take everything very
seriously, because my life appears to me to be an infinitely serious thing.

I am not going to worry anymore. It is enough for me to be.

Have read *La suite dans les idées* by Drieu de La Rochelle.[55] Obscure, brutal, and unpleasant, written in an athletic and overly vigorous style; some
very nice pages, especially in the beginning. Who will cause me to lose my
fondness for literature? Is it a deformation to adore beautiful sentences,
some of which are "more moving than the body of an adolescent girl?" I
feel more at home in the gallery of 143 when Jacques turns beloved pages for
me than in Belleville's library, where the sympathy for others and the facility of action deliciously relax me, and than in Baruzi's class, where beautiful
and austere ideas give me a serious and passionate fever. Arland, Larbaud,
and Rivière are my peers. If only I could go for all of my life from Belleville
to the Sorbonne and from the Sorbonne to the books that I love! But from
day to day, I continue to take shape [*me précise*] and the diverse possibilities [*possibles*] refuse to harmonize [*se mettre d'accord*]. The one that I have
chosen is the one that I prefer.

There are a lot of things in me that resist it, so I turn towards the others; but if I were familiar with them, there would be even more things that
would resist them. Besides, I will not lose any of all this; I will not let go of
any treasure. I have faith in myself. I have faith in myself.

I would like to copy every page of this book by Rilke! Life has a strange face on certain days: solitude, impulses hidden in the depths of ourselves. Psychological analysis will always be my passion, and what can one say about it when it is dramatized in this way.

Silence, faces, and death, the different deaths of different beings, the fear, the verses, "the existence of the dreadful in each particle of air," especially the prodigal child who did not want to be loved, and the death mask of the drowned woman; the smiling face and the knowing face, the young man and glory, his illness: his cries as he was overcome by himself.[56]

Monday, May 2

I am reading *Les possédés* [Demons] by Dostoyevsky and *Les âmes mortes* [Dead Souls] with an ever greater admiration for these magnificent and so profoundly human Russian novels—they alone know how to create life in this way. Balzac is crude and artificial next to them. Nevertheless, there is *Le Père Goriot*, but what about *L'idiot* [The Idiot]?[57]

I understand Mauriac's Thérèse Desqueyroux really well![58] *Really* well! Any deed will do to destroy the odious familiarity of daily life. One of the simplest and most soberly moving works by Mauriac.

To read: Adrienne Mesurat, *Défense de l'Occident* [Defence of the West], *Aline.*[59]

Spent the day yesterday at the Tuileries exhibition first with Zaza, then alone. Even today and philosophy class (getting 14 on my presentation, congratulations from Rey, "the charming idiot," etc.) have not yet calmed the exhilaration of this joy of walking with anticipation towards a work bound to delight you, of filling your eyes with the beautiful painting encountered, of touring each room ten times to compare and renew feelings of admiration, and finally, of going home intoxicated with forms and colors.[60] Especially this feeling: these people are there for me; they obediently wait until I come to see them; I am alone, and I have three long hours to interrogate them one after the other. The pleasure of rediscovering old friends and also of being stopped by someone unknown who suddenly touches your shoulder when you were going to pass by with indifference. I still have doubts about my artistic judgement, but at least I know clearly why I like or dislike a work.

Three great passions:

- Matisse's *The Dancers* in white dresses posed next to quite clear blues and blacks—an impression of plenitude that only Matisse's paintings give me.[61] It is intentional [*voulu*] and well done [*réalisé*].

- Severini's portraits, especially the one with the black collar whose folds match the waves in the hair—the rigor and severe beauty of a living theorem—it is intellectual, and yet not abstract nor theoretical. The guitars and the countryside are curiously treated; I like them less.[62] A woman by Waroquier, between two well-executed landscapes but without anything special (for Waroquier, I mean)—the woman's stare and smile are sober, precise, and secret. I would have questioned her for hours.[63]

I also like: André Lhote's beautiful Negresses, admirably constructed; the two landscapes are beautiful also; Maillol's dancers who stand out pink with black hair from the spread-out whiteness of their skirts; Favory's clear and frank nudes.[64]

The three by Vlaminck (man in a top hat, dark street, and especially, mysterious black-and-silver still life).[65]

I hate the ones by Desvallières.[66] Maurice Denis presents the same Christ in the same crude colors. (Why do painters paint when they no longer have anything to say? Why do they repeat the same painting on ten canvases?)[67] The ones by Guérin look like all his paintings. (The eighteenth-century paintings are annoying; the portraits good, but when I think about the guitarist in the Salon d'Automne!)[68] The Besnards are decent.[69]

At first, I could not convince myself to like Utrillo's three landscapes.[70] Some Marvals (white flowers, young girl in black); you see right away that it's a woman; thus she is not a painter.[71]

I was forgetting a nice Gromaire, dry, a little bit big but really *very* good, better than any other Gromaire that I have ever seen.[72]

I quickly greeted Lardareau-Deshayes, Quiliré[?], Chabaud, and Flandrin like acquaintances, of whom I have nothing to say, no, really nothing.[73]

And the others, the unknown? First, three nudes by Borchard that I like very much, very much, especially the tall half-naked woman stretching out her arms against a green drape: not geometric, not angular, and yet . . . and then warm colors . . . I do like it.[74] Conrad's mill, a brown house in R. Blum's dark green trees.[75]

A beached boat by Bompard is curious and rather appealing despite the crudity of the tones.[76] Interesting paintings by Léger, but too decorative for my taste—placing one object next to another is not how to make a painting, and then there is the artifice and insincerity found in literature (a man's thoughts).[77]

I adore six Kislings; I feel that it is rather clever painting, not too far from le Grand Palais, but nevertheless how can one not be taken with these childish women's heads with black hair, an ocher-colored complexion, and astonished, smiling, or fearful eyes?[78] The woman in green who is bending down towards a rose . . . The blond enveloped in her shawl . . . I do not want to discuss my pleasure. I could have cried over these canvases.[79]

From Marbois: a beautiful dog, and energetic landscapes. (There are a lot of landscapes; the impressions produced by roofs and windows are so trite! But then many receive only a trite approval).

Some Survages interested me a lot: this prejudice for bright yellow, this brutality (bullfight) of luminous colors; it doesn't mean anything profound to me but I am detained, interested.[80]

I like a gray-and-red harbor by Moinelot. The rest at random: Arman-Jean, violets, awful.

Morisset (Perrault's fairy tales), pretty and silly.[81]

Two beautiful drawings by Quiliré[?] and especially by Boureau that I like a lot.

Grianchon's circus.

Marcel Lenoir—Despujets—Delorme—Ivanned[?]—[82]

Schonkhaeff (brutally detains me, but I think that this painting is detestable: seascapes, bread, umbrella and hat). Bionère (hideous). Claire Fargue (portraits). Ch. Denier: Wedding at the photographer's (More literary artifice and insincerity [*Littérature*], false customs officer Rousseau—awful).[83]

Gluchoneaux—etc. etc.

I would have to come back here in a month after I have read some critics to orient myself.

I retain that: Severini, Matisse, Lhote, and Waroquier delighted me.[84]

Borchard, Survage, Kisling especially were revealed to me.

Today, wandered in Paris with some girls who go to l'École Normale: saw a Utrillo, a Chirico, a Picabia, some surrealists, a Braque, a charming Van Dongen (woman standing on a chair, green grass, billiard cloth)—and especially: Foujita! Foujita! Foujita![85]

Ah! Paris! . . .

Tuesday, May 3

Saw Mademoiselle Mercier. Lemonade again, I believe. Attempt at a novel or maybe working on my Greek, but it is so pretty out, and it would be so pleasant to make up beautiful stories with moving sentences—magic of words harmoniously organized. What craziness it is to deceive oneself with literature like this.

DIARY OF A PHILOSOPHY STUDENT

How sad I was to reread the things that I wrote last year, young, new and courageous because I believed. Believed in what? In life probably. I really need three quiet months in England.

Friday, May 6

No, no pity for my vanished past. Live in the present. It is beautiful enough if I know how to make it so.

This morning I experienced a strange minute whose memory has not yet died for me. I had just seen Barbier again, who had so spontaneously come towards me with his slightly slow voice and his cold stare that seemed to seek his thoughts in his very depths, and this amiable, human, intelligent smile, so gentle under his hard eyes. He talked to me about myself, philosophy, and literature with an obvious interest. And then, in the hot library where the students were nothing more than insignificant imbeciles, for an instant, I held a completely new life in my hands. This was true for as long as it lasted; I thought about the love that could have been between us; I *saw* myself between his and Jacques's love. Well really! I was not chained to the past. A new passion was blossoming in me. Splendid. I loved him. How can I put it? It was not speculation or reasoning, or dream or imagination. For an instant, it was. Still a bit even now, my life is no longer a traced path where, from the point that I have already reached, I can discover everything and have nothing more to do than to place one foot after another. It is an unmarked trail that my walking alone will create. I am thinking back to Baruzi's class and Schopenhauer: empirical characteristic, intelligible characteristic.[86] Yes, it is only by free decision and thanks to the interplay of circumstances that the true self is discovered. I told Mademoiselle Mercier that for me a choice is never made, but constantly in the making; it is repeated every time that I become conscious of it; this is quite true! Well, this morning I chose Barbier. The horror of the definitive choice is that we engage not only the self of today but also that of tomorrow.* And this is why marriage is fundamentally immoral. Thus, we must try to determine which one repeats our changing self the most often. One must create a sort of abstract self and say to oneself: this is the state in which I find myself the most often; this is what I want the most often; thus, this is what suits me. First, one can be mistaken, and even if one is not mistaken, "most often" is not always. (Hence Claudel's phrasing that I understand better than ever, "That which

---

* This sentence is highlighted with a line in the margin.

246

is more necessary than oneself, there is but a single remedy, which is to make it the strongest forever!" Yes, but at the cost of what sacrifices of everything else that hasn't chosen *that* and which nevertheless counts.)[87] Naturally, I haven't asked myself the question for the definitive choice; but it's Barbier and not Jacques who fits the present self.

For an instant I was free, and I experienced it: me, abandoning the friend to whom I was attached by so many tender memories, for the unknown person who knew how to conquer me. In fact, if he loved me (no danger of this because he loves that young brunette), I don't know if I wouldn't love him. I don't know if I wouldn't let go of Jacques. Yes, but Jacques would come back into view whereas in fact he has been far from my eyes for two weeks, and from my heart for even longer. (This does not mean that I don't love him, but rather that I love him like a friend so close that you no longer think about him; besides I find it quite good that we do not need one another.) It is very complicated. I must bit by bit kill all but one of these possibilities [*possibles*] in me. This is how I see life: thousands of possibilities [*possibles*] in childhood fall by the wayside bit by bit, and so much so that on the last day there is no longer anything but *one reality;* you have lived *one life.* But it is Bergson's *élan vital* that I am rediscovering here, that which divides, letting go of one tendency after another so that a single one can be realized [*réalisé*].[88]

There used to be the possibility [*possible*], charitable work—Garric, etc. It is dead; it is very much Jacques who killed it. I regret it when I see Mademoiselle Blomart, when I relive a memory with intensity, but it is basically rather artificial; it is not for it that I am made; experience has taught me. Then the possibility [*possible*], dilettantism—art—Jacques—tranquility, really revolted me at first, then later, dominated and satisfied me. Now it often weighs on me! There is the serious possibility [*possible*], austerity— philosophy—Barbier; oh, its very strong attraction, my need to realize what I feel within me, to do something, to believe in something!* My intellectual passions, my philosophical seriousness! Things that Jacques dismisses with a smile. Naturally one can demonstrate the vanity of all things in terms of intelligence, but what if this becomes as important as a living presence? Jacques would say, and so would I—I say this on numerous days when I resemble him—what good is it to dedicate your life to philosophy when you know that you won't discover anything? But what if I like this vain search? I cannot resolve to do nothing, simply to live pleasantly. No! I will

---

* From "Then the possibility" through "its very strong attraction," this passage is highlighted with a line in the margin.

not.[89] I have only *one* life and many things to say. He will not steal *my* life away from me.*

In a while, tomorrow, wearied or recaptured by his charm, I will cry out to him and ask for forgiveness. But no, I must not be ashamed: my *self* does not want to let itself be devoured by his. It's awful! I didn't do anything this year (in terms of my own thoughts) for the image of a calm life next to him convinced me so strongly of the uselessness of an effort in any other direction, but when I have this life, when I am there, established, I will do even a lot less. But this is the supreme defeat! Oh, it's not a matter of success, of a brilliant intellectual future that I would so willingly sacrifice for him! But of what I *am* and what he will keep me from being. Why? Well, because I will think like him, nothing will sustain me, and I will not know what I want. I do not know, even at present. If Barbier had loved me! If we had come towards each other still "available"! I would have loved to work protected by his gravity, to think, to seek the truth. To say that I love him, what does that mean? Does the word itself have a meaning?

I tell myself that what attracts me is his way of dominating, of being strong and such that one can walk in the light simply reflected by his eyes, whereas Jacques does not impose himself upon me. Maybe if I got closer to Barbier, I would find the same weaknesses in him. Maybe in some years, Jacques will have the same assuredness. (To think that he will never know the depths that my love and my indifference have attained!) I see him, as a whole: his subtle intelligence, his exquisite sensibility, the *elegance* of his entire person, his entire soul.† I see his tenderness and my own great tenderness for him. But it already seems to me that this affection is no longer love. (It probably will be again later.) It's because we no longer have anything to say to each other. It is also because I *judge* him.

I am writing nonsense. However, this is true: it is not by free choice that I will marry J.; it is because circumstances threw us together. I could have loved another and with a love that would, perhaps, have been better made for me. There I am telling myself cruel things that are not completely true, not more so than certain passionate pages. I know what precious things Jacques's love gave me, its delicate charm, and its gentleness. If I reflected calmly, above all if I knew B. as well as him, I would perhaps prefer Jacques. But there is a lot of truth in this.

I don't love Barbier, since at the moment I desire not to love anyone,

---

* Starting with "Jacques would say," this paragraph is highlighted in the margin.

† The passage from "I see him" to "certain passionate pages," in the next paragraph, is highlighted in the margin.

since I am not sad at the thought that I will no longer see him again. But I feel that if I wanted to love him like G. last year, if I evoked his face often, I would again know the senseless passion that I felt for G. and J. Never have I been so frank with myself: what then is love? Not much, not much; I come back to this idea. Sensitivity, imagination, fatigue, and this effort to depend on another; the taste for the mystery of the other and the need to admire; wonderment. I don't see why for different beings this would not start over again often, like with books and paintings for which one can have a passion successively. It was a great joy to sense this feeling being reborn in me and to feel an entire novel acting itself out so intensely that I have no regret about not being able to realize it. What is worthwhile, is friendship. It is why, that which is between G. and me leaves me cold today and why, if I stopped loving J., there would always be this profound mutual confidence between us, and this joy of knowing that the other exists.*

I want Barbier to be my friend. (Oh! What my life would have been by his side: philosophical, literary, liking ideas without being among the intellectuals that I abhor, idealistic, serious, and so gaily young and strong and very affectionate I think—working with him, developing myself under his direction.) And I will no longer see him; worse, I will no longer think of him. Because this love that could have been and that I would have at least kept as a memory, this love is not.

I will see him Friday. I will tell him, "I would like to chat with you." He would give me a piece of advice. I would say to him, "I am intellectually very alone and very lost at the entrance to my life; rid of all of my prejudices, I tackled action, literature, and philosophy, haphazardly, looking for a direction. I feel that I have worth, that I have something to do and say, but my thoughts spin aimlessly: Which way shall I direct them? How can I shatter this solitude? What shall I achieve with my intelligence?" And still, "Do you believe that duties are imposed upon us? Must we achieve something or is being happy about having a pleasant life enough? I am in great distress at the moment of deciding my life. Can I be satisfied with what is called happiness? Or must I walk towards this absolute that attracts me? Help me with your experience; tell me what one can demand of life and what it demands of us. I am addressing you as though you were an elder who possessed a few certainties, like Cébès (me), "new man among unknown things," addresses Simon (you), who possesses strength.[90]

I will say this, and I will try to make him understand and respond.

* This final sentence in the paragraph, beginning "It is why . . . ," is highlighted with a line in the margin, and "yes" is written in the margin and underlined in brown ink.

If it depended on me to make him love me, would I do it? Yes. I would not hesitate to put everything into question.

And that is why, whereas this should be sad, I am joyous and young because nothing is decided anymore. I have resolved only to act in full accordance with my self.

* * *

Whatever tears one may shed, in the end one always blows one's nose.
H. Heine[91]

Monday, May 9

The evening at Buttes Chaumont, I really cried over this self who will not be. Then, that charming party where I met Deffontaines also made me feel how many things B. would make me sacrifice. The next day, I saw Jacques again during a charming car ride, and I understood how much I was a slave. Strange day! After such joyous camaraderie in the hot streets, my conversation with G. Lévy in the Luxembourg Gardens, then this emotional class with Baruzi where he spoke to us about our "charming and profound" schoolmate, so suddenly dead.* Yesterday, Mademoiselle Ionnis talked about the death of Pallio. My heart was wrung with emotion at the difference between such faith and the distressing emptiness [néant] of the words that Baruzi was saying. Ah, if only they still existed! But no, Saturday night while "the class went on without him who had always been present in past classes," I felt it: there is nothing. The death of these thousands and thousands of states of consciousness that a being represents! An irreplaceable being and who is snuffed out . . . irrevocably. I feel before death not the greatness but the smallness of man. It is impossible for all of it to be so important since the destruction of all of it is so rapid and especially happens so unobtrusively because even those who cry continue to go on living. And in this way, love appears to me to be a beautiful thing that at least assures a being that when he is dead, the other will not be able to live; he must only love the other enough for the life of this other woman, taking on an infinite meaning, to give an infinite meaning to his own . . .

And then, the death of a young being is a tragic thing, but isn't it even more tragic for him to live? At the moment I am happy in the sense that I have the life of which I dream: the charm of the Équipes Sociales, the good

---

* From "The next day, I saw Jacques" up through "so suddenly dead," this passage is highlighted.

that we do, and the easy camaraderie—the charm of the Sorbonne and the serious friendships that are born there (the philosophy group from which I've just come, intellectual sympathies); books; theater; and the paintings Friday in rue La Boétie for two hours; and the beauty of the weather; and Jacques; and my very strong capacity for thought; and myself, finally, myself rediscovered and whom I so like! But when I gather my thoughts to reflect, what tragedy I feel around me! These millions and millions of states of consciousness, Schopenhauer, they die as much in life as in death and more painfully. What will this young man do? What part of his dreams, of himself will he realize? There is so much to be abandoned, to be renounced on his route. It is so vain to live that in order not to cry out over this vanity, men are obligated to grab onto happiness which keeps them from thinking about it, but happiness will never be anything but a diversion.*

G. Lévy shed some light for me on what I felt next to Barbier: when you love beings as we love them, not for their intelligence, etc., but for what they have in their very depths, for their soul, how can you legitimize a choice? You love them equally: they are entireties, perfect inasmuch as they are (to be = perfection). Why then is there this desire to get closer? To know them, and thus to love them more perfectly for what they really are. What is surprising is not that we love them all, but rather that we prefer one of them. So it is with Jacques's friends about whom he says to me "they are better than me"; something sharp runs through me which is my love for them; I feel that I love them as much as Jacques for what they each have that is different and irreplaceable. This is not intellectual love. This is a love for souls, from all of me towards all of them in their entirety.

This explains to me why the choice is so painful. But it is, however. Ah, it's because from all the things just as beautiful that we would lament, there is one, however, which is closer to our heart. I should not choose myself over a similar other, and I have often felt this strange detachment. Yet, I know how much I have transformed this servitude chaining me to myself into a preference. Yes, I would sacrifice my happiness for another, but I would not want to be another. That's the key. And so, the one who is my other self, I can refrain from loving him more, as a being, and yet for being another self, I cherish him more than any other.[92] And this choice is a beautiful thing. Resolves nothing, because even two people confined together are still confined; but helps.

It amuses me to think about what J. would say if he knew that on the sub-

---

* Opposite this line, on the facing page, in brown ink is written: "May 1929—*No* with all my strength, no—only the life of the real exists because death cannot be thought."

ject of my love for him, I ask questions about the one and the many, about finite and absolute modes, about ideas and being. He probably would not understand because few people can understand what it is to feel ideas and that just because a love is not sentimental does not necessarily mean that it is intellectual. (In fact, it is often one or the other.) But there is a deeper question, and I am once again curiously finding myself thinking the same things as last year about this incommunicable self.

* * *

The way in which the character develops its properties can be compared to the way in which every body in unconscious nature reveals its properties. Water remains water with the properties inherent in it. But whether as a calm lake it reflects its banks, or dashes in foam over rocks, or by artificial means spouts into the air in a tall jet, all this depends on external causes; one state is as natural to it as is the other. But it will always show one or the other according to the circumstances; it is equally ready for all metamorphoses, yet in every case it is true to its character, and always reveals that alone. So also will every human character reveal itself under all circumstances, but the outward signs resulting from it will be in accordance with the circumstances.
[Schopenhauer][93]

Existence itself, is a constant suffering, and is partly woeful, partly fearful.
[Schopenhauer][94]

The world, as a represented object, gives the will the mirror by which it becomes conscious of itself.
[Schopenhauer][95]

Sometimes when we think back to the thousands of years that have passed, to the millions of men who lived in them, we ask, What were they? What has become of them? But, on the other hand, we need recall only the past of our own life, and vividly renew its scenes in our imagination, and then ask again, What was all this? What has become of it? As it is with our life, so is it with the life of those millions of men. Or should we suppose that the past took on a new existence by its being sealed through death? But our own past, even the most recent, even the previous day, is no longer anything but an empty dream of the imagination, and the existence of all those millions of men is the same. What was all of it? What is all of it today?
[Schopenhauer][96]

Why is this now here, my own now, precisely now?
[Schopenhauer][97]

Rather have we to know the present as the only form in which the will can manifest itself. One cannot tear the present away from the will anymore than one can tear it away from the present. Therefore if there is a being who is satisfied with life as it is, and who is attached to it in every way, he can confidently regard it as endless (. . .) the form of all life is the present (. . .) Conversely, whoever is oppressed by the burdens of life (. . .) cannot save himself through suicide (. . .) the form of life is the endless present.

[Schopenhauer][98]

The real existence of the human individual is only in the present, whose unimpeded flight into the past is a constant transition into death, a constant dying. (. . .) thus his existence is a continual transformation of the present into a lifeless past, a perpetual death.

[Schopenhauer][99]

Life swings like a pendulum to and fro between pain and boredom (. . .) after man had placed all pains and torments in hell, there was nothing left for heaven but boredom.

[Schopenhauer][100]

The desire to live is what occupies every living being, and keeps him in motion. When existence is assured, we do not know what to do with it.

[Schopenhauer][101]

If a great misfortune, at the mere thought of which we shuddered, has now actually happened our frame of mind remains on the whole much the same as soon as we have overcome the first pain. Conversely, experience also teaches us that, after the appearance of a long-desired happiness, we do not feel ourselves on the whole noticeably better or more satisfied than before. It is only at the moment when these changes come upon us that they strike us with unusual force, as deep distress or shouts of joy; but both of these effects soon disappear, because they rested on illusion. For they did not spring from an immediately present pleasure or pain, but rather from the hope of a truly new future that we anticipate in them.

[Schopenhauer][102]

Men are like clockwork that is wound up and goes without knowing why.

[Schopenhauer][103]

Genuine friendship is always a mixture of self-love and pity.

[Schopenhauer][104]

What moves us to tears is not our own suffering, but rather a foreign sorrow. Why? It is because in our imagination we put ourselves in the sufferer's place; we see in his fate the common lot of humanity, and consequently above all our own fate. Thus in a very roundabout way, we always weep about ourselves; we feel pity for ourselves.

Schopenhauer[105]

Wednesday, [May] 11

Sunday, circus. Last night Atelier (*Voulez-vous jouer avec moâ?* [Do you want to play with meee?] and *Antigone.*)[106] The weather is still just as nice; life is perfectly charming. The Sorbonne populated by known faces is perfectly charming. I ask this question of every young man whom I approach: are you as good as Jacques? And if I view them as really very good, but less so than he, then I am happy.* Because it is useless to deceive myself; all my life I will be a slave to this type of smile that he has, to this affirmation of himself. Yesterday in the nocturnal chill of la place Dancourt I felt it again; even if his life displeases me, I will always love him. I say smile because in this smile I read his soul, slightly ironic, but very much a dreamer at heart. I suffer only when I see a being of his worth doing nothing because, as Spinoza explains to us, there is nothing to do except to observe what is. But if I consider this worth in itself, I rejoice that it is. Why did I sometimes make him responsible for this drama of life so pitifully described by Eucken in the lines that I copied; the contradiction between the push towards a superior life and the complete emptiness of this painfully conquered life. It is the absurdity of existence that we were thus supposed to struggle with in the emptiness.[107]†

Oh, to love him again very simply as I sometimes knew how to do.

Only know this: despite what I wanted, my love must maintain limits, and whatever does not fit into this love must not be sacrificed because of it.

These days I understand to the point of tears the line by Ramuz, "The things that I love do not love each other." Jacques negates Barbier; Barbier negates Garric. Having chatted Monday with Alain's student enlightened me on several points. (This boy, who for two hours so intensely relived for me his year of study with a "master," was charming.) He taught me a lot. "To think well is a pleonasm," said Alain; "you think well as soon as you think." This man seeks with an absolute intellectual probity that is his entire ethics (Spinoza again), *his* truth. He does not construct a system. He does not know

---

* The next few sentences of text are highlighted, up to "I read his," and written in brown ink in the margin is, "May 1929 How my ideas (!) have changed and how my heart repeats exactly the same words! . . ."

† The passage from "contradiction," in the previous sentence, to the end of this paragraph is highlighted in the margin.

how to speak. For him, philosophy is the personal work of each individual, one's life itself. He does not make an external unity; he is his unity.

Mademoiselle Mercier spoke yesterday in a very profound way about the life of the mind, the difficulty of maintaining side by side the experience and the real, the wearing away and the horror of collapsed syntheses for anyone who does not have the strength to reconstruct any of them.

I must reconstruct. I want to live. I must therefore be able to live. In order for this I must make *my* unity.* I must not care about what others think and do. I give a profound meaning to this: the opinion of any other does not worry me. I mean that I must adopt my own system of values without ever judging in function of a neighbor's system. This is where I get lost.† I must walk directly and energetically in my own direction. Live according to me, not according to others. I am *myself.* I am wrong, in determining my acts, not to act directly according to myself, to worry about the values established by others that are legitimate for them and not for me. I am not all that I love.[108] I must live according to what I am and not according to what I love.

Move forward. Don't endlessly turn back to see if it wouldn't be better to commit myself [*m'engager*] to another path that I've left behind. Whatever one I have chosen, even poorly chosen, if I follow it to its end, I will arrive. Besides, it is not poorly chosen unless I cannot arrive at its end.

But arrive where?

Yes, I know what [I] am asking from life, to realize myself. They say that it is useless. Most certainly. Euclid's postulate is not certain. But besides, every judgment is absurd; it is a tendency that comes out of something deeper than intelligence. It is the law of my being.‡

To do something is not what I want. The written work only interests me because I unleash power into it and not for what it is once it's accomplished. But it is false to believe what Jacques says, that to be somebody it suffices to lie down and sleep.

This is important, and let's clear up any ambiguity [*équivoque*]; he would be right to answer to anyone who would tell him to get up, "Who will make me do so?" No law can be imposed from the outside onto any of us. Those who depend on exterior principles are "barbarians."[109] This is even how a barbarian is recognized.§ When you raise yourself above them, you start

---

* This sentence and the previous two are highlighted with a vertical line in the margin.

† The passage from "This is where I get lost" through the end of the paragraph is highlighted in the margin.

‡ This paragraph is highlighted with a line in the margin.

§ From this point, the rest of this paragraph is highlighted in the margin.

by "destroying the idols." But once this is done, you might find a deep call-ing [*appel*] in yourself. Or you might not find anything. When you judge a being, you must keep yourself from confusion. Did he, or did he not, com-plete his circular path? That is the only question. If it is a rule from outside, you can always destroy it, but if a being says, "This is my law itself," it is as stupid to deny such a law as to deny such a being. (This is to affirm to myself that criticism does not discredit the position that I may take.)

*   *   *

> Children do not keep their promises; young people very rarely, and if they do keep their word, it is the world that doesn't honor them.
> Goethe[110]

Friday (May 13)*

After having chatted with Mademoiselle Lévy yesterday at her house, played chess last night with Jacques and just a little while ago exchanged a few words with Barbier; I find myself alone crying in this library. Barbier is nothing to me. G. Lévy is barely intelligent but very far from me since plea-sure is enough for her. Jacques is my dear friend, but isn't our love already worn out? We are both so demanding! It's good to love one another in truth and even in weakness, but it is so painful to see the weaknesses. And then well, it's nothing but that! Still . . .

Thus, I want to realize myself and live now that I know all that you can about life, admitting and understanding everything. For that, I must first know the extent to which I am alone. I speak mystically of love; I know its price. But I know also that it does not put an end to my solitude. Besides, it is not made for that. I am too intelligent, too demanding and too rich for anyone to take care of me entirely. Nobody knows or loves me completely. I have only me.†

I must not try to evade this solitude by giving up what I alone can bear. I must live, knowing that nobody will help me to live. My strength is that I esteem myself as much as any other. I may well envy one or another for a certain quality, but nobody's worth seems to me to surpass my own. I have just as much.

Alone I will live, strong with what I know how to be. I must once again, like last year, pass by secretive and distant, without letting my glance turn

---

* In the brown ink she used for later comments, Beauvoir has added: "May 13."
† The final four sentences of this paragraph are highlighted in the margin.

away from my own route. I must no longer be the plaything of my desires' caprices.

I don't want to neglect anything that gives life its charm, but I don't want to be its slave either. I will do good deeds, I will chat, I will help or awaken souls, but all without desiring anybody's approval. And it will be essential to obtain the profound unity of my thoughts, to have my point of view on all things without caring about other possible points of view. It is a mistake to look for a work in which I will express myself for one audience or another. I must haughtily write my work for myself even if nobody will read it and only my death will finish it.

But I must guard against limiting myself to a rigid ideal. I must be sincere, said Barbier when he explained his ethics to me. Yes. But, today already, I no longer have Wednesday's fervor for the serious image of myself. Thus this image is not entirely correct. If I feel like doing silly things and chatting with imbeciles, I must do so. I must be careful only and always to allow myself the possibility of not doing so. No artificial unity. I sense so keenly that underneath this apparent dissipation there is a strong unity of my self! If I judge myself from the outside only I am frightened to see myself passionate with the Équipes Sociales, intellectual here, crying and demoralized at home, sensual and silly elsewhere. All of this is me. My beliefs like my confusions. I must only establish a hierarchy so that I can recognize myself and have a fixed home base from which to proceed.

Here is what I am going to do: in this notebook I will recount my experiences that I accept as varied and even absurd; this will be in terms of my weaknesses. Then I will attempt a work of thought in which everything will result in a strong, detached, and disdainful judgment. There will be no dilettantism or splitting in two.

I see myself as having a very hard face at the moment; this hardness is very profound in me. Yet I love Meaulnes and Francis Jammes profoundly too. But does one cry less sincerely, are tears less valuable because one knows the value of all human despair? This hardness, on the contrary, makes my tenderness more willed and my compassion more pitiful. I feel so well how no two things in me are mutually exclusive, but rather complete and explain each other!

Thus: bite into life on the outside, have fun with it, savor it as though it were a show performed for me. Become attached to the inner life, take it seriously and sacrifice everything for it. Never let my experiences from the first plane ruin my inner beauty, but don't believe either that personal perfection requires the sacrifice of anything on another plane that cannot reach it.

257

There is no effort here to reconcile irreconcilables. It is rather their separation that is artificial.

But, after all, how, in what form, shall I realize my inner life? With which part of my thoughts shall I start? It's always the right one, says Alain. But still, you have to find one, and one that I could hold onto for all of my life. Thus, my marriage will have little importance. My deepest life will not be affected by it. Neither critique, nor novel that treated beings and things aside from myself would satisfy me.

I will see, I will think. I will find.

(Rereading the first pages of this notebook, I marvel at the wealth of lucidity and precision in the analyses and at my gift for describing the states that I was going through. I am moved by this as though these pages were written by another. Thus, could I too do something? I must work on a work in which I believe and for which I would not desire any praise. A novel about inner life or something similar.)*

Let me leave for England! Two months in Limousin in a tête-à-tête with Mama, I can't!

(Multiply the precise analyses—a good exercise and perhaps fruitful.)

I support every word that I wrote on April 23.

Write "essays [*essais*] on life" that would not be novelistic, but rather philosophical, by linking them vaguely with fiction. But let thought be the essential and let me seek to find the truth, not to express or to describe the search for truth: a) irrationality of life; the given is irrational, b) the powerlessness to analyze it, c) the uselessness of life. Link these meditations with short narratives and quick scenarios.

Schopenhauer's fourth book contains the most beautiful pages that I have ever read! The definition of time, of the present is splendid, and problems are posed in such a direct and human way!

* * *

> The belief that a being participates in an unknown life to which his or her love may win us admission is, of all the prerequisites of love, the one which it values most highly and which makes it set little store by all the rest.
>
> Proust[111]

---

* The foregoing sentences enclosed by parentheses are highlighted in the margin.

Thursday, [May] 19

These miserable efforts for being! Ah yes! I know, I know it well. What more? Sometimes, from being simply seated in the sunny courtyard where nice students walk around as they chat, I experience one minute of plenitude. I had some beautiful hours this week, beautiful from accepted solitude, from strength without pride. Life had a new and spicy taste (for example the trip to Choisy, alone in the train where every minute contained all the marvels that I wanted to see). But what? And is that truly all?

I have peace and almost joy, because books, chats, and the sweetness of the air are so dear to me. But in my depths, masked by this day's diversions, the same emptiness! Certainly, today is equilibrium: neither great despair, nor infinite lassitude, nor even resigned coldness. I am living with enough ardor and pleasure, satisfied with each day's task and distractions. How unimportant all of that is! I repeat the magnificent prayer of Marcel Arland in *Étapes* [Stages], this book in which I would have signed every page, every line: "a total exigency."[112] I like this man for having shown the greatness of our effort in its very uselessness and the stifling feeling of what we owe to this self that we drag everywhere without respite, without anything rational to justify this duty.

But yesterday how I envied M. de Wendel for being so pretty and so simple! Without pride or envy, I cried at the thought of the destiny reserved for me, the strength and the tension required for me to be able to find it preferable to all others.

G. Lévy revealed to me that happiness would really be enough for her. Henriette is young and asks only to be happy. Jacques manages to lose himself by having fun. I myself keep my emptiness inside of me, and this certainty that I am alone, that nothing can satisfy me, that my happiness will have to be willed so strongly, so severely that it will be more of a fatigue than a peace.*

I cannot find anything greater than myself, and I know how small I am! For Marguerite *being* happy is like breathing. If only I could scorn this happiness! But no, Marguerite is perfect in her total ignorance, and my pitiful knowledge does not make me look more beautiful. Neither pity nor disgust for myself. I am going to do some Greek.

---

* In the margin next to the sentence starting, "I myself keep my emptiness inside of me," is the comment, "May 1929. Thank you, my nineteen-year-old sister[,] for having willed it so strongly that today, without anyone's help, it seems to me to be an unexpected gift."

The day that I feel very loved, maybe I will take heart again; especially the day that I will love more.* But will I love more? Probably, it is only because I haven't seen him in a long time . . . But also, "I know that it was something entirely different, incompatible with everything."

Friday in a moment of strength I established a program for living [*programme de vie*]. In such instances my solitude is an intoxication: I am, I'm in control, I love myself, and I scorn everything else. But I too would so much like to have the right to be very simple and very weak, to be a woman. In what a "desert world" I walk, so arid, with my bouts of intermittent esteem for myself as my sole oases.[113]†

> Yet I am not truly sad tonight either. I count on myself; I know that I can count on myself.
> But I would really like not needing to count on myself.

Friday, [May] 20

And then, with all its meanness and its insufficiencies, life is truly beautiful anyway, isn't it! Impression of a juicy fruit that suddenly melts deliciously in your mouth. I like that in the bus the lady spoke to the elderly gentleman. I like the Luxembourg Gardens to be dusty and full of people underneath the fountains. I like this summer to be hot and splendid, for it to be four o'clock, and for me to be nineteen years old! I also like that *Gold Rush* is such a masterpiece in the empty movie theater where Charlie Chaplin seems to be acting for me alone. I like to walk, to breathe, to be. I like life!

So much!

And to think that I almost passed up these easy and profound joys! My childhood summers were carefree, last summer was painful and serious. Now, out of all of my repressed pains, I will build splendid, sunny afternoons. Now I know, and I know that I know. My periods of happiness are thus conquests. That of today is a smiling conquest.

Is it because I chatted for two hours with Miquel this morning under the Sorbonne's clock that should have been marking some moments of work?[114] Maybe. There is in this boy something upright, simple, and so com-

---

* In line with the sentence starting, "The day that I feel very loved," in the margin is written: "Dear external circumstance!—September 1929." The external circumstances of September 1929 that contribute to her feeling of being loved include primarily her close relationships with Sartre, Jacques, and Maheu.

† On the opposite page, in line with the sentence starting "In what a 'desert world' I walk," is the comment, "May 18, 1929—Could I stand to suffer again like I suffered in writing these lines?"

pletely sincere! Nothing from those tricks of literature or that artifice that he denounces in Rivière and that Jacques is sometimes troubled by (or tries to get rid of, which is the same). A joyous optimism, a manner of walking in his own direction, which confines him a bit and keeps him from understanding everything but which assures him of a beautiful and simple unity. He is very young and spontaneous with this intelligent and funny quickness in conversation that I so like, but without the touch of disdain that makes J. so seductive. He is original. He said very intelligent things to me that I do not tire of hearing to confirm what I think at heart: you must treat yourself as an end, it is on yourself that you must build; if this is only a game, at least let us take the game to heart; this will be justified by itself, this bears in itself its reason for being.[115] He is right. Marcel Arland is also right. But Marcel Arland does not say anything to the contrary. He made some very amusing remarks about Massis, "who plays with safety nets and who falls constantly in the nets." This manner of remaining apart [*étranger*] from so many things appeals to me despite everything because truly "it is so foreign to him that he doesn't even see why it could be useful." So he passes by, even without disdain, no, he didn't notice anything . . . And intelligent, very intelligent.

So much for the lengthy discourse on him. Ah! More than anything I like beings, and even simple companionship is a very precious good! In it alone I can tear myself away from my own manner of thinking. It would be curious to study how this education of one another takes place.

To him I owe the ability not to scorn leisurely walks, futility, young laughter (because Jacques's laugh is not so lacking in ulterior motives.* It appears that he is giving up [*s'abdique*] or else more profound feelings ripple beneath his smile. I don't even desire to see him; I cannot pretend that he doesn't fatigue me even when he is the simplest; it is because I feel that he is profoundly maladjusted to existence, so much so that none of his gestures appears to me to respond to his inner face. Others express themselves entirely with each breath of air, as Miquel would say, but it is not true for everybody. Besides, it doesn't matter. Today, even Jacques will make me joyous).

* * *

To love is to identify with the object that one loves; it is to want oneself in the other.†

---

* The rest of this paragraph is highlighted in the margin.

† This quotation is placed across from the paragraph starting, "In practice," of the May 21 entry in the manuscript.

Saturday, [May] 21

I continue my meditations on Miquel, Alain, Lagneau. But in trying to think them, I well believe that I am in the process of finding myself once and for all, of daring to be me [de m'oser]. It is a lesson for me that this boy who was speaking to me about movies yesterday morning got himself profoundly congratulated by Baruzi this evening, as is also the fact that Barbier, lover of the naked truth, made me read Schwob's book.[116] I observe how much I have matured since last year despite my belief that I was losing myself, how something strong was born from the painful experiences survived and from the numerous minutes that I believed were wasted. I no longer confine myself to Garric or Jacques; too many diverse but equivalent [également comprises] syntheses have obliged me to construct my own. And that is infinitely simple. Georgette Lévy aggravates me (although I'm very pleased to see her) with her need to put problems everywhere and to imprison herself in her indecision. I myself know that there is only one problem and one that has no solution, because it does not perhaps make sense. It is the one formulated by Pascal, much closer to me Marcel Arland.[117] I would want to believe in something—to meet with total exigency—to justify my life. In short, I would want God. Once formulated as such, I will not forget this. But knowing that this noumenal world exists, that I cannot attain, in which alone it can be explained to me why I live, I will build my life in the phenomenal world, which is nevertheless not negligible.[118] I will take myself as an end.

(Curious to see how I build: my departure point is what a being has revealed to me about his position, and from this premise I try to deduce an entire system. Let's continue on, but where are *my* premises?)

Lagneau's expression is beautiful, "I have no support but my absolute despair."[119] I would not want another motto. On this despair I will build my joy; I will overcome the inexplicable. Courageously every day, rebuild everything: this is good because each time, the building is more solid and rises higher. It is enough not to abdicate, but you must hold up until the last day, without worrying about "possibilities [*possibles*], better named impossibilities [*impossibles*]." So here I am settled in. After having tossed and turned on my pillow, I have finally found a cool place.[120]* It is good to think, to understand, and to love. Wandering about is more precious to me every day: the tapestries of Marie Mounier, Antigone, or Charlie Chaplin are profound enrichments, new visions of the universe.

---

* The rest of the paragraph is highlighted by a vertical line in the margin.

It is exactly what I wrote the other day. I must affirm to myself that the truth is in my strength and not in my weakness, that this evening I am right, and not in the morning when upon opening my eyes, the anxiety of having to live again oppresses me even when the day's program is attractive.* Love, too, will have to submit to this discipline. It could be marvelous to help in the achievement of this other end that Jacques is, and reciprocally, to help myself through him, but without letting myself be troubled by the attempt to fuse our two inner lives.[121] I know that I will not succeed and that my sentimentality will treat this as intellectualism. Yet, I'm right. This profound self whose voice haunted me last year is here and speaking tonight. J. is no longer necessary, as he was this winter, for me to be. I have gone beyond that. He is only necessary for me to live.

Danger, ah! The danger of love when one believes that something is higher than love! Naturally, one seeks compenetration, the creation of a "we" that is neither me nor you.[122] This is Mademoiselle Blomart's conception, but she has a God outside of herself. *I* have no other god but myself. Will I mutilate this god, thus also mutilating the other's god through mutual concessions? What a hideous word!

Come on, my critical mind! Cry out: but any value judgment is stupid; what difference does it make if you give up [*abdiques*]! This need to be, this duty, in relationship to whom, in relationship to what?

Well! No. I myself suffice for imposing laws upon myself. I feel that I *must* walk in this direction. I will walk in it.

Yes, it is simple. I will play the game as if it were not only for laughs. Besides, no, people do not play for laughs. They play, that's all. (Only I am really afraid of the day when the game will no longer amuse me.)

In practice: continue to live (inner culture because Baruzi knew how to fascinate me), live with ardor and imagination without rigidity or harshness, start to think. Why don't I write a meditation every day? I will let myself be carried away by my pen instead of directing it. Beside these notes and these clarifications, more concentrated reflections would be the best of disciplines for me. Shall we try? We shall try.

(Why can't I keep myself from being so ironically conscious that the forty-nine positions that I have left out have just as much worth as the fiftieth that I have adopted? Barrès or Lagneau? The *N.R.F* or *L'Esprit?*[123] Ah! if only I could sometimes have tunnel vision!

Well! No! Even this apparent contradiction is not really one. This appar-

---

* This sentence is highlighted with a vertical line in the margin, from "this evening" to its end.

ent contradiction is me. There is A. There is B. I have within me some A and some B. I moan, thus I am neither A nor B! Thus I don't know what I am! Oh, yes I do. I am C = f(A,B).)

So strongly sure of myself that I think that I no longer fear anything from others. Good, that. Let's hope that some miserable little nervous tensions do not come to get in the way of this.

I am sure of how to live. Will I manage to get rid of the why that perhaps makes no sense but without which perhaps also the how makes no sense.

* * *

> There is indeed nothing more profound in love than the vow to be happy. What can be more difficult to overcome than the boredom, sadness, or unhappiness of those we love? Every man and every woman should always keep in mind the fact that happiness—I mean the happiness one conquers for oneself—is the most beautiful and most generous gift one can give.
> Alain[124]

Tuesday, May 24

Chatted again yesterday with Miquel, who turns out to be communist. I understood that one could be intelligent and be interested in politics. But he is not close to me because for me what value could I put on the search for humanity's happiness when the much more serious problem of its reason for being [*raison d'être*] haunts me? I will not make one move for this earthly kingdom; only the inner world counts.* However, thanks to these chats, this inner world is no longer a cloister for me, and I am enriched by all these passions that I do not share.

Saw an Epstein film Sunday: $6\frac{1}{2} \times 11$ at Ursulines and yesterday *Hamlet* with Pitoëff; so beautiful and profound![125] I suffered once again upon feeling man crushed by an excessively heavy destiny; love powerless to save him, and death itself full of mysteries. Neither Shakespeare nor Schopenhauer allows us to trust even in that!

Letter from Mlle Blomart to whom I respond by defending myself for being "enthusiastic and ardent." I explain to her how my happiness, my acts, my loves are willed and how fatiguing it always is to will.

Chatted with G. Lévy; truly better than I thought. Above all: continued to read Lagneau and to live philosophically.

---

* The text from "because for me" through "world counts" is highlighted in the margin.

* * *

If I told you that I love you, would you find the response?
No, right?
So I prefer to keep quiet.
    Bost[126]*

Saturday, [May 28]

My heart is sleeping under the weight of my philosophical meditations. Communism and love have held my attention this week. My thoughts are clearer and clearer [*s'affermit*]. G. Lévy is almost becoming a friend. I owe it to her to have defined the exact nature of my hurt and understood as a result how I would have to live: by delving deeply into Lagneau's words. In Alain I found a splendid sentence that I am quoting here. How many times have I thought that, forcing myself to be happy in order to prove my love, and suffering from Jacques's boredom as if from a painful proof that he still did not love me enough to make the effort to be happy? It is also because of it that love frightens me so, because of this necessity that it will impose upon me to be joyous. But the happiness of the other will compensate for that and go beyond it.

How far he is from me, "the other"! Yet, even though I have filled my feelings with intelligence and my life with philosophy, I do not feel or live any less. Spinoza does not exclude Francis Jammes.

If I am less sad, it is because, being more absolutely in despair, I met the meaning of my despair and accepted it, made a place for it [*installé*] instead of trying to flee from it. But also I hardly have to wait. If I easily bear the nonfulfillment [*inaccomplissement*] of my desires, I have hardly any desires, do I?! Here I am like the wise man from antiquity, so disdainful of human things that neither good nor bad ones can reach me. I pass by like someone who is not supposed to join in but only watch the show and go away. I understand resigned philosophers. Until recently, I thought that in the words that they were saying, they were seeking intellectual reasons to persuade themselves. But no, I am living it, and it is entirely something else.

And yet, I remain profoundly human: I too know how to plunge occasionally into the fray. I cried yesterday about leaving the one who shook my hand so nicely, "I wish you many good things." I will never see you again, "oh you whom I could have loved ... ," who knew it perhaps![127] When I

---

* In the manuscript, this quotation is placed across from the paragraph in the May 28, 1927, entry that starts "And yet."

think about what Papa means by "to love" and my discussion with him the other night; services rendered, affection, gratefulness! So many people have thus never known love! I mean unique love, which is neither desire nor routine affection where one loves only oneself, because for me, somebody who distinguishes between two loves has not known either of them. There are only degrees, but not differences. I do not love for the good that one has done for me, above all, I do not love because one loves me.

The feeling that the other has for me is probably the sign that something in him is made to agree with something in me. Once I love, I probably desire to be loved. And to found a true love, this reciprocity is necessary, but if I love, it is because this being is what I want him to be, because I feel his perfection; because he imposes himself upon me and penetrates into me.[128] On all this, there would be many things to say, but to me it seems so elementary to recognize that gratitude never creates love! (Love = friendship = affection etc . . .) On the contrary, I love less the one of whom I am too sure (unless I am sure because I love less). For this I am treated as coldhearted, and there are probably very few beings I love. But insofar as I love, this love is truly addressed to them and not to me; "insofar as" . . . because even for the most beloved there is a measurement [*mesure*] since he is not God. In fact, maybe not . . .

I will go more deeply into this for my thesis.[129]

I wanted only to say the pain of having encountered him, and of never meeting him again, he whom I loved in the strongest sense of the word. I think that love is purer and less strong in the beginning of an affection because the other has not yet been penetrated with you enough for one to love oneself in him.[130] More pure does not mean more beautiful. The penetration of one by the other is the juicy fruit of familiarity. Even then, one must respect some moderation [*mesure*]. Ah! Love is so great and so small! If it were only small! Or if it were only great as it is for the young girl full of wonder! Go on! I will have no part of this profound and charming being that an almost fraternal sympathy inclined me towards. The very memory of this beautiful friendship that could have been will disappear. Thanks, at least, my young male friend, for what you have given me of yourself.

Perhaps it is only in the name of the love that I had for Jacques that I will be obligated to love him again and to protest against this sentence that I am writing!

In his presence alone I will rediscover a desire for him.

How sad it is to be sad no longer . . .

Friday, June 3

Charming book by Pierre Bost, *Homicide par imprudence* [Homicide through Negligence]. Profound and magnificent book by Ramon Fernandez that I will surely reread (lent to Miquel, and I am happy to bring something to him). Ballets Russes for a break; all of this has aroused thoughts or dreams in me.[131]* But I want to speak of Jacques, glimpsed yesterday, Sunday, without joy and until Wednesday indifferent, or rather of Jacques, Wednesday, rediscovered by me who didn't know that I had never lost him.

I went to his home, my heart heavy with all that I have never said to him, and especially with what he had vainly told me so often when I could not hear him. I was radiant when I left because our souls had touched in a simple and profound sincerity.

Sometimes, even alone with me, he takes on a disdainful or carefree mask that embarrasses me. So I myself tense up, too, and inwardly I assert that I am against him. I know that more love annoys the one who loves less, so I try to stifle my tenderness, believing myself less loved. And also, as I judge him on his life of the moment, which is not worthy of him, a doubt, a discouragement is born in me.†

I have sworn so often, after a real presence, not to be the plaything of these "intermittences of the heart" any longer, and above all to believe that I am loved![132] What's more, I am right, if love must not be established [*posé*] once and for all but unceasingly created in a perpetually renewed youth.

Since I saw that no God was waiting for me on the incomprehensible route where I was seeking total Exigency, the reason for the world, and for my life, and since I exhausted the bitterness of the great metaphysical sorrow without seeking, as others do, to make each of the moments of my human life divine, let me peacefully turn instead towards this human life, with such poignant uncertainty. Let me not forget the great emptiness.

Let me no longer delude myself with the hope of filling it, but let me become attached to what is most solid and sure in life when one asks life alone for its reason.

Jacques said to me, "Already tired of seeking?" No, but I have found. I have found that it does not matter so much to know and to understand in order to want and to love. For all of my life, I will try to advance as far as possible into the heart of the problem with my intelligence alone, but I will

---

* This last sentence was highlighted by a double line in the margin.
† This entire paragraph was highlighted in the margin.

accept the given and live the given without expecting to possess the absolute. The philosopher well versed in mind games comes back to common sense, which he knows to be more true than his reasoning. In the same way, I presently think that it suffices to live well and truly [*bellement*], doing what I find good to do and loving what my love finds meritorious, without asking the absurd, "What good will it do?" It is not to be justified. It is, if I create it.[133]*

Why therefore would my love be sad? Wednesday, I passionately suffered from this act of adherence, of consent to the other. It is infinitely more than any intellectual notion that one may give of it.

And darn philosophy anyway! (Although now it is coexisting peacefully with my somewhat more wisely mastered heart, because it is truly and for always assimilated into my life "joyous and strong equilibrium.")

If I analyzed and justified love when I loved less, was it not to be able to love more fully and more uniquely when I would love?

Paul Valéry and Francis Jammes. But so profoundly the one and the other, that one might no longer know that one could be the one, when one *is* the other.

Being stretched out on the wet grass of the woods and thinking of you. Putting my face in some roses and thinking of you. Listening to Garric and Claudel giving interminable lectures and seeing all these people living socially by their convictions once they are set down [*posées*], and thinking of you inwardly and freely. Being here in this living room, your letter in front of me, and thinking of you.

Of you, not of me in front of you, but of you in this secret intimacy that is reserved only for me alone perhaps. I have such confidence! No, you will not be "mediocre," you will not say no to your youth—not useless and in despair. Your male friend died from being intelligent; the two of us will live from it!

We know that happiness is only that! But we will support one another so strongly that we will know how to withstand the great vertiginous void. We will not fall into the abyss. I will really force you to love yourself if you love me because the image of you that you will see in my eyes will be beautiful and true. Each will be strong from the other's weakness.

I have felt quite close to our lips the infinite words that neither of us has said. I know that you have felt them too. I know that you believe in love.

Would it be true that you are timid? That you wish, perhaps without

---

* This entire paragraph was highlighted in the margin.

daring it, what I desire so for you to dare. Yes, I often feel like being nice, Jacques, and since you have almost told me that I will never displease you by being so, I will dare to be even more so.* Why suppose that you are so different from me? Maybe you too are not certain of not bothering me. I would like for you to say "I love you" because of the response that I would know how to give. I am really cowardly when I harden my heart. So let him read all of my tenderness. Of what importance is it to me?

It seems to me that tonight this love is splendidly gratuitous, because I finally feel so disengaged and saved from you. I understand how truly this love is free, voluntary, that no necessity imposes it on me.

Despite the silly distractions and the somewhat cowardly compromises, despite too many hesitations and a facility to flee from you that I dislike, in the depth of my mind, I think that you are worth much more than me.

I think this because I have often thought the contrary and because I am sure that you never judged yourself as the best.†

This is a sudden bedazzlement. Oh! This humility so simple next to my unavowed pride and my complacence towards myself! Oh! Such sincerity, such disconcerting sincerity, such confidence! I am asking for your forgiveness. I am asking for your forgiveness!‡ I doubted you! Because you always say, "I am not much of anything," I almost believed that it was true. But now, I will be faithful to that minute when I saw you face to face. It is so much easier to doubt than to believe, as Rivière says. In spite of you perhaps, I will believe.

Truly tonight, it is not "me and the other," it is us. And this is thanks to you who so decently took me with you Wednesday evening, oh my friend, my friend forever.

Monday, June 20

Exams, soccer games at the Sorbonne, theater and cinema, secret nocturnal outings, chats with G. Lévy, with Miquel, reading and walks, I continue.§

Why have I gotten closer to the barbarians in this way? Why when I am

---

* On the opposite page, across from "Yes, I often feel like being nice, Jacques," is a comment written by Beauvoir years later: "May 1929 I can still see this couch where I was settled, the armchair where you were seated; I hear your voice; I love you more than life itself. Come back, I beseech you so that I may tell you everything that I didn't know how to say."

† This paragraph and the next one are highlighted with a vertical line of dashes in the margin.

‡ Near the sentences where she says Jacques is worth more than she, and where she asks for forgiveness, Beauvoir later wrote the comment, "May 1929: Yes, with all my heart."

§ This foregoing paragraph was highlighted with a vertical double line in margin.

so full of scorn, do I lead a silly life that I could scorn? The weather is so beautiful and in these relaxing games I leave so little of myself! Probably, I like myself better when I am haughty and solemn. Probably. But my pathos is well exhausted. I hate artificial emotions. It is better to live rashly than to give in to boredom and disgust.

Do you remember the Monday when he came, when once he left, you came downstairs with a heavy heart and for an hour in the Luxembourg Gardens you moaned as though you were going to die? A soaked handkerchief in one hand, what good is an argument next to that? There was only this suffering that I didn't understand; I didn't know why I was living through it, and I felt myself dying, awfully. Those minutes were awfully in vain and already past, and an infinite weakness invaded me, a desire to let myself slowly slide. Irony even in my pain, which made it more sincere and more harsh; I repeated Heine's words, and the fact that these tears were worthless made them flow more bitterly. Why so mean to myself?

Scene on Saturday with Mama when it hurt me so much that she meddled in my affairs. But I saw J. again and everything is like before. My friend . . . but love?*

Équipes Sociales etc. All of that has no importance. What is important enough for me to plunge myself into it?

Are they the same, the one who has a profound, moving, rich and voluptuously sad life, and the one who laughs indifferently, who sleeps and no longer finds tears on her eyelashes because the absolute of her despair has diverted her from strong and beautiful things? I must meditate a bit and see:

what I am in comparison to G. Lévy

in comparison to Miquel

with Jacques!

what is life for me today, what love is, where my pride is and how I resolved my problem. What I can do to love myself again, to love again . . .

Wednesday, [June] 22

Jacques came. Jacqueline is perhaps going to come. I am alone, marvelously alone. G. Lévy, intelligent little girl who naively takes her childishness and her inner discoveries seriously; annoying with her logic, her need to reduce

---

* Opposite these last two sentences Beauvoir later added the comment, "May 1929—A while ago I 'could still vividly remember' Jacques! He was standing on the other side of the table, under my eyes, with words that created happiness in me? I did not dream up this past in which he said 'a friendship like ours is very rare.' Oh! Jacques!"

everything to a formula and also her desire to explain herself. Brings every emotion back to concepts. I let her study me, but I escape her. It would be falsifying myself to submit to her.

Miquel, nice, but simple. He believes in himself and in Lagneau. No culture or these subtleties that I like.

You are all barbarians, even if you might be right, O you who are not me!

It is not that this self is so brilliant. Am I truly having fun being successful? Having an easy sense of companionship? Now that I have shaken myself up a bit and I have scorned these pleasures, it gives me a charming feeling of independence vis-à-vis my acts. Jacques's influence? Maybe. Maybe it is to understand him better that I let myself drift a bit and to be able to tell myself "I am not better than he." But it hardly bothers me. The memory of Barbier no longer makes me wince with remorse. Something, I know, is going to come of all of that and my heart's private indifference: a work, a passion or a more reliable [*sûr*] self, I don't know. But I know that only good will come of it.

I am no longer seeking "adventure" because nothing for me will ever be an adventure again. I watch myself living indifferent and distant, precious to nobody and without love for anyone, unconscious and almost gay, in the calm expectation of an unknown and more beautiful "presence."

I am profoundly certain that tomorrow will make something beautiful of the nothing that is today.

It's not true; it is not true! What do I want to come of it? Nothing but a life, a poor human life.

Ah! How humdrum life is!

In this office two years ago, I was ignorant of everything, everything: everything that was love, books, and friendships. I didn't know that the Sorbonne, Belleville, works of art, or bars existed. Nor tears, nor laughter, nor beings. Nothing. I didn't have a hint of anything. My universe was sufficient for me. Now I have traveled through all the universes (mine and those of others). Now I have lived, already lived so much in eighteen months, even in six months. Only that much! Only that much! And still that much! Ah! Tears over the cloistered and muffled days of ignorance that my calm youth lived through during warm summers!

I have just faced death for a split second. Reaching my arms towards it, I asked it, "What?" It answered me, "Nothing! Nothing!" And I tottered into a great void. To take a step, support my weary head there is only this pale void. This is not possible! I will not! Oh! Die right away rather than carry within me a death, which slowly, implacably devours me. I felt my death, I was conscious of the death that imperceptibly settled within me before the so total ruin of my past. I am dead, I am dying, ah! Not that! And nothing from so much suffering, so many cries, desires, from so much love. Nothing from me. Nothing from him. Next to that, how can even the joy of loving matter?

once again

face to face with the absolute

This weight on my heart—

my head on fire

the horrible face of reality before my eyes

And everything retreats: complications, distractions, friendships, everything, everything. I do not envy happy people. I do not understand anything, I do not accept anything.

G. Lévy is right. A single oppressing problem, which suddenly seizes you by the throat when you believed it to be asleep. Nothing exists except for me and the veiled and snickering monster named God, life or reality. It snickers because it has seen my powerlessness and because happiness and indifference do not shield us from its claws. It is there, it is watching me intently.

I'm afraid.

(And I could fall back into the world where men have faces, where one studies problems, where words have meaning. I will live; I will believe in life even while detesting it for having seen what I've seen and knowing what I know.)

But I will say it.

Here is the only truth.

Kill yourself instead.*

This poor book that I just read is stupid and sad enough to make you cry; ah! "this pitiful farce that is life." At least the young sorrowful and well-raised young girl believes in love. Me? Tonight in Belleville speaking solemnly on a subject of ethics, tomorrow joking at the Sorbonne. Ah!

Pitiful farce, too sad, I don't want it. My friends, you my unknown friends who suffered so, if only we could find you again and moan together. Laforgue

. . .

---

* Opposite this line Beauvoir later added the comment, "May 1929—Even with my most intense cry for life I cannot deny the horror of this day; I know quite well that 'it' is always there. No, I cannot say that I wasn't right before."

Wednesday, June 29

Exams—pleasure of chatting with nice young people, of having a snack with Lautman in the "bateau"; pleasure of feeling myself surrounded by the joyous politeness of this *likable* barbarian.* Slightly feverish excitation, study project and companionship; it seemed for a moment desirable for me to study for the *agrégation* and I felt like I had the soul of a Normalian![134]

And then last night such a heartsick feeling in the solitary courtyard when night was falling and on my bed after returning from the Sorbonne! I dreamed of Jacques in *Les Thibault,* who clenches his fists while shouting, "They have reduced me to this."[135] Me too, they have reduced me to "this"! Ah! No, let's shake off this scholarly dust. Jacques exists after all.

Jacques exists above all.

How lucky I was to be initiated by such a maladjusted person that the barbarity of others appeared quite evident to me. I felt how much, for example, G. Lévy is to be excused for so often being wrong.[136] These intelligent and charming boys, we refuse to classify them as barbarians. For very little, we would resign ourselves to being like them; at least, we would feel uneasy if we felt that we were different. Fortunately I know, moreover, how much this is in vain! I hear Lautman praising a companion. Immediately afterward, this little twinge that I experience every time I feel slightly touched by a being who is worthy of having us endure his life, and then he continues: he will be someone like Rauh or . . . Léon Blum![137] In that case, no!

I am not very happy with myself.

I feel quite stupid with fatigue, a bit diminished by my successes that were too deeply felt by my companions, and diminished by the sympathetic curiosity that they feel towards a "young girl of worth." What have I really done with this year? Nothing.

I am not very nice. I deny having opinions that I like in order to gain the favor of people whom I despise. I am unfaithful to ideas to become attached to some beings. Probably, end of the year fatigue. But all of this is very base; I have very little pride.

After all! Since I am "barbaric" tonight, let's stay that way. This played itself out well. For a minimum of work, a maximum of return. The Greek coup especially was funny; and in this case, I really attributed the right importance to this exam.

---

* "Likable" is underlined in the brown ink she used in May 1929 and "ah?" is written across from it.

Projects for next year:

a) *Work:* study psychology, ethics, philosophy in depth, homework for Baruzi, readings.
b) Discussions: There are M. Blomart and Zaza outside of the Sorbonne. At the Sorbonne: Miquel (who is worth more than all of these Normalians who attract me more due to stupid cultural and educational reasons) in Baruzi's class, and at the library. Lautman, in ethics and sociology, who only half interests me.

Pontrémoli, to whom I would like to get close, because he appears to have a *rich inner life,* such a sad look, and this kind of desire, that he appears to have, to get close to me.[138]* G. Lévy, of course. I am not speaking of Quartier nor of G.P., who gave me everything he could give me with a soccer game and a few glasses of lemon-lime soda. Surely *Merloponti* [*sic*], so offended at being beaten by me but so likable (externally I fear, and for poor reasons in which vanity plays a part).[139]† I cannot get close to Lagache after what G. Lévy told me; why isn't she incensed?[140] It is probably my Catholic heredity that arouses me like this. I know very well that all ethics are unethical; I like Gide, but in reality I only tolerate the beings who aim at the same values as I, whose internal aesthetic is similar to my own. I will not even try to get over this. It is a profound repugnance, whatever may be its so-called great worth.

Gandillac if I have the chance.[141]

All of this is already faded; they are all so far, so far away from me!
c) *do something:* "two pages per day and some genius," says Stendhal.[142] Force myself to think for two pages per day or something of the sort.
d) music: Colonne, Pasdeloup, etc.[143] Painting, literature, theater, all of this in rather strong doses and with as much extravagance as I like. Take walks, chat, have fun.
e) live.

I wasn't absorbed in the Équipes Sociales, or Neuilly, or my family and my milieu. I will not let myself be absorbed in the Sorbonne. Don't be "Mlle Bertrand de Beauvoir." Be me. Don't have a goal imposed from outside, a social framework to fill. What works for me will work, and that is all. Remain haughty and pitiful.

So now my diversions are settled. If only I could settle the fate of my soul in the same way.

---

* In the clause "Pontrémoli, to whom I would like to get close, because he appears to have a *rich inner life*," "rich inner life" is underlined in the brown ink used for 1929 comments, and there is the marginal comment next to it, "unbelievable!"

† "Merloponti" is underlined in the brown ink often used for later comments. ·

Thursday, July 7

To think that last Thursday, all morning and afternoon at Mademoiselle Mercier's home, I sobbed from nervous tension. This is it! A nice successful life, I thought! Oh! Emptiness! Nothingness, vanity . . .

Once again, here I am strengthened by the love that others have for me. Charming afternoon at G. Lévy's home reading verse together and touching beautiful books. Long conversations with Miquel, who is becoming very dear to me. Simone Weil, who always comes back to Chartier. Mademoiselle Mercier. Lastly Pontrémoli. Then met José, and the joy of doing her some good.[144] Wrote to Jacques, less because I felt like it than because he might have felt like it. Then [I] read Stendhal, Amiel.[145] How far have I gotten?

I gained two things this year: the liking for and the habit of philosophy and the knowledge of beings. Last year I learned to know myself, to know Jacques, literature, and art; I discovered the inner world, I got a hint of life.

My winter was occupied almost uniquely with love and suffering. The end of this year put me in contact with the life of others, with life, period, and taught me, thanks to books and conversations, to formulate my problems philosophically and rigorously. I like them so much and so passionately! I dare say, whenever I perceive that the actors in this really wonderful drama live it and bear it like me, I am overwhelmed with distress and everything dissolves into tears. But when I look at the show from the outside, how I love it and what rapture! I am in communion with them. I recreate them, and I penetrate them. I become drunken with their existence. And if I see myself as an actor among these other actors, I applaud myself as a truly beautiful success. At the moment, the passion for this great game fills my heart. Life is so beautiful as long as I am creating it! So painful when it is a given that must be endured. Live, act, be wholeheartedly! This is how I want to do something! I refuse to let these ideas, these riches that swell up in me be lost. Take heart!

Unendingly I make resolutions that I never keep. However . . . Next year I will have almost nothing to study. And there won't be too many books left for me to read. I must make a work of my own. On the one hand, keep a journal every day with precise descriptions of what I have done, seen, thought (and not lose myself in vague raptures and imprecise ramblings). On the other hand, consecrate two hours per day to the work that I will have chosen between now and October. I will be twenty years old in a few months. My education will be almost finished. I will have learned, read, seen everything essential and well beyond. I will have lived with my intelligence and my heart and known a rather wide world. I will even have begun to think by myself; there will be no wasted time. But then it will be advisable to put myself to work. If I live, I must fully accept the game; I must have the most beautiful life. I don't know why I am here, but since I remain here, I will construct a beautiful edifice. One has to keep busy . . .

(Besides, this energy that I got from my conversation with Pontrémoli will soon subside, but it doesn't matter).

First, one must take risks.* Am I perhaps afraid of ridicule? I have always congratulated myself for having confronted it. Afraid of work? No, indeed. I will establish myself [*m'affirmerai*]. Indeed, a friendship to support me would be precious. Neither Zaza, nor M. Blomart, nor any young girl. Maybe G. Lévy. Surely even I can speak to her about it, discuss it with her, but she is too interested in herself to support me truly. Jacques intimidates me too much and takes nothing seriously enough. I would infinitely like the friendship of Pontrémoli, who is of average intelligence but profound, serious, sensitive and attentive, who understands literature and philosophy as I do, and whose sympathy for me is so evident. (His friend who wrote him such a nice letter about Alain will be someone to know and to cultivate.)

What has become of Jacques in the midst of these more and more profound and important friendships? I have understood that others besides him carry an infinity within themselves. I have absolutely no need of him any longer in order *to be;* he would bother me instead. But every time that his presence succeeds his slightly dormant image in the depths of myself, a great wave of love washes over me. "I often think of you," I wrote to him; it is true. I will sacrifice my exams for him, but not my written work if I can do one, nor myself.† Besides, he will not ask me to do this. Impossible for me to fall asleep in a love, refusal to submit to any slavery.

And deep down I don't know—maybe I will sacrifice everything, everything for him, and it will not be a sacrifice.

What should I do? First, don't scatter myself in fragmentary works. When ideas interest me, take note of them but without following them, carefully keep them in the greatest disorder—either I will rediscover them and integrate them into the chosen work, or they will become the point of departure for a new work once I will have exhausted the first. Don't hurry, but work

* The first eight sentences in this paragraph—up through "Lévy"—are highlighted in brown ink in the margin.

† From the beginning of the third sentence in this paragraph through the end of the next paragraph, Beauvoir's sentences are highlighted with a vertical line in the margin. The word "oh!" written later appears opposite "I will sacrifice my exams for him."

two hours per day, genius or not, even if I believe that it will come to nothing, and confide in someone who will criticize me and take me seriously: Baruzi, G. Lévy or Pontrémoli.

Two tendencies in me: a) To describe and to create. Unceasingly I recreate life. I close my eyes and unfold a splendid and moving reality according to what experience has made me know. I create myself. I create my story. I live and make others live complicated and ardent novels. Whence the need to make all of this turn into a written work, into a written work that would say everything, that would analyze souls in minute detail while breathing life into each body. I see what I desire and will never attain, this type of objectification of the inner world that perhaps no procedure will ever make it possible to attain.

Thus I must seek and try in this way: clarify my desire and proceed by trial and error in order to prepare what would eventually be a great written work.

b) Analyze, understand, and descend more deeply into myself. That must be achieved; it is feasible. It is not about creating life, but about thinking already created life, it is there, I think, that it is imperative to begin. The questions that interest me must be studied in great depth.

There is this subject of "love," which is so fascinating and for which I have sketched the outline. It would be necessary to go on from there, to bring it together with the problems of the personality that love formulates so exactly—the problem of the act of faith that so closely touches the first two problems.

And then as an easier, yet related subject: friendship; its dangers; the nature of the education it provides; in brief, how souls can interact with one another. It would be fascinating to write some very brief and lofty descriptive treatises about this and at the same time [*parallèlement*] some didactic studies. It would be necessary to have the courage to write, not to expound ideas but to discover them, not to clothe them artistically but to animate them. The courage to believe in them.

How about if for two hours every day I forced myself to look into *my* thoughts instead of ingesting those of others! And then I must not repeat the same thing fifty times. I always leave everything sketched out without development. I am going to impose upon myself, during vacation, without books or anything, the task of taking up the subject of love, perfecting it in October, and presenting to Baruzi at the beginning of November at least thirty condensed and coherent pages. I will see what he says.

"I admire you because you are a force." I would like to quote this line to G. Lévy, whom I miss more than I would have believed. It doesn't surprise me, coming from Lydia Kleimann's stupidity and Hélène Alphanderi's childishness, but it makes me contemplate some things: my strength and my weakness!

* * *

> I do not notice tolerance in the arts nor in geometry. This frees me from this sad friendship that would mean to me, "You are other and I am other; let us bear one another because we cannot do any better." With this indulgence, all gifts are lost from the start. Great friendship, great fraternity is more demanding. Goethe said this admirable thing, "Forgive everyone and even those we love." Admirable words because we cannot follow them. For if someone shows himself to be insensitive to the arts, or stubborn towards geometry, we can only be consoled by scorning him. It is perhaps too much to ask, but we do not have the right to ask for less. The most beautiful thing is that with all the severity possible, we cannot use force since it is what is free that we want. What we want is what makes one oneself; there is my likeness. He refuses to be it, and I myself want him to be it . . . This type of severity is the only thing in the world that is good. Charity doesn't give, it asks.
>
> Alain[146]

Friday, July 8

Evening too gray and too sad after this awfully humdrum day. From the bed where I am stretched out with Léon Paul Fargue's poems that are too much the color of my soul, I see some birds fly by in a cottony sky.[147] There is a letter that I desire and will not receive. What emptiness, what boredom! I hang on to some likable faces, but the too well loved face unendingly smiles at me with sorrow. For what indefinite crossing have I embarked at this precise point in time and space as though in the middle of an immense sea? A crossing whose goal is unknown . . .

This story is of no interest.

Sunday, July 10

To Miquel and Pontrémoli yesterday I said good-byes full of laughter. Yesterday, too, José was joyful to discover that she had a friend. But what do I myself get out of what people attribute to me? I am thinking of all of those who hold me dear, and it is very sad because I care so little about them! The only one who matters is he whom I know nothing about today.

Mademoiselle Mercier is trying to convert me; she talks to me about Abbé Beaussard, who would like to see me, and I think of the words of G. Lévy, "You will be tempted in that domain."[148] It's true. This morning while racing in vain to St. Cloud, I passionately desired to be the young girl who receives communion at morning mass and who walks with a serene certainty.[149] Mauriac's and Claudel's Catholicism, for which Jacques has not completely lost his liking, how it has marked me and what a place remains in me for it! And yet, I know that I will no longer know this; I do not desire to believe. An act of faith is the greatest act of despair that could be and I want my despair to preserve at least its lucidity. I do not want to lie to myself. Besides, this infinite God saves me only as a *person;* and it is my entire individual that I want to save. I must clearly spell out my philosophical ideas, and maybe I will begin the narrative that I would like to write. So many ideas that have matured with my meditations and become more precise through my conversations. I should take stock of my eighteen months of thought, reassess and go more deeply into problems that enticed me, to which I gave overly hasty solutions.* The theme is almost always this opposition of self and other that I felt upon starting to live. Now has come the time to make a synthesis of it. Foreign influences are remote, and also the desire for affectation in writing. I will write my work in my own style seeking only to express well what I feel.

This page by Alain that I have copied: Does Socrates really want to find himself in his likeness? I know that the laws of the mind are the same in all men. But it does not seem to me that there is only one way to judge sanely. It depends on postulates that each man has implicitly or explicitly accepted, and the choice of his postulates is left to each man. It depends on his temperament, his sensitivity, and the irreducible given that constitutes the individuality of each man. I should read Leibniz for I feel so vividly the principle of indiscernibles![150] I hate the mechanism that, reducing the quality to the quantity, makes the quality disappear. Likewise, to reduce men to similar but diversely combined tendencies explains nothing; whether the difference be in the combination or in the elements, there is always a given that excludes the identical. That is why I feel myself to be not phenomenon but noumenon; quality is a reflection of noumenon on the plane of experience. I believe that, and I perceive it as something almost uniquely qualitative. But why then this relative objectivity? Why can't we not accept

---

* The rest of this paragraph is highlighted with a line in the margin of the diary.

geometry? Because there the postulates are explicit, and also the step which makes us pass from one truth to the other; we observe a truth that we do not create—the same as in formal logic. But once we truly think, we must in some way create our truth. In the same way when we appreciate the work of art, whereby following the spontaneity of . . .[151]

Claude came and spoke to me of Jacques, who is bored. It's really sad! It is really sad! I am here, he is there—we can only think a little about each other, but we are alone, so alone: "There is no path" . . .[152] If only you wanted it, Jacques.

Monday, July 11

Another overwhelming day. The strong odor of rain in the Sorbonne court-yard where my routine brings me back. Yet in the Luxembourg Gardens the cool morning heavy with perfumes was an invitation to the easy life. Have reread *L'inquiète adolescence* [Restless Adolescence] by Chadourne—all of this already has the attraction of a memory.[153]

Oh! My God! My God! How could one express in any work the body's lassitude, the mind's great fatigue, the heart without desire? And if I were to express it, of what use would it be? Rereading the book later would I still understand it?

Tuesday, [July] 12

Letter from Pontrémoli that fills me with a strange feeling. He must have had some liking for me, to come to Porte Dauphine every day to see me. Besides, I definitely felt that something stronger than a banal companion-ship was forming since I myself had thought of writing to him after his sad good-bye. I would be pleased to become his friend. But there are many unwritten things between the lines of this letter, and I am afraid of a feeling too intense for my already occupied heart. I will not break it off, for if I must engage others there, I will risk everything in my life; but it often appeared to me that this boy loved me, and this confirms my idea. I will loyally tell him from the start how things are; not to do so would be to act like a flirt. His friend [*amie*] and nothing else.

Curious. I don't know him. All I know of him I like, and yet I prefer Jacques, who cares perhaps less about me. What if I had entered into Pon-trémoli's life by another door? I don't know. I know only that I imagine him pensive, alone with a big tender heart that has pounded at the idea of a possible affection. Lagneau's precept comes back to mind "Do not pretend to do good—have only the ultimate will to avoid doing harm."[154] And I know that Lagneau is right, and that in order to avoid doing harm it would be necessary to avoid responding, but I care too much about Pontrémoli to have such rational coldness.

I like the courageous decision with which he wrote me. But how curious it is to imagine the face that I must have in his life and the rapidity with which I entered into it.

(1 rond point Bugeaud. Paris. XVIe.)

One idea I am contemplating: the astonishment one feels upon finding what one considers to be the most important in another place in someone else's life, a book for example. *Aimée*, which is for me the initiation to a more difficult world, amazing to become aware that such an other has not read it![155] Or understanding Picasso, which appeared to me to be the supreme goal; one can be intelligent and not like him, and so on. Think this through again.

Thought a lot about Pontrémoli. I answered him right away with all the details. "Even if my life is already established around a deep affection, each prospective friendship will find me no less entirely available." Come what may.

Saturday, [July 16]

Thought much more again about Merleau-Ponti, whom I met yesterday at Normale and with whom I just chatted deliciously for two hours in the Luxembourg Gardens. Oh! The wife of this young, frank, simple, so gay and so serious boy will really be lucky! How I rebelled today against you, my difficult and disappointing love, you so uncertain, complicated and yet without artifice, so sincere but also so weary, disenchanted—you who do not write, you whose love I have sometimes felt quite near, who let me glimpse a profound tenderness, but who never gave me the refreshing exchange of your affection! All that comes to me from you is grave and heavy. Dreaming of this more industrious boy, who is less purely emotional and sensitive however, from this so likeable boy, I have understood how little certain ardent pages of these notebooks link me to you, the shivers before your door, the frantic errands in Paris, and how easily one love can replace another, but also how much any stifled "thank you," any "adieu, old girl," any smile of confident tenderness used to make me the slave of our affection.[156] Love, small thing; but this great friendship, I will not run away from it. And I suffered to know this; it is when I love you the most that I hate even more the love that I have for you.* Bizarre love. Through your fault and mine. Sure enough for me to live, far enough away for me to experience all the sentiments and the despairs that I would feel if I were alone.[157] For me to conserve it despite everything, you must really be of a very rare essence. Before seeing him again I believed him to be of the same quality as you. Now, liking him more than ever, desiring him ardently for a friend, I find him a bit similar to others, all the same. But such a charming frankness, such a concern for essential things, so much cordiality and especially intellectual probity. He likes me for what is young in me. Maybe I am so, despite everything, from the energy with which I stand back up and come back to life [*ressuscite*] from my numerous deaths.

The branches are numerous and new at the moment. They completely mask the abyss that is underneath.[158]

I will explain everything to him Monday: how I started with action, to flee self-worship for the necessary action—Barrès and Péguy; then how I saw the illusion of that and that life demanded nothing from me; how I am seeking an exigency and how I find that nothing is worth it; my despairs and the position I am in now: no longer waiting or hoping for anything, neither able to accept nor to refuse life.[159]

Sunday, July 17

All today again, I thought about this charming companion with whom I was immediately on equal footing and calm. Life really has another "look" that depends on the being at the center of it! The afternoon slipped by easily, brightened by letters written to girlfriends brought close by my joy. Thanks to him, I have sunny hours.

And I've just reread the pages that I wrote on June 3. You, more secret and more rare, more bitter also, must I truly say excuse me to you for this lassitude that I have for you sometimes like for myself too? I don't know. I write and you don't respond; I cannot make out your face, you are as though you were not; so I say to myself: what am I to him? I remember vague remarks, inconsistencies, everything that fills me with a vague malaise once your firm presence is no longer there to dissipate them. Ambiguous face even for anyone who loves you and knows you well.† Probably, my timidity and your own have impeded the conversations where one tells all. Probably we have

---

* The preceding clause is highlighted in the margin.
† The last two sentences are highlighted in the margin.

spoken too much through silences. So I say to myself, what is he?—and I know that this is bad, that an entire confidence is necessary, that you merit more than these doubts, than these feelings of anxiety or indifference, that you are difficult, and that precisely because of this you need me to understand you. I say to myself, I foresee the tears of remorse that I will shed just as sometimes I have shed them! But it is so much as if everything was over! As if everything was over!

And it's my fault. It's when I love less that I feel less loved. I cannot imagine what you are today: maybe you are thinking of me, maybe you are sorrowfully meditating. Oh my friend, forgive me! No, it isn't over since I am already crying from remorse about these too charming days spent without you—in order to relax, to let you sleep in my heart. It isn't very decent, but I consent to it; but to judge you when you are not there to defend yourself, to declare that this is dead, never again.

How awkward, uncertain, and highly complicated we are! Why never similar to others, just a little bit similar?

But what nostalgia I have for this perilous affection—how all the same, the calm and sure love that a Merleau-Ponti would offer has less power in his smile than yours seen through my tears!

Why so awfully powerless to imagine what I am for others? Agitation on the threshold of their secret life, this no longer belongs to me. The worth that some attribute to me, and Jacques, who has me, what worth does he assign to this wealth? I well feel that for others I have the infinite appeal of all that of which they are ignorant, and that he loves me sadly, faithfully, sternly like a poor finite being who is nothing but that! Oh! Those weren't stories, those frightened words that I wrote at the beginning of the year, "a woman is only one part of the world's beauty . . ."; others love me, and I love them in an illusion, whence the charm of our relationships—in fact [en vérité] we love each other so cruelly.

Jacques, I hurt when I think of you; I don't know why your life is tragic. And now the great, tearful desire that I knew so well this winter is being revived. The desire for your presence, for your tenderness, simply for your smile!

Monday, July 18

Luminous conversation with Ponti, for whom my sympathy has become profound affection.

I am still new since I haven't even lived for two years. At first, painful enthusiasm, but enthusiasm all the same: Garric, action, self-worship. Then, collapsing of such values: no exigencies and the influence of disillusioned, ironic, and too easily discouraged Jacques, then despair.

Ah well! Ponti is right. *I do not have the right to despair.* I accepted that despair was justified, but it demands to be demonstrated—to say, "nothing is worth it," and to sit idly by with your arms crossed, to have the certainty that no certainty is possible; this is still dogmatism. This is what Mlle Blomart used to say awkwardly to me, and what I have understood through contact with Ponti. I am still too much of a woman. I say, "I am seeking what I need and not what is, but I know that what I need cannot be." I too am setting forth a postulate: it is first necessary to seek what is, then, I will see if I must still despair.

How well they said in *L'Esprit* that those who like the search for the truth more than the truth will not be saved.[160] I do not hunger enough for the truth. It is no longer about all my stories: tall tales. I will use my vacation to seek what I believe.

But: if in trying to think without passion I say, "I have no reason to choose despair," I also say, "I have no reason to move towards Catholicism rather than any other way." Indeed I don't want an optimism like the one that Guindey explained, a human truth justified by a categorical imperative, or an ethic without metaphysics. I want God or nothing, but why the Christian God?

And on the contrary, it is because Catholicism speaks too much to my heart that my reason distrusts it: traditions, heredity, memories that direct me to give my support to it. Without all that, why turn to it rather than elsewhere? Raised differently, Merleau-Ponti, would your reason stripped of all passion attract you to Catholicism? You have said yourself that the manner of asking the question was of considerable importance and almost implied the response. If you therefore say, I am examining Catholic dogma but in complete impartiality, aren't you making a mistake? The impartiality is in the manner in which you ask the question.

Tuesday morning, [July 19]

I slept poorly last night; thought too much about all these things. And then, my dear friends, you don't like young girls, but remember that they not only have a reason to satisfy, but also a heavy heart to subdue [*comprimer*]—and in this way I want to remain a woman, still more masculine by her brain, more feminine by her sensibility.[161] (Moreover, everyone recognizes in approaching me that I am not like other young girls. Oh Ponti, how nicely you said so to me in the splendid Luxembourg Gardens on the gilded night. So humble, you too my *friend,* so simple, so charming!)

I have examined my conscience, and here is what I have found: prideful, selfish, and not very good. Jacques also made me feel this. Yes. I often have disgust for myself. I think that I could be very humble before God, but I am not humble before men. I have closed myself in my ivory tower, saying, "Who is worthy of entering here?" I would sometimes open the door and that is all, but there are some people profoundly better than me, and this haughty attitude is stupid.

Egoist—I love others only inasmuch as they are me; I easily scorn, and scornful, I no longer try to do my best.

Not very good—how severely I judge and with what right? Even the boys who sing ignoble songs, I should love them with pity and indulgence. I laugh with scorn; I should suffer with gentleness. I am hard, hard and proud. Become conscious of your own poverty, my girl, and of all of your cowardice! You walked for five minutes in a beautiful garden, then you arrived in a desert of stones and behind you the door was closed. You walked for five more minutes, then you lay down on the ground, and you cried from not being able to find any suitable position after having sought one all year. People passed by, saying, "There can only be stones there." You said, "Why?" You were right, but you said within yourself, "There are only stones," and then, "Why?" All you have to do is to get up and to walk on until your last day.

And this position seems so evident! Benefit of the contact with others— upon seeing another point of departure, we become conscious that ours does not impose itself; we analyze it and the hidden defect suddenly stares us in the face. I now see the sophism. I used to say, "One must seek, walk; I don't have the right to remain thus." And right away, "What good will it do, in relationship to whom, in relationship to what?" And indeed, to this, "What good will it do?" I cannot answer anything, but the answer will come at the same time as the complete response if there is one. If there isn't one, then indeed, "What good will it do?"[162] But I will only have the right to say this when, having carried on regardless, I have truly found that there isn't anything. And besides, does one ever find this? Even if everything were to say "no" to me, I can never know if there isn't one remaining question to which a "yes" would answer; to abandon the hunt, is always too hasty an induction, and unjustified discouragement.

I have covered my own cowardice with sophisms—oh! You see, you must give me credit after all, because I have only been doing philosophy for barely ten months, because I have almost never chatted with intelligent people.[163] I made myself in spite of barely favorable circumstances, and in spite of others, in a great intellectual solitude. And then I truly have no vanity, a great goodwill and a complete sincerity.

If only I could live with people in whose worth and sincerity I had great confidence. I was so enclosed in my own judgment—basically, it is in supporting myself with my reason that I doubt my reason. All of that must be changed. One must love the truth and not the search for the truth.

(But I am afraid that, at any rate, nobody's questions will influence me—and yet this time it really appears to me that this is something really essential!)[164]

Only, let's get back to my comparison. One must get up and walk on, yes. Ponti says, "There is this path (of Catholicism) I want to see if it is possible." I say, why this path? I believe it to be impossible. Probably I do not have the right to affirm this before I have gone all the way. But I fear the loss of time that I could more usefully spend on another path.

My essay where I denied substance contradicts this realism that I explained to G. Lévy. I am too easily satisfied with contradictions. But here is the explanation: I must have all or nothing. Ponti says, "It is better to sacrifice becoming than being." Me, once I see a defect in a system, I want to sacrifice the entire system. I doubly detest the things that I would love if they were perfect and that are essentially unfinished.

To believe that I will find the truth with my reason? But why me and not my concierge? Those who are not philosophers are thus condemned to error—they do not need the truth? Why do I need it then?

The intelligent people who are Catholic . . . yes, but do they think without passion? By definition, no, since they invoke grace. Gandillac, etc., do not doubt Catholicism, only found it on reason within Catholicism. Reason alone cannot lead to Catholicism; grace is necessary.

All explicative philosophy puts us in front of a remainder.[165] Reason gives only the human element, necessity of a mysticism. Isn't the first crime to think? That is why I do not believe that philosophy will ever tell us the secret of the world; we are enclosed in reason and can judge reason only with itself: vicious circle.

I must reread and contemplate Kant, Bergson, and Descartes.

All the same, he departs from an act of faith in reason. I believe with Kant that one can not attain the world of noumena . . .

Being does not equal substance—there is some being in the order of phenomenon. I said, "I believe in substance"; as I said, "I believe in causality." I meant, "I imagine things under the order of substance as under the order of causality," but this does not mean that there is a substance. Separate reason from noumena with Kant and Bergson, while you admit that reason can grasp noumena.

I started by examining my conscience and making an act of contrition; I have recognized that I was supposed to seek, but not in Catholicism.

I scared myself with my inconsistencies. Then, in delving into them, I saw all the same that my philosophy was not as up for grabs as it appeared.

Ponti supports his with faith in reason, I on the powerlessness of reason. Who proves that Descartes prevails over Kant? I am maintaining what I wrote for the Sorbonne—use your reason, you will end up with remainders and irrational elements.

But precisely in religion there is a mysticism, "act of faith"—act of defiance in reason. If I am logical with myself, I must admit it. I have understood the act of faith, for at least a split second.

Five o'clock—I didn't tell him anything about all that because we stayed at Normale, where you can't chat. But tomorrow at nine o'clock I will see him. What simple and total sympathy between us! He has the same complexion, the same hair, and the same color suit as Jacques. The charming smile when he is mocking someone, such a childlike look, such youth—and such seriousness, such gravity when we are alone.

In Normale's courtyard, seated on the grass . . . telling me about Lautmann near to Baruzi, so similar to me, so pleasantly ironic, so, so . . . and I was really happy to do this little favor for him.

Deep down, I do not regret knowing him only now. These daily conversations interspersed with meditations in Paris on vacation are charming. We will see each other again next year.

Delight of the beginnings of friendship.

Maurice Merleau-Ponti . . . I like him so already! Why "already"! On the contrary, alas! Normale is such a dump: dirty, poorly kept . . . but the courtyard with the fountain is nice, and it is interesting to see once (especially when Ponti is there).

Wednesday, July 20[166]

I have learned things. Now I must continue to learn things, but above all, I must want the truth. I am ashamed! I am ashamed! When I see Merleau-Ponti, I am ashamed of my indifference. I am sad, I am feverish; I believe that I am beginning to like him too much.

Of two things one remains—either there is a truth inaccessible to reason, and so by no means will I attain it—or there is a truth accessible to reason, and I will have it only by using my reason. In any case, I must opt for reason. Even if there were ninety-nine chances for the first hypothesis to be correct, logically one chance remains anyway for me *to have to* use my reason, and I therefore no longer have the freedom of indifference. This is certain. If I ever say, "What good is this?" it will be out of cowardice; let me be warned once and for all. I am committing myself to do something difficult. It won't be pleasant for me, but I must do it as long as there is one chance that I must inevitably do it.

Don't do philosophy as a game anymore. Systematize my thoughts and believe in the value of thought. Read as if this had happened and not with the unavowed certainty that this is false. Delve more deeply. Take all of this seriously. Be more pitiless towards myself and less skeptical with regards to others.

How many projects, under the influence of diverse sympathies, have I thus imposed on myself? But this one combines the others.

(All the same, isn't there a sophism there? Catholicism is not proven to be true, thinks the unbeliever; I am abandoning it. Is it proven to be false? answers the priest. You must stay with it. What if there are not any decisive proofs in either sense?—extrarational element of belief.

He seeks justification, not discovery; why not seek to justify Buddhism or any other doctrine?

If a religion is true, upon seeking it honestly with your reason, you cannot find it to be false. If it is false, you can find it to be true. And that is why before the number of people who are not believers and those who are believers, the first impress me more.)

Don't be worried about religion for the moment. Do philosophy seriously by proceeding in order. Stop only in front of the evidence. Write conclusions once they are acquired.

In essence: reread *l'Esprit* and study mysticism; meditate over Kant and Bergson; study Plato, Leibniz, and Thomism; study post-Kantian philosophy.[167] Challenging program for a school year, but I will do it.

And above all: think for myself.

(Oh! Tired, irritated, sure of getting nothing out of this desperate recourse to philosophy, and yet I *want*, I owe it to myself to do it. Who will help me to do it? Me.)

The first two points of departure must be the idea of truth and the idea of God.

Is there a truth? Within or outside of us? Created or received by me? Ontology or criticism? This already presupposes the nature of intelligence. What is truth?

Oh! My God, my God, is this being whom we would like to love and to whom we would give all, does this being truly not exist? I know nothing, and I am weary, weary. Why, if he is, does he make seeking him so difficult?

And there you have it! Before holding the first link, I have almost decided not to try anything because it appears impossible to me to ever seize the last one. Forbid this to myself. Reason coldly. Ah! There is a lot to do to make a philosopher of me!

Why wouldn't God be? Oh! Peace, my soul, peace. I would like to see Abbé Beaussard tonight.[168]

Friday, July 22 (Square de la Sorbonne)

A curious little sadness in a kind of vague joy—some hope and some regret, a waiting, an abandonment, a final goodbye with the hope of a renewal . . .

O my crucifying affections that sometimes chain me, crush me, and enslave me with any vocal inflection (and so fragile is my happiness thus hanging on some stranger), that sometimes leave me lonely, hard, lonelier still to think how much my friends live without me.

Exquisite days, filled with the wait for the already habitual mornings: I arrive at 9:30, I sit down, I listen to the questions (for the *agrégation*), I start to say is he going to come? And he arrives, without a hat, young, smiling, even childlike. We stay ten minutes, and then we walk towards the Luxembourg Gardens where we chat at length, slowly. Winged conversations, easy and profound, will I ever again find anything that measures up to this? This which is, nevertheless, going to end . . . religion, politics, and our lives also: his mother, the meagerness of their resources with his very joyful courage, so much honesty!

But how much simpler than I is he, acting already as though what he seeks were found, having a fixed direction! How lonely I find myself to be with my heavy and unsatisfied heart! He will love the young girl whom he will love simply . . . whom I don't want, whom I do want to be. Even closer in any case my friend, close enough that I can confess my weaknesses to you. It hurts me to have to leave you soon without having given you more, it hurts me to give up this adorable and brief period of our life.

"The multiplicity of compossibles," Rivière, how I suffer from it.[169]

At least, he gave me the sincere ardor for truth. But he does not love himself as I love myself. His satisfied thoughts, his profound but well-behaved heart will leave him in peace. He lives; he will know how to live. And me, and me . . .

Yet I believe that I am walking sincerely towards a serious simplification. Literature, paradoxes, the liking for complications have fallen away from me. More stripped, more serene and confident, more reliable too; will I manage to bear life better? I will seek the truth with all of my force. With all of my force, I will do what I decree is good, which maybe *is* good—good books, smiling friendships will help me perhaps, perhaps . . .

". . . and you want a discreet heart . . ."

Why turn everything into sorrow? Ah! Wearying analyses, will I ever abandon you? Every corner of these Luxembourg Gardens hurts me with an encountered memory.

Proust says well that it is a small misfortune to regret a lost possession once one has detached oneself from it; "One must then, even when one possesses it, foresee this loss."[170] I am doing so. At the same time that I take pleasure in any profound affection, I feel that it is dead; my regret doubles my possession. I feel very bad. And never will I detach myself from these human things. Never will I cease to love others and myself passionately because infinity is within us. And for each one, I will suffer awfully from his not being everything in my life. Torture of this happiness that I imagine, that I sense and that I do not have even the right to desire. Horror of being obligated to choose! For a non-external choice that modifies the entire being, this would be easy, but profound . . . to choose *oneself* in choosing another.

The same tears as last year after the car ride with Jacques . . . "The harvesting of a dream to the heart that stole it."[171] Why is the loved one absent? Above all, why does one love? And I love him so, so much that I hurt from an unavowed pain, from an obscure malaise that I do not understand.

Less and less I understand this "Love" that people talk about, peaceful once it has met its object. I myself don't have any unused love, but each encounter imposes a new irreplaceable one on me, unique like the being for whom I feel it.*

Awful to die and awful to endure. Awful not to be able to vanish totally [*s'anéantir*] into every minute, horror that each minute vanishes totally.

If I had God, I would still suffer from that, but aren't these simply love's heartrending tortures such as I knew them for Jacques? All the more torturous in that I cannot even wish for the mutual enthusiasm [*élan*] that would

---

* This paragraph is highlighted in the margin of Beauvoir's manuscript.

make the two of us only one—too strong and too weak; I love and do not prefer. But will the possession of such a beautiful rose console me for leaving such a really beautiful carnation? And again, there only my pleasure is engaged, whereas here I must also give up the happiness that the other would have received from me.

I desire and don't desire for Jacques to be here.

I am distressed, but it is a rather gentle pain since I know that my friend loves me too and that I will see him again tomorrow.

But the act of loving, stripped of jealousy, of fear as of hope, the pure act of love is really a heartbreaking thing.

Desires for work, for success, for intellectual certitude at least. Too tired to start a systematization. But I can no longer read anything but books going back to the essential and think about essential things.

I would want God, and yet God frightens me because then this pain, this love, this past minute would be little ephemeral things and would no longer contain infinity. But before knowing if what is pleases me, it is necessary to know what is.

I will do it, but I know so well in advance that this will not take away any of my reasons to suffer. "Nothing beautiful but what lives, and life is what dies."

So many tears on the terrace! Such bitterness! So many hopes! And then death at the end! And then death at the end! His tranquil certitude of being eternal, but I myself am afraid—he and I, who were here yesterday elegant, young, smiling, and friends, one day underground both of us, and nothing will tell of our passage—nothing. If I felt like this near you, will I ever be able to forget you?

I don't want to die!

Start by seeking the things that I am sure about. Then arrange the questions about which I am uncertain, read and reflect on them.

I have some negative certainties. Sure that mechanism doesn't explain the world, sure that my body doesn't explain my soul, sure that materialism is false. I am going to do a philosophy class as though I were addressing students.

List of essential questions: truth—is it? what?—the self (personality, hence ethics)—the world: from where does it come, where is it going, why is it: *God*—God's relationship to me.

Saturday, [July 23]—So tranquilly joyful!

Because it is an immense friendship that is being born in these analyses, these confidences, these walks, these smiles—because my love for Jacques is affirmed when I see Ponti so like a kid at heart—because the two go well together and are both infinite and as great as if each were alone.

Here I find my advantage: I have lived more than he even if I have thought less. He is astonishingly naïve sentimentally; I would not be able to be loved by him. Besides, I feel that he has no desire to love me. As a female friend, indeed, he desires me, but who will take care of me for all of a lifetime? Will Jacques himself dare?

When I chat with anyone, I realize how simple he is compared to us, and feel this even when we are perfectly sincere and simplified. I have done experiments that have not resulted in anything. Ponti does not experiment; he advances only as and when his route becomes clear. "Looks like Mauriac," Georgette Lévy used to say. Thus, I had placed him among the people to get to know for next year. But I did not suspect that he would be a *friend*.

How young, childlike, intelligent, serious, nice he is!

Sunday, July 24

In these friendships, these letters (G. Lévy, Pontrémoli . . .) I scatter a lot of myself. But so what! I am on vacation. Saw M. Blomart. She told me things about love that make me laugh, especially since Jacques and I are far from them (physical love, etc.); it is true that we are not like everyone. I think back to my strange dream. On religion, really precious information: she believes because she needs something, so she says this something is, but her reason rebels; she believes with her heart against her intelligence. Too passionate in terms of sentiments, too near a Bloy, a Daudet and not enough of a Fournier.[172] I so much prefer my weak, my poor Zaza! My poor Zaza! Ah! In the letter that I wrote her while crying, let her find some comfort. But it is not the struggle that frightens me; it is what she will conquer with this struggle! She is going to found her future on a past; she is following a destiny. As for me, I feel so free, so much like the creator of my present . . . poor Zaza! I didn't suspect any of this.

I saw five curious novels taking shape this year: Poupette and Jean, small romance without significance; M. Blomart and her fiancé, profound love, but (shall I say it?) banal.[173] G. Lévy and her "partner," but this girl barely has a heart; me and Jacques—that's another story; finally, Zaza and this sad love that she knows is unworthy of her without being able to tear herself away from it. How young you are, Ponti; you who are ignorant of the pathos of all of this.

Such faith in Jacques, such total and peaceful certainty in me, somewhat certain, despite the doubt that she wanted to deposit in me. I do not understand well, but I believe, and this without any effort. My beloved . . .

Unreal and precious world where here I am plunged anew. Wouldn't it always be necessary to live there? Far from them, far from difficult problems, from fatigues, from efforts, outside of time and space, in a completely new today where waves of love surged. Meaulnes's enchanted land where I have so often wandered, why can't I stay there?[174]

Indifferent, alone, sumptuously sad . . . Those who have "grace," as J. says, they live there. If Georgette is speaking of this when she speaks of marvelous moments, she is perhaps right: they are sufficient in themselves. Verses float around me, verses of languor and beauty; fraternal souls are quite close. This is my paradise rediscovered.

But what is its worth?

Thursday, July 28

I envy him, the simple and strong boy who lives a tranquil life next to a tenderly cherished mother and calmly seeks a truth that he hopes to find. "Aristocrat" did he say to me? It is true. I cannot get rid of the idea that I am alone, in a world apart, witnessing this world as if at a show. Hardness, scorn? Perhaps, but rather indifference. I am not judging. Only there are people who do not exist for me, others who do exist, that's all.

He forbids himself dreams. Ah! I myself find riches in them that I do not want to do without. Drama of my affections, pathos of life and this unreal Alain-Fournier who I often am. Indeed, I have a more complicated, more nuanced sensibility than his and a more exhausting power of love. Those problems that he lives in his mind, I live them with my arms and my legs. Has he ever known months when all the days were only tears? I do not want to lose all that.

But why lose it? Only I must make myself stronger in order to walk on despite my burden. Two cowardly attitudes: keep the burden and sit down— (this is very cowardly)—throw off the burden and walk on. One good one: keep the burden and walk on. I will walk on.

I say "skepticism," he says "laziness." He is right. My laziness has excuses. Yes, but one must not need to be excused.

Friday, July 29

Why did I go see the Abbé B.?[175] I don't know. He told me that reason is not sufficient to arrive at faith. I suspected as much. Zaza, Poupette, Mlle Blomart believe with their hearts. I don't think that I will ever be Catholic. But after all, whatever the final response must be, I will seek.

The year is ending. Let's liquidate it.

It brought me incalculable riches, friendships, ideas, sentiments; I have lived intensely. I must learn how to move forward. Until now my thoughts have always been engaged in feelings, but Ponti is right to say, "Feeling is a failed idea." I do not want any failures.

I was superstitious about life. Hypnotized by Rivière, Fournier, Jacques, I didn't know how to surpass them. That is why, rereading my notes, I noticed that I was at a virtual standstill. To think, however, is to live. I will think.

I will not refuse love, this extraordinary creation of values, but I will know that it is not the essential thing. During the last vacation, I was writing a cry of revolt against this love that hides what's uniquely necessary from me; and it's true: one must not transport infinity into love; one must know that it is a human thing.[176] Hence, my cries of revolt against Jacques this winter. I was struggling against myself in the darkness. On how many obscure routes did I commit myself? Now, I know.

I occupied my intelligence only by thinking my feelings, only by withdrawing into myself. It made me richer, but now I have lingered too long; it's enough.

In my intelligence, I am similar to men; in my heart, how different! It seems to me that they have a wider and less profound heart. More cordiality, an easier access, more indulgence, more pity, but also this does not descend into them as in me. For me, to love is the painful thing that Benda describes and blames, this identification with the other, this total "compassion." This hardly touches them, does not penetrate into their internal universe: a refuge, a pleasure, not an avidity of the soul.[177]

I cannot, I do not want to give up these tortures and these subtleties of the heart that they sell short. And yet . . . But why judge myself, compare myself? I must be taken as I am.

What does it matter that they judge as weakness or illogicality what comes from a greater complexity? I love Jacques more passionately than ever for this weakness that is also his.

"Make something" . . . "fulfill one's duty towards men." It seems to me that I owe them so little, except those whom I love! I myself also believed that I had something to do, and now . . .

Don't like the complicated for the complications. Be of an absolute, inflexible honesty and do not escape with a pirouette. Don't cherish worry; don't have complacence for my suffering or for his. Have the most profound and sincere desire to be simplified on the order of intelligence.[178] Never take feeling for an idea. Love the idea for the beautiful emotion that it awakens. Don't be worried about what is elegant, go sternly to the truth, and unveil the pettiness of what might seem seductive. Be tough, tough on my mind and on my heart inasmuch as it wants to serve my mind. Don't take fatigue for skepticism, discouragement for proof that everything is bad. Choose what's most difficult. Be demanding, severe, refuse to flee from myself—no more of these opiums with which I have numbed myself. A true intellectual life, austere, implacable, that carries on regardless. Consecrate at least two hours each day to a meditation that is not dreaming. Don't let myself be absorbed by others; take from them only what is useful for me. Practice the asceticism that was so familiar to me last year. Never take an attitude; never act without knowing exactly why. And if I say, "What good will all of this do?" I respond with Péguy, "It is not from virtue for we barely have any, / It is not from duty for we do not love it," but it is the profound law of my being, and the means of finding the peace that I want.[179] I am not giving any moral value to this resolution. (At least not yet, for a point to examine is the source of these imperious orders from which we cannot extract ourselves and "this voice that all of our life is spent trying to understand . . ." Whence comes this need to understand the truth, to conform oneself to the truth? I don't know. Illusion. But illusion of what? And besides, there is no other way to assure oneself that it is worthwhile or not worthwhile except in obeying it.)[180]

What's more: live ardently anyhow and do not reject any dream, any love. I hate those who split their lives in two, but I also hate those who deny themselves without reason. As long as I am not sure that human things are not worthwhile, I will passionately give myself to human things. Besides, they are worthwhile since *I* am worthwhile. One must be complete, and to be complete, it is not like Ponti appears to believe, to juxtapose two diverse tendencies; it is to live according to each as completely as if it were alone. He tells me that I am strangely double. There isn't any duplicity either. There is only one unique essence expressing itself completely in each of its attributes.

One must love *and* judge. Up until now I have only loved and to judge seemed arbitrary to me. This is why when I say, "I don't love," I condemn, whereas Ponti, who judges, is capable of more indulgence. But judge in relationship to what? Precisely; I must find truths that can serve as norms for me. What? Is it reconstructing the world and organizing it into a hierarchy instead of choosing the chaos where I have lived this year? Probably, but I myself will construct only if the plan truly imposes itself on me and not as Alain does by virtue of a free decree. This is why I fear not coming out of the chaos.

My undisciplined heart that wants to remain so, my wise and well-behaved mind that wants to be more so, will you live well together? Attractions of uncertain youth, it is with a sigh that I give you up, but my renunciation is really total. This experimentation is only worth the fruit that my finally decisive hand will pick.

Ah! This equilibrium that I promised myself, will I attain it? Without sacrificing anything, will I save myself? Yes, if there is a salvation.

Starting tomorrow, August 1, during all of vacation and all of the year consecrate *two hours* every day without exception to systematic reflection, pen in hand—(see the notebook of concordances).

I don't see anything at all; not only no answer, but no presentable way to ask the question. Skepticism and indifference are impossible; a religion is impossible for the moment—mysticism is tempting. But how will I know the value of a thought that does not leave room for thought? On what can I base my rejection or acceptance of it?

Accept to spend two years in reading, conversations, fragmentary meditations. I am going to work like a dog: I don't have a minute to lose.* And not neglect anything: link up with Baruzi, do homework, try to know, to know.

Oh! I see my life well now: not action, the professoriate or whatever. But a passionate, boundless research. No love will eclipse this. If I marry, my philosophy will have to be taken with me. This is essential, so much so that in order to possess it, I would almost accept not getting married.

No, because love is from life, and my philosophy must be from life. Marvelous intoxication of thought, solitude of the mind. I will dominate the world. Literature, works, undertakings—what are all these next to my austere resolution.

Like a dog, I will work like a dog until I know.†

---

*The text is highlighted in the margin, from approximately "I am going to work like a dog" through "my philosophy will have to be taken with me," in the next paragraph.

† This sentence is highlighted in the margin.

When I write to Ponti, I will explain this: that I resemble a wild horse that is allowed to exhaust itself as it pleases in unbridled galloping until finally, with the bit between its teeth, it is both ardent and disciplined, but the horse's fatigue was in vain, and it is finally conquered whereas my feverish race in life has enriched me. Not only more human, but also more understanding, more educated and mature finally. But it is the same ardor that I will pour into my thoughts, now that I have recognized that the most profound part of my life is my thoughts. I was unaware that one could dream of death out of metaphysical despair, sacrifice everything for the desire to know, and live only to save oneself. I didn't know that every system is something ardent and tormented, effort of life, of being, drama in the full sense of the word, and does not engage only abstract intelligence. But I know it at present, and that I can no longer do anything else.

That's Ponti's defect: he has remained a schoolboy, he is disciplined by external rules, and he is not passionate [*violent*]. The kingdom of God is for the passionate—he is well behaved. He obediently prepares for his exam, he is indulgent towards everyone, he advances prudently. I feel that I am so other! If I believed, perhaps I would be in a convent! My exams turn out however they may, and people must take me as I am; I really have other things to do!

It is not pride, but I know well that I am so different from all of them! That my friends cannot understand me because they compare me to themselves. Illogicality, contradictions, that is what they call whatever astonishes them. Who will follow me? Who will be faithful to me until the end? "They" did not understand Péguy, "they" never understand those who are different, they excuse precisely what should be loved. And then, what difference does it make to me? I will not allow myself to be devoured by them. I will keep what's most cumbersome, what's most different of myself..

August 1

Said goodbye to Ponti this morning without any sadness and was light-hearted tonight at Jacques's house. I found him to be so indifferent, or rather I was so indifferent to his indifference! Like someone foreign, forgotten. Whereas I was saying, "Yes, this is a friendship, but my love is for another and will revive once I see him again," it is this friendship that little by little was gliding into first place. I looked at J. as if I had never seen him. So what does he have that is so extraordinary after all? Oh! Such frivolity, such lack of seriousness; he is so N.R.F with his stories of bars, bridge, and money![181]

And my conscientious, fervent friend not only withstood comparison, but also took first place. And it is probably unfair: for it is the most secret part of Jacques that is rare and of value—it probably cannot be done away with so easily, and that is precisely what is most terrible!

My life would be so tranquil and happy with Ponti! No feverish love; no admiration; not a total understanding; for I am so much older (morally) than he, more complex and difficult; but a peace without a desire for anything else; a sure esteem; an exquisite intimacy. No, I do not "love him," but after all what is loving? Feeling dominated. It is too late now; I can no longer feel dominated (except perhaps in my flesh but I scorn that).* Ponti has nothing of what is imperative for me to relinquish myself in favor of him, for me to give in and to be finally unburdened of myself, but near him, I would cheerfully carry my burden.

How far away Jacques is! No matter how much I evoke dear memories, I only manage to suffer from feeling that they are dead. I regret a tenderness that I had, but I judge him so well! It was so difficult and painful for me to get myself in unison with him; and now, I have so quickly gotten out of tune! If only I hadn't known him first, if only he hadn't subjected me to his influence because I loved him, would I have been affected by his influence? And yet there are in him rarer things than in another, but also something so pitifully lacking!†

Already I am no longer thinking what I am writing here and what I thought a little while ago. Already, no longer scrutinizing my heart to come (poor ardent heart, hesitating, conflicted), I have confidence in him and in me. I will not fail him. Not because of the kind of fidelity possessed by Zaza, which would be a defeat for me, but because I *know* what he is worth and that this wicked spell is attached to him to make those who love him suffer, to make them doubt him, misjudge him; it is imperative to love him doubly to compensate for it—irritating, inexplicable. It is precisely for this that I myself want to be there.‡

I have only to let things happen. But, in any case, how alone I will be! More intelligent and more mature than the one, more serious and so different from the other! An instant in the Luxembourg Gardens, I felt faint with sadness, thinking that after eighteen months of such passionate love affairs,

---

* The comment "It is too late now; I can no longer feel dominated" is highlighted in brown ink in the margin and Beauvoir has written, "What denial! 1929"

† This entire paragraph is highlighted in the margin.

‡ In the margin of the opposite page, facing the words "because I *know* what he is worth," the following words are written in brown ink: "But what if I no longer know? What is left?" The next paragraph is also highlighted in the margin.

I found myself with an empty heart and knowing that *the one who would fulfill everything* doesn't exist.*

Courage, be everything to yourself. Seek your truth; construct your life, a beautiful life; be strong and passionately cherish yourself to console yourself for being so alone in the midst of all those who love you. Again, this necessity to be strong! To be alone always if I do not give myself up! I had a moment of vertigo, without anything to grab on to. He tells me that I am individualistic; I feel so strongly that nobody can do anything for me, that I can count only on myself, that I only have myself—and how can I lose myself? Nobody is great enough to merit the total gift of myself.†

I have one hope left, that a love that I have known would be born again from a Jacques such as I have sometimes seen him to be possible. But even then, I know so well that to be happy it would be imperative to give up the best of myself!‡

I can love him with emotion, passion, as an "other," but to chat amiably, but to live together, will this be possible? So few things in common. It is imperative for him to be everything to me, for me to forget myself for him. If I think of myself, I suffer, for he loves me so little for my differences! For my weaknesses, not for my strength.§ Love of a child and a dreamer. *But a man's intelligent love?***

Fear, astonishment, hope. I will see what happens.

But how dear Ponti has become to me, oh! Normale's courtyard where he was seated on the green grass, the edge of the fountain basin on which he was approaching, our race in the rain when I took his arm, our chairs close together in the Luxembourg Gardens, our returns by bus when he paid (or didn't pay) for my seat, our meetings when he was always late, the smiles, the half confidences, the way he speaks about his mother, about Gandillac. Such a manner of not displaying his tastes, of being indulgent and so simple. He has all that for which I loved J.‡‡ And it is so much more soothing.

---

* Beauvoir underlined the words in the last sentence in brown ink and wrote and underlined in the margin, "*Sartre—1929.*"

† This paragraph is highlighted, from "nobody can do anything for me" to its end. Opposite the last sentence of this paragraph, the following is written in brown ink: "Someone is—but then it isn't needed."

‡ This last sentence was highlighted in the margin.

§ Opposite this last paragraph, through "not for my strength," is written in brown ink in the margin, "Absolutely right all of this—and in reversing the terms we have what Sartre knows how to be for me."

** From "So few things in common" to the end of the paragraph, this passage is highlighted in brown ink. Beauvoir also underlined the last sentence in brown ink.

‡‡ This sentence is highlighted in the margin with the remark, "really!!"

One does not live with impunity for two weeks with an exquisite soul in the most exclusive intimacy. I left a lot of myself there. And him? What am I for him? He had drafted a nice note. I would want his letter.

If he loved me, it would be him whom I would love.* But he can be happy without me, and I believe that J. needs me. In any case, poor me!

Write Ponti to tell him that of all of my very painful friendships he alone was both understanding and soothing.

August 2

Sadness of departures; less than last year when my heart almost burst with tears, but vague hurt to leave thus with an uncertain heart.

"Have I loved; do I love?"[182] Ask the question alas! No matter. If ever *he* speaks out, I will only say yes after having seriously explained everything. If he doesn't speak out, I am sure that whenever I want, the other will speak out; and how I will say yes then! Someone strong, good, simple! Someone who would be my living rule, near whom it will be easy to follow my law.[183] So passionately last year I desired one smile from Jacques, I sobbed over his absence! Ah! Cauterets, where I shed such heavy tears; and now, now . . .

I say that this is not love because my first two love affairs were fever and waiting, but this calm, this sure habit, this confidence, couldn't it be true love? Go on! Don't get carried away by absent Ponti, when his presence is not there to modify the idea that I have of him. There is nothing to do but wait. I have two years ahead of me before I choose, at least two. There is no hurry.

(What's most comical is that I don't know at all if he would want to marry me. But it is always necessary for me to choose, to decide and to know what I would do if . . . need to direct, at least ideally, my destiny.

I am so sure that the one who would truly be all, understand all, profoundly be the brother and equal of myself does not exist! There are only men.)†

I reread letters written this year: awful distress, dream, crazy dream and these words, "I do not see any other use for my intelligence than to serve my heart!" I no longer think thus, alas! Here I am precise, intellectual; I would no longer write the unsent letter to Marcel Arland that depicts an entire period of myself.

---

* In line with this sentence is a marginal note in brown ink: "No—but I placed in him all that I knew was not in J."

† This brief paragraph is highlighted in the margin.

Say to Ponti, "You are not in a hurry because life as it is appears accept-able to you. You seek out of a worry to fulfil a duty rather than out of a necessity that you have come up against; if God didn't exist, you would not kill yourself. As for me, I need to know right away because if there is no rea-son for me to live, I will go away. My future, my career, and even my heart's adventures are of so little importance to me! I have attained such depths of suffering! I have seen so much around me . . ."

He does not have a feeling for the irreparable, the irreplaceable.

Have reread Pontrémoli's letters. How curious it is that a sentence I hesi-tated to pronounce out of timidity distressed him thus! Such efforts to get close to me afterwards! Such swiftness in coming to see me and responding to me! I wrote to him twice: once to accept his offer while clarifying the boundaries of the friendship that I would grant him, the other telling him my story, my initial intoxication with living, then my despair before a mean-ingless life, my desire to die, the coldness of my friendships, and finally my effort to find, my act of faith in philosophy.

To G. Lévy, wrote about my willingness to question everything because I believe this to be a duty, to reject any postulate, even to give up what I believe.

August 4

This type of pilgrimage in the neighborhood that I made the night before last made priceless moments of those that often appeared to me to be insipid. Each step that I took brought up a thousand memories: this place in the courtyard where Barbier told me goodbye, this other one where Miquel was smoking next to me, this stone bench where we were playing at making faces. All of this was empty and deserted as if it would never come back to life. And *this* will indeed never be reborn! Oh! This perpetual and necessary passing of things and of ourselves! Sameness [*le même*] bores us and no lon-ger satisfies us, and yet in it alone there is rest and not regret. Crazy desire for being that would be becoming at the same time. With everyone, I was spiritually united [*communié*] in tears; even Lautman played a part in this sorrow; I even saw Lévy's silhouette outlined on the steps of the stairwell where we were describing people.

These games, these books read in this courtyard, the classes taken, the library work, the wonder of ourselves that Georgette and I discussed, the communism into which Miquel initiated me, all of it mixed together had the exciting and desolate flavor of beloved and finished things. Why does a certain insignificant gesture (Miquel's fanning away the smoke from his cigarette, for example) become so priceless? I stopped at the corner of the street where he spoke to me of Alain and where we had stopped. I relived all of my friendships with a marvelous and heart-rending intensity. And then I went back to the beginning of my great fifteen-day-old friendship, in la rue d'Ulm, this bench where I was waiting for him to arrive, his face brightened by a smile, rue Soufflot that we went down side by side, and the Luxembourg Gardens. And sometimes I shiver with joy and emotion as if it were the beginning of something eternal. At other times it hurts me to see it sink into a vertiginous void.

This arrival, about which I had barely thought, gave me great pleasure. Here too, dear memories accompany my steps and the imperceptible nuance of my past youth lives again. The stages gone through, the dreams, the diverse books according to the year and the place, and which led to this today. This relaxed today, ready for a slow, smiling repose in a muslin dress under the gloriously blue sky. No longer the grimness of last vacation and every day in tears, but a little of the easiness of two years ago. Why do I tense up? I am strong enough not to fear anything from others. Why not welcome "the simple and easy life," the rediscovered scent of flowering dark wheat and this sun on the chestnut groves? Yes, I know. Such a Proustian need for perfect analysis that, without having read Proust, I used to make into a law, this need to live in intense exaltation. I was sure then that infinity was in me, and I adored it. Today, I would be closer to this unreal Alain-Fournier who moves effortlessly in his dream. I am no longer *alone*, but I have discovered tender and feverish beings with whom I live in profound communion; and thus, pacified, simplified, I will seek only in joyous hours this truth that I summon [*appelle*] in pain, without however, distrusting a joy that I am well capable of bearing.

For this is the immense difference: last year I pushed joy away to avoid letting myself be caught back up in the easy life; today I will accept it.

I *understand* Ponti. What a difference between this restlessness that merely mutes his adapted and tranquil life, this restlessness from the brain, and my tortures painfully lived! He tells me that he is tempted by animal life, capable of becoming like everyone again; at the moment, I am like that. But how small I would feel if it were to last!

Stronger, more reliable than a year ago. I will no longer stupefy myself with idiotic books. Intelligence put back in its place. Splendid and perfect equilibrium.

Thursday, August 5

Letter from Pontrémoli, with whom I am less and less pleased because I believe that he is above all a man of letters.[184] He tells me to write. But to write for me would not be to reveal [*découvrir*] myself since I portray myself here as I like; it would be for me to express myself.* And I fear two things: mistaking diversion for what's essential, losing myself in the desire for literary glory, for approval, all the things that I scorn. I will write if what I have to say could be useful. Ask advice from Merleau-Ponti. This boy will be my conscience, like a living rule, because he is stripped and simplified, the best and the most profound of myself.[185]

To write, delicious temptation! But my written work would not be that of one day or two months of vacation. But I will not have the time to manage exams, the search for truth, and the expression of myself. G. Lévy says that I don't have to fear splitting into two; try? Like this, without notes, simply start a written work again?†

Let's organize my time. In the morning from nine to eleven, letters and journal. From eleven to one, philosophy (meditation), from three to five (philosophy, reading), from five to eight, writing? After dinner ad libitum (reading nonphilosophical books, prolongation of reading, philosophical meditations etc.) Yes, but . . . can one reflect over *two* things at once? And if I am truly passionate about what's essential, will I give time to the rest?

What is necessary is to read less. I have read what is most important. Read only books from which I can profit. Meditate more, pen in hand, and try even awkwardly to systematize. Continue to write letters and to chat; the best of myself expresses itself usefully in this way as José's letter shows me. Reflect over this work that I will write one day in any case, if not right away. Probably in Paris I could consecrate all of my time after dinner to it. But is it worth the trouble?

(Ask Mlle Blomart and Zaza.) And then I fear that the creation of this world of mine will turn me away from the true world. And especially that this will encroach upon what's essential. For Pontrémoli hasn't understood anything. O Merleau-Ponti, my living conscience, how I would like to chat with you at the end of this Gidean letter of one who will not be saved if he continues. ("They have lost the eternal part of themselves.")

---

* The rest of the paragraph is highlighted in the margin.
† This paragraph is highlighted in the margin.

Saturday, August 6

I wrote Ponti a long letter full of friendship where, telling my story, I wanted to justify myself in his eyes: wondrous discovery, sudden collapse, all my weakness and the weight of my friendships, and also the restlessness in my heart and my passion for analysis.

Probably last year I studied myself more anxiously. But some useless books read here, some days of awful distress, what came out of it that was better than what came out of my studious application? No longer emotions, but ideas now, and this is better. No longer a child, truly a woman. No longer the avidity for living, the feverish becoming: equilibrium. But isn't this death? Oh! No, I still bring so much fervor to living. I take all of it so much to heart. No desire for glory, for happiness. Complete disdain, he would say, "Superhuman," for all contingent things. Only and always this "mysterious calling [*appel*] that all of our life is spent trying to understand without a voice."[186]

He likes religious things (prayer, mass, gospel) in an earthly way.*
He likes the earth: situation—test—politics.
I myself am not satisfied—the earth's uselessness weighs on me, I would like a "superhuman exigency," and yet for human things to be justified.
Disgust, sadness—I feel that nothing is worthwhile; hence my lack of concern for many questions.
All the rest is diversion; nothing but diversion, some branches to keep from sinking.[187]
He lives, he wants to live.
I don't live: things get done but outside of what necessity imposes on me, I don't do anything, I don't strive for anything, I don't desire anything, but to forget myself.
Living? Indeed, I can ardently hang on to everything, but so scornful of life.
Brûlard, letters, journal, the abbess[188]
Disraëli, Schwob, Bopp, Delacroix[189]
Baruzi, Robin, Plato.[190]

---

*The passage from "He likes religious things" to the line ending "Baruzi, Robin, Plato," was written on a loose page, of thick, tan paper and inserted before the August 19 entry of the manuscript.

Friday, August 19

These fifteen days have been peaceful with work. Have read, meditated seriously, and started this book, that looks to me like it's working, that I want to write and to which I don't attach too much importance. Beautiful studious days. Sometimes the regret of controlling my life better and of living less, but is to live only to feel? Wrote lots of letters in which I give a bit too much of myself; received a very beautiful response from Mlle Mercier and a very touching letter yesterday from M. Blomart, "Doubt about everything and everybody is too strong in me." Oh! Such awful weakness often in the strongest souls. I myself say that I do not want to doubt. I affirm that they are right to be what they are. I don't ask them for anything, but yet how sad I am then not to receive anything! This letter from Ponti that I was expecting and that hasn't yet come. And I think so much about him; I count so much on his friendship!

And then the other one, the other one who did not say the word I was waiting for, who probably won't ever say it now; as H. Heine says, "We have played hide-and-seek so well."[191] I remember certain evenings, certain words, certain facial expressions of his whose lack of constraint makes me feel faint. And then I recall my indifference and his from the past, and everything I reject in him. I do not know if he will ever say, "I love you." I do not know, if he said it, how I would respond to it! Yesterday, upon setting foot here, I remembered my soul of a year ago so exactly that I sobbed on the avenue all evening long because it was only from the past: to have loved so much, suffered so, and yet not to desire anything anymore. Let's see, it was yesterday that in this bedroom I thought so deliciously of him. Alas! All of these hours have not vanished; they are waiting for me in every corner, and I am rediscovering all of them. At least I know what suffering is; I will never suffer more; it is not possible. But I will also never love more, never as much. I have really hung him as a commemorative plaque in "this heavy heart of my adolescence."[192] What is truly going to spring forth from this more secret and more bitter spring that Mauriac promises me?

I want to read L'éthique [Ethics]; but this will not keep me from dreaming and suffering. "Feeling is a failed idea," but not love, or sorrow, or the heart that yields completely.[193] Be stronger, but also remain weak and powerless. Believe more in reason, but don't deny my heart. I cannot detest myself; I pity myself who alone cares for me.

Here again: Work—and remember alas!

I love him again. Him? Or the idea of him? What he was or what he is still? Who are these tears for? And this "Jacques" that I whisper, to whom is it addressed?

"Ah! my child do you know what I haven't known? And the infinite words that I haven't shouted?" To think that he almost said them! And that I was so awkward, so silly! How far away again is the Sorbonne and my "social" self! There is only my soul passionately seeking yours, my friend, my friend who loves me perhaps still after all! I loved you too much; you were too timid. And now I no longer know anything, neither of my heart nor of yours . . .

Jacques if you thought of me once in all those Parisian evenings, let my heart of this evening go to unite itself with your dream of that evening.

Jacques!

Jacques, whom we don't know, whose frivolity seems to hide too many promises, then against whom we are thus too severe, out of disgust! Who hurt me, who made me happy, who loved and neglected me, who forgets, who is magical and ironic, disappointing, worrisome, and so simple also! I remember you as one remembers a dead man.

"We played hide-and-seek and we lost ourselves and each other so well . . ."194

I remember having loved you, having been right to love you. Come now, it is not possible that he's dead, the one who . . . the one who . . .*

And it's irreparable. What if we love each other without being able to tell each other? Where are those tears we shed, that unknown tenderness?

Jacques, help Jacques.

Sunday, [August] 21

Admirable letter from Ponty. It is not yesterday's tears that are worthwhile. But the judgment that I will make in full daylight, lucid and voluntary. Answer him.

Monday, [August] 22

The letter I wrote in response is there. And I have reread some pages from this notebook. Yes, now thanks to him, I will no longer lose myself in a vain contemplation of myself. I live by very pure "presences" in a finally attained marvelous equilibrium. In these friendships and this book that I am writ-

---

* Beauvoir did not finish her sentence.

ing, all of what I used to be is of service, and I know why I am living: to find and help others to find. The ethics that I want to serve, all of this purity, this strength and this simplicity returned without any vain complacency. Yes, no longer "ardent and disillusioned," but ardent and pure, clairvoyant and strong; strong with my hope. More feverish, but living, and this synthesis is finally definitive whatever may be the content of my thought. No longer death, life.

And so we have two closed periods: of magnificent discovery (Garric), of discouragement, experiences, and disgust (Jacques). The one beginning under the aegis of Ponti will be for all of my life, I hope, not part of the becoming, but for the duration. Definitive (this synthesis) because not a single regret accompanies it; everything is found here; it conforms to all of my desires that my intelligence alone persists in frustrating. I have sure rules for judging; I have lost my fondness for what is not the essential. In the other syntheses I felt how much effort of will it took to support them. This imposes itself on me. It responds to what I craved all year. I am finally convinced.

But it implies that I will live according to this conviction. That if J. is undermining me as I fear, I will have the strength to carry on regardless, or if he cares about me, the strength to keep all of myself in marrying him. And to follow Alain's advice: to hold myself to what I think now without letting myself be swayed by others' opinions. Not to give in to what J. will say; to hold firm. And perhaps write him frankly towards the end of vacation to ask him what we are to each other. Our friendship was so elevated! I intensely feel how difficult it will be to resist it, even if it is necessary. But after all, don't worry about it. Make myself more decided every day. Live ardently, purely. I am happy, peaceful as I have never been for the past eighteen months. That makes one long month that this has lasted. Thank you Ponti. Jacques taught me indulgence. You have given me the right to severity.

Friday, [August] 26

Yes, and yet recalling a smile or a vocal inflection is sufficient to be no longer anything but a crying thing, "the woman who wanted to eat all the flowers," or "being selfish together."[195] Is it over? Oh! No, it's not is it? If I have not rediscovered, in our last conversations, the one I used to love before, tell me that he will return. And that I will know how to make something strong and beautiful out of this awkward tenderness! I am torn. I don't *want* to be selfish together; I don't *want* to fail him. If truly the one who loved me is dead, it will be relatively easy. And then again no, how awful, what heart-rending regrets! To have lost his love through my own fault. If he loves me still . . . ah! I will not fail him, as dangerous as it may be. I will run the risk and will not fall. Not selfishness together. But seeking together. I will only subject myself to the best that can be in him or in me. I love you. I am right to love you. That you are less able than others to help me to keep to my own path is certain. But love is a fact to which one must submit. The only sin is idolatry. Don't think too much about this! Alas! Life is less and less simple for those who want to feel and think their feelings. To others, also, I would have wanted to make this gift of my entire self, others in whose eyes it would have been worth more than in yours. But here, reason is not the judge. I love you. I want you to be truly you. We can dominate our sensibility, not deny it. And yet so many things, so many things in him make me suffer. Wait. But I will not keep myself from crying for, in any case, it *was* great. The memory of it will always be great.

Wrote to Pontrémoli on, "Why is more spirituality important?" the need for friends in my life, what my written work will be, and the vision for my future; asked the question about death.

Thursday, September 1

The night's beauty! Where does it come from? (To be studied)—wind carrying the vague scent of dark wheat, Poupette's white dress and moon in this so pure sky, and me with all of my life, with all of those I love, and suddenly nothing anymore, nothing anymore but this star in an abyss of night and my soul that was ignorant of all except its existence. I come home and read pages on Jacques, Ponty, etc. Who is right? Would it suffice if this self without memory and detached from what is not truly itself were eternal? The pure self, the simple consciousness of being; and all the successive states of consciousness thus have no importance? Or is it imperative, as I wanted, to save *everything*? My memories and each of my states of consciousness?

I remember having passionately opted for this: just the day before yesterday, in the unbelievably beautiful sunlit fields, writing, yet another note card. Tonight, it seems to me that these human things are not worthy of being cried over in such a way. This self, absent from the rest of the earth, absent from what it was, alone, in a beautiful solitude, is enough. Thus walk the others in a similar solitude, and it is good.

I know that I am not a pure mind. I remember bouts of crazy sensitivity: not too long ago one night at this same window; I remember even my trembling flesh on nights of nervousness. But truly there are hours when I feel how much all of it is nonexistent, not only their senseless life turning each other away from essential solitude, but even what I called my life and passionately cherished. How shocking in the fields under the moon the highest love would have been! How much *it* alone matters at the moment, *it* to which I cannot give a name! There are hours when my soul alone lives. (Descartes says that the passions come from the body.) My "selfishness" is affirming itself: government, happiness, etc.—what men do is not important; what is important, Mlle Weil, is not that the factories run; it's that the poor as the rich, the barbarians as the civilized, save their souls. Senseless, those who impose as an end, and a duty, only that which is average; life's matter and not anything else![196] Men's folly, this great folly, if they call it "selfish," so what—I am selfish. And for all time: my dear solitude, my anxious interrogations, my intoxications in the beauty of the countryside, far from all of them. Paris is them and I feel ill at ease there; and what's secondary takes precedence over what's essential; everything is complicated, intellectualized. I notice that others are living; here it is only me. And the great enigma, so maladjusted that nobody is maladjusted in comparison to me; superficial life is possible for them at least as a diversion. This intensity in me frightens me a bit, this extreme manner of living, of burning up life, of thinking only *of this all the time*—no half-measures.

I like these very simple beings such as Jeanne and the little children who are tranquilly themselves and don't need to raise themselves above the life they live; what I detest are those who, wanting to reflect on it, reflect poorly, the "wise or good people," the "writers", etc.

Even from literature I feel *very* detached—writing sentences with anxiety, no—it is first useful to become aware of this anxiety, it supports, it is beautiful—but afterwards! One must lean on others only as long as one is not big enough to walk alone. Indeed, I do not really know what I want. It is for this reason that it is necessary to try to know what is and not what I want.

This life is peaceful and beautiful for the moment.

(Role that others can have: ideas mixed with emotion—don't judge the ideas according to the emotion, but the others don't feel the emotion; they judge objectively.)

Sunday, September 4

Again this taxing anxiety: the metaphysical anxiety of man alone in the unknown. How does one not become crazy? There are days when I cry out in fear, when I shed tears of ignorance, and then I take hold of myself again. I tell myself, "Let's work sensibly," but alas! I know well that I will die without knowing! Last year when I used to sob saying, "That is what true Life is like," far from men and the best of what they offer, that's what was stifling me, but I hadn't become clearly conscious of it then. And then the anxiety also of all of them, of these souls that I love too wildly despite the hardness that I hide behind, these souls that will never suspect how passionately I have taken care of them. "They smile at you with feeling and then goodbye." Oh! Don't believe it, not one soul. I dream of you throughout the gloomy days; I tremble for you. Like one who, seeing some bold and treacherous feat, holds his breath and trembles with powerlessness, so I watch you, and I am afraid.

And for myself also, because I cannot accept my "multiple and fragmented" death; was the little star right? As long as I do not know, I often feel hurt, as in reliving those hours from last year when "this heavy heart from my adolescence" finished bleeding. Now the spring promised by Mauriac gushes forth from it. And this spring is right, and my "heavy heart" is not useless since the spring would not be without it; but I am crying over the heart itself, and not only the heart itself as something useful to today. And I am also crying over all the futures that will not be, this obligation to choose; I am afraid of this route going I don't know where. There is nothing to do but wait, hanging on to that of which I am sure, to what's essential. But waiting is not forgetfulness.

How real all of this is, more real than the world where they live. This presence [présences] of souls, this presence of the past, of the future, and of the *true face* of the present. Ponty used to admire the intensity of my inner life. Every day it is greater. How will I manage to live? Already I no longer hear the words; I no longer see what they see. And who, knowing this, will want to take care of me? Who would not be afraid of me!

And sometimes I take refuge in the simple sweetness of friendships. Like yesterday in that car. For one hour, life seemed to me to be a beautiful story, so beautiful, and I was proud that *my* life was the most beautiful; of these souls who opened themselves up to me, who leaned on me, who loved me; and of my own strength. Mlle Blomart and Marie Louise wrote to me. Sweetness for a minute to feel that I was attractive and in blossom, enveloped with respectful tenderness. There is a strange charm in these friendships between young girls and young guys when both are simple, straightforward, and loving; something precious and rare, very fragile too. Thus, I oscillate between the exhilaration of an ardent life, so much like I had dreamed it, and the horror of this tragic adventure that this life is turning out to be. And I am moving towards a greater and greater solitude, a more and more complete meditation, and yet without losing any of this great human passion, this restless power to suffer because of others, from the least negligence of others. For does one suffer less by knowing that this suffering must be controlled? And what of the sensitivity of *souls;* this is what has not been said and must be said.

Monday, [September 5]

And say also the dream, the memories, the joy of rediscovering everything at the moment when one believes to have lost it all, the past that still lives and to which one offers this future that he imagines, and that has become part of the present, the beauty of the evenings, of life, everything that I have just written to Zaza. Joy, joy! Immense friendship, like my heart, which will not end.

Tuesday, September 6

I feel it now: I am strong enough forever; no fear of losing myself. M-P would be peace, simple and sure affection; Jacques; the difficult steps towards the other; work that is never completed and always to do; anxiety. Thus, it is Jacques who must definitively be chosen; confident enough to rest my happiness in his hands, strong enough to continue to live if he cannot give this happiness back to me. I can do something for Jacques. For the other, it would only be joy. A couple of days from now I will write a long letter to Jacques.

Ah! How irreparable, even only in the imagination, are evenings of great sacrifices!

Wednesday, September 7

Rereading this notebook, I understand my year; oscillation between the discouragement brought to me by love, the only great human thing in which I felt the nothingness of the entirety of what's human, and the desire to seek, the confused hope that there was something to do. Ponty did not change me so much. He gave me the strength to affirm the second tendency. I stick to everything that I wrote since I saw him.

For the essential, my path is determined [*fixé*].

For the rest, I oscillate between the taxing anxiety of living, the beauty of *my* life in which everything that is, is perfect, and the pride of having conquered such a life.

Tuesday, September 27

Fifteen days of rest. Adorable closeness with Zaza and feeling that she is for me, along with Poupette, what no other will be because we have lived together and because saying nothing together forms a bond stronger than any. I am not overestimating her worth, but she is perfect in all that she is. I love her. Sentiment that it is "the two of us" and the others. The beauty of friendship when there is no longer a word that dares not be said.

I have lived almost without thinking; long vacation. However, letters sent to or received from Jacques, Ponty, Pontrémoli. Crisis of despair in front of Xavier de Moulin. Felt too well the distance between them and me and the sophism in which they would want to enclose me.[197] My thoughts on this were expressed in my letters.

Saw: G. and J. de Neuville, nice, intelligent, personal within impersonal surroundings.[198] Xavière Beaudon, elegant and penetrating, and a guy who truly *is:* Xavier du Moulin.

Oh! Walks, readings together of Jammes, Radiguet, Laforgue! Chats and the return trip!

Defeat before the immanence of departure. Having all that I love in Paris, I recoiled at having to come back because it is what I love that weighs heavily. Like awakening, even to a beautiful day! And that awakening was a year ago, and new years succeed the old. Then joy, now that life is not going to resume but has resumed. Saw the neighborhood again, already chatted with Miquel, who has given me almost all he can, and made a date with Pontrémoli. I have no news of those whom I love as much as they love me, but I will soon.

I compare a life weary of being to this painful return where a sole person kept going. I have joy today. I want to live, and *I* suffice for *myself.**

Let's organize this life and hold ourselves to it.

> Get up 8 AM; 9 AM to noon: personal work in my room.
> 2 to 6 PM: serious study—6–8 PM: conversations, painting, reading, without vain strolls to which I have no *right*. This year everything must be *useful*.

---

* This paragraph is highlighted in the margin.

9 to 11 PM: preparation for my classes, for the club, make up what didn't get done.

11 to 12 PM: journal, on books and especially on people; also on facts.

Three mornings sacrificed, one for the concert, the others for classes must be replaced at night.

This will be organized when I know my class schedule. In the month of October, give especially to personal work.

It is imperative to do two assignments for Baruzi, to write my book, to complete my degrees [*licenses*].[199]

To read every two weeks four or five journals and two new publications—few novels—don't read any relaxing books when I could read others. Especially books on ideas and the great foreigners—reread slowly every Sunday a hundred pages marked as essential.

To read with the note cards that I have started—meditations, and comprehensive work. Analysis of the conversations held, etc. Work seriously from October first on.

My bibliography is well made. Stick to it. Read little. Write a lot. *Finish* between now and January the first part of my book and between now and November my assignment for Baruzi.

Wednesday, [September] 28

Go on, it really is the same person that I rediscover with all my promises of strength. After this day spent with Zaza in a very similar atmosphere, here I am the same. It is as if all the newcomers were not. I have habitual life and the indecisive liking for 7 PM in the illuminated office. I will see *him* again tomorrow. He who?

I remember last year in this office at this time, having thought passionately about him, having remembered wanting him. I don't want him and nevertheless remember. Would this precisely be love? The effort to turn away and despite oneself, without knowing if he is worth it, without expecting anything or regretting, a vague anxiety, a vague desire. Not to see him. If he were a thousand kilometers away! But since he is not a thousand kilometers away, to see him, yes, to face his presence. Will I see him? Oh! To see him without seeing him, to speak without speaking, to know nothing . . .*
Like last year.

It was easy, huh? When he wasn't there, when he wasn't prowling around

---

* Beauvoir did not complete her sentence.

my soul? But my strength will be to rediscover the same slight frictions forgotten at twilight every day and not to give way, not to ignore them.

Even *more* the same than in the past!

Have I loved? do I love? . . .[200]

I am not even thinking of him. I *feel* his existence. He is part of me. And that is when it must be affirmed that these analyses of my uncertainties are not the essential. This spell must be broken! And yet no . . . it is enough to know that tomorrow, that now if it *is imperative,* I *can* save myself. But living is good too, and it is necessary to be a little weak.

You . . . who?

I am afraid only of the unknown. When I know, I face up. I don't know. I am not acquainted with it.[201]

Thursday, September 29[202]

Saw *him* again. It seemed to me that he loved me and desired to see me. I will go on Monday. Day spent at Pontrémoli's home, so far from me, so incapable of thinking, so far from my restlessness. Promises of new acquaintances, books, groups formed, etc. I am no longer very sensitive to this. Great intellectual asceticism. I like it very little. But it stimulates my desire to work.

All of this or J. alone? J. no longer represents at all a superior life from which I am excluded, on the contrary. He no longer has anything but himself. I believe that it is enough for him. Oh! No literature! What a man of letters M. Pontrémoli is. He has no hardness, no pride, neither fear nor disgust. He lives through others. He has no strength in himself.

I must write my book to assert *myself.* And I would so like to see once again (past are the indecisive days when I confront all a bit fearfully), my dear, my very dear male friend, my living conscience.*

Mauguë, Baruzi, Pontrémoli, these people whom I interest, disgust! It is imperative to work, to become again as in my attic in Meyrignac, myself and God, and the others only inasmuch as they are with God.[203]

Friday, September 30

Have read *Le docteur Faustroll,* which I don't like much.[204] Chatted at length with Mademoiselle Mercier. Her God is far from me. Freed from those who

---

* This short paragraph is highlighted in the margin.

want to lead me astray, far from myself. And rediscovered Jacques in the deepest part of my heart. My brother.

Thought also with sweetness of my very dear male friend to whom I would send a note. What a strange and powerful thing love is! "I have rediscovered the things from last year . . ."[205] Yes, even in putting my tenderness in its place, I did not diminish it. Just as passionately present as in the other winter's anxious evenings. I love you, Jacques, you know.

Tuesday, October 3

Saw Madeleine Blomart again with pleasure.

Merleau-Ponty put me back before the big problems again. No more impulsiveness. I am going to continue my book, my friendships, my studies while coldly seeking the solution. Don't hurry and do neatly write out my thoughts.[206] I will tell him on Thursday all that disconcerted me upon my return: family, study groups, literature and above all . . .[207]

And above all that I saw Jacques yesterday very close by and that I am going to see him again in a little while and that he is the one I love and that I am a bit afraid. Don't scatter myself in these charming friendships. What are my *thoughts* on all this?*

Two questions: what is, and the value of what is. Resolve the first one, to start. But the second one, then, is formulated differently.

We chatted seriously.† He acknowledges my position, without taking it too seriously. He himself is passive, he accumulates, he loves life, he is perfectly right.

I feel hurt.

He is at the stage of *Nourritures terrestres.* He wants to live. I turn my back on that; I am separating myself from life. Is this true? Yes, it is a renunciation of the sweetness of the night for example, of other pleasures . . . "This is really abstract for twenty-year-olds, Simone." Alas! . . . I remember exquisite intimacies. Oh! This "thanks" from last year; it was my whole life. How severe this chat was; what severity in me—that he took seriously. But he is far away. And I believe that I love him. The great game, risk even in feeling.

---

* This paragraph is highlighted in the margin.

† The passage from "We chatted seriously" through "'This is really abstract for twenty-year-olds, Simone,'" two paragraphs hence, is highlighted in the margin, and on the facing page in brown ink is the following: "How right he was, how the memory of this chat upsets me. I could respond to it today, and I don't want to—my poor Jacques, I am very unhappy—September 1929."

This is so foreign to me; everything hurts me so deeply. These things that I say become heavy truths when I say them.

I will tell this to Ponty, this law from which I cannot remove myself, this subtle and intentional heartbreak. For it is so hard to continue alone on the route laid out together.

I have before me three burdensome years of study, some of them in this home of mine that weighs on me, with street lamps in the somber night and head colds. Then . . . probably an indefinite solitude instead of that tenderness that was offered one day. A husband, children, a warm hearth . . . Does one marry a woman like me?

Everyone understands in me only what he has in himself; this is right [*juste*]. I love Beucler's book *La ville anonyme* [The Anonymous City][208]*

I adore Zaza.

I am happy to see Georgette Lévy again. I would like to cry. Why? Because of what I have decided. Besides I am not choosing; I am outside of life.

Useless to waste my time describing my illness.

Jacques is perfectly harmonious. Maybe he loves me. And me? What does it matter?†

I dream of immense sacrifices, but I have nothing great enough to give it as a useless gift.

Crucifixions, vain tears, irreparable in one move! No such thing.

Seriously, I have obeyed my unknown will. Isn't this a dream?

He had one expression, "It would be impossible to live like that." How much time will I live, I who choose untenable positions. Oh! Shout this into my book to free myself [*me délivrer*] of it! Shout, then, keep quiet forever, unless the response is dazzling.‡

Saturday, [October] 8

Sweetness of walks with Ponty in the woods gilded by autumn, near lakes where there are swans and rowers. We chat about our companions, about

---

* This paragraph and the previous one are highlighted in the margin.

† Written opposite the sentences concerning Jacques is the following comment from 1929, written in brown ink on the facing verso of the manuscript: "May 1929—Can one suffer so and be such a silly child when Jacques simply exists! When he is there! Odious abstract girl who didn't know how to understand him! I pity you and I thank you for having been this ignoramus whose gravity allows me this friendly reproach today—today when I am a wiser woman who would know so well how to love you and be happy. (If she loved you—alas! September 1929.)"

‡ This paragraph was highlighted with three parallel lines in the margin.

Claudel, about Mauriac, about Thomism, about everything, about nothing. And sometimes I think of him with a great tenderness: simple, straightforward, thrusting upward with a single branch like a smooth and young trunk, almost naïve. No "genius," no extraordinary gift, a bit of facility for superficial life, but a perfect harmony of young, pure, and strong gravity in its intentional ignorance of anything that is not it.

I saw G. Lévy again, on Wednesday. Without affection. Tells me stories of Lautmann and overwhelms me with inextricable complications; so many "plans," "viewpoints," "stages," and such classifications, such necessity to share her opinion.[209] Not my girlfriend, no. Adorable Thursday. A small baguette and a pound of grapes on a lakeside bench reading *Zéno*.[210] Then, afternoon in the very nice room of Pontrémoli, whom I am beginning to like a bit. Saw Mauguë, in whom I like the slightly distracted look, the sensitivity, the elegance, despite his too great concern for elegance, the profound distinction.[211] "Barbarian," says G. Lévy. My God! He is not a "saint." Nor even a philosopher, nor I believe a "great artist," but he loves art and feels it; he is sensitive, charming, and it was a rather great pleasure to witness the intimacy—a bit too tender—of these two souls with nothing in common. Weak arguments, astonishing ignorance, and in Mauguë, great rashness, but friends to cultivate and to whom it would perhaps be good to get a bit closer.

I ardently desire seeing Gandillac; alone great enough for me and in whom I like in advance the severity, the asceticism, the reserve, and the strength. What inner solitude is his. I judge him according to my own.

At the Lamoureux concert with Z.[212] Very beautiful, Bach's Brandenburg Concerto, and also *Tannhaüser*'s overture.[213] I like less Mozart's *Jupiter* symphony, and Rimsky-Korsakoff's piece. It is better not to talk about Chabrier.[214]

Concert, painting, theater, cinema, literature. With all that, continue to write my book.

Whom do I love? There is no longer anyone whose death would bring about my own. Will I ever love more? Not loving, will I marry, happy with a strong affection? Well, it's in God's hands. But my youth will have been beautiful. Three more years!*

I am living now. The future will bring little that's new.

---

* The last two sentences in this paragraph are highlighted with double lines in the margin.

Saturday, [October] 15

Sunday at the Ursulines: *Nyu* idiotic and that adorable film *La petite Lotie.*[215] Saw G. Lévy again in the morning and also Monday afternoon in the little Luxembourg Garden. Interesting chats, "Proustian concierge"; the expression suits her. At heart she is really not very disdainful in the importance she gives to the least of her disdains! She does not know how to make herself loved because she only knows how to understand herself. Always justifying what *she* does! Still she has certain qualities and lives somewhat according to her thoughts.

Caught sight of Jacques without emotion.*

Saw Pontrémoli Friday. Banal chat: I am waiting for his book.

I am studying sociology. I started my classes with pleasure.

At Colonne heard: Prélude to *Lohengrin,* Beethoven's 5th, Bachelet's "Scemo," Debussy's "Fêtes" and "Nuages," and some Rimsky-Korsakoff.[216] It was beautiful.

Chatted with Mlle Bourdel, very nice with simplicity, sincerity, not *very* intelligent, but private, a bit hard, as I like people to be.

G. Lévy told me about Lagache, who is perhaps lesbian.

In the woods this morning with Ponty, my dear, dear friend and so removed from all the things that make "the lives of sensitive beings voluptuous and sad things."[217]

In short, I am living. I am no longer thinking.

* * *

He played with burning coal as if it had been pebbles.
  Browning[218]

(Wouldn't the sentence be just as beautiful thus: "He played with pebbles as if they had been burning coals . . ."?)

Monday, [October] 17

He said to me so sadly, "I so regret coming to you without bringing you anything." How could I not have known to respond that you were bringing me something more precious than anything, your presence, your straightforward and serious presence that so firmly supports me; don't you know? And

---

* There is a comment written later (probably in 1929, like the other comments) on the opposite page in brown ink: "I would give so much today for the emotion of catching sight of him!"

all my great tenderness that puts tears in my eyes upon thinking of you, very dear young friend, a bit weak, a bit simple, without much ardor, but scrupulous, straightforward, and so stripped of irony despite your kind gibes!

I always take for granted things that nobody else does, except Jacques, who was the first to take my hand to lead me into these roads where he has not followed me. I no longer love Jacques. He has my affection, forever. Will he ever find my love again? In fact, there is something in me that would like to see him grown up. No, I will never love again. Nobody is great enough to be loved. Perhaps, however, I will get married. What does it matter?

Have read *L'état de grâce* [State of Grace]. A bit too affected stylistically. Too literary. But, I like certain things a lot.

At the concert yesterday Franck's "Redemption."

Mozart's "Symphony in B flat."

Chopin's "Concerto in F minor."

"Pavane pour une infante"—Ravel.

"Poème de l'extase"—Scriabine.[219]

Very beautiful.

Friday, [October] 21

Caught sight of Merleau-Ponty again. Saw Pontrémoli a little while ago. "I am looking for Nicole," he told me. I rerouted the conversation. I am afraid that he will take me for Nicole. Too bad for him. I am not looking for anything. I have my strength within me. I love and keep myself; I give myself without losing anything. I don't need anybody! Oh! My strength that does not impede a great tenderness! I should have told him, "You *must* not look for Nicole; each person is alone, and that is what is beautiful." Jacques taught me that, painfully, for I loved him. Ponty is teaching me this in joy; beautiful friendship without severity, without abandon, spontaneous, new, happy and tender, and that asks for nothing more than what it is good to give. Goodnight you . . .[220]

NOTES

1. The source of the quotation is unknown; my translation. Alain is the pseudonym of Emile-Auguste Chartier (1868–1951), a student of Lagneau and later a philosopher and essayist who wished to make people understand philosophy as something that would lead them to wisdom and a control of their passions. He is well known for his short essays called *Propos*, which appeared in the paper *Libres Propos* and journals including *La Nouvelle*

Revue Française. As Beauvoir had acquaintances who had studied with Alain, it is possible that she is quoting what she heard from his students rather than what she read.

2. Paul Valéry, "Palme," *Charmes, Oeuvres,* 1:153; my translation.

3. Arthur Schopenhauer, *The World as Will and Representation,* trans. Payne, fourth book, section 57, 1:311. The entire quotation in context is: "Ultimately death must triumph, for by birth it has already become our lot, and it plays with its prey only for a while before swallowing it up. However, we continue our life with great interest and much solicitude as long as possible, just as we blow out a soap-bubble as long and as large as possible, although with the perfect certainty that it will burst." Schopenhauer (1788–1860), the German philosopher, was best known for his philosophy of pessimism, his opposition to the teachings of Hegel, and his work *The World as Will and Representation.* He maintained that intellect and consciousness are instruments to be used by the will, that the world is full of unsatisfied desires and pain caused by conflicts between individuals, and that the only possible escape can be found temporarily in philosophy and art forms and permanently in the renunciation of all desire.

4. Jules Lagneau (1851–94) was a French philosopher made famous posthumously thanks mainly to his student Alain. Lagneau is known for his search for the universal spirit beyond the finite self through an analysis of both perception and judgment. He maintained that seeking an individual and egotistic self results in mistakes and evil. The sentence quoted in Beauvoir's diary appears to be an approximation of a quotation from a letter from Lagneau to Paul Desjardins, January 2, 1893, in Lagneau, *Célèbres leçons,* 9; my translation. To my knowledge, no published English translation currently exists.

5. The exact origin of this quotation is uncertain; my translation. On Bergson, see note 22 in Beauvoir's 1926 diary. Bergson wrote and lectured extensively.

6. Exact source of quotation unknown; my translation. Rudolf Christoph Eucken (1846–1926), a German idealist philosopher and winner of the Nobel Prize in 1908, maintained that an individual is a composite of nature and spirit, that one must strive to be more spiritual, and that personal ethical and creative effort plays a greater role than intellectual idealism in the amelioration of life. He revised his works over several decades. Some of them exist in more than twelve editions, which is why it is difficult to locate the exact source for this quotation. His major works include *The Problem of Human Life as Viewed by Great Thinkers from Plato to the Present Time; The Struggle for a Spiritual Content of Life; The Truth of Religion; Life's Basis and Life's Ideal: The Fundamentals of a New Philosophy of Life;* and *The Meaning and Value of Life.* The last named contains many of the same ideas as the quotation furnished by Beauvoir.

7. Nietzsche, *The Will to Power,* trans. Kaufmann and Hollingdale, section 1032, 532. Friedrich Nietzsche (1844–1900) was a German philosopher known for his rejection of Western bourgeois values. He was the author of *The Will to Power,* in which he proposes that only a man's creative will to power would make him rise above "the herd" of mundane humanity.

8. Louis Aragon, *Le paysan de Paris,* trans. Taylor, *Paris Peasant,* 203. Aragon (1897–1982) was a French writer and one of the founders of surrealism, the movement in art and literature devoted to blurring dreams and reality in order to express the imagination without the conscious control of reason or convention.

9. Pensée to Orion in act 1, scene 3, of Claudel's *Le père humilié,* trans. Herald, "The Humiliation of the Father." For Claudel, see note 3 in Beauvoir's 1926 diary.

10. The title of Mallarmé's poem "L'après-midi d'un faune" was left untranslated by Aldous Huxley, although its literal translation in English would be "The Afternoon of a Faun." For Mallarmé, see note 56 in Beauvoir's 1926 diary. Philippe is the male protagonist of *Le jardin de Bérénice* by Barrès. For Barrès, see notes 18 and 336 in Beauvoir's 1926 diary.

11. The reference here is to Barrès, *Sous l'oeil des barbares,* in *Romans et voyages,* 84; my translation. This work is also quoted in entry of October 5, 1926, of Beauvoir's diary. See notes 133, 134, 135, and 142 in Beauvoir's 1926 diary.

12. As with the 1926 diary, the feminine form of "friend" in French, *amie,* has been translated throughout the 1927 diary as "female friend" or "girlfriend," according to the context, unless otherwise indicated. As in English, the use of the word "girlfriend" may but does not necessarily refer to a romantic relationship.

13. The French, "Peut-être la vaut-elle," could also be translated as "Maybe it is worthy of her."

14. This phrase is a repeated reference to Goethe and Cocteau. See note 73 in Beauvoir's 1926 diary.

15. For Strowski, see note 143 in Beauvoir's 1926 diary.

16. Jean Baruzi (1881–1953), a French philosopher, was a professor at the Sorbonne and a specialist on Leibniz, Saint Paul, Angelus Silesius, and Saint John of the Cross. His publications include *Leibniz et l'organisation religieuse de la terre* [Leibniz and the Religious Organization of the Earth] and *Saint Jean de la Croix et le problème de l'expérience mystique* [Saint John of the Cross and the Problem of Mystical Experience].

17. Léon Brunschvicg (1869–1944), a French philosopher and professor at the Sorbonne from 1909 to his death, extended the teachings of Kant and Hegel and also referred to Plato, Descartes, Spinoza, and Pascal. He regarded God as whatever enables individuals to live the life of the spirit. His major works include *La modalité du jugement* [The Modality of Judgment]; *Les étapes de la philosophie mathématique* [Stages of Mathematical Philosophy]; and *Le progrès de la conscience dans la philosophie occidentale* [The Progress of Consciousness in Occidental Philosophy]. Brunschvicg's wife, Cécile Brunschvicg, was a prominent feminist who fought to give girls access to the *baccalauréat* (Offen, "The Second Sex and the Baccalauréat," 266). I am grateful to Margaret Simons for this information on Cécile Brunschvicg.

18. Maeterlinck, "Silence," *Le trésor des humbles,* trans. Sutro, *The Treasure of the Humble,* 5, 19. Maurice Maeterlinck (1862–1949) was a Belgian author famous for his lyrical dramas and philosophical essays. His works are notorious for inaction, fatalism, mysticism, and the constant presence of death. *The Treasure of the Humble* develops many of his mystical ideas.

19. Mallarmé, "Renouveau" verse 2, line 1, 34; my translation. For Mallarmé, see note 56 in Beauvoir's 1926 diary.

20. Maine de Biran (1766–1824), a French philosopher, stressed the importance of inner consciousness of the self and found the basis of morality in the consciousness of volitional activity. His writings are published as *Oeuvres inédites de Maine de Biran.* William James (1842–1910) was an American philosopher who is often considered the father of American psychology. He was the author of *Principles of Psychology,* which viewed consciousness as an evolutionary process. His theory of emotions claims that our emotions depend upon our physical reaction to things. For example, we feel sorry because we cry, or we feel afraid because we tremble.

21. Nikolaï Nikolaïevitch Evreinov or Evreïnoff (1879–1953) was a Russian playwright, drama theorist, and director who settled in France in 1925.

22. Beauvoir is probably referring to Paul Vérola's *Au grand large* (Paris: Illustration, 1927), an adaptation of the play *Outward Bound* by Sutton Vane (London: Samuel French, 1924). George Bernard Shaw (1856–1950), the Irish playwright and critic, was a freethinker who defended women's rights and equality of income. He supported the abolition of private property and argued for radical change in the voting system. He was awarded the Nobel Prize for Literature in 1925.

23. Zarathustra is the main character of *Thus Spoke Zarathustra* by Friedrich Nietzsche (1844–1900), a German philosopher who, using Zarathustra as his mouthpiece, claims that religion is a comforting but limiting self-delusion, that each human is responsible for creating personally meaningful ethics and abiding by them, and that a "superman" or "overman" would create a new heroic morality affirming life and its value as opposed to shunning them and the world in favor of an imaginary afterlife.

24. On Spinoza, see note 317 in Beauvoir's 1926 diary.

25. Source of quotation is unknown; my translation. For Charles Ferdinand Ramuz, see note 4 in Beauvoir's 1926 diary.

26. Beauvoir might be referring to her cousin Madeleine. See *Mémoires,* 116–25, *Memoirs,* 85–87.

27. Ludmilla Pitoëff (1895–?) was a Russian actress famous for her interpretation of female roles on Parisian stages between 1922 and 1939. *Saint Joan* was a play written by Bernard Shaw.

28. The original French for the translation, "internalized it," is "enfermée en moi."

29. Beauvoir is perhaps referring back to Bergson's ideas of the two different "selves" that she cited before the August 12, 1926, diary entry. See also note 22 in the 1926 diary.

30. Marcel Arland's *Les âmes en peine* is a collection of short stories about a variety of people who pursue their elusive dreams without ever realizing them. For Arland, see note 45 in Beauvoir's 1926 diary. Rainer Maria Rilke (1875–1926) was an Austrian writer renowned for his lyricism, his thematics of erotic and spiritual love between men and women, and a search for an ethics without God. His *Die Aufzeichnungen des Malte Laurids Briggs,* translated by Stephen Mitchell as *The Notebooks of Malte Laurids Briggs,* concerns the search for love in a seemingly lonely and uncaring world. This work by Rilke is notable in terms of Beauvoir's development for its continual questioning of gender roles and its portrayal of women and love.

31. This sentence refers to Gide's *Les nourritures terrestres.* See the quotations next to Beauvoir's September 26, 1926, entry.

32. These descriptions refer to characters in Arland's *Les âmes en peine.*

33. From Mallarmé's "Apparition," trans. Lewisohn. Beauvoir also quoted this poem on October 6, 1926. In Beauvoir's 1926 diary, see note 56 for Mallarmé and note 126 for the October 3, 1926, entry.

34. Philippe is the main male character of Barrès, *Le jardin de Bérénice.*

35. Drieu de la Rochelle, *La suite dans les idées,* 110–11, my translation. There is no other published English translation of this work, to my knowledge. For Rochelle, see note 330 in Beauvoir's 1926 diary.

36. Rilke, *Notebooks of Malte Laurids Briggs,* trans. Mitchell, 4.

37. Ibid., 6.

38. Ibid., 10.

39. Ibid., 16.

40. Ibid., 20.

41. Ibid., 24. I have modified the translation to make it correspond more closely to the French quoted by Beauvoir.

42. Ibid., 63. I have modified the translation to make it correspond more closely to the French quoted by Beauvoir.

43. Ibid., 87. I have modified the translation by adding "[accomplissement]" to show that it was used in the French translation quoted by Beauvoir, although the same term is translated as "fulfillment" in the English translation. The word accomplissement became important to Beauvoir's philosophy.

44. Ibid., 95. I have modified the translation to make it correspond more closely to the French quoted by Beauvoir.

45. Ibid., 251–52. I have modified the translation to make it correspond more closely to the French quoted by Beauvoir.

46. Ibid., 253. I have modified the translation to make it correspond more closely to the French quoted by Beauvoir.

47. Ibid., 253.

48. Ibid., 254. I have modified the translation to make it correspond more closely to the French quoted by Beauvoir.

49. Ibid., 260. I have modified the translation to make it correspond more closely to the French quoted by Beauvoir.

50. My translation of the ending quotation provided in French by Beauvoir, which does not seem to correspond to the published English translation. Many of the quotations of Rilke correspond to his interpretation of the biblical tale of the Prodigal Son, who tries to find God and love while ironically attempting to escape from both during part of his search.

51. For Cocteau, see notes 19 and 35 in Beauvoir's 1926 diary.

52. "Don't be too intelligent" is from Le Potomak by Cocteau. See notes 19, 35, and 164 in Beauvoir's 1926 diary.

53. I have consistently used "restless" to translate inquiet and "restlessness" to translate inquiétude throughout Beauvoir's 1926–27 diary. In her Mémoires, Beauvoir says that she was studying Barrès, Gide, Valéry, and Claudel, all authors who worshiped inquiétude, which James Kirkup translates less colloquially as "disquiet"; see Mémoires 269; Memoirs 194–95.

54. This refers back to Laforgue's verse that Beauvoir quoted before the November 5, 1926, entry: "it's really you and not another." See note 270 in her 1926 diary.

55. For Drieu de la Rochelle, see note 330 in Beauvoir's 1926 diary.

56. These are all images found in Rilke's Notebook.

57. Les âmes mortes was written by Nikolai Vasil'evich Gogol (1809–52), a Russian novelist and playwright often viewed as the founder of critical realism in Russian literature and known for exposing the faults of human character. Le père Goriot was written by Honoré de Balzac (1799–1850), the French author famous for the ninety-five novels portraying French society and characters in minute detail that compose The Human Comedy. Le père Goriot contains many of the key figures in the series and recounts the story of a father who sacri-

fices his own happiness for his daughters who eventually abandon him. *L'idiot* (The Idiot), by Fyodor Dostoyevsky (1821–81), was noted for its presentation of the religious intensity of the author's world. Its main protagonist is a pure being in the image of Christ.

58. François Mauriac's *Thérèse Desqueyroux* tells the story of a young married woman who, feeling oppressed by her family and societal role, tries to escape by poisoning her husband.

59. *Adrienne Mesurat* is a novel by Julien Green. *Défense de l'occident* [Defense of the West] was written by Henri Massis. *Aline,* a novel by Charles Ferdinand Ramuz, tells the story of Aline, whose mother believes that good girls know how to cook, work in the fields, and knit, and that they should never have fun. To escape from such a destiny, Aline falls in love with Julien, who impregnates her and then abandons her. Everyone views her pregnancy as her fault alone. When Aline learns of Julien's imminent marriage to another girl, she kills her three-month-old sickly son and hangs herself on an apple tree. Her mother's reward for abiding by societal rules is thus loneliness and imminent madness.

60. French students are graded on a scale of twenty. Fourteen is a very good grade. It is rare to attain a grade higher than eighteen. Ten is considered average and a passing grade.

61. Henri Matisse (1869–1954) was a French leader of the Fauve movement in painting around 1900.

62. Gino Severini (1883–1966), an Italian Futurist painter who migrated to Paris, mixed with the avant-garde and was noted for theories of dynamism in art.

63. Henry de Waroquier (1881–1970) was a French painter, sculptor, and printmaker heavily influenced by impressionism and Oriental art.

64. André Lhote (1885–1962) was a French cubist painter and sculptor. Aristide Maillol (1861–1944) was originally a painter in the Nabi group, which included Maurice Denis, Edouard Vuillard, and Pierre Bonnard. Maillol later revolutionized the art of sculpture. André Favory (1888–1937), a classically trained artist, experimented for some years with cubism and is known for his cubist painting *Woman with a Fan.*

65. Maurice de Vlaminck (1876–1958) was a French fauve painter.

66. Georges-Olivier Desvallières (Paris 1861–1950) was a French painter who studied with Gustave Moreau and who befriended Maurice Denis.

67. Maurice Denis (1870–1943), a French painter who was one of the founders of the Nabi group.

68. Charles François Guérin (1875–1939) was a painter known for portraits, nudes, and figural compositions. His illustrations appeared in many books. He was heavily influenced by the poetry of Francis Jammes and used a mixture of realism and romanticism to produce art celebrating the young girls of the past. For the Salon d'Automne, see note 236 in Beauvoir's 1926 diary.

69. Paul Albert Besnard (1849–1934) was a French painter and graphic artist.

70. The French painter Maurice Utrillo (Paris 1883–1955) concentrated on landscapes and scenes of Montmartre.

71. Jacqueline Marval (1866–1932), a French painter, was a member of the Parisian avant-garde.

72. Marcel Gromaire (1892–1971) was a French expressionist painter who made his reputation with *La guerre* (1925).

73. Beauvoir is referring to Eugène Deshayes (1868–1939), an Algerian painter of portraits and landscapes; Auguste Chabaud (1882–1955), a fauve painter; and either Hippolyte

Jean Flandrin (1809–64), a French painter best known for his religious paintings and por- traits, or Jules Flandrin (1871–1947), a French painter from Grenoble and friend of Matisse and Georges Rouault, well known between the two world wars for his experimentation with impressionism, symbolism, fauvism, and other modernist techniques.

74. Edmond Borchard (1848–1922), a French painter from Bordeaux, was known for his compositions that often feature robust horses.

75. Beauvoir is probably referring to Robert Frederick Blum (1857–1903), an American painter and illustrator.

76. Beauvoir likely referred to Pierre Bompard (1890–1962), a French marine painter.

77. Fernand Léger (1881–1955), a French painter of Argentinean origin, was influential in the development of cubism and the exposition of urban and technological culture. "There is the artifice and insincerity found in literature" is the translation for "il y a de la littérature."

78. Le Grand Palais was built on the Champs-Elysées for the 1900 Universal Exposition and is known for its complicated architecture of stone, steel, and glass, and for its varied decoration, including art deco ornamentation and a mosaic frieze that extends the length of the facade.

79. Beauvoir is describing works by Moïse Kisling (1891–1953), a French painter of Polish origin, who was first heavily influenced by French impressionism and later by the modern and more imaginative styles of Amedeo Modigliani, Georges Braque, Pablo Picasso, Max Jacob, André Salmon, and Chaïm Soutine.

80. Leopold Survage (1879–1968) was a Russian cubist painter.

81. Perhaps Beauvoir is referring to Henri Morisset (1870–?), a French painter known for his portraits, landscapes, and still lifes, as well as mural paintings in churches. He was a student of Gustave Moreau and is associated with the Barbizon School of painting.

82. Jules Oury, known as Marcel-Lenoir (1872–1931), was a painter, sculptor, poet, and ceramist.

83. Henri Rousseau (1844–1910), was a French painter and innovator of Naïve art who was employed for a time in the customs service in Paris. He is the archetypal untutored artist. See also note 235 in the 1926 diary.

84. André Lhote was an artist who taught painting in Paris.

85. Normalians are students attending the École Normale Supérieure (ENS) on the rue d'Ulm in Paris, the most rigorous and highly esteemed teacher's training college and one of the most prestigious of the French elite university-level schools in Beauvoir's day. See also note 134. Francis Picabia (1879–1953), a painter, drawer, and poet, participated in impres- sionism, cubism, dadaism, and surrealism. Kees Van Dongen (1877–1968) was a Dutch fauve painter. For Foujita, see note 189 in Beauvoir's 1926 diary.

86. Schopenhauer says that being free does not necessarily mean that we could have done anything else than what we have chosen to do, but that each of us is free in a higher sense because one's sense of responsibility reveals an innate character that is self-deter- mining and independent of experience, and one's actions manifest that person's respective innate or intelligible character. A person's intelligible character is a timeless act of will that the person essentially is. See Schopenhauer, *The World as Will and Representation,* trans. Payne, section 28. Both the concept of the intelligible character and the concept of the empirical character (the intelligible character as it expresses itself through action) come from Kant (*Critique of Pure Reason,* A539/B567). Viewing these concepts as useful for resolv- ing the problem of freedom and determinism, Schopenhauer believes that the more we

learn about ourselves, the more effectively we manifest our intelligible character and thus the more "artistically and methodically" we play our designated role (*WWR*, section 55).

87. This is an approximation of some of the verses of Claudel's "Saint Louis," quoted across from the August 21, 1926, diary entry.

88. *Élan vital* is the creative principle and fundamental reality held by Bergson to be immanent in all organisms and responsible for evolution. See also Bergson, *L'évolution créatrice,* 283, trans. Mitchell, *Creative Evolution,* 284.

89. "Je ne veux pas," which I have translated as "I will not," could also be accurately translated as "I do not want this" in this context.

90. Cébès and Simon are characters in Claudel's play *Tête d'or.* In the first part of the play Cébès introduces himself as an "imbecile and ignorant, a new man among unknown things"; my translation. The play presents Cébès's struggle against the barbarians and his search for spiritual growth.

91. Heinrich Heine (1797–1856) was a German author noted for his poetry and prose showing his lyricism, his satire, his barbed wit, and his embittered criticism of romanticism, patriotism, society, and politics. The original source of this remark, widely attributed to Heine, is unknown in the *Columbia World of Quotations* (1996). It is attributed to Heine as quoted in Simone de Beauvoir, *Mémoires,* 320, *Memoirs,* 232.

92. This sentence is my translation for Beauvoir's "Et alors, celui qui est l'autre moi-même, je peux ne pas l'aimer plus, en tant qu'être, et pourtant d'être un autre moi-même je le chéris plus que tout autre."

93. Schopenhauer, *WWR,* trans. Payne, book 2, section 26, 139. I have modified Payne's translation to make it correspond more closely to the French quoted by Beauvoir.

94. Ibid., book 3, section 52, 267.

95. Ibid., book 4, section 54, 274–75. Payne's translation of the German text is as follows: "the mirror of the will has appeared to it in the world as representation. In this mirror, the will knows itself in increasing degrees of distinctness and completeness."

96. Ibid., 278. I have modified Payne's translation to make it correspond more closely to the French quoted by Beauvoir.

97. Ibid., 279. I have modified Payne's translation to make it correspond more closely to the French quoted by Beauvoir.

98. Ibid., 280–81. I have modified Payne's translation to make it correspond more closely to the French quoted by Beauvoir.

99. Ibid., section 57, 311. I have modified Payne's translation to make it correspond more closely to the French quoted by Beauvoir.

100. Ibid., 312.

101. Ibid., 313. I have modified Payne's translation to make it correspond more closely to the French quoted by Beauvoir.

102. Ibid., 316. I have modified Payne's translation to make it correspond more closely to the French quoted by Beauvoir.

103. Ibid., section 58, 322.

104. Ibid., section 67, 376. I have modified Payne's translation to make it correspond more closely to the French quoted by Beauvoir.

105. Ibid., 377. I have modified Payne's translation to make it correspond more closely to the French quoted by Beauvoir.

106. *Voulez-vous jouer avec moâ?* was written by Marcel Achard (1924). *Antigone,* by Cocteau (1927), is a musical tragedy based on Sophocles's play.

107. For lines by Eucken, see the quotation given before Beauvoir's April 17, 1927, entry.

108. The line "Je ne suis pas tout ce que j'aime" could also be translated as "I am not all that I like." The end of the next sentence, which I give as "according to what I love," could be translated as "according to what I like," since it is not clear from the French context if Beauvoir would have chosen "like" or "love" in English.

109. Beauvoir is again referring to Barrès's concept of "barbarians." See notes 18, 133, 134, 135, and 142 in her 1926 diary.

110. The exact source of the quotation is unknown; my translation. Johann Wolfgang von Goethe (1749–1832), the German poet, dramatist, novelist, and scientist, was probably best known for his dramatic poem *Faust.*

111. Marcel Proust, "Combray," trans. Moncrieff and Kilmartin, *Remembrance of Things Past,* 108. I have modified the Moncrieff and Kilmartin translation to make it correspond more closely to the French.

112. Marcel Arland's *Étapes* is a series of essays exploring the human search for the meaning of existence. Several of Arland's ideas reappear in Beauvoir's 1927 diary, such as the goal of self-fulfillment instead of self-utilization (*Étapes,* 50) and the desire to be great without self-deception (28). About exigency, Arland writes, "Almost all doctrines have a common characteristic: that is to be founded on a single part of the soul, but not to take into account the exigencies of the entire being. Almost none of the doctrines contemplates the upheavals that the future can bring about in us; the doctrines are conceived according to a state of mind that must necessarily change. If the doctrines have not foreseen this change: how would they be valid once it is accomplished?" (56). The prayer referred to by Beauvoir is against demons; for Arland, the demon changes "thoughts into words, execrable coinage, coin of deceit; it is the demon that makes us happy to be deceived. The demon is called habit, and it is above all what he is called; for habit is the beginning of death and that is the true name of the demon" (22). Part of the prayer is as follows: "Nevertheless, demons, I do not want for my life to be rendered false and in vain by you. If I only bring a moderate ardor to certain exteriors of life, it is perhaps because another life, locked within and secret . . . seems to be the only real one. I will enter into death trembling with fear, perhaps, but not with my eyes closed and my ears plugged" (23). All translations of Arland's *Étapes* are my own.

113. The expression "desert world" (*monde désert*) alludes to an image of a desert carried over by the use of the term "oases" and also to an uninhabited place. It might be an allusion to Pascal's use of the expression "desert island" (*île désert*) from fragment 198 of *Pensées:* "En voyant l'aveuglement et la misère de l'homme, en regardant tout univers muet et l'homme sans lumière abandonné à lui-même . . . j'entre en effroi comme un homme qu'on aurait porté endormi dans une île déserte et effroyable, et qui s'éveillerait sans connaître et sans moyen d'en sortir." [Upon seeing the blindness and poverty of man, upon watching every mute universe and man without light abandoned to himself . . . I enter in fear as a man who would have been carried sleeping onto a frightening and desert island, and who would awaken without knowing and without the means of getting away]; my translation. "Monde désert" might also be an allusion to the 1927 novel *Le monde désert* by Pierre Jean Jouve, in which the main female character falls in love with a young man named Jacques, for whom

she must suffer enormously, and who did not dream of her but "only needed her presence, a regular and daily need that, once satisfied, left him joyous" (64); my translation.

114. Miquel is Jean Mallet in her *Mémoires*.

115. Jacques is probably referring to Immanuel Kant's idea of ends in *Critique de la raison pure* [The Critique of Pure Reason]. Kant (1724–1804) says that we can divide the world into beings with reason and will like ourselves (ends-in-themselves) and things that lack those faculties (means-to-ends). Ends-in-themselves are autonomous beings with their own goals, who, if they failed to recognize their capacity to determine their own actions, would be impeding their own freedom and undermining reason itself. Hesitating between alternative courses of action, ends-in-themselves need not consider means-to-ends (such as buildings or rocks) in deciding what goals to have and what means to use to achieve them. However, ends-in-themselves (people) are reasoning agents and thus warrant careful thought in relationship to the goals chosen and the means used to accomplish them. Moral actions, for Kant, are actions ruled by reason, which means that people are responsible for carefully considering other beings who act according to their own goals, reasoning, and thoughtfulness for others. See McCormick, "Immanuel Kant, Metaphysics."

116. Marcel Schwob (1867–1905) was a French writer whose principle works include *Coeur double* (chronicles and short stories), *Le livre de Monelle* (a symbolist vision of compassion that features the mysterious heroine Monelle and her adventures), and *Les vies imaginaires* (voyages into the world of the fantastic). As a child, Schwob fell in love with *Treasure Island* by Robert Louis Stevenson, and it influenced many of his later works. Often putting into play the question of why evil exists, Schwob leads readers to wonder whether he is writing fantasy or philosophy. He is also noted for French translations of English works such as *Hamlet*. The *Oeuvres completes* [Complete Works] of Schwob appeared in 1927, which makes it difficult to know which of his works Beauvoir read.

117. Blaise Pascal (1623–62) was a French scientist and religious philosopher. In *Pensées* Pascal states that reason cannot satisfy men's hopes and that only mystic faith can allow men to give meaning to the universe. See also note 113 in Beauvoir's 1927 diary. For Arland, see note 45 in Beauvoir's 1926 and note 112 in the 1927 diary. The phrase "much closer to me Marcel Arland" is a literal translation for "plus près de moi Marcel Arland." In my translation, I prefer to respect the ambiguity of Beauvoir's phrasing. She may have meant that Arland was closer to her than Pascal, or vice versa.

118. Immanuel Kant, the German philosopher, maintained that things beyond the realm of possible experience are noumena (things-in-themselves, such as God, freedom, and immortality) and are unknowable, although we presuppose their existence. Phenomena (objects of experience) can be perceived in sensibility, space, and time, but they can be understood only if they possess characteristics of causality and substance—structures of phenomenal experience. See also note 115 in the 1927 diary.

119. For Lagneau, see note 4 in Beauvoir's 1927 diary.

120. The idea of finding a cool place on her pillow after tossing and turning refers to Laforgue's line, "A cooler place on the feverish pillow." See the verses before the entry of November 5 and note 261 in Beauvoir's 1926 diary.

121. "This other end" refers again to Kant. See note 115 in Beauvoir's 1927 diary.

122. Compenetration is in general the mutual interfusion of two ideas. It is a term often used to discuss Christian theology and especially the teachings of Thomas Aquinas on the theory of being and on the substantial and individual nature of the ego. According to his

ideas, consciousness protects against the compenetration of one person's ego with that of another.

123. The *NRF,* or *Nouvelle Revue Française,* was a literary journal; *L'Esprit* was a philosophical one. See notes 55, 308, and 332 in Beauvoir's 1926 diary.

124. Alain, trans. Cottrell and Cottrell, *Alain on Happiness,* 248. On Alain, see note 1 in Beauvoir's 1927 diary.

125. Jean Epstein (1897–1953), a French movie director, was noted for his book on film theory, *Bonjour Cinéma* (1921), and for his poetic and imaginative films. The 1927 film *Six et demi onze* (*6½ × 11*), considered a black-and-white silent masterpiece, tells the story of female infidelity that causes a man to commit suicide. The dead man's brother starts to have an affair with the same woman, but then discovers a $6\frac{1}{2} \times 11$ film negative of his brother, which complicates things further. Georges Pitoëff (1884–1939), a Russian actor and director, was famous for his performances on Parisian stages during 1922–39. He was married to Ludmilla Pitoëff when they immigrated to France in 1922. She became the director of his professional theatrical company upon his death in 1939. See also note 27 in Beauvoir's 1927 diary. Studio des Ursulines was the cinema where films were often shown for the first time in Paris during Beauvoir's youth.

126. Bost, *Homicide par imprudence,* 121; my translation.

127. This refers to Baudelaire's poem "A une passante," the last line of which literally translates as "O you whom I could have loved, o you who knew it!" Baudelaire, *Les fleurs du mal,* 101; my translation.

128. These thoughts on loving beings who impose themselves upon Beauvoir evoke her comments about Jacques on October 23, 1926; about herself and Zaza on November 27, 1926; and about Barbier on May 6, 1927.

129. I have translated *mon diplôme* as "my thesis." The undergraduate degree is called a *licence,* which required the completion of four *certificats.* Most students usually finished one *certificat* each year. The teaching degree, a type of graduate degree necessary for teaching in secondary schools, required the presentation of a thesis (on a philosophical topic, for Beauvoir). The most highly competitive exam, the *agrégation,* consisted of both a lengthy written essay or thesis and an oral test. It was required to teach in certain high schools (*lycées*) or in universities (*Facultés*). Part of studying for the *agrégation* entailed preparing nine or ten topics, one of which would be chosen for the written exam. To pass the oral, among other feats, a candidate had to draft a lecture on a previously unprepared topic within a few hours. Successful completion of the *agrégation* guaranteed a job for life as a civil servant in the French educational system (Moi, *Simone de Beauvoir,* 43, 52, 53).

130. Beauvoir's usage of the French term "pénétrer," which literally means "to penetrate," most likely must be understood more in the sense of understanding or permeating the other than in any sexual way. Nevertheless, both the English and French terms do evoke a sexual image—one that I have maintained to respect Beauvoir's ambiguous choice of words.

131. Ballets Russes was started by Diaghilev in 1913. See also note 289 in Beauvoir's 1926 diary.

132. The expression "intermittences of the heart" comes from Proust, *Sodome et Gomorrhe,* in *A la recherche du temps perdu* [Cities of the Plain, in Remembrance of Things Past]. It is a moment in which a series of past sensations is unexpectedly reproduced and thus evokes a strong memory and a poignant but momentary re-becoming of the past self that initially experienced the sensations in relationship to an event.

133. Beauvoir also discussed self-delusion and the meaning of existence in her August 7, 1926, diary entry. See also notes 19 and 35 in her 1926 diary.

134. As previously stated, the *agrégation* is the highest competitive exam for teachers in France. A Normalian is a student at the École Normale Supérieure (ENS). In 1925, studying at the ENS in the rue d'Ulm would not have been possible for Beauvoir as women students were not yet allowed (Moi, *Simone de Beauvoir,* 49). See also note 196 in Beauvoir's 1927 diary.

135. *Les Thibault* was a series of novels (*roman-fleuve*) under this title by Roger Martin du Gard concerning the evolution of individuals and families in a rapidly changing France. The novels appeared from 1922 to 1940.

136. Beauvoir recreates G. Lévy as Blanchette Weiss in her *Mémoires* 331–32; 337–38; *Memoirs,* 239–40; 243–44.

137. Léon Blum (1872–1950), a French writer and politician, was known first for his literary criticism and later for his work with the socialist party. His works include *Nouvelles conversations de Goethe avec Eckermann* [Goethe's New Conversations with Eckermann] and a critical essay, *Le mariage* [Marriage].

138. Pontrémoli is Michel Riesmann in Beauvoir's *Mémoires.*

139. Beauvoir apparently did not know "Merloponti," that is, Merleau-Ponty (appearing as Pradelle in her *Mémoires*), well enough yet to spell his name correctly. Maurice Merleau-Ponty (1908–61) was a French philosopher who believed in the reality of a world that transcends consciousness of it. He stressed the primacy of perception with an emphasis on the bodily levels of conceptualization as preconditioning mental concepts necessary to access the real. His later work focuses more on the role of language in perception.

140. Daniel Lagache (1903–72) was a philosopher, doctor, psychoanalyst, and criminologist who passed the *agrégation* examination in philosophy after having studied at the École Normale Supérieure with Aron, Sartre, and Nizan.

141. Maurice de Gandillac (Pierre Clairaut in her *Mémoires*) served as a professor at the Sorbonne (1946–77) and was the author of numerous texts on philosophy.

142. Stendhal, pseudonym of Marie Henri Beyle (1783–1842), is considered to be one of the great French novelists. He is most well-known for *De l'amour* [On Love], a psychological analysis of love; *Le rouge et le noir* [The Red and the Black] and *La Chartreuse de Parme* [The Charterhouse of Parma], both novels; and his autobiographical work *La vie d'Henri Brulard* [The Life of Henry Brulard], published posthumously.

143. Edouard Colonne (1838–1910), a French conductor and violinist, in 1871 founded in Paris the Concert national, which later became known as the Colonne Concerts. Jules Étienne Pasdeloup (1819–81) founded the Concerts populaire at the 1861 Winter Circus in Paris, making musical culture available to the population at large. After a long interruption, these concerts were started up again as the Pasdeloup concerts.

144. José Le Core (known as Lisa Quermadec in *Mémoires*), who was also preparing a degree in philosophy, was a rather shy student who spent hours sharing her innermost thoughts and secrets with Beauvoir during their university studies.

145. Henri Frédéric Amiel (1821–81) was a Swiss critic and philosophy professor heavily influenced by the philosophies of Hegel and Schelling and noted for the scrupulous self-observation found in the fragments of his posthumously published 1847–81 diary, *Journal intime* (1883).

146. Alain, "Mon semblable," in *Propos,* 700; my translation. For Alain, see note 1 in Beauvoir's 1927 diary.

147. Léon-Paul Fargue (1876–1947), a French poet, was noted for his free verse and poetry written with lyricism, imagination, and melancholy.

148. "Abbé Beaussard" may be the same person Beauvoir refers to as "abbé Beaudin" in her *Mémoires* (342; *Memoirs*, 247).

149. "While racing in vain to St. Cloud" (*pendant cette vaine course à St. Cloud*) might also be translated as "while on that pointless errand in St. Cloud."

150. Gottfried Leibniz (1646–1716), a German philosopher and mathematician, was the author of *Essais de Théodicée sur la bonté de Dieu, la liberté de l'homme, et l'origine du mal* [Theodicy]; *Monadology;* and *Nouveaux essais sur l'entendement humain* [New Essays Concerning Human Understanding], his view of Locke's *Essay Concerning Human Understanding*. Leibniz maintains that the universe is the result of a divine plan. Monads or simple substances each represent the universe from a different point of view and have perception or consciousness but cannot act. Only rational monads have apperception (self-consciousness). Beauvoir wrote a thesis on Leibniz during her studies. She appears to have studied Leibniz's view of sufficient reason, which claims that everything that happens is explicable and every question has an answer, and his principle of the identity of indiscernibles, which states that if two things are alike in all ways, they are the same object. So it must be the case that no two things are ever exactly alike or God would have had no reason for making two of them. See the discussion in Douglas Burnham's "Gottfried Wilhelm Leibniz."

151. Beauvoir did not finish her sentence.

152. This phrase refers back to a verse from Claudel's "Ténèbres" found on the opening page of Beauvoir's 1926 diary.

153. Louis Chadourne (1890–1925)was a French poet and a novelist of exotic adventures. *L'inquiète adolescence* [Restless Adolescence] is a coming-of-age story in which Paul Demurs slowly loses his religious fervor as he discovers his desire for women.

154. Lagneau to Paul Desjardins, November 19, 1893, in *Célèbres leçons,* 9–10. See also note 4 in Beauvoir's 1927 diary.

155. For *Aimée,* see note 2 in Beauvoir's 1926 diary.

156. "Frantic errands in Paris" (*les courses éperdues à Paris*) could also be translated as "the frantic races in Paris."

157. "Sure enough for me to live" (*assez sûr pour que je vive*) could also be translated as "safe enough for me to live."

158. In *Mémoires,* Beauvoir indicates that this image of the branch comes from one of François Mauriac's heroes who considered his friendships and his pleasures as branches that would support him above nothingness (319; *Memoirs,* 230). This image most likely comes from Mauriac's *La chair et le sang,* whose young hero is named Claude. For Mauriac, see note 9 in Beauvoir's 1926 diary.

159. "To flee," which appears early in this sentence, translates what I have deciphered as the word *fuir.* An alternate deciphering renders the word as *puis,* which would translate as "then." This passage about self-worship evokes what Beauvoir wrote on the same subject in her diary entry of October 12, 1926.

160. For *L'Esprit,* see notes 308 and 332 in Beauvoir's 1926 diary.

161. For the Beauvoir Series project and this diary, I have chosen to translate *féminin* as "feminine," and *masculin* as "masculine."

162. For other references to this discussion of self-delusion and the meaning of existence involving the question, "What good will it do?" see note 133 in the 1927 diary.

NOTES TO PAGES 286-93

163. The "you" is this sentence is rendered by *vous* and is thus definitely not Jacques. See note 149 in Beauvoir's 1926 diary.

164. An alternate translation to "But I am afraid that, at any rate, nobody's questions will influence me" (*Mais j'ai peur que toujours les questions de personne ne m'influencent*) would be "But I am afraid personal questions will always influence me." Beauvoir is thus either frightened that she is so intelligent that she will never find anyone good enough to challenge her, or she fears that she is too dependent on context and emotions to have a fixed view of anything; perhaps, given the ambiguity of the passage, both interpretations must exist simultaneously.

165. Explicative philosophy is a philosophy that functions through logic and language and that offers a ready-made doctrine, as opposed to a pre-Socratic or Oriental philosophy that provides a practical wisdom entailing mental discipline.

166. I have corrected this date according to the 1927 calendar and the dates Beauvoir assigned to entries surrounding this one. Beauvoir mistakenly wrote July 21.

167. The teachings of the Greek philosopher Plato (427?–347 B.C.) are among the most influential in the history of Western civilization. A friend and student of Socrates, Plato wrote his earliest group of dialogues as conversations with Socrates. These Socratic dialogues include the *Apology,* defending Socrates; the *Meno,* asking if virtue can be taught; and the *Gorgias,* exploring the absolute nature of right and wrong. Plato's later dialogues, *Republic, Phaedo, Symposium, Phaedrus, Timaeus,* and *Philebus,* argue that a rational relationship exists between the soul, the state, and the cosmos. The highest idea is the Idea of the Good; the principal path is illustrated in the *Republic* by the metaphor of the cave, in which the uneducated man is chained in a world of shadows. Through study, or a constant questioning of assumptions and a formulation of postulates (dialectic), humans can move up to the highest good. The *Republic* states that the philosopher is the only one capable of ruling the just state since only the philosopher understands the harmony of all parts of the universe in their relationship to Good. Thomism, comprising the teachings of Saint Thomas Aquinas (1225–74), an Italian philosopher and theologian, is declared to be the official Catholic philosophy. Saint Thomas affirms being, argues that all human knowledge is grasped through the senses, and maintains that we can discover God by reason and come to know of God's existence through the knowledge of things. For *L'Esprit,* see notes 308 and 332 in Beauvoir's 1926 diary.

168. For Abbé Beaussard, see note 148 in Beauvoir's 1927 diary.

169. For Rivière, see note 2 in Beauvoir's 1926 diary. The term "compossible" is linked to the Leibnizian concept of compossible worlds. Although there are infinite possible substances, Leibniz called the finite number of substances that can exist together in the same world "compossible" substances.

170. The exact source for the quotation of Marcel Proust is unknown; my translation.

171. Beauvoir quotes this and other verses from Mallarmé's "Apparition" in her October 5, 1926, entry.

172. For Bloy, see note 10 in Beauvoir's 1926 diary. Léon Daudet (1867–1942) was a French author most noted for his criticism of democracy and as co-editor, with Charles Maurras, of the right-wing daily *Action Française.* For Fournier, see diary entries for November 3 and 4, 1926, along with the quotations Beauvoir copied.

173. "Jean" is most likely Jean Giraudoux. See Hélène de Beauvoir, *Souvenirs,* 122.

174. For Meaulnes, see note 137 in Beauvoir's 1926 diary.

175. For Abbé B, see note 148 in Beauvoir's 1927 diary.

176. "What's uniquely necessary" is a translation for "l'unique nécessaire," which may also be translated in philosophical jargon as "the unique necessary."

177. Julien Benda (1867–1956), a French novelist and critic, led an attack against the romantic philosophy of his time, especially that of Bergson. Beauvoir may have read his 1927 work *La trahison des clercs* [The Treason of the Intellectuals], in which he accused his contemporaries of abandoning truth and succumbing to political passions. After a short association with Péguy and a collaboration on *Cahiers de la Quinzaine,* he baptized himself "the free man" and began to defend in his novels and essays the superiority of rational knowledge linked to freedom over everything in the emotional or intuitive domain.

178. "The order of intelligence" seemingly refers back to Beauvoir's entry of October 16, 1926, in which she writes, "Nothing ever sleeps in me; nothing needs to wake up. Everything maintains a life of an extraordinary intensity; in particular, everything remains *present* for me, on the sentimental order, as well as on the intellectual order."

179. This approximates two lines in Charles Péguy, "Prière de confidence," 132. For other references to the question of what good it will do, see notes 133 and 162 in Beauvoir's 1927 diary.

180. The phrase beginning "this voice" is a verse from Claudel's "Saint Louis." See August 21, 1926, diary entry and corresponding note.

181. "N.F.R." stand for the journal *Nouvelle Revue Française.* See note 123 in Beauvoir's 1927 diary.

182. "Have I loved; do I love?" repeats the words of Mauriac quoted at the beginning of the 1926 diary. See note 9 in Beauvoir's 1926 diary.

183. "Living rule" (*règle vivante*) might also be rendered as "living rules" or "living measuring device." It does not indicate a "governing authority" in this context.

184. "Man of letters" (*littérateur*) is often used pejoratively in French to depict a professional writer who writes more to impress an audience than from the heart.

185. For "living rule," see note 183 in Beauvoir's 1927 diary.

186. This quotation refers back to a line in Claudel's "Saint Louis," which Beauvoir quoted opposite one of the pages of the entry for August 21, 1926.

187. For the meaning of the branch imagery, see note 158 in Beauvoir's 1927 diary.

188. Beauvoir may be referring to works by Stendhal: *Vie de Henry Brulard; Journal: oeuvre posthume, 1801–1814* [The Private Diaries of Stendhal]; *Correspondance inédites* [Unpublished Correspondance]; or *L'abbesse de Castro* [The Abbess of Castro].

189. Perhaps Beauvoir is referring to *La vie de Disraëli* [Disraeli's Life] by André Maurois or *Disraëli* by Maurice Courcelle. For Schwob, see note 116 in Beauvoir's 1927 notebook. Léon Bopp (b. 1896), a French author, wrote fictional, historical, and philosophical texts including *Jean Darien, Interférences: romance critique* [Interference: Critical Romance], and *H. F. Amiel: essai sur sa pensée et son caractère d'après des documents inédits* [H. F. Amiel: Essay on His Thought and His Character According to Unpublished Documents], all of which Beauvoir may have read or planned to read in 1927.

190. The works of Léon Robin (1866–1947), a French philosopher and specialist in Greek philosophy, include *La théorie platonicienne des idées et des nombres d'après Aristote* [Plato's Theory of Ideas and Numbers According to Aristotle], in which he attempts to reconstruct Plato's theory from Aristotelian testimony.

191. A longer poetic translation of the original German into English published by Louis

Untemeyer gives insight into the full signification of this verse by Heine: "And finally playing like children that go / At hide and seek in the woodland together, / We managed to stray and to hide ourselves so / That each of us now are lost to the other." Heine, "Lyrical Intermezzo #27, trans. Untermeyer, 58.

192. This quotation refers to Mauriac's epitaph, found in *Le coeur gros* by Barbey, which Beauvoir talks about reading in her August 17, 1926, entry. See note 52 in her 1926 diary.

193. Beauvoir may be referring to *L'éthique* [Ethics] by Spinoza.

194. See note 191 in Beauvoir's 1927 diary for a lengthier English translation of verses in this same poem, "Lyrical Intermezzo #27," by Heinrich Heine.

195. "Being selfish together" is my translation for "faire de l'égoïsme à deux."

196. Simone Weil (1909–43), who became a writer and philosopher, was, unlike Beauvoir, a student at the École Normale Supérieure (1928–31). She prepared for the ENS entrance exam in the preparatory classes, called by students "l'hypokhâgne" (first year) and "la khâgne" (second year) at lycée Henri IV, with the philosopher Emile-Auguste Chartier (1868–1951), known as Alain (see note 1 in the 1927 diary). The preparatory classes for the ENS consisted of two years of intensive memorization, and upon entering the ENS, many of the students had almost completed a *licence*. When Simone Weil entered the ENS in 1928, Beauvoir was already preparing her *agrégation*. A disciple of Alain, Weil was much more keenly aligned with the working class and ideas of revolution than was Beauvoir. See *Mémoires*, 330–31; *Memoirs*, 239; Moi, *Simone de Beauvoir*, 49, 55.

197. The same episode with a lengthier description of Xavier Du Moulin is recounted in *Mémoires*, 355–57; *Memoirs*, 256–57.

198. G. de Neuville is perhaps Geneviève de Bréville in *Mémoires*.

199. For an explanation of French degrees, see note 129 in the 1927 diary.

200. "Have I loved? Do I love?" repeats Mauriac's lines once again. See note 9 in Beauvoir's 1926 diary.

201. This entry for Wednesday, September 28, was written on a separate sheet of thin white paper, torn off of a bank deposit slip of some kind and inserted between the pages for the Tuesday and Thursday entries.

202. Beauvoir mistakenly wrote September 28.

203. Beauvoir seemingly recreated Mauguë as Jean Mallet in her *Mémoires* 331–32, 337–38; *Memoirs*, 239–40, 243–44.

204. Beauvoir is referring to *Gestes et opinions du docteur Faustroll, pataphysicien: Roman néo-scientifique* by Alfred Jarry.

205. Beauvoir is probably slightly misquoting from memory the poem by Jammes that appears before the September 29, 1926, entry. See note 116 in the 1926 diary.

206. "Neatly write out my thoughts" translates "mettre au net ma pensée."

207. "Study groups," which translates "équipes" in this context, is probably another of Beauvoir's references to the Équipes Sociales.

208. André Beucler (1898–1985) was a French author most noted for his novel *Gueule d'amour*, which was later transformed into a movie by the director Jean Grémillon, starring Jean Gabin. During 1920–30, Beucler also hosted frequent radio programs.

209. "Plans" (*plans*) might also be rendered as "planes."

210. This probably refers to *La coscienza di Zeno* by Italo Svevo (1923), translated into French in 1927 by Paul-Henri Michel as *La conscience de Zéno*.

211. For Mauguë, see note 203 in Beauvoir's 1927 diary.

212. Charles Lamoureux (1834–99), a French violinist and conductor, founded Les Nouveaux Concerts (1881), an association that later became the Lamoureux Concerts. He is noted for bringing Wagner's repertoire to France.

213. The German composer and organist Johann Sebastian Bach (1685–1750) brought polyphonic baroque music to its culmination. *Tannhaüser* is an opera by the German composer Richard Wagner (1813–83), who was noted as a master of romanticism.

214. Emmanuel Chabrier (1841–94), a French composer, was noted for his vitality, his imaginative inventions, and his colorful melodies. He was a friend of Manet, Verlaine, Duparc, and Fauré.

215. For Studio des Ursulines, see note 125 in Beauvoir's 1927 diary.

216. The Colonne Orchestra has offered concert series since 1873. *Lohengrin* is an opera by Wagner. The German composer Ludwig van Beethoven (1770–1827) was a musical rebel who was difficult to classify. He was noted for the extraordinary emotion in his compositions. *Scemo* is a lyrical drama by Alfred Bachelet (1864–1944), a French composer. The French composer Claude Debussy (1862–1918) was an exponent of impressionism who developed a new fluidity of form and experimented with harmony and dissonance.

217. "The lives of sensitive beings, voluptuous and sad things" is a repeated reference to Barrès, *Le jardin de Bérénice*. See note 336 in Beauvoir's 1926 diary.

218. The exact verse is from Browning's "Light Woman"; it reads, "You think of my friend, and the burning coals / He played with for bits of stone."

219. César Auguste Franck (1822–90) was a Belgian-French composer and organist whose music is rooted in the polyphonic and chromatic techniques of Bach. The Austrian musician Wolfgang Amadeus Mozart (1756–91) composed works noted for their grace and technical perfection. Frédéric Chopin (1810–49), a composer who was of French and Polish parentage, brought romantic piano music to unprecedented expressive heights. "Pavane pour une infante" is a piano composition by Maurice Ravel (1875–1937), a French composer. He was a leading exponent of impressionism, along with Debussy, and was noted for his original, fluid music. *Poème de l'extase* is a symphonic work by Alexandre Nicolaïevitch Scriabin (1872–1915), a Russian composer and piano virtuoso.

220. Beauvoir's 1927 journal ends with this unfinished thought.

Bibliography

Achard, Marcel. *Voulez-vous jouer avec moâ? Pièce en trois actes.* Paris: Paris-Théâtre, 1949.

Alain. *Propos.* Bibliothèque de la Pléiade. Paris: Gallimard, 1920.

———. *Propos sur le bonheur.* Nîmes: Fantaisie, 1925. Translated by Robert D. and Jane E. Cottrell as *Alain on Happiness* (New York: Ungar, 1973).

Alain-Fournier. *Le grand Meaulnes.* Paris: Emile-Paul, 1914. Translated by Françoise Delisle as *The Wanderer (Le grand Meaulnes)* (New York: New Directions, 1928).

———. *Miracles.* Paris: Nouvelle Revue Française, 1924.

Aragon, Louis. *Le paysan de Paris.* Paris: Gallimard, 1926. Translated by Simon Watson Taylor as *Paris Peasant* (Boston: Exact Change, 1994).

Aristotle. *Politika.* Edited by Panarges Lekatsas. Athens: I. Zacharopoulos, 1979. Translated by Thurot as *La politique* (Paris: Garnier, 1926). Translated by Benjamin Jowett as *Politics* (New York: Newton Abbott, 2000).

Arland, Marcel. *Les âmes en peine.* Paris: Nouvelle Revue Française, 1927.

———. *Étapes.* Paris: Nouvelle Revue Française, 1927.

———. *Étienne.* Paris: Nouvelle Revue Française, 1924.

———. *Monique.* Paris: Gallimard, 1949.

Bair, Deirdre. *Simone de Beauvoir: A Biography.* New York: Summit Books, 1990.

Balzac, Honoré de. *Le père Goriot.* Paris: Gallimard, 2000. Translated by Burton Raffel as *Le Père Goriot* (New York: Norton, 1994).

Barbey, Bernard. *Le coeur gros.* Paris: B. Grasset, 1924.

337

Barnes, Hazel. "Simone de Beauvoir's Journal and Letters: A Poisoned Gift?" *Simone de Beauvoir Studies* 8 (1991): 13–29.

Barrès, Maurice. *Le culte du moi.* Paris: Plon, 1922.

———. *Un homme libre.* In *Romans et voyages.*

———. *Le jardin de Bérénice.* In *Le culte du moi.*

———. *Romans et voyages.* Paris: Robert Laffont, 1994.

———. *Sous l'oeil des barbares.* In *Romans et voyages.*

Baruzi, Jean. *Leibniz et l'organisation religieuse de la terre.* Paris: Alcan, 1907.

———. "Le problème du salut dans la pensée religieuse de Leibniz." In *L'intelligence mystique,* edited by Jean-Louis Vieillard-Baron, 122–39. Paris: Berg International, 1985.

———. *Saint Jean de la Croix et le problème de l'expérience mystique.* 1924. Paris: Alcan, 1931.

Baudelaire, Charles. "A une passante." In *Les fleurs du mal,* 101.

———. *Les fleurs du mal.* In *Oeuvres complètes,* 40–131. Translated by James McGowan in a French-English edition as *The Flowers of Evil* (Oxford: Oxford University Press, 1997).

———. "Le masque." *Les fleurs du mal.* Translated by James McGowan as "The Mask," 43.

———. "Moesta et errabunda." *Les fleurs du mal.* In *Oeuvres complètes,* 80. Translated by Carol Clark as "Moesta et errabunda," in *Selected Poems,* 71–72. Translated by James McGowan as "Moesta et errabunda" in *The Flowers of Evil,* 129–30.

———. *Oeuvres complètes.* Paris: Seuil, 1968.

———. *Poésies diverses.* In *Oeuvres complètes,* 132–43.

———. *Selected Poems* (French with English prose translation). Translated by Carol Clark. New York: Penguin, 1995.

———. "(LXXVI) Spleen." In *Selected Poems.* Translated by Carol Clark, 74–75. Translated by James McGowan as "Spleen (II)" in *Flowers of Evil,* 146–47.

Bauer, Nancy. *Simone de Beauvoir: Philosophy and Feminism.* New York: Columbia University Press, 2001.

Beauvoir, Hélène de. *Souvenirs.* Paris: Séguier, 1987.

Beauvoir, Simone de. *Les belles images.* Folio. Paris: Gallimard, 1966. Translated by Patrick O'Brian as *Les belles images* (London: Fontana, 1985).

———. *Le deuxième sexe.* Paris: Gallimard, 1949. Translated by H. M. Parshley as *The Second Sex* (New York: Knopf, 1968).

———. *Force de l'âge.* Paris: Gallimard, 1960.

———. *L'invitée.* Folio. Paris: Gallimard, 1943. Translated by Yvonne Moyse and Roger Senhouse as *She Came to Stay* (London: Fontana, 1984).

———. *Journal de guerre.* Edited by Sylvie Le Bon de Beauvoir. Paris: Gallimard, 1990.

———. *Lettres à Sartre.* Edited by Sylvie Le Bon de Beauvoir. 2 vols. Paris: Gallimard, 1990. Translated by Quintin Hoare as *Letters to Sartre* (New York: Arcade, 1992).

———. "Littérature et métaphysique." *Les temps modernes* 1, no. 7 (1946): 1153–63. Translated by V. Zaytzeff and F. Morrison as "Literature and Metaphysics," in Beauvoir, *Philosophical Writings,* 269–77.

———. *Les Mandarins.* 2 vols. Paris: Gallimard, 1954. Translated by Leonard M. Friedman as *The Mandarins* (Cleveland: World Publishing, 1956).

———. *Mémoires d'une jeune fille rangée.* Folio. Paris: Gallimard, 1958. Translated by James Kirkup as *Memoirs of a Dutiful Daughter* (New York: Harper and Row, 1959).

———. *Philosophical Writings.* Edited by Margaret A. Simons, Marybeth Timmermann, and Mary Beth Mader. Urbana: University of Illinois, 2004.

———. "Préface." In *L'existentialisme et la sagesse des nations.* 1948. Paris: Nagel, 1963. Translated by M. Timmermann as "Preface" in "Existentialism and Popular Wisdom," in Beauvoir, *Philosophical Writings,* 216–18.

———. *Pyrrhus et Cinéas.* Paris: Gallimard, 1944. Translated by Marybeth Timmermann, as "Pyrrhus and Cineas," in Beauvoir, *Philosophical Writings,* 89–149.

———. *Quand prime le spirituel.* Paris: Gallimard, 1979. Translated by Patrick O'Brian as *When Things of the Spirit Come First* (New York: Pantheon, 1982).

———. *Tous les hommes sont mortels.* Folio. Paris: Gallimard, 1946. Translated by Leonard M. Friedman as *All Men Are Mortal* (Cleveland, Ohio: World, 1955).

Bell, Susan Groag, and Karen M. Offen, eds. *Women, the Family, and Freedom: The Debate in Documents. Volume 2, 1880–1950.* Stanford: Stanford University Press, 1983.

Bergoffen, Debra. *The Philosophy of Simone de Beauvoir.* Albany: State University of New York Press, 1997.

Bergson, Henri. *Essai sur les données immédiates de la conscience.* 1927. Paris: Quadrige/PUF, 1997. Translated by F. L. Pogson as *Time and Free Will* (1910) (New York: Harper and Row, 1960).

———. *L'évolution créatrice.* Paris: Alcan, 1914. Translated by A. Mitchell as *Creative Evolution* (New York: Modern Library, 1944).

Beucler, André. *La ville anonyme.* Paris: Gallimard, 1998.

Bonal, Gérard, and Malka Ribowska. *Simone de Beauvoir.* Paris: Seuil/Jazz Éditions, 2001.

Bost, Pierre. *Homicide par imprudence.* Paris: Société des Editions Fast, 1920.

Browning, Robert. "Light Woman." *Dramatic Romances,* edited by Anders Thulin. http://eserver.org/poetry/browning-dram-romances.txt (accessed November 2, 2001).

Burnham, Douglas. "Gottfried Wilhelm Leibniz." *Internet Encyclopedia of Philosophy.* http://www.utm.edu/research/iep/l/leib-met.htm (accessed March 4, 2002).

Butler, Samuel. *Erewhon, or Over the Range.* London: Jonathan Cape, 1921.

Chadourne, Louis. *L'inquiète adolescence.* Paris: A. Michel, 1920.

Charrier, Edmée. *L'évolution intellectuelle féminine.* Paris: Albert Mechelinck, 1931.

Claudel, Paul. "Cantique du coeur dur." *La cantate à troix voix.* In Claudel, *Oeuvre poétique,* 362–66.

———. *L'échange.* Paris: Mercure de France, 1964. Translated by Donald L. Holley and Jean-Pierre Krémer as *The Trade* (Woodbridge, Ont.: Albion, 1995).

———. *Les feuilles de saints.* In Claudel, *Oeuvre poétique,* 597–696.

———. *Oeuvre poétique.* Bibliothèque de la Pléiade. Paris: Gallimard, 1967.

———. *Le père humilié.* In *Théatre II,* 489–569. Bibliothèque de la Pléiade. Paris: Gallimard, 1965. Translated by John Heard as *The Humiliation of the Father,* in *Three Plays: The Hostage, Crusts, The Humiliation of the Father* (New York: Fertig, 1991).

———. "A la mémoire de Georges Dumesnil." In Claudel, *Feuilles de saints,* 603–4.

———. "Ode jubilaire." In Claudel, *Feuilles de saints,* 675–89.

———. "Sainte Thérèse." In Claudel, *Feuilles de saints,* 624–33.

———. "Saint Georges." In Claudel, *Feuilles de saints,* 608–11.

———. "Saint Louis." In Claudel, *Feuilles de saints,* 651–62.

———. "Saint Philippe." *Corona benignitatis anni dei.* In Claudel, *Oeuvre poétique,* 415–16.

———. "Ténèbres." From *Images et signets entre les feuilles*. In Claudel, *Oeuvre poétique*, 430. Translated by Joseph T. Shipley as "Shadows," in *Modern French Poetry* (New York: Greenburg, 1926), 72.

———. *Tête d'or*. Paris: Mercure de France, 1959. Translated by John Strong Newberry as *Tête d'or: A Play in Three Acts* (New Haven: Yale University Press, 1919).

Cocteau, Jean. "L'adieu aux fusiliers marins." From *Discours du Grand Sommeil*. In Cocteau, *Oeuvres poétiques complètes*, 449–51.

———. *Antigone: tragédie musicale en trois actes*. Paris: M. Senart, 1927.

———. *Le Cap de Bonne Espérance suivi du Discours du Grand Sommeil*. 1925. Paris: Gallimard, 1967. Translated by unidentified translator as *The Cape of Good Hope* (New York: Quarter Horse, 1965).

———. *Oeuvres poétiques complètes*. Bibliothèque de la Pléiade. Paris: Gallimard, 1999.

———. "D'un ordre considéré comme une anarchie." From *Le rappel à l'ordre*. In *Poésie critique*, vol. 1. Paris: Gallimard, 1959. Translated by Rollo H. Myers as "Order Considered as Anarchy" in *A Call to Order* (New York: Holt, 1926).

———. *Orphée: tragédie en un acte et un intervalle*. Paris: Stock, 1927. Translated by Carl Wildman as *Orphée: A Tragedy in One Act and an Interval* (London: Oxford University Press, 1933).

———. *Le Potomak*. Paris: Librairie Stock, 1950.

———. "Tentative d'évasion: Maladresses pour s'évader de la terre." In Cocteau, *Le Cap de Bonne Espérance*.

———. *Thomas l'imposteur*. Paris: Gallimard, 1923. Translated by Lewis Galantière as *Thomas the Imposter* (New York: Appleton, 1925).

Conrad, Joseph. *Heart of Darkness*. In *Longman Anthology of British Literature*, edited by David Damrosch, vol. 2, 2018–72. New York: Addison-Wesley, 1999.

Dayan, Josée, and Malka Ribowska. *Simone de Beauvoir: Un film*. Paris: Gallimard, 1979.

Dostoyevsky, Fyodor. *Besy: roman v trekh chastiakh*. Moscow: Soglasie, 1996. Translated by Victor Derély as *Les possédés* (Paris: Plon, 1886). Translated by Richard Pevear and Larissa Volokhonsky as *Demons: A Novel in Three Parts* (New York: Knopf, 1994).

———. *Idiot: roman v chetyrekh chastiakh*. Kishinev: Izd-vo "Kartia moldoveniaske," 1969. Translated by Albert Mousset as *L'idiot* (Paris: Gallimard, 2000). Translated by Henry and Olga Carlisle as *The Idiot* (New York: Signet Classic, 2002).

Duhamel, Georges. *La possession du monde*. Paris: Mercure de France, 1919. Translated by Béatrice de Holthoir as *In Sight of the Promised Land* (London: Dent, 1936).

Dumont, E. "Dolorosa." In *Les plus belles chansons de 1900 à 1940: Collections de 110 Succès*, 28–29. Paris: Paul Beuscher, n.d.

Fabre, Lucien. *Rabevel ou le mal des ardents*. Paris: Nouvelle Revue Française, 1923.

Fallaize, Elizabeth. "The Housewife's Destiny: Translating Simone de Beauvoir's 'The Married Woman.'" In *Cinquantenaire du Deuxième Sexe*, edited by C. Delphy and S. Chaperon, 101–14. Syllepse: Paris, 2002.

Farrington, Frederick E. *French Secondary Schools*. 1910. 2nd ed. New York: Longmans, Green, 1915.

Francis, Claude, and Fernande Gontier. *Simone de Beauvoir: A Life, a Love Story*. Translated by Lisa Nesselson. New York: St. Martin's, 1987.

Fromentin, Eugène. *Dominique*. Paris: Plon, 1876. Translated by Edward Marsh under the same title (New York: Chanticleer Press, 1948).

340

Fullbrook, Edward. "*She Came to Stay* and *Being and Nothingness.*" *Hypatia* 14, no. 4 (Fall 1999): 50–69. Reprinted in Simons, *Philosophy of Simone de Beauvoir*, 42–64.

Fullbrook, Edward, and Kate Fullbrook. *Simone de Beauvoir and Jean-Paul Sartre: The Remaking of a Twentieth-Century Legend.* New York: Basic Books, 1994.

Galster, Ingrid. "'Une femme machiste et mesquine': La réception des écrits posthumes de Simone de Beauvoir dans la presse parisienne." *Lendemains* 61 (1991): 53–62.

Gibson, Michael. *Le Symbolisme.* Paris: Taschen, 1999.

Gide, André. *L'immoraliste.* In *Romans.* Translated by David Watson as *The Immoralist* (New York: Penguin, 2001).

———. *Les nourritures terrestres.* In Gide, *Romans.* Translated by Dorothy Bussy as *Fruits of the Earth* (London: Secker and Warburg, 1962).

———. *Paludes.* In Gide, *Romans.* Translated by George D. Painter as *Marshlands,* in *Marshlands, and Prometheus Misbound* (New York: McGraw-Hill, 1965).

———. *La porte étroite.* Paris: Le Mercure de France, 1909. Translated by Dorothy Bussy as *Strait Is the Gate* (New York: Knopf, 1924).

———. *Le retour de l'enfant prodigue.* Paris: Nouvelle Revue Française, 1919. Translated by Dorothy Bussy as *The Return of the Prodigal* (London: Secker and Warburg), 1953.

———. *Romans: récits et soties, oeuvres lyriques.* Bibliothèque de la Pléiade. Paris: Gallimard, 1958.

———. *Si le grain ne meurt.* Paris: Gallimard, 1928. Translated by Dorothy Bussy as *If It Die: An Autobiography/André Gide* (New York: Random House, 1957).

———. *Le voyage d'Urien.* In Gide, *Romans.* Translated by Wade Baskin as *Urien's Voyage* (New York: Citadel, 1964).

Gogol, Nikolai Vasil'yevich. *Mertvye dushi.* Moscow: Sovremennik, 1974. Translated by Arthur Adamov as *Les âmes mortes: ou les aventures de Tchitchikov* (Lausanne: La guilde du livre, 1956). Translated by Richard Pevear and Larissa Volokhonsky as *Dead Souls* (New York: Vintage, 1997).

Green, Julien. *Adrienne Mesurat.* Paris: Fayard, 1994. Translated by Henry Longan Stuart under the same title (New York: Holmes and Meier, 1991).

Hegel, G. W. F. *Philosophie des Geistes.* In *Encyklopädie der philosophischen Wissenschaften* (1830). Translated by Véra Augusto as *Philosophie de l'esprit* (Bruxelles: Culture et civilisation, 1969). Translated by William Wallace as *Hegel's Philosophy of Mind* (Oxford: Clarendon, 1971).

Heinämaa, Sara. "Simone de Beauvoir's Phenomenology of Sexual Difference." *Hypatia* 14, no. 4 (Fall 1999): 114–32. Reprinted in Simons, *Philosophy of Simone de Beauvoir*, 20–41.

Heine, Heinrich. "Lyrisches Intermezzo." In *Buch der Lieder.* Leipzig: Insel, 1978. Translated by Albert Mérat and Léon Valade as *Intermezzo: poème* (Paris: Lemerre, 1868). Translated by Louis Untermeyer as "Lyrical Intermezzo" in *Poems of Heinrich Heine* (New York: Holt, 1927).

Holveck, Eleanore. *Simone de Beauvoir's Philosophy of Lived Experience.* Lanham, Md.: Rowman and Littlefield, 2002.

Jammes, Francis. *Almaïde d'Etremont, ou, L'histoire d'une jeune fille passionnée.* Paris: Mercure de France, 1901.

———. *Clara d'Ellébeuse, ou, L'histoire d'une ancienne jeune fille.* Paris: Mercure de France, 1899.

——. *De l'angelus de l'aube à l'angelus du soir.* In Jammes, *Oeuvres complètes.*

——. "Elégie huitième." From *Le deuil des primevères.* In Jammes, *Oeuvre poétique complète,* 76.

——. "Elégie troisième." From *Le deuil des primevères* (1898). In *Anthologie de la poésie française du XXè siècle.* Paris: Gallimard, 2000. Translated by William Alwyn as "Third Elegy" in *Prayers and Elegies,* 32.

——. *Oeuvres complètes.* Geneva: Slatkine Reprints, 1978. Selected prayers and elegies translated by William Alwyn as *Prayers and Elegies by Francis Jammes* (Youlgrave, Eng.: Hub Publications, 1978).

——. "J'ai vu revenir les choses . . ." From *Le deuil des primevères.* In Jammes, *Oeuvre poétique complète,* vol. 1, 1891–1919 (Biarritz: J and D Editions, 1995), 310.

——. "Prière pour demander une étoile." From *Quatorze Prières.* In Jammes, *Oeuvres poétiques complètes,* 1:318. Translated by William Alwyn as "Prayer for the Gift of a Star," in *Prayers and Elegies,* 8.

——. "Prière pour louer Dieu." From *Quatorze Prières.* In Jammes, *Oeuvres poétiques complètes,* 1:326–27. Translated by William Alwyn as "Prayer in Praise of God," in *Prayers and Elegies,* 15.

——. "Prière pour que les autres aient le bonheur," 1:317. Translated by William Alwyn as "Prayer for the Happiness of Others," in *Prayers and Elegies,* 7.

Jarry, Alfred. *Gestes et opinions du docteur Faustroll, pataphysicien: Roman néo-scientifique.* Translated by Simon Watson Taylor as *Exploits and Opinions of Doctor Faustroll, Pataphysician: A Neo-Scientific Novel* (Boston, Mass.: Exact Change, 1996).

Jouve, Pierre Jean. *Le monde désert.* 1927. Paris: Mercure de France, 1960.

Kant, Immanuel. *Kritik der reinen Vernunft.* Hamburg: Felix Meiner, 1956. Translated by A. Tremesaygues and B. Pacaud as *Critique de la raison pure* (Paris: PUF, 1963). Translated by Norman Kemp Smith as *Critique of Pure Reason* (New York: Palgrave Macmillan, 2003).

Klaw, Barbara. "Desire, Ambiguity, and Contingent Love: Simone de Beauvoir, Sexuality, and Self-Creation or What Good Is a Man Anyway?" *Symposium* 51, no. 2 (Summer 1997): 110–23.

——. "Intertextuality and Destroying the Myth of Woman in Simone de Beauvoir's *Tous les hommes sont mortels.*" *Romanic Review* 89, no. 4 (November 1998): 549–66.

——. *Le Paris de Beauvoir/Beauvoir's Paris.* Paris: Syllepse, 1999.

——. "The Rewriting of Sexual Identity from Colette's *Chéri* to Beauvoir's *L'Invitée.*" *Simone de Beauvoir Studies* 21 (2004–5): 77–92.

——. "Sexuality in Simone de Beauvoir's *Les Mandarins.*" In *Feminist Interpretations of Simone de Beauvoir,* edited by Margaret Simons, 193–221. State College: Pennsylvania State University Press, 1995.

——. "Simone de Beauvoir and Nelson Algren: Self-Creation, Self-Contradiction, and the Exotic, Erotic Feminist Other." In *Contingent Loves: Simone de Beauvoir and Sexuality,* edited by Melanie C. Hawthorne, 117–52. Charlottesville: University Press of Virginia, 2000.

——. "Simone de Beauvoir, du journal intime aux *Mémoires.*" In *Genèses du "Je,"* edited by Philippe Lejeune and Catherine Viollet, 169–79. Paris: Centre National de la Recherche Scientifique, 2000.

——. "Update on Simone de Beauvoir." *Women in French Studies* 9 (2001): 253–68.

342

Kruks, Sonia. *Retrieving Experience: Subjectivity and Recognition in Feminist Politics*. Ithaca, N.Y.: Cornell University Press, 2001.

——. *Situation and Human Existence*. New York: Routledge, 1990.

Lacoin, Elisabeth. *Zaza: Correspondance et carnets d'Elisabeth Lacoin, 1914–1929*. Paris: Seuil, 1991.

La Fayette, Mme de. *La princesse de Clèves*. Paris: Gallimard, 2002. Translated by Walter J. Cobb as *La Princesse de Clèves* (New York: Meridian, 1995).

Laforgue, Jules. "Ah! que d'Elle-même . . ." (first line of poem "IX," untitled). In Laforgue, *Oeuvres complètes*, 2:177–78. Translated by Peter Dale as "If of her own accord . . . ," 425–27.

——. "Avis, je vous prie." *L'imitation de Notre-Dame La Lune*. In Laforgue, *Oeuvres complètes*, 1:275. Translated by Peter Dale as "Advise, I Beg You," *The Imitation of Our Lady the Moon*, in *Poems*, 260–61.

——. "Couchant d'hiver." In Laforgue, *Le sanglot de la terre*, 43.

——. "Crépuscule de dimanche d'été." In Laforgue, *Le sanglot de la terre*, 40.

——. "Curiosités déplacées." In Laforgue, *Le sanglot de la terre*, 24.

——. *Derniers vers*. In Laforgue, *Oeuvres complètes*, vol. 2.

——. "Dimanches III." In Laforgue, *Derniers vers*, 2:151. Translated by Peter Dale as "Sundays III" in *Last Poems* in *Poems*, 396–99.

——. "Eclair de gouffre." In Laforgue, *Le sanglot de la terre*, 53.

——. "L'hiver qui vient." In Laforgue, *Derniers vers*, 2:143. Translated by Peter Dale as "The Coming Winter," *Poems*, 387.

——. "Hypertrophie." In Laforgue, *Le sanglot de la terre*, 39.

——. "Marche funèbre." In Laforgue, *Le sanglot de la terre*, 25. Translated by Patricia Terry as "Funeral March" in *Poems of Jules Laforgue*, 19.

——. *Moralités légendaires*. In *Moralités légendaires: Les deux pigeons*. Paris: Mercure de France, 1917. Translated by William Jay Smith as *Moral Tales* (New York: New Directions, 1985).

——. "Nobles et touchantes divagations sous la lune." *L'imitation de Notre-Dame-La Lune*. In Laforgue, *Oeuvres complètes*, 1:268. Translated by Peter Dale as "Noble and Touching Digressions under the Moon," *The Imitation of Our Lady the Moon*, in *Poems*, 250–55.

——. *Oeuvres complètes*. 2 vols. Geneva: Slatkine Reprints, 1979. Reprint of 1922–30 edition. Selected poems translated by Peter Dale as *Poems* (London: Anvil Press, 2001). Selected poems translated by Patricia Terry as *Poems of Jules Laforgue* (Berkeley: University of California Press, 1958).

——. "Petite Chapelle." In Laforgue, *Le Sanglot de la terre*, 45.

——. "Rosace en vitrail." In Laforgue, *Le sanglot de la terre*, 32.

——. *Le sanglot de la terre*. In Laforgue, *Oeuvres complètes*, vol. 1.

——. "Soir de Carnaval." In Laforgue, *Le sanglot de la terre*, 14.

——. "Solo de lune." In Laforgue, *Derniers vers*, 2:168. Translated by Peter Dale as "Moon Solo," *Last Poems*, in *Poems*, 415–19.

——. "Spleen des nuits de juillet." In Laforgue, *Le sanglot de la terre*, 18.

Lagneau, Jules. *Célèbres leçons et fragments*. Paris: PUF, 1950.

Lahr, Le Père Charles, S.J. *Manuel de philosophie résumé du cours de philosophie*. 2nd ed. Paris: G. Beauchesne, 1926.

Larbaud, Valéry. *A. O. Barnabooth, ses oeuvres complètes: Fermina Márquez; Enfantines; Beauté, mon beau souci . . . ; Amants, heureux amants . . . ; Mon plus secret conseil. . . .* Paris: Gallimard, 1995.

——. *A. O. Barnabooth, son journal intime.* 1913. Paris: Nouvelle Revue Française, 1923. Translated by Gilbert Cannan as *A. O. Barnabooth: His Diary* (London: Quartet Books, 1991).

——. *Fermina Márquez.* In Larbaud, *A. O. Barnabooth, ses oeuvres complètes.* Translated by Hubert Gibbs as *Fermina Márquez* (New York: Quartet Books, 1988).

Lejeune, Philippe. *Le moi des demoiselles: Enquête sur le journal de jeune fille.* Paris: Seuil, 1993.

Léna, Marguerite. "Jeanne Mercier, lectrice de Maurice Blondel." In *Maurice Blondel et la quête du sens,* edited by Marie-Jeanne Coutagne, 109–17. Paris: Beauchesne, 1998.

Maeterlinck, Maurice. *Le trésor des humbles.* Paris: Mercure de France, 1898. Translated by Alfred Sutro as *The Treasure of the Humble* (New York: Dodd, Mead, 1898?).

Maleprade, Henri. *Léontine Zanta (1872–1942): Vertueuse aventurière du féminisme.* Paris: Rive Droite, 1997.

Mallarmé, Stéphane. "Apparition." From *Poésies.* In Mallarmé, *Oeuvres complètes,* 30. Bibliothèque de la Pléiade. Paris: Gallimard, 1945. Translated by Ludwig Lewisohn as "Apparition" in *The Poets of Modern France* (London: Kennikat Press, 1918).

——. "L'après-midi d'un faune." From *Poésies.* In Mallarmé, *Oeuvres complètes,* 50–53. Translated by Aldous Huxley under the same title (London: Golden Cockerel Press, 1956).

——. *Les poésies.* Brussels: Edmond Demon, 1899. Translated by Roger Fry as *Poems* (New York: New Directions, 1951).

——. "Renouveau." From *Poésies.* In Mallarmé, *Oeuvres complètes,* 34.

Margueritte, Victor. *La garçonne.* Paris: Flammarion, 1922.

Martin du Gard, Roger. *Les Thibault.* Paris: Gallimard, 1972. Translated by Stuart Gilbert as *The Thibaults* (New York: Viking, 1941).

Massis, Henri. "André Gide ou l'immoralisme." In *Jugements.* Paris: Plon, 1924.

——. *Défense de l'occident.* Paris: Plon, 1927. Translated by F. S. Flint as *Defence of the West* (New York: Harcourt, Brace, 1928).

Mauriac, François. *L'adieu à l'adolescence: Poème.* Paris: Stock, 1911.

——. *La chair et le sang.* Paris: Emile-Paul, 1920. Translated by Gerard Hopkins as *Flesh and Blood* (New York: Farrar, 1955).

——. "L'étudiant—Départ II." *Les mains jointes.* In *Oeuvres complètes.*

——. *Oeuvres complètes.* Vol. 6. Paris: Fayard, 1951.

——. *La province.* Paris: Hachette, 1926.

——. *Thérèse Desqueyroux.* Paris: Calmann-Levy, 1927. Translated by Gerard Hopkins as *Thérèse* (London: Eyre and Spottiswoode, 1947).

Maurras, Charles. *La musique intérieure.* Paris: Grasset, 1925.

Mayeur, Françoise. *L'enseignement secondaire des jeunes filles sous la Troisième République.* Paris: Presses de la Fondation Nationale des Sciences Politiques, 1977.

McCormick, Matt. "Immanuel Kant, Metaphysics." *Encyclopedia of Philosophy.* http://www.iep.utm.edu/k/kantmeta.htm (accessed April 11, 2005).

Mercier, Jeanne. "Deux livres sur la pensée." *Bulletin de l'Association des anciennes élèves de l'Université de Neuilly.* Quoted in Léna, "Jeanne Mercier, lectrice de Maurice Blondel," 109.

——. "La philosophie de Maurice Blondel." *Revue de métaphysique et de morale* (July 1937). Quoted in Léna, "Jeanne Mercier, lectrice de Maurice Blondel," 110.

——. "Remarques sur *L'Action, t.I: Le problème des causes secondes et le pur agir.*" *Teoresi* 5 (1950): 113–22.

——. "Le ver dans le fruit: A propos de l'oeuvre de M. J.-P. Sartre." *Études,* February 1945, 232–49.

Merleau-Ponty, Maurice. "The Battle over Existentialism." 1945. In Merleau-Ponty, *Sense and Non-Sense,* 71–82.

——. "Metaphysics and the Novel." 1945. In Merleau-Ponty, *Sense and Non-Sense,* 26–40.

——. *Sense and Non-Sense.* 1948. Translated by Hubert L. Dreyfus and Patricia A. Dreyfus. Evanston, Ill.: Northwestern University Press, 1964.

Miomandre, Francis de. *Écrit sur de l'eau.* Paris: Henri Falque, 1908. Translated by William A. Drake as *Written on Water, Écrit sur de l'eau* (New York: Brentano's, 1929).

——. *La jeune fille au jardin.* Paris: J. Ferenczi, 1924.

Moi, Toril. *Simone de Beauvoir: The Making of an Intellectual Woman.* Cambridge, Mass.: Basil Blackwell, 1994.

——. *What Is a Woman? and Other Essays.* New York: Oxford University Press, 1999.

——. "While We Wait: The English Translation of *The Second Sex.*" *Signs* 27 (4): 1005–35.

Nerval, Gérard de, trans. "Le roi de Thulé." *Oeuvres diverses.* http://www.poetes.com/ nerval/roi_thule.htm (accessed March 15, 2005).

Nietzsche, Friedrich. *Ainsi parlait Zarathoustra = Also sprach Zarathustra.* German-French bilingual edition. Translated into French by Geneviève Bianquis. Paris: Aubier, 1992. Translated by R. J. Hollingdale as *Thus Spoke Zarathustra* (New York: Penguin, 1969).

——. *Der Wilte zur Macht.* Leipzig: Alfred, Kröner, 1918. Translated by Henri Albert as *Volonté de puissance* (Paris: Mercure de France, 1923). Translated by Walter Kaufmann and R. J. Hollingdale as *The Will to Power* (New York: Vintage, 1968).

Noailles, Anna de. *Les éblouissements.* Paris: Calmann-Lévy, 1907.

Offen, Karen. "The Second Sex and the Baccalauréat in Republican France, 1880–1924." *French Historical Studies* 13, no. 2 (Fall 1983): 252–86.

Pascal. *Pensées.* Paris: Seuil, 1962.

Patterson, Yolanda. "Entretien avec Hélène de Beauvoir." *Simone de Beauvoir Studies* 5 (1988): 12–31.

——. "H. M. Parshley et son combat contre l'amputation de la version américaine." In *Cinquantenaire du Deuxieme Sexe,* edited by Christine Delphy and Sylvie Chaperon, 475–81. Paris: Syllepse, 2002.

Patterson, Yolanda Astarita. "The Man behind *The Second Sex:* A Smith Professor's Letters Reveal the Story of the English Translation." *Smith Alumnae Quarterly* 83, no. 2 (Spring 1992): 12–16.

Péguy, Charles. *Le mystère de la charité de Jeanne d'Arc.* Paris: Nouvelle Revue Française, 1910. Translated by David Louis Schindler Jr. as "The Mystery of the Charity of Joan of Arc" in *The Portal of the Mystery of Hope* (Grand Rapids, Mich.: Eerdmans, 1996).

——. "Prière de confidence." *Les cinq prières dans la Cathédrale de Chartres,* in *Les tapisseries.* Paris: Gallimard, 1957.

Petrement, Simone. *La vie de Simone Weil.* Vol. 1, 1909–34. Paris: Fayard, 1973.

Prévost, Abbé. *Histoire du chevalier des Grieux et de Manon Lescaut* (1731). Paris: Gallimard,

2001. Translated by Helen Waddell as *The Story of Manon Lescaut and the Chevalier des Grieux* (New York: Heritage Club, 1938).

Proust, Marcel. *A la recherche du temps perdu.* 2 vols. Bibliothèque de la Pléiade. Paris: Gallimard, 1954. Translated by C. K. Scott Moncrieff and Terence Kilmartin as *Remembrance of Things Past* (New York: Random House, 1981).

Ramuz, Charles Ferdinand. *Aline.* Lausanne: Librairie Payot, 1905.

Raynal, Paul. *Le maître de son coeur: comédie en trois actes.* Paris: Librarie Stock, 1932.

Régnier, Henri de. *Poèmes, 1887–1892.* Paris: Mercure de France, 1897.

Rilke, Rainer Maria. *Die Aufzeichnungen des Malte Laurids Brigge.* Munich: Deutscher Tachenbuch, 1997. Translated by Maurice Betz as *Les cahiers de Malte Laurids Brigge* (Paris: Seuil, 1980). Translated by Stephen Mitchell as *The Notebooks of Malte Laurids Briggs* (New York: Random House, 1982).

Rimbaud, Arthur. "Aube." In Rimbaud, *Illuminations,* 80, 82. Translated by Louise Varèse as "Dawn," in *Illuminations and Other Prose Poems,* 81, 83.

———. "Fleurs." In Rimbaud, *Illuminations,* 84. Translated by Louise Varèse as "Flowers," in *Illuminations and Other Prose Poems,* 85.

———. *Illuminations.* In *Oeuvres,* edited by Suzanne Bernard, 245–309. Paris: Garnier-Flammarion, 1960. Translated by Louise Varèse as *Illuminations and Other Prose Poems* (New York: New Directions, 1957).

———. "Mystique." In Rimbaud, *Illuminations,* 78. Translated by Louise Varèse as "Mystic," in *Illuminations and Other Prose Poems,* 79.

Rivière, Jacques. *Aimée,* Paris: Gallimard, 1993

Rivière, Jacques, and Alain-Fournier. *Correspondance, 1905–1914.* 2 vols. Paris: Gallimard, 1926.

Rochelle, Drieu de la. "A vous Allemands." *Interrogation* (1917). In *Écrits de jeunesse: Interrogation, Fond de cantine, Suite dans les idées, Le jeune Européen.* Paris: Gallimard, 1941.

———. *La suite dans les idées.* Paris: Au Sans Pareil, 1927.

Romains, Jules. *La vie unanime: poème.* Paris: L'Abbaye, 1908.

Sarment, Jean. *La couronne de carton, Le pêcheur d'ombres.* Paris: Librairie de France, 1921. *Le pêcheur d'ombre* translated by Frances Keene and Adrienne Foulke as *Rude Awakening: A Play in Four Acts* (Boston: Poet Lore, 1939).

———. *Je suis trop grand pour moi.* In *La Petite Illustration,* May 3, 1924, 1–36.

———. *Le mariage d'Hamlet.* In *La Petite Illustration,* December 30, 1922.

Sartre, Jean-Paul. *Being and Nothingness.* 1943. Translated by H. Barnes. New York: Philosophical Library, 1953.

———. *Literary and Philosophical Essays.* Translated by Annette Michelson. New York: Criterion Books, 1955.

Schmitt, Louis, ed. *Contes choisis: Les frères Grimm.* Paris: Garnier, 1886.

Schopenhauer, Arthur. *Die Welt als Wille und Vorstellung.* Berlin: Bibliopgraphische Anstalt. 1891. Translated by E. F. J. Payne as *The World as Will and Representation,* 2 vols. (New York: Dover, 1969).

Seneca, Lucius Annaeus. *Sénèque. Lettres à Lucilius: III.* Available in Latin with French translation at http://site.voila.fr/scolaires/snq/trois.html (accessed April 4, 2002). Translated by E. Phillips Barker as *Letters to Lucilius* (Oxford: Clarendon, 1932).

Shaw, Bernard. *The Doctor's Dilemma.* London: Constable, 1925.

——. *Saint Joan: A Chronicle Play in Six Scenes and an Epilogue.* New York: Penguin, 1946. Translated by Augustin and Henriette Hamon as *Sainte Jeanne* (Paris: Presses du Compagnonnage, 1968).

Simonet-Tenant, Françoise. *Le journal intime: Genre littéraire et écriture ordinaire.* Paris: Nathan, 2001.

Simons, Margaret A. *Beauvoir and "The Second Sex": Feminism, Race, and the Origins of Existentialism.* Lanham, Md.: Rowman and Littlefield, 1999.

——. "Bergson's Influence on Beauvoir's Philosophical Methodology." In *The Cambridge Companion to Simone de Beauvoir,* edited by Claudia Card, 107–28. Cambridge: Cambridge University Press, 2003.

——. "L'indépendance de la pensée philosophique de Simone de Beauvoir." *Les Temps Modernes* 57, no. 619 (2002): 43–52.

——. *The Philosophy of Simone de Beauvoir: Critical Essays.* Bloomington: Indiana University Press, 2006.

——. "The Silencing of Simone de Beauvoir: Guess What's Missing from *The Second Sex.*" *Women's Studies International Forum* 6, no. 5 (1983): 559–64. Reprinted in Simons, *Beauvoir and "The Second Sex,"* 61–71.

Simons, Margaret A., and Hélène N. Peters. "Introduction" to "Analysis of Claude Bernard's Introduction to the Study of Experimental Medicine." In Simone de Beauvoir, *Philosophical Writings,* edited by Margaret A. Simons, Marybeth Timmermann, and Mary Beth Mader, 15–22. Urbana: University of Illinois Press, 2004.

Spiegelberg, Herbert. *The Phenomenological Movement: A Historical Introduction.* 3rd ed. The Hague: Martinus Nijhoff Publ, 1982.

Spinoza, Benedictus de. *Ethica: Ordine geometrico demonstrata et in quinque partes distinca.* Munich: Rupprecht-Presse, 1920. Translated by Roland Caillois as *L'éthique* (Paris: Gallimard, 1993). Translated by G. H. R. Parkinson as *Ethics* (New York: Oxford University Press, 2000).

Tacitus, Cornelius. *The Agricola.* In Latin. Edited by Duane Reed Stuart. New York: Macmillan, 1909.

——. *Agricola.* Translated by Maurice Hutton. Rev. ed. 5 vols. Cambridge, Mass.: Harvard University Press, 1970. Latin and English on opposing pages.

Tagore, Rabindranath. *Fruit-gathering.* New York: Macmillan, 1916. Translated by Hélène DuPasquier as *La corbeille de fruits* (Paris: Nouvelle Revue Française, 1920).

——. *Gitanjali.* London: Macmillan, 1914. Translated by André Gide as *L'offrande lyrique* (Paris: Gallimard, 1963).

Thorpe, Wayne. Review of *French Marxism between the Wars: Henri Lefebvre and the "Philosophies,"* by Bud Burkhard. *American Historical Review* 106, no. 2 (April 2001): 1–3.

Valéry, Paul. *Eupalinos, ou l'architecte.* Paris: Gallimard, 1924. Translated by William McCausland Stewart as *Eupalinos, or the Architect* (London: Oxford University Press, 1932).

——. *Oeuvres.* Vol. 1. Bibliothèque de la Pléiade. Paris: Gallimard, 1957.

——. "Palme." *Charmes.* In Valéry, *Oeuvres,* 1:153–56.

——. *Variété* (1924). In Valéry, *Oeuvres,* 1:423–1512. Translated by Malcolm Cowley as *Variety* (New York: Harcourt, Brace, 1927).

Verlaine, Paul. "La bonne chanson X, XIII." *La bonne chanson.* In Verlaine, *Oeuvres poétiques complètes,* 133–57.

——. "Kaléidoscope." *Jadis et Naguère.* In Verlaine, *Oeuvres poétiques complètes,* 321–22.

——. "Langueur." *Jadis et Naguère*. In Verlaine, *Oeuvres poétiques complètes*, 370–71. Translated by C. F. MacIntryre as "Apathy," in *French Symbolist Poetry* (Berkeley: University of California Press, 1964), 33. Translated by Norman R. Shapiro as "Languor" in *One Hundred and One Poems by Paul Verlaine* (Chicago: University of Chicago Press, 1998), 134.

——. *Oeuvres poétiques complètes*. Bibliothèque de la Pléiade. Paris: Gallimard, 1962.

Vildrac, Charles. "Avec moi-même." In Vildrac, *Livre d'amour*, 81–82. Translated by Witter Bynner as "By Myself" in *A Book of Love*, 79–80.

——. "Commentaire." In Vildrac, *Livre d'amour*, 14–17. Translated by Witter Bynner as "Commentary" in *A Book of Love*, 5–7.

——. "Gloire." In Vildrac, *Livre d'amour*, 64. Translated by Witter Bynner as "Glory" in *A Book of Love*, 59.

——. *Livre d'amour suivi des premiers vers*. Paris: Seghers, 1959. Translated by Witter Bynner as *A Book of Love* (New York: Dutton, 1923).

——. "Sans Espoir de Rien." In Vildrac, *Livres d'amour*, 21. Translated by Witter Bynner as "Happy-go-lucky" in *A Book of Love*, 15.

——. "Tristesse." In Vildrac, *Livre d'amour*, 42–43. Translated by Witter Bynner as "Dejection" in *A Book of Love*, 37–38.

Vintges, Karen. *Philosophy as Passion: The Thinking of Simone de Beauvoir*. 1992. Translated by Anne Lavelle. Bloomington: Indiana University Press, 1996.

Vocabulaire Européen des Philosophes: Dictionnaire des intraduisibles. Paris: Seuil, 2004.

Wilde, Oscar. *Complete Works of Oscar Wilde*. London: Collins, 1976.

——. "The Critic as Artist." In Wilde, *Intentions and The Soul of Man*, 97–224.

——. "The Decay of Lying." In Wilde, *Intentions and The Soul of Man*, 54–56.

——. *Intentions and The Soul of Man*. London: Methuen, 1969.

——. *Lady Windermere's Fan*. In Wilde, *Complete Works of Oscar Wilde*, 385–430. London: Collins, 1976.

——. "Pen, Pencil, and Poison." In Wilde, *Intentions and The Soul of Man*, 61–95.

——. *The Picture of Dorian Gray*. In Wilde, *Complete Works of Oscar Wilde*, 17–167. London: Collins, 1976.

Index

and Beauvoir's early philosophy, 31; Beauvoir's writings in Fourth Note-book about, 228, 235, 239, 240, 259, 292, 294, 308, 312; Beauvoir's writ-ings in Second Notebook about, 110, 165, 168, 192–95, 198; and literary and historical context of Beauvoir's early writings, 23–24

Beauvoir, Simone de: aspirations of, 8–9, 29, 30–31, 32–33; barriers to scholarly research about, 2–4; birth of, 24; calling [appel] of, 304; debates about works of, 7–8; family back-ground of, 24; greatest claim to honor of, 124; public image of, 21, 27n10, 27n13; reevaluation of works of, 7–8; as role model, 27n10; as teacher, 35–36, 46, 157, 183

Beauvoir Series, 4

becoming, 44, 156, 286, 301, 304, 307

Beethoven, Ludwig van, 318, 335n216

being: and Beauvoir's early philosophy, 44; Beauvoir's writings in Fourth Notebook about, 233, 248, 252, 255, 259, 275, 286, 301, 308; Beauvoir's writings in Second Notebook about, 57, 68, 84, 90, 104, 108, 110, 119, 132, 163, 164, 183; Bergson's views about, 61; "irreplaceable," 108; and literary and historical context of Beauvoir's early writings, 11; Mallarmé's views about, 205n56; Merleau-Ponty's views about, 286; Rilke's views about, 238; Rivière's views about, 155; in She Came to Stay, 11; sterility of, 119; and stories Beauvoir would like to see written, 84

Being and Nothingness (Sartre), 2, 43

beliefs, 242, 257, 262, 284, 288, 301

Les belles images [Pretty Pictures] (Beauvoir), 11

Benda, Julien, 18, 294, 333n177

Bérard decree (1924), 31, 47n11

Berger, Gaston, 205n55

Bergoffen, Debra, 43

Bergson, Henri: and actions, 60; and

Alain, 203n37; and art, 61, 66–67, 87; and art of writing, 87; Baruzi as student of, 40; and Beauvoir's early philosophy, 29–30, 34, 36, 38–40; Beauvoir's writings in Fourth Notebook about, 226, 247, 286–88; Beauvoir's writings in Second Note-book about, 58–61, 66–67, 70, 87, 126; and being, 61; Benda's attack on, 333n177; and consciousness, 34, 58–59, 60; and eduction of women, 47n9; élan vital of, 39, 247, 326n88; and feelings/emotions, 58–59, 67, 73; and future, 61; and happiness, 61; and hope, 61; and ideas, 60; influence of, 49n30, 202n22; and intuition, 49n30; and language, 59, 60; and literary and historical context of Beauvoir's early writings, 14; and love, 58–59; and memories, 61; Mercier's work on, 49n20; and opinions, 59–60; overview of, 202n22; and phenom-enology, 49n30; and "Philosophies" group, 222n308; and philosophy, 66–67, 226; and psychology, 67; and reality, 61; and reflection, 60; and self, 34, 59, 60, 322n29; and soul, 58–59; and space, 60; and suffering, 61; and time, 60

Besnard, Paul Albert, 244, 324n69

Beucler, André, 316, 334n208

Bibliothèque Nationale (Paris), 1, 2

Bionère (artist), 245

Biran, Maine de, 23, 222n312, 231, 321n20

Blake, William, 70, 206n58

Blomart, Mademoiselle: Beauvoir's writ-ings in Fourth Notebook about, 230, 239–40, 247, 263–64, 274, 276, 284, 292, 294, 303, 305, 310, 315

Blondel, Maurice, 49n20

Bloy, Léon, 23, 54, 200–201n10

Blum, Léon, 273, 330n137

Blum, Robert Frederick, 244, 325n75

body, 7, 13, 45, 104, 161, 233, 234, 309

Bompard, Pierre, 244, 325n76

353

Contributors

BARBARA KLAW is a professor of French at Northern Kentucky University. She is the author of *Le Paris de Simone de Beauvoir* and numerous essays on Beauvoir and on French and Francophone literature and culture in scholarly journals and books.

SYLVIE LE BON DE BEAUVOIR is the adopted daughter and literary executor of Simone de Beauvoir. She is the editor of *Lettres à Sartre* and many other works of Beauvoir.

MARGARET A. SIMONS is a professor of philosophy at Southern Illinois University Edwardsville. She is the author of *Beauvoir and "The Second Sex"* and editor, most recently, of Beauvoir's *Philosophical Writings* and *The Philosophy of Simone de Beauvoir*.

MARYBETH TIMMERMANN is a certified translator of the American Translator's Association and the Alliance Française de St. Louis. She has taught French at St. Louis Community College and at Southern Illinois University Edwardsville.

BOOKS IN THE BEAUVOIR SERIES

Series edited by Margaret A. Simons and
Sylvie Le Bon de Beauvoir

Philosophical Writings
  Edited by Margaret A. Simons
  with Marybeth Timmermann
  and Mary Beth Mader
  and a foreword by
  Sylvie Le Bon de Beauvoir

Diary of a Philosophy Student:
Volume 1, 1926–27
  Edited by Barbara Klaw,
  Sylvie Le Bon de Beauvoir,
  and Margaret A. Simons,
  with Marybeth Timmermann

The University of Illinois Press
is a founding member of the
Association of American University Presses.

Composed in 10.25/13 Adobe Minion
with Meta display
by Jim Proefrock
at the University of Illinois Press
Designed by Copenhaver Cumpston
Manufactured by Thomson Shore, Inc.

UNIVERSITY OF ILLINOIS PRESS
1325 South Oak Street   Champaign, IL 61820-6903
www.press.uillinois.edu